EDUCATION FOR LIVING SERIES

UNDER THE EDITORSHIP OF

H. H. REMMERS

Techniques of G

Techniques of Guidance

TESTS, RECORDS, AND COUNSELING

IN A GUIDANCE PROGRAM

ARTHUR E. TRAXLER, 1900—

Associate Director Educational Records Bureau

NEW YORK   LONDON

HARPER & BROTHERS, PUBLISHERS

To the Memory of My Father

EDWIN C. TRAXLER

*Teacher and Counselor
of Kansas Youth
for more than a generation*

CONTENTS

Editor's Introduction xi

Foreword xiii

I. *Background and Orientation* 1
Meaning of Guidance—Influences That Have Created Guidance
Programs—Staff Organization for Guidance—Costs of Guidance—
Cooperation, the Ultimate Solution—The Relation of Guidance to
Education in a Democracy

II. *Opportunities for Young People* 14
The Nature of Opportunities for Youth—Sources of Information
About Opportunities

III. *Kinds of Information Needed; Use of Interviews and Questionnaires
in Collecting Information* 20
Needed Information About Individual Students—Procedures for Collecting Information—The Interview as a Means of Gathering Information—Use of Questionnaires in Collecting Information

IV. *Appraisal of Aptitudes for Guidance Purposes* 42
What Is Aptitude?—Kinds of Aptitude Tests—Aptitude and Intelli-
gence—Tests of General Academic Aptitude—Tests of Aptitude in
Special Fields—Annotated List of Aptitude Tests

V. *Evaluation of Achievement in a Guidance Program* 68
Achievement Test Batteries for the Elementary School—Secondary
School Achievement Tests—Annotated List of Reading Tests—An-
notated List of General Achievement Tests: Elementary School—
Annotated List of Achievement Tests: Secondary School and Junior
College

VI. *Appraisal of Personal Qualities—Tests* 98
Extent of Attempts to Measure Personality—Definition of Personality
—Survey of Procedures for Appraising Personality—Validity and
Reliability—Use of Results of Personality Tests—Selected and An-
notated List of Personality Tests

VII. *Appraisal of Personal Qualities—Rating Scales, Anecdotal Records, and
Behavior Descriptions* 130
Rating Scales—Anecdotal Records—Characteristics of a Good Anec-
dote—Steps in an Anecdotal Record Plan—Limitations and Cautions

in the Preparation of Anecdotes—Values and Uses of Anecdotal Records—Sample Anecdotes—Relation of Anecdotal Records to Personality Ratings and Behavior Descriptions—Annotated List of Rating Scales and Behavior Description Forms

VIII. *Planning and Administering a Testing Program for Guidance Purposes* 155
Steps in Planning and Conducting a Testing Program—Test Information for Students—Need for Plan of Using Test Results

IX. *Scoring, Organizing, and Reporting Test Results* 164
Scoring Procedures—Plainfield High School Testing Program—Reporting Procedures

X. *Use of Results of Objective Tests in Improving the Instructional and Counseling Program of the School* 185
Administrative and Supervisory Uses of Tests—Instructional Uses of Tests—Use of Test Results in Counseling—Limitations to the Use of Tests in Instructional and Guidance Programs—How to Improve the Usefulness of Tests

XI. *Basic Principles and Main Types of Pupil Personnel Records* . . 202
Some Basic Principles—Main Types of Personnel Record Systems

XII. *Cumulative Records in a Guidance Program* 215
What the Cumulative Record Is—Variations in Record Forms—American Council Cumulative Record Forms—Recording Test Scores in Terms of a Common Criterion Group—Cumulative Records Employed in Different School Systems—A Suggested Simplified Cumulative Record—Basic Concepts in the Construction of a Cumulative Record System

XIII. *Reports to the Homes* 235
Marking Systems—Trends in Forms for Reports to Parents—Criteria for Report Forms—Types of Report Forms with Illustrations—The Need for Experimentation with Various Plans of Reporting

XIV. *Case Study Procedures in Guidance* 284
Origin of Case Studies—What the Case-Study Method Is—Assembling and Organizing Data in a Case Study—Outlines for Case Studies—The Case-Study Method Illustrated—Points to Be Observed in Making a Case Study—Distribution of Case Studies—Value of Case Studies

XV. *The Role of the Teacher in Guidance* 308
Is It Desirable to Combine the Functions of Guidance and the Functions of Teaching in the Same Person?—Should not Guidance Procedures Be Carried on by Specially Trained Persons?—If I Try to Do Guidance Work When My Schedule Is Already Full, Will not This Extra Load Reduce My Teaching Efficiency?—What Can I Do About the Guidance of the Pupils in My Classes, Whom I See in Groups for

Forty or Fifty Minutes Each Day, Most of Whom I Did not Even Know by Name Before They Entered the Class, and About Whom I Know Little or Nothing?—What Can I Do to Help Make the Testing Program of the School Effective?—What Use Can I Make of Cumulative Records and How Can I Contribute to the Records?—How Can I Make Maximum Use of the Cumulative Test Histories in Diagnosing the Learning Difficulties and Improving the Instruction of My Pupils?—How Can I Assist in the Adjustment of the Pupils in My Classes to Their In-School and Out-of-School Environment?

XVI. *Follow-up of Students and School Leavers* 317
Aspects of a Follow-up Program—Purposes and Nature of Follow-up of School Leavers—The Continuous Follow-up Survey—Forms Used in Follow-up Surveys—Salient Characteristics of a Follow-up Plan

XVII. *Guidance in the Adjustment of Individuals* 334
What Is Adjustment?—The Danger of Labels—Mechanisms of Escape from Reality—Steps in Counseling for Adjustment—Characteristics and Professional Training Desirable for Counselors

XVIII. *Reading Resources for Counselors* 343
Child Psychology and Mental Hygiene—Educational Guidance, Counseling, and Personnel Work—Vocational Guidance—Studies Related to Guidance—Interests and Their Measurement—Testing in a Guidance Program—Case Studies—Cumulative Records—Visual Aids to Guidance—Bibliographies—A Selected Library for Counselors

Appendix: *Guidance and Placement of Persons Whose Education Has Been Interrupted* 366
Index 383

EDITOR'S INTRODUCTION

IT IS A PLEASURE AND SATISFACTION TO INTRODUCE THIS BOOK IN THE SERIES "Education for Living," characterized as it is by its high level of insight and competent craftsmanship. It is gratifying, too, to note its insistence throughout on the need for scientific, objectively verifiable data as a basis for valid guidance.

In this volume Doctor Traxler has marshaled, organized, and clearly presented the best of modern techniques and procedures available for the complex and all important job of counseling and guidance. For all of his insistence upon objectivity, he has not fallen into the not unknown error of mistaking means for ends. Measuring instruments, record forms, and forms of organization of guidance programs all have, as their only reason for being, the more adequate adjustment of the individual to the society in which he must live and work. The book, in other words, continues the point of view of holism to which the first volume in this series adheres as the most valid philosophical principle of approach to the problems of guidance.

Counselors, teachers, and administrators, whether in training or in service, will find the book a useful, authoritative, and practical guide in their most important professional activities—that of aiding in the continuous adjustment of individuals to a dynamic and increasingly complex society.

H. H. REMMERS

FOREWORD

FOR ABOUT NINE YEARS I HAVE BEEN ASSOCIATED WITH THE EDUCATIONAL RECORDS Bureau, the main function of which is to assist its member institutions in the use of objective techniques in guidance. The Bureau helps the schools plan two testing programs annually; fills orders for the tests recommended for these programs; provides scoring, statistical, and reporting services; maintains a cumulative-record service; carries on research with the test results; and makes suggestions concerning the uses and limitations of the results by means of personal interviews, correspondence, and publications.

Since coming to the Bureau I have written for our member schools a considerable number of articles, bulletins, and other manuscripts on testing and guidance. Some of these have been published and some are in unpublished form This book consists of an organization, revision, and synthesis of these materials, together with other material written specifically for it.

The approach to guidance as represented by this book is relatively uncomplicated, objective, straightforward, and matter-of-fact. The central idea is to gather as much relevant information as possible about each pupil, organize it so that it shows both status at any given time and growth over a period of years, and use these data with understanding in the distribution and adjustment of individual pupils. If this book is able to help schools apply these procedures, it will have accomplished its main purpose.

Since questions received from those who perform guidance functions show that specific information and concrete suggestions are especially needed and desired, I have included in the book much detailed explanation concerning tests and other instruments of evaluation and a large number of illustrative record forms.

For consistent encouragement and sympathetic criticism in the first preparation of much of this material, I am deeply indebted to Professor Ben D. Wood, of Columbia University, director of the Educational Records Bureau, and to Mrs. Eleanor Perry Wood, formerly associate director. I was persuaded to put the material into book form by Professor H. H. Remmers, of Purdue University, to whom I am grateful for advice and editorial criticism. I also wish to express my appreciation to Professor Ruth Strang, of Columbia University, who read part of the manuscript and made helpful suggestions, and to Professor

W. C. McCall, of the University of South Carolina, who gave constructive advice concerning the scope and organization of the book. Mrs. Ann Nappi Petersen rendered efficient assistance in typing the manuscript and checking numerous details.

Finally, I owe an especial debt of gratitude to the 380 member institutions of the Bureau and to numerous faculty members of these schools who through their consistent use of tests and cumulative records in instruction and guidance are translating into action the basic ideas I have tried to set forth in this book.

ARTHUR E. TRAXLER

New York City
January, 1945

Techniques of Guidance

CHAPTER I

Background and Orientation

WITHIN THE LAST TWENTY-FIVE YEARS GUIDANCE HAS BECOME ONE OF THE MOST common words in the vocabulary of education. Its rapid development in the schools has been due mainly to new social conditions and needs, a new psychology which has emphasized individual differences, and new techniques for studying individuals.

Psychologically, a need for guidance is found wherever the environment is sufficiently complex to permit a variety of responses and whenever individuals are not equipped to react instinctively to the stimulus of the environment. Among animals and in primitive social orders, the guidance of youth is taken care of by the parents. Even in a fairly advanced civilization which maintains a certain homogeneity, the home can continue to be the chief guidance agency. Thus, in the largely agrarian society which obtained in the United States until approximately 1900, there was no keenly felt need for organized guidance other than that provided by the family.

It is unnecessary to point out that within the last half century our environment has become exceedingly complex. The astonishing development of pure and applied science and the mechanization of industry have led to minute vocational specialization and an infinite number of vocational choices. The growth of huge industries and the pyramiding of the financial structure have led to dense concentration of the population in certain areas and to dependent sociological problems. The attempt of the schools to keep pace with the growing need for social and industrial education has so expanded the curriculum that the pupil is presented with a bewildering array of subject choices, frequently with little or no information concerning those for which he is best fitted. The peacetime needs for guidance created by these comparatively new conditions were greatly intensified by the speed-up and tension attending the war effort.

I

At the same time that the changing environment has placed much greater responsibility upon young people for the making of wise choices, educational agencies have become aware of large differences among individuals in their potentialities for success in different areas. The application of mathematics and measurement techniques to psychological problems has indicated that individuals tend to distribute themselves widely on almost every measurable characteristic and that in many instances the distributions assume the appearance of the normal, or bell-shaped, curve.

A complex environment and an awareness of individual differences make an attempt at guidance in the schools inevitable. Such an attempt would be characterized largely by trial and error were it not for the fact that techniques of measurement and the recording of observations have laid the basis for an applied science of guidance. The main purpose of this book is to try to provide a description and illustration of the application of this new science to the problems of youth.

It is true of course that schools have always provided some type of guidance for their pupils even though they may not have used the word guidance at all. The very routine of enrolling pupils, holding classes, and carrying on the work of instruction makes it inevitable that pupils will be guided to some extent. In the past, however, schools have infrequently taken full advantage of their opportunity for guidance because they have not clearly recognized their responsibility in this respect and because they have often been more concerned over the details of the curriculum than over the distribution and adjustment of young people to the school environment and to the broader environment of postschool life. Until recently, the guidance afforded by most schools has not been based on an organized, well-planned program but has been left largely to the individual initiative of the principal and the teachers. Systems of planned, organized guidance began to appear in the schools of the United States about 1910. So rapidly has the movement grown that at the present time nearly all the more forward-looking high schools and many of the elementary schools attempt to provide some type of individual guidance for their pupils.

MEANING OF GUIDANCE

Guidance is one of the most difficult of all educational subjects to discuss because there has been, and there continues to be, confusion and uncertainty concerning its nature and functions. Some authorities feel that guidance is as broad as all education and that the whole program of the school should be set up for guidance purposes, whereas others would restrict it to some relatively narrow aspect such as vocational guidance or moral guidance. Some guidance programs consist chiefly of courses in occupational information. The main emphasis in other guidance programs is on the placement of pupils in courses designed to eliminate or reduce failure. Still others stress therapy and the treatment of maladjustment as the central purpose of the counseling relationship. Not infrequently, character building is thought to be the main purpose and function of guidance. Too often, one fears, the guidance programs of schools consist of little more than lip service to a nebulous concept which is useful in the publicity relations of the school but which has almost no influence on the lives of the individual pupils.

Not only is there lack of agreement concerning guidance in its totality but there is also misapprehension with regard to the main divisions of the guidance field. Notwithstanding the critical attitude adhered to for years by various authorities on guidance, there continues to flourish a popular misconception that there is a logical cleavage between educational guidance and vocational guidance. It should be clearly understood that the two are inextricably interwoven and that while there may be differences in emphasis on one or another of these aspects at various grade levels, no realist will try to separate them.

The division of guidance into adjustment and distribution as advised by Koos and Kefauver[1] and others is a much more pertinent distinction, but even in this case the division is one for convenience in thinking rather than one that can be applied functionally. In working with individual cases, counselors often find that the key to adjustment is better distribution of the pupils to the offerings of the school.

In the practice of guidance, the whole process is as unitary as the lives of the individuals with which it deals. No school can successfully conduct a few selected functions of guidance, for the reason that the personalities of individuals cannot be divided into compartments. Hence no school should attempt a guidance program unless it is willing ultimately to undertake all phases of it.

Ideally conceived, guidance enables each individual to understand his abilities and interests, to develop them as well as possible, to relate them to life goals, and finally to reach a state of complete and mature self-guidance as a desirable citizen of a democratic social order. Guidance is thus vitally related to every aspect of the school—the curriculum, the methods of instruction, the supervision of instruction, disciplinary procedures, attendance, problems of scheduling, the extracurriculum, the health and physical fitness program, and home and community relations. This of course implies the closest kind of cooperation between guidance functionaries and all the other members of the staff. Although guidance is closely related to all areas of the school, those charged with responsibility for the guidance program cannot be specialists in all these fields. Their functions are to collect and systematize accurate information about pupils,

[1] Leonard V. Koos and Grayson N. Kefauver. *Guidance in Secondary Schools.* New York: The Macmillan Company, 1932, pp. 15–22.

to provide an individual counseling service, and to carry on a dynamic educational program among their colleagues and among the pupils and their parents that will lead to intelligent use of the information that the guidance department is able to provide.

INFLUENCES THAT HAVE CREATED GUIDANCE PROGRAMS

The somewhat varied status of guidance in American schools may be traced in part to the diversified nature of the factors which have been influential in the development of guidance programs. The present guidance movement stems mainly from five divergent and highly dissimilar sources. One of the oldest of these is *philanthropy,* or *humanitarianism,* which stresses benevolent regard for the welfare of mankind. The philanthropists or humanitarians look upon life and, seeing the many misfits, they say, "People should be guided when they are young so that these maladjustments will not occur. This is a job for the schools." All social workers and nearly all the people in educational work have philanthropic tendencies. They exert a certain amount of pressure on the schools to develop guidance programs.

Another old source of the guidance movement is *religion.* The religious man looks upon the world and he sees what he interprets as a constant struggle between the sources of righteousness and those of evil. In turn he says, "We must get hold of people when they are very young and train them for the good life. We must build character in our youth." And so he looks to the educational system to help him with this task. Nearly every school administrator has, on occasion, felt the relentless pressure of this guidance group.

A third, and much newer but in some respects similar, guidance source is *mental hygiene.* This school of thought sees in maladjustment a need for mental therapy. According to this point of view, people should learn when they are young to get a correct perspective on their abilities in relation to life goals; to prefer overt, frank, open behavior to retiring, secretive behavior; to understand the significance of sex and to take a rational attitude toward it; to meet their problems squarely rather than to retire into fantasy and other forms of escapism; to avoid infantile fixations detrimental to the development of a set of maturing interests; to evolve gradually from a state of parental dependence to one of self-dependence through demonstrated achievement in fields within their own capacity; and to assume other qualities which characterize a healthy, adult mental and emotional state. Anyone who has ever seen a psychiatrist struggling through an hour interview with a shy, introverted child, seeking to draw him out and to understand the organization of his tight little personality, knows that here is an intricate and sometimes extremely difficult aspect of guidance. There are clinics to care for this type of guidance so far as markedly neurotic individuals are concerned, but even individuals within the normal range also occasionally need guidance in mental hygiene. For the great mass of children this function must be performed by the school; so another guidance force impinges upon the school.

A fourth source of interest in guidance manifests itself so notably through the administrative aspect of the school that we are sometimes misled into thinking that it originates with administrators, when as a rule it stems from *social change*. It is unnecessary to dwell upon the familiar fact that before the war effort created abnormal employment demands, technological unemployment, a world-wide depression, rising ethical standards with respect to child labor, compulsory attendance laws, and similar forces literally drove into the secondary schools thousands of young people who had no marked desire to be there, had no clear idea of why they were there or what they expected to get from their secondary school training, and did not know where they were going when they left school. The pressure of numbers and the essentially non-academic character of these pupils created a whole set of new problems for administrators. As a natural first step, they have greatly broadened the curriculum to provide for this horde of young people, but they have seen clearly that this is not enough. They have found that the outstanding need is individual attention and counsel to help each individual marshal his assets of aptitude and previous training and find his way through the complex school environment and the still more complex environment outside the school to a kind of personal and economic self-dependence and security. The administrator, realizing his inability to cope with the situation singlehanded, has naturally tried to utilize the counseling resources of his staff, notwithstanding the fact that the staff may have no previous training for this work and no real knowledge of the pupils as individuals. Thus, from this source, many guidance programs have been introduced, some of which have been successful but many of which cannot function effectively because the teachers are almost as bewildered by the situation as are the pupils, and neither teachers nor pupils have any tangible basis on which to begin the personnel work.

The last of the major sources of the guidance movement is one that has usually been identified in our thinking with the measurement movement in education but which, when it is analyzed, is seen to involve a concept much broader than educational measurement alone. Basically, it is the simple yet fundamental thesis that the first duty of the school is to *know its pupils as individuals*. It involves, first, a recognition of the essential dignity and worth of the individual and, second, a willingness to study him by every means which the resources of the school can command. Those who take this approach to guidance point out that in any large high school it is virtually impossible for any one person to know more than a very few of the pupils well enough even to attempt to provide guidance on the basis of personal acquaintance alone. The solution for this seeming impasse, they insist, is for each school to make a systematic attempt to collect information about each individual and then to pool its essential knowledge year after year. The physical manifestation of this pooling of information is what has come to be known as the cumulative record. Objective tests are the most important instrument yet devised for the collection of data for the cumulative record, but they are by no means the only instrument. Social history records, health records, rating scales, anecdotal records, and other procedures can contribute pertinent information to this record.

When the guidance movement is seen as resulting from so many influences, there can be little wonder that the field of guidance is confused and uncertain. The concept of the cumulative record and of the systematic collection of information for it by means of regular testing and other procedures was the last to develop among the sources contributing to the growth of guidance programs. This has been unfortunate, for this last aspect of guidance is essential to the successful functioning of all its other aspects. The development of a dynamic guidance program in the schools of this country depends, in large measure, upon a realization that we must first marshal the facts about our students, that we must first of all make personnel work a kind of science, and then add those overtones of personal relationship and those inspirational qualities which can contribute a great deal provided they are founded on understanding.

Many schools, when planning a guidance program, begin by giving detailed attention to the kind of guidance *organization* that should be adopted. This is of considerable importance, but it is not the matter of first importance. The first duty of those charged with the development of a guidance program is to build a plan that will enable the school to *know its pupils*. This is "the major strategy of guidance." Without it, no type of guidance organization can have any important effect upon the lives of the pupils. With it, a school can achieve considerable success with almost any kind of guidance setup, provided the data are interpreted with the understanding that arises from working with many individuals. It will be desirable, however, to consider briefly the general types of guidance organizations which have been developed in our secondary schools.

Staff Organization for Guidance

The guidance organization and the functionaries by whom guidance is carried on vary greatly from school to school. In most small schools the principal is the chief guidance officer. In many fairly large ones the work of guidance is carried on by the assistant principal or dean of girls and dean of boys. In others home-room teachers conduct the guidance program. In some small schools and a few large ones an attempt is made to utilize all the teachers as advisers. Some large school systems employ a staff of trained counselors, quite apart from the staff of teachers, to perform the guidance functions. Visiting teachers are the chief guidance agency in a number of these large systems. Finally, in a considerable proportion of large and medium-size schools, committees of advisers, specially selected by the principal from the teaching staff, carry on the guidance work.

Because of differences in local situations, it would not be advisable to try to recommend the adoption of any one type of guidance organization to the exclusion of all others. Two rather definite trends, however, may be noted. One is the tendency to separate as much as possible the functions of guidance from those of administration. Good administrative officers who perform their tasks with imagination will of course always do important guidance work, but experience shows that the relationships between the pupils and those who are charged with the special responsibility of counseling are likely to be more natural and cordial if the counselors perform no administrative or disciplinary functions. In schools where a major share of the counseling is done by deans of girls and of boys, emphasis should be placed upon the *guidance* functions of deans, and discipline should be a minor part of their work. The well-qualified dean considers his most important function that of working with and through teachers, teacher-counselors, home-room teachers, or whatever type of organization is used to provide a counselor for every student.

The other trend in guidance organization is toward the bringing about of a closer relationship between guidance and teaching. It is desirable that the guidance director be a person with special training in both personnel work and educational measurement, and to fill this position it may be necessary to go outside the local school system. But many, and in some cases all, of the counselors may be drafted from the regular teaching staff. Teachers have always, of necessity, performed many of the functions of guidance; consequently, every experienced teacher has already had some experience in this field even though he may never have considered his work in that light. Not every teacher will make a good guidance officer. Some authorities, in fact, go so far as to say that a school is fortunate if one-fourth of its teachers can be trained for guidance work, but nearly all of them agree that a school's own staff is its most important source of counselors. Even the teachers who do not have direct responsibility for counseling can contribute a great deal to the guidance program of a school. All the teachers should be instructed in the guidance philosophy of the school and in the use of guidance records.

If a school adopts a policy of drawing all or nearly all its counselors from its teaching staff, one important question still remains to be decided. Shall the counselors be withdrawn from teaching entirely (except perhaps for the giving of courses in occupations) and their places on the teaching staff filled by new

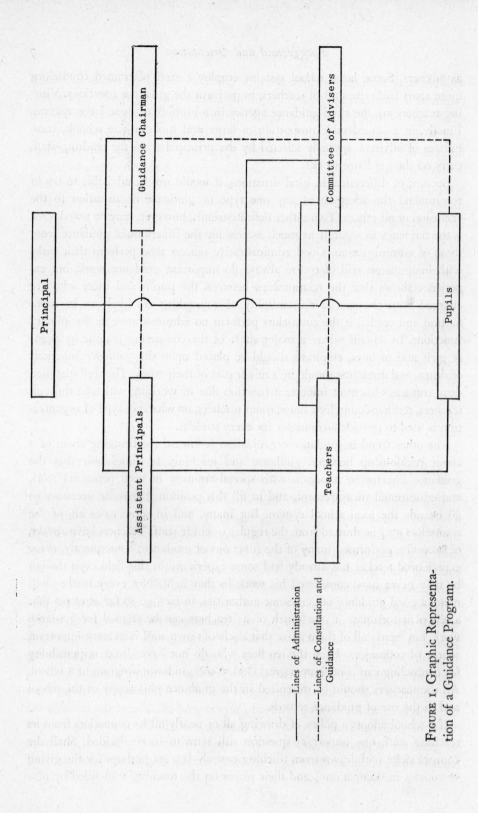

FIGURE 1. Graphic Representation of a Guidance Program.

appointees, or shall the guidance work be spread as widely as possible and each counselor retain perhaps four-fifths of his former teaching load? There are advantages to both plans and successful programs of both types are in operation. If the counselors give all or nearly all their time to personnel work, their interests will center in it and they will not have their loyalty and effort divided between guidance and teaching. On the other hand, if they continue to teach, it is possible to arrange the pupils' programs so that the counselors have in class those pupils who are in their own guidance group, and thus close acquaintance and mutual confidence between pupils and counselors is fostered.

Perhaps the strongest argument for favoring close relationship between counseling and teaching is that in both it is necessary first of all to know each individual pupil before the objectives can be realized. Thus the initial stages of both individual guidance and the individualization of instruction are almost identical, and it therefore seems economical and efficient to have the same functionaries engage in both types of activity.

A graphic representation of lines of relationship in a guidance program which was organized on the basis of a committee of advisers, consisting of twenty-five classroom teachers under the chairmanship of a specialist in guidance and testing, is shown in Figure 1. It will be observed that in this plan the lines of consultation and guidance are carefully differentiated from those of administration.

Costs of Guidance

Most school administrators will agree that the essentials of guidance—namely, a comprehensive testing program, a cumulative record, and a staff trained to interpret and use the guidance data—are fine in theory but frequently they will insist that these are not possible in so far as their own school is concerned because of the expense involved. The question of cost is therefore one of the most crucial ones that can be raised about guidance.

The costs of guidance may be grouped under three main headings: (1) personnel, (2) clerical services for the maintenance of records, and (3) testing programs. The cost of guidance personnel varies greatly in different schools depending on the plan adopted. At one extreme, there are schools in which the salary of a counselor for every two hundred or three hundred pupils is added to the budget as well as that of a director of guidance. At the other extreme, there are schools in which nothing is added for personnel because of the fact that the work of guidance is absorbed by the existing staff. In the first group the cost of guidance is probably greater than it needs to be; in the second, guidance usually suffers because of the rigid economy, for the guidance program is likely to start without the full approval of the staff and to be conducted in a desultory manner because it represents an added burden for each teacher.

The guidance program in the Providence Public Schools, under the direction of Richard D. Allen, seems to have met the problem of cost of personnel with exceptional success.[2] In that school system the group guidance instruction (including occupational information) has a recognized standing in the curriculum. Each counselor gives three-fifths of his time to group guidance instruction, one-fifth to other subject instruction, and one-fifth to individual interviews with pupils. Since the four-fifths of his time that is devoted to instruction would have to be taken over by other teachers even if the guidance program were dropped, it is felt at Providence that the only cost for guidance personnel is the one-fifth of each counselor's time that is given to interviews—the interviews being so scheduled that the counselor regularly has one fifteen-minute conference each term with each pupil in the group. At Providence, the annual cost of replacing, through employment of new teachers, the time that is taken from instruction and given to individual interviews is approximately one dollar per pupil; that is, it is necessary to add one beginning teacher at a salary of twelve hundred dollars a year for approximately every twelve hundred pupils interviewed by the counselor. If it were impossible to afford new teachers, it is estimated that the cost of interviewing could be absorbed by adding one pupil to each class in the school.

Admitting that this plan may involve some costs which do not appear on the surface, one must still be impressed by the relatively small cost of counseling personnel in one of the foremost guidance programs in America. It should also be pointed out that the apparent cost may be more than balanced by the effect of the guidance program, not alone in values to pupils but in actual dollars and cents. Dr. Allen states that when the guidance program was introduced into Technical High School and Commercial High School in Providence, the savings resulting from reduction in failure and elimination of small elective courses that it had been necessary to maintain when the pupils did not have adequate guidance were "equal to approximately five times the additional cost of the guidance department in these schools."

The costs of clerical services for the maintenance of cumulative records depend upon the nature of the records, the care with which they are kept up-to-date, the degree of detail in the entries, the prevailing rates for clerical work, and various other factors. Published data on the cost of maintaining cumulative records are almost non-existent. Some figures on this point have been made available, however, by the Plainfield, New Jersey, High School, one of the schools which cooperated in the Public School Demonstration Project of the

[2] Richard D. Allen. "The Costs of Guidance in a Secondary School," *Clearing House,* XIII (October 1938), 73–77.

Educational Records Bureau.[3] This school uses the American Council cumulative record folder adapted for a visible file and keeps all parts of the record, including the graph of test results. The cost per pupil has been found to be about five and one-half cents for the record itself (folder and titled insert) and twenty-five cents a year for servicing it, or approximately $1.05 for the four high school years. It is doubtful if that amount could be invested in the education of the pupil in any other way to yield such high returns in increased educational efficiency.

The testing program is one of the main elements in the cost of guidance. As will be indicated in greater detail later, the basic program should consist of at least five tests annually—a test of academic aptitude or reading on alternate years, and achievement tests in English and three of several other fields, such as mathematics, science, social studies, foreign languages, commercial subjects, fine arts, and practical arts—depending on what the pupil is studying. The annual cost of five test booklets for each pupil is about thirty-five cents, but this is usually the smallest part of the cost of a testing program. Under ordinary conditions the scoring and the necessary statistical work are more important items of cost. Teachers are subjected frequently to the drudgery of scoring, but if the average teacher's time is worth more than that of the average scoring clerk, this is one of the most expensive ways of getting the scoring done.

If the tests for the guidance program are to be scored locally by hand or sent to a test service agency, probably the minimum amount that should be allowed for a testing program is one dollar per pupil annually. A large school system can reduce its testing cost materially through the use of the electrical test scoring machine produced by the International Business Machines Corporation. These machines are not for sale; they are installed at a rental and service charge of four hundred and eighty dollars a year.[4] With a special type of pencil the pupil marks his responses on an answer sheet inserted in the scoring machine, with the result that the entire test is scored in one operation. A speed of scoring as high as five hundred tests an hour is not uncommon. Since the pupils make no marks on the test booklets, the same booklets may be used repeatedly; thus a part of the cost of the rental of the machine or of obtaining outside machine-scoring services may be met by the reduction in the total cost of test booklets. The scoring machine may be used in scoring teacher-made tests as well as standardized tests.

It is obvious of course that only a fairly large school system can afford to maintain a test scoring machine for its own exclusive use, but it is feasible for a number of medium-size school systems in the same locality to cooperate in

[3] *Guidance in Public Secondary Schools.* Educational Records Bulletin No. 28. New York: Educational Records Bureau (October 1939). Pp. xxv + 329.
[4] Conditions created by the war have temporarily retarded the distribution of scoring machines to schools.

the use of a scoring machine in connection with a guidance program.[5] The possibilities of solving some of the problems of testing and guidance by cooperative effort are sufficiently great to deserve special consideration.

COOPERATION, THE ULTIMATE SOLUTION

The thesis is now widely accepted that the backbone of any guidance program worthy of the name is an individual cumulative record and that the most important source of data for the cumulative record is a well-organized testing program. It seems probable, however, that for years to come only a small proportion of the schools in this country will adopt either a cumulative record or a thorough testing program if left to their own devices. Inertia, prejudice against anything new or different, lack of understanding of what is involved, and doubt of ability to pay for the minimum program that any specialist in guidance is willing to recommend seem almost insurmountable obstacles to the average school. Apparently these obstacles can be met in only one way, through the cooperation of the schools in each locality working under the leadership of those who are conversant with both measurement and personnel work. The first big problem is to place a testing program within the reach of all schools. For this purpose the state seems to be the logical unit as far as public schools are concerned. Some eighteen states now have state-wide testing programs ranging in scope from the elaborate Iowa Testing Program, which includes the construction of an extensive battery of tests as well as the reporting of results, to programs that consist of little more than the recommendation of a uniform set of tests throughout the state which may be used in establishing state-wide norms. Some of the newer state testing programs in which the International Test Scoring Machine is utilized for the central scoring of the tests given in the various schools show that it is possible to conduct a state-wide testing program on a very economical basis; however, in the larger and more populous states it may not be feasible to try to service the schools of an entire state by one scoring installation. For schools that do not yet have access to a scoring machine through a state testing program, certain service agencies, such as the Educational Records Bureau, make scoring services available at nominal prices.

States which have testing programs need to go one step beyond providing the best possible machinery for the administration and scoring of the tests. They need to conduct a program for educating the schools in the use of the results for guidance purposes. The lack of information about the proper uses of tests is probably the greatest weakness in the average testing and guidance program. Gradually, however, materials on the use of tests prepared especially

---

[5] For example, a cooperative program of this kind has been set up by a number of suburban schools in the Philadelphia area in connection with a scoring machine at Drexel Institute.

for teachers and counsellors who are not highly trained in statistics are being made available by various organizations. It is believed that the use of such materials in preparing the staff to carry on the functions of guidance should be as much a part of a testing program as the administration of the tests themselves.

THE RELATION OF GUIDANCE TO EDUCATION IN A DEMOCRACY

It has been pointed out many times that one cannot train individuals for life in a democratic state merely by rules and indoctrination or by the establishment of emotional loyalty. The only effective training for citizenship in a democracy is practice in democratic living. The facts concerning each individual's potentialities, his interests, the things to which he responds with emotional satisfaction, his skills, his rate of development, and his major points of strength and weakness must be accurately ascertained and assembled as objectively and dispassionately as possible, and out of the whole picture he must be led to evolve for himself a satisfactory level of living and at the same time maintain a balance between his own welfare and that of the group. Thus, training for living in a democracy and guidance as exemplified by carefully organized personnel programs are one and the same process.

The point will bear repeating that guidance as defined by those who approach the problem rationally implies first of all recognition and understanding of the individual and creation of conditions that will enable each individual to develop his fullest capacities and ultimately to achieve the maximum possible self-guidance and security both economically and socially. This concept of guidance epitomizes our democratic philosophy. It is as enduring as democracy itself, for basically it is democracy applied to the life of the school.

CHAPTER II

Opportunities for Young People

ONE OF THE MOST IMPORTANT FUNCTIONS OF GUIDANCE IS TO HELP BRING ABOUT A better distribution of young people to the offerings of the school and to vocations. In connection with this area the main responsibilities of counselors are, first, to become familiar with the opportunities for young people and to acquaint them with these opportunities; second, to know the aptitudes, interests, and achievements of individual pupils and to help the pupils understand the significance of the test data and other information concerning their aptitudes, interests, and achievements; and third, to develop a continuing program of individual counseling which will lead young people to discover and recognize the opportunities best suited to their potentialities.

The Nature of Opportunities for Youth

The counselor's program should include provision for the intelligent guidance of individual boys and girls toward the immediate opportunities provided by the school and the community and toward long-time educational and vocational opportunities available after secondary school is finished. The opportunities for any given individual are dependent both upon his environment and upon his own aptitudes and personal qualities.

One of the main areas of opportunity within the school is of course the curriculum. When there is only a single curriculum consisting of constants which all pupils are expected to take, as was true of many schools a half century ago and is true of some smaller high schools even today, the possibilities of guidance in relation to the curriculum are of course decidedly limited; but with the many curricula offered in modern metropolitan high schools or under conditions where there is a curriculum consisting of constants supplemented by a wide offering of variables, there must either be a careful individual program of guidance of pupils toward the offerings best suited for them as individuals or there will inevitably be a great waste of teacher and pupil effort, which will eventuate in many cases of failure and maladjustment and increased costs for school support.

The extracurriculum affords a second area of opportunity for boys and girls of school age. The extracurriculum, which in the early history of the secondary school was very limited in scope, has expanded tremendously during the present century. In all but the smaller schools there is now such a variety of sports, clubs, and hobbies included under extracurriculum activities that some aspect of it should appeal to the interests of every normal pupil. School people recognizing its educational value are tending to an increasing extent to accord the extracurriculum a place closely parallel to the curriculum itself.

Boys and girls vary greatly in the degree to which they take advantage of the opportunities provided by the extracurriculum. The average pupil takes part in three or four of these activities. At one extreme, there are individuals to whom the extracurriculum is by far the most important aspect of school life and who participate so extensively in extracurriculum activities that there is great interference with the learning process fostered by their regular curriculum. At the other extreme, there are timid, backward, solitary, retiring individuals who do not take part in a single extracurriculum activity unless participation in at least one such activity is a requirement laid down by the school. The pupils at both these extremes are greatly in need of guidance leading to the choice of a moderate number of the activities best suited to them.

The community provides a third area of immediate opportunities for young people. Many of the opportunities afforded by the community are educational and they may be used to supplement and reinforce the program of the school. In fact, it would be entirely possible to replace most elements of the school curriculum by a program based on a study of the resources of the community. Broad contacts with the business life, the civic organization, and the civilizing influences provided by the agencies of literature and art will do much to infuse the curriculum which the pupil pursues in school with real content and meaning. In a rural or small-town environment the young people may be so well acquainted with the community educational resources that little guidance in this area is needed, although even in such a case the counselors have some functions of this kind to perform. In a complex metropolitan environment, however, boys and girls are likely to be acquainted with only certain types of community resources which are along the line of their special interests or which are in their neighborhood, and they need guidance in getting a balanced sampling of the community opportunities.

Part-time work opportunities are also available for a considerable number of pupils of secondary school age, and guidance into these is a function of counseling. From a long-term guidance point of view, the chief objective in this type of vocational counseling is not so much to help the student economically as it is to provide him with a background of work experience which will be useful when he is ready to choose a lifetime vocation.

Opportunities for young people at the end of secondary school may be classified broadly into those of higher education and those of the vocations. Guidance toward the opportunities in both of these areas were temporarily paralyzed by the war. For the past several years, very few physically fit boys have received more than a few months of higher education unless they were taken into the College Training Program of the Army or the Navy. Girls continued to have potential opportunities for college training, but many well-qualified girls have foregone these opportunities because of an understandable desire to participate in the war effort.

Most physically fit boys who recently finished high school have been engaged in one occupation—a military one. Girls have gone into a variety of occupations, but there has been a strong tendency to choose those which had an obvious relationship to the war program regardless of native aptitudes.

Present-day counselors have an obligation to take a long view and to try to see ahead to the vocational situation that will develop as this country gradually adjusts to postwar conditions and the young people whom they are counseling will be free to resume their interrupted careers. They must keep in mind the fact that guidance toward these distant educational and vocational opportunities is not only more difficult but also more necessary than it is under normal conditions. The pupils whom they are counseling need, as never before, to be given an abiding understanding of and faith in their own aptitudes, and a knowledge of the more enduring goals which are in line with those aptitudes.

SOURCES OF INFORMATION ABOUT OPPORTUNITIES

Counselors, as well as pupils, need to be instructed concerning the opportunities available to young people. The counselor's information concerning opportunities afforded by the school will be obtained mainly through reading school catalogues, detailed study of course outlines, and conferences with faculty members. The counselor not only should become thoroughly informed concerning all aspects of the opportunities which the school provides but he also should be alert to inadequacies in the total school program and should use his influence to improve and broaden the opportunities.

A common and frequently used source of information concerning the post-school opportunities of college preparatory pupils is of course college catalogues. There should be available for use by both counselors and pupils a complete and up-to-date file of the catalogues of all colleges to which the school customarily sends students. Every counselor should try to become familiar with the pertinent guidance information in these catalogues.

Surveys of college entrance requirements and procedures are a second valuable source of information. A recent report of the Committee on School and College Relations of the Educational Records Bureau summarizes the responses of approximately four hundred colleges to a series of recommendations looking toward the liberalizing of certain entrance requirements.[1] The report not only provides a summary of the replies of the whole group of colleges but it also gives detailed information concerning the answers of each college. Comments on the recommendations received from most of the state departments of education are also included. It is believed that every counselor could use a report of this kind to good advantage in his work with individual pupils.

Among the many sources of information concerning vocational opportunities, several are almost indispensable to the counselor. One of these sources is the *Dictionary of Occupational Titles*[2] prepared by the U. S. Employment Service and published in four separate books. Part I, *Definitions of Titles,* contains definitions of more than 17,000 separate jobs and gives more than 12,000 alternate titles. Part II, *Titles and Codes,* classifies each job with the other jobs to which it is related. The other parts are Part III, *Conversion Tables,* and Part IV, *Entry Occupational Classification* (Preliminary Edition). Parts I and II are intended for the classification of applicants who are already fully qualified to perform specific occupations. Part IV is intended for classification of applicants into kinds of work in which they have not had experience or specific training.[3] Supplements containing new job definitions and new code numbers are issued from time to time.

Another source of information relative to vocational opportunities is found in the publications of the Occupational Information and Guidance Service, U. S. Office of Education, Washington, D. C. W. J. Greenleaf has prepared many of the helpful publications in this series including such titles as *Eighty New Books on Occupations* and *Trends in Occupations and Vocations,* both of which were published in 1940.

The publications of the Science Research Associates, Chicago, Illinois, form a third source of information about vocational opportunities. This organization publishes a variety of materials, including monthly issues of *Vocational*

---

[1] *Fourth Report of the Committee on School and College Relations of the Educational Records Bureau* (Eugene R. Smith, Chairman). New York: Educational Records Bureau (February 1943). Pp. v + 55.

[2] *Dictionary of Occupational Titles.* U. S. Employment Service, Department of Labor, Washington, D. C., 1939. For sale by the Superintendent of Documents, Washington, D. C.

[3] For a helpful brief discussion of the uses of the *Dictionary of Occupational Titles,* see H. H. Remmers and N. L. Gage, *Educational Measurement and Evaluation.* New York: Harper & Brothers, 1943, pp. 66–67, 314–316, 320.

Trends, Occupational Monographs, and *Occupational Outlines of America's Major Occupations.*

A fourth source of information about vocational opportunities is provided by *Monographs on Careers,* published by the Institute for Research, Chicago, Illinois. This series consists of a hundred or more booklets, each of which contains a careful appraisal of an important occupation.

Much additional information on vocational opportunities is to be found in numerous books and magazines. Among the helpful discussions in various books may be mentioned Part II of Bingham's *Aptitudes and Aptitude Testing.*[4] This part, entitled "Orientation within the World of Work," discusses manual occupations, skilled trades, clerical occupations, and the professions.

One of the most helpful journals is *Occupations, the Vocational Guidance Journal,* published monthly from October to May, inclusive, by the National Vocational Guidance Association, Inc. Another valuable publication in this field is *The Occupational Index,* published by Occupational Index, Inc., New York University.

The sources of information for the counselor may also be used in providing the pupil with information concerning opportunities. In addition, information about opportunities available in the school is often given through locally prepared pamphlets telling new pupils in an interesting way about the school equipment, customs, social activities, and so forth. School orientation books, such as *Your School and You,*[5] *High School and You,*[6] *Making the Most of High School,*[7] and *Social Studies, an Orientation Handbook for High School Pupils*[8] have long been standard materials in this area.

The school newspaper also can be used to give pupils helpful information relative to opportunities in the school. Occasionally, an entire issue of the school paper may be devoted to a discussion of the opportunities and advantages of the local school.

Vocational orientation courses are probably the most generally used means of informing pupils in a systematic way relative to occupational opportunities. The success of such courses is largely dependent upon the initiative, industry, imagination, and enthusiasm of the instructor. Much work and planning is required to render such courses thoroughly dynamic and strictly up-to-date.

Exploratory courses form another very important means of disseminating

[4] Walter VanDyke Bingham. *Aptitudes and Aptitude Testing.* New York: Harper & Brothers, 1937. Pp. x + 390.
[5] Walton B. Bliss. *Your School and You.* Boston: Allyn and Bacon, 1927. Pp. x + 248.
[6] Irvin T. Simley. *High School and You.* Rockville Centre, New York: Acorn Publishing Co., Inc., 1937. Pp. xxii + 328.
[7] Clyde M. Hill and Raymond D. Mosher. *Making the Most of High School.* Chicago: Laidlaw Brothers, 1931. Pp. 288.
[8] William McAndrew and others. *Social Studies, An Orientation Handbook for High School Pupils.* Boston: Little, Brown and Company, 1937. Pp. viii + 465.

information about occupational opportunities among young people. These courses allow pupils at the junior high school level to sample the work experiences of various kinds of occupations within a relatively brief period of time. This type of direct experience should be supplemented by visitation and observation in local business and industrial plants. Visitation trips need to be carefully selected and planned, for they are time-consuming, but with young people they no doubt leave more lasting impressions concerning occupations than any which can be secured through reading alone.

REFERENCES

Brewer, John M. (assisted by Elizabeth J. Cleary, C. C. Dunsmoor, Jeanette S. Lake, Calvin J. Nichols, Carol M. Smith, and Helen Parker Smith). *History of Vocational Guidance*. New York: Harper & Brothers, 1942. Pp. viii + 344.

Germane, Charles E., and Germane, Edith G. *Personnel Work in High School*. Chapter XIII: "Looking at the Curriculum from the Personnel Point of View," pp. 221–256; Chapter XVII: "Why Vocational Counseling?" pp. 350–375; Chapter XVIII: "Pertinent Suggestions for Counseling in Vocational Guidance," pp. 376–407; Chapter XXI: "Carrying on a Group Guidance Program," pp. 457–473. New York: Silver Burdett Company, 1941. Pp. xv + 599.

Hamrin, Shirley A., and Erickson, Clifford S. *Guidance in the Secondary School*. Chapter VI: "Guidance and the Curriculum," pp. 145–182; Chapter VII: "Guidance and the Extracurriculum," pp. 183–213; Chapter XI: "Guidance for the Next Step," pp. 308–332. New York: D. Appleton-Century Co., Inc., 1939. Pp. xii + 465.

Judd, Charles H., and Russell, John Dale. *The American Educational System: An Introduction to Education*. Boston: Houghton Mifflin Company, 1940. Pp. xvi + 555.

Koos, Leonard V., and Kefauver, Grayson N. *Guidance in Secondary Schools*. Part I: "Informing Students Concerning Opportunities," pp. 31–187. New York: The Macmillan Company, 1932. Pp. xi + 640.

Reed, Anna Y. *Guidance and Personnel Services in Education*. Part II: "Information on Educational and Occupational Opportunities and Community Resources," pp. 69–146. Ithaca, New York: Cornell University Press, 1944. Pp. xi + 496.

Strang, Ruth. *Pupil Personnel and Guidance*. Chapter III: "A School Environment Conducive to Child Development," pp. 73–120. New York: The Macmillan Company, 1940. Pp. xiii + 356.

Terry, Paul W. *Supervising Extra-Curricular Activities in the American Secondary School*. New York: McGraw-Hill Book Company, Inc., 1930. Pp. xi + 417.

Williamson, E. G., and Hahn, M. E. *Introduction to High School Counseling*. Chapter IV: "Group Work with Students," pp. 86–101; Chapter V: "Student Personnel Work and the Curriculum," pp. 102–123; Chapter VI: "Personnel Work in the Classroom," pp. 124–145. New York: McGraw-Hill Book Company, Inc., 1940. Pp. ix + 314.

CHAPTER III

Kinds of Information Needed; Use of Interviews and Questionnaires in Collecting Information

NEEDED INFORMATION ABOUT INDIVIDUAL PUPILS

THERE ARE AT LEAST TEN AREAS OF THE HISTORY AND DEVELOPMENT OF THE INDIVIDUAL pupil within which we need information for guidance purposes. In this chapter these areas will be listed separately for purposes of definition and discussion, but it should be kept in mind that although at first glance these areas may seem to consist of separate bits of information, they contain factors which are closely interrelated. One of the primary functions of the counselor is to obtain from these varied factors a developing picture of the student as a whole that has unity and proper emphasis on factors which may dominate the individual's whole adjustment.

One of the ten areas is *home background.* It is desirable to obtain facts concerning the parents including type of occupation, education, religion, health, birth place, citizenship, and language spoken. Likewise, the names, sex, birth dates, education, and health of the siblings should be listed. In addition it is helpful to have information in regard to type of community in which the home is located, study conditions in the home, availability of books and magazines for home reading, and other factors, such as "broken home."

A second type of information has to do with *school history and record of class work.* Information should be available concerning names and types of schools attended, achievement in subjects and activities, and school difficulties encountered. There should, of course, be a complete record of the subjects studied by the pupil and of his progress in these subjects. This has, from the beginning, been the common kind of information kept for individual pupils in schools and it is probable that this is still true in the majority of schools in the United States. While all schools keep a record of the class work of their pupils, not all of them make the record in identical terms. This situation is to be expected, for we are in a period of transition with respect to records of class work. The conventional bases of reports of class work—the Carnegie Unit and the school mark—are under fire. Many schools, colleges, and other groups, including the Carnegie Foundation for the Advancement of Teaching, have begun recently to favor the abandonment of the Carnegie Unit and have pointed to its limitations, including its tendency to cause the accumulation of credits to be the major objective of many students and its inapplicability to the curricula of many modern secondary schools. As for the other time-honored basis of reports of class work, dissatisfaction with the indefinite and unreliable nature of marks and with their tendency to vary widely from one institution to another has caused some schools to abandon them in favor of a verbal statement of success achieved in the different fields of study. The guidance value of records of school work will be greatly enhanced if the information is made available in meaningful, qualitative terms instead of, or supplementary to, marks and credits expressed in units.

A third kind of information needed for guidance is the *mental ability or academic aptitude* of each pupil. It is generally recognized now that academic aptitude is not entirely an innate characteristic but is a combination of native capacity and training. The appraisal of the intelligence or academic aptitude of each individual might be done by means of rating procedures, but tests are so much more reliable than opinion that they have become the standard procedures for use in investigating aptitude.

Most secondary schools now administer one intelligence, or academic aptitude, test to their students at some time during their high school course, and a considerable number obtain the results of two or more such tests for each individual. Schools commonly employ tests yielding just one mental age and I.Q. and while the results of tests of this kind are helpful, in general the more diagnostic the test the more valuable are its scores in placement and guidance. Other things being equal, a school should give preference to an academic aptitude test that yields, in addition to a gross score, separate scores for at least linguistic aptitude and quantitative aptitude, or language and non-language aptitude.

Nearly all tests of academic aptitude call for a considerable amount of reading, and the results are highly correlated with reading test scores. It is desirable, nevertheless, for the school to obtain reading test results as further evidence of academic aptitude. Reading ability is so important in school and college that students with special reading disability are almost certain to experience difficulty with courses in the humanities, social studies, and natural sciences.

A fourth kind of guidance information concerning the individual has to do with *achievement and growth in different fields of study*. The class record furnishes information concerning the achievement of a student, but it is determined partly by the subjective judgment of the various teachers and is inevitably influenced to some extent by the effort, interest, enthusiasm, and personality of the student. The school should, if possible, supplement the class record with objective evidence of achievement based on comparable tests. A comprehensive achievement testing program should include for each pupil four or five tests which are usually administered near the end of the year. The tests commonly used in such a program are an English test, a language test if the pupil is studying a foreign language, and either broad field tests or the appropriate subject tests in mathematics, science, and social studies. The results of the tests should be recorded cumulatively in either tabular or graphic form, or both.

Information concerning achievement and growth obtained in the secondary school not only is valuable for guidance while the pupil is in school but is also helpful in making reports for selection and guidance purposes to higher institutions and to business and industrial organizations. One of the recommendations that the Committee on School and College Relations of the Educational Records Bureau submitted recently to colleges was that in considering a candidate for entrance, colleges should give full weight to the results of comparable tests constructed, administered, and scored by competent persons. Of the four hundred colleges which replied to the questionnaire, more than three-fourths favored the recommendation.

A fifth type of guidance information deals with the *health* of the individual pupil. This kind of information may be obtained from questionnaires, interviews with the pupil, tests, and records of examination by the home or school physician.

In the cumulative folder or file for each pupil there should be a generally available and quickly read summary of the health and physical characteristics of the pupil, including vigor or lassitude, assets, and disabilities or limitations. In addition there should be a more detailed record of health including periodic physical examinations and a disease history record. This information will usually be filed in the physical education office or office of the school physician.

A sixth type of information needed in guidance consists of notes on the *out-of-school experiences* of the pupil. This type of information will be secured mainly by questionnaires and personal interviews. Special attention should be given to summer experiences and work experiences. Information in regard to work experiences should cover such items as type, duration, hours per week, earnings, and the degree to which the individual liked and enjoyed the work.

A seventh type of guidance information is concerned with the *educational and vocational interests* of the individual pupil. The newer psychology emphasizes the dynamic role of interest in all aspects of mental and emotional development. Interests should invariably be one of the reference points in personnel work with individuals.

The school should secure two kinds of information about the interests of each pupil. In the first place it should keep a record of his activities as an indication of functioning interests. In the second place it should be able to make a summary statement concerning the interests of the pupil on the basis of observation and scores on standardized interest questionnaires.

In the interpretation of interest data the counselor should keep in mind the fact that the interests of many individuals change markedly during the secondary school years. Trends in interest development may be fully as important as the pattern of interests at any given time.

At present, many secondary schools record information concerning the activities in which the pupil has engaged. They also attempt to summarize the student's interests, but the value of this report depends upon the accuracy of the counselor's judgment. Few schools have much objective data on interests, although the number that recognize the importance of this phase of the student's development and the need for adequate information concerning it is significantly larger than it was a few years ago.

Closely related to interests is an eighth aspect of pupil development about which the school should obtain information for guidance purposes. This type of information includes the student's *special aptitudes*—art, literature, music, mechanical skill, and so forth. In the case of many students, perhaps the majority of them, the secondary school cannot record anything very significant under this category, for a large proportion of the pupils have no unusually marked aptitude in any one field; but when a pupil has exceptionally high aptitude of a particular kind, the counselor should be informed of this fact as soon as possible. Awareness that the student possesses the aptitude will unquestionably influence the counselor's advice concerning courses and other relationships in the school, and plans for future education and vocational choice. Information in regard to a pupil's special aptitudes may be obtained from the record of his activities in the school, the comments of his teachers and others who know him well, and the results of various aptitude tests. Few schools use special aptitude tests extensively, and the main reliance will usually be placed on more subjective criteria of evaluation.

A ninth, and very important, area in which the guidance department needs information about individual pupils is that of *personality*. The eight categories already considered are indirectly related to personality, but here we are concerned more directly with a complex of qualities which acting together tend to shape the personality of the individual.

There is close agreement among teachers and counselors at all levels of the school that much attention should be given to personality development. It would, however, be impossible to suggest a list of personal characteristics which would be satisfactory to all educators. Every group that has tried to formulate a comprehensive set of personality traits has come out with a somewhat different list, although all of them overlapped to some extent. The components of personality may ultimately be isolated by means of factor analysis, but in the meantime lists of personal characteristics formulated as a result of a subjective analysis must be used as the basis of appraisal. One list that will undoubtedly be used extensively is included in the "Description of Behavior" in the new revision of the American Council cumulative record form. It covers responsibility, creativeness, influence, adjustability, concern for others, seriousness of purpose, and emotional stability.[1]

Some schools, especially the thirty schools which cooperated in the Eight-Year Study of the Progressive Education Association, have recently given much attention to the appraisal of the personal qualities of their students. Most schools, however, are probably less well prepared to furnish valid information concerning this aspect of the status and growth of their pupils than about any of the other categories discussed in this chapter.

If schools in general are to be able to supply their guidance departments with really valid information in this area, they must devote much time and thought to the improvement of procedures for appraising personality. Ratings made hastily by one individual, perhaps the principal or the counselor, at the end of the pupil's high school course are subject to large error. Personality tests are of some value in a counseling program if they are used cautiously along with other information about the pupil, but they have not reached the stage of development where they can be employed with a high degree of confidence. Anecdotal records have marked possibilities as a basis for personality appraisal, but few schools have as yet solved the problems of obtaining systematic records from all the teachers and of summarizing the anecdotes. Behavior descriptions of the type devised by the Reports and Records Committee of the Progressive Education Association probably provide the most workable procedure for the evaluation of personal qualities thus far developed. Through this plan, behavior descriptions can be obtained at regular intervals from all staff members acquainted with the individual, and summarized when the pupil is graduated from the secondary school. Experience indicates that when a summary of behavior descriptions or of ratings of personal qualities is made, the school should not merely average them—for the average rating may not be the rating assigned by any one of the staff members—but it should also de-

---

[1] *1941 Revision of American Council on Education Cumulative Record Card for Junior and Senior High Schools.* Prepared by the Committee on the Revision of Cumulative Records (Eugene Randolph Smith, Chairman). Washington, D. C.: American Council on Education, 1941.

termine the most frequent rating and the spread of the ratings. Variability in behavior or in personality characteristics in different situations may be very significant from the personnel point of view.

The last area of guidance information which will be mentioned here is *plans for the future*. This area should include educational and occupational plans as indicated by the pupil, his parents, and the counselor. The information will be obtained chiefly from interviews and questionnaires.

It will be observed that in connection with the foregoing list of kinds of information needed, certain techniques for the collection of the information were mentioned repeatedly. These techniques included questionnaires, interviews, rating scales, behavior descriptions, objective tests, records in the form of anecdotal material, and cumulative records. These techniques will be discussed in considerable detail in the next section and in the following chapters.

PROCEDURES FOR COLLECTING INFORMATION

As indicated in the first part of this chapter, a considerable amount of the information about individuals which is needed for guidance may be obtained from tests and other objective techniques. For those areas in which they are applicable, objective techniques should be preferred, for they provide data whose reliability and impersonal quality is highly desirable as a starting point in counseling. It is obvious, however, that certain kinds of information must necessarily be collected directly from the parents or the pupil, not through objective procedures but by means of interviews or questionnaires. These kinds of information include especially home background, social history, certain aspects of the school history, certain aspects of the health history, extracurriculum activities, work and summer experiences, interests, school subjects preferred and those disliked, conditions for study outside the school, voluntary reading, and educational and vocational plans.

THE INTERVIEW AS A MEANS OF GATHERING INFORMATION [2]

If time were available for extensive individual conferences, there can be little doubt that the most satisfactory procedure for the collection of information in the areas listed would be a personal interview with each individual. The interview is a particularly fortunate medium because of its flexibility, the possibility of pursuing main questions through a series of more detailed questions, and the opportunity for drawing pupils out and getting them to express themselves freely concerning activities, interests, plans, and so forth. It is the most

[2] For an extensive and authoritative discussion of this topic, see Walter V. Bingham and Bruce V. Moore, *How to Interview*. New York: Harper & Brothers, 1941 (revised). Pp. x + 263.

extensively used technique in personnel work. In independent schools,[3] which are well-staffed in proportion to the number of pupils enrolled, and in some of the smaller public schools, it may be possible to dispense with questionnaires altogether and to handle the collection of background information entirely by means of interviews. The interview of course has many other uses, some of them therapeutic, but we are here concerned with the value of the interview in gathering information.

When guidance information is to be derived from interviews, the counselor should of course prepare carefully for each interview. He should formulate a definite series of questions, and he should have them so well in mind that the interview will take on a certain objective and scientific character notwithstanding its freedom and latitude.

Although the counselor should be prepared to ask certain important questions in a predetermined way, he should avoid allowing the interview to seem stereotyped and formal to the pupil. He should spend a few moments at the beginning of the interview in establishing rapport and his questions should seem to arise naturally in the course of a pleasant conversation. The carrying out of a definite line of questioning in an informal and cordial setting is a difficult achievement which calls for natural sympathy and diplomacy, and considerable experience. Properly applied, however, it is the most satisfactory technique for obtaining information in the less tangible areas.

Care should be used to see that the interview does not take on the character of an inquisition or even that of an oral questionnaire. Too direct a line of questioning may defeat the purpose by arousing a feeling of antagonism and resentment. The pupil should be encouraged to talk freely and to volunteer information which he feels is important.

When the counselor is obtaining information for use in guidance later, he will of course need to make a written record of the pertinent facts. Nevertheless, he should do as little writing as possible during the interview. A counselor whose memory is good can probably avoid writing anything while the interview is in progress, while one who does not easily recall factual statements may need to make occasional notes. In this event the writing should be done so briefly and easily that the thread of the conversation is not broken. Immediately after each interview the counselor should make a detailed written summary of the information secured. He cannot afford to depend for long upon his memory, nor should he, even if he could hold the facts in mind indefinitely, for a brief written record of the interviews which take place between pupil and counselor, and also between the counselor and persons who know the pupil, will be an important addition to the cumulative record.

[3] Independent schools, as the term is used in this book, include private college-preparatory schools, church-supported schools, military schools, and all other schools not publicly maintained and controlled.

INTERVIEW RECORD

Name of Student:_____

Name of Counselor:_____

Date

_____

_____

_____

_____

_____

_____

Form 1.

The interview record may be set down in the form of notes or paragraph statements, or it may be made on a specially prepared blank. Some schools have their own blanks for this purpose, and a few such blanks are distributed commercially by various organizations. One of the most extensive blanks of the latter kind is a form entitled *Aids to the Vocational Interview*,[4] published by the Psychological Corporation. In contrast to that elaborate and detailed record form, a very simple blank will often serve the counselor for everyday use in interviewing pupils. This type of record is illustrated in Form 1.

Use of Questionnaires in Collecting Information

Notwithstanding the advantages of the interview as a means of gathering information, it is not practicable for counselors in a large school to try to interview every new pupil at the beginning of the school year in order to secure the information needed as a starting point for the guidance of the individual. In gathering the required data most schools will necessarily resort to a printed or mimeographed information blank or questionnaire. Questionnaires have often been criticized for their unreliability, but their reliability can be greatly increased if they are used as standardized interview forms and are filled out under careful supervision.

It is preferable to have the information concerning social history and home background supplied by the parents rather than the pupils themselves; in fact, this is the only reliable procedure if the children are young. In private schools and in public schools in small communities it may be possible to have one of the parents, usually the mother, of each pupil come to the school and fill out the social history questionnaire under supervision. A plan of this kind has been used for years in connection with the Records Office of the University of Chicago Laboratory Schools. Regardless of whether the child is entering the kindergarten, the elementary school, or the high school, one of the parents is asked to come to the Records Office and fill out an extensive social history blank. The questionnaire is based directly on the master record cards, and all the information requested is needed in filling out the cards. A representative of the Records Office is always present to answer questions and assist the parents in providing the needed information.

In large public schools it is seldom feasible to try to get the parents to fill out the questionnaire under supervision, and the school must either send it to the parents to be filled out and returned or depend on getting the information from the pupils. In junior and senior high schools the latter plan is probably preferable, for the pupils can readily be assembled and instructed to fill out,

---

[4] Paul S. Achilles. *Aids to the Vocational Interview*. New York: Psychological Corporation. 10 cents each; $2.00 for 25; $7.00 for 100.

QUESTIONNAIRE FOR HIGH SCHOOL PUPILS

To the pupil.—Please fill out this questionnaire so that your counselor may have more information about you and thus be in a better position to help you with any problems that may arise. The information will be treated confidentially.

1. Name_____2. Date_____
           Last   First   Middle

3. Address_____4. Tel. No._____

5. Birthplace_____6. Date of Birth_____
          City   State   Mo. Day Year

7. Nationality_____8. Citizenship_____
         (Scotch, Irish, etc.; not citizenship)

9. Father's name_____10. Father's occupation_____

11. Mother's name_____12. Mother's occupation_____

13. Do you live in a house or in an apartment?_____

14. Do you have a separate room?_____

15. Number of older brothers_____Number of older sisters_____

    Number of younger brothers_____Number of younger sisters_____

16. Names of brothers and sisters who have attended or are attending this school

_____

17. What elementary school or schools did you attend?_____

_____

18. Have you attended any high school other than this one?_____If so, what one?

_____What high school years?_____

19. Date of entrance to this school_____Grade entered_____

20. What subject or subjects in school do you like best?_____

_____Why?_____

_____

21. Are there any subjects that you dislike?_____What ones?_____

_____

Form 2.

22. Do you study at home?____How many hours per day, on the average?____

23. Have you ever repeated a school subject or grade?_____If so, state what subject or grade_____

24. Do you play a musical instrument?_____What one?_____

25. Do you take part in interscholastic sports?_____What ones?_____

_____In intramural sports?_____What ones?_____

_____ _____

26. Why do you prefer the kind of athletics in which you take part?_____

_____

27. Estimate the number of hours you spend in recreation outside school each day

_____

28. To what school clubs do you belong?_____

_____

29. What school offices have you held before this year?_____

_____

30. What school offices are you holding now?_____

_____

31. Do you expect to go to college?_____To what college?_____

32. In what department do you expect to specialize?_____

33. Have you selected a vocation?_____If so, what one?_____

34. Do you enjoy reading?_____If so, what type of book do you prefer?_____

_____

35. Who are your favorite authors?_____

36. What magazines do you read?_____

37. How often do you attend the movies?_____

Form 2 (cont.)

38. What kind of movies do you like best?_____

39. How did you spend your past summer?_____

_____

40. Name any summer camps you have attended and give dates_____

_____

41. Have you traveled in this country or abroad?_____If so, state the nature and

extent of travel_____

_____

42. Do you have any responsibilities or duties at home?_____If so, describe

briefly_____

43. Do you participate in any church activities?_____If so, what ones?_____

_____

44. What special interests do you carry on during your spare time and approxi-

mately how long have you had each special interest?_____

_____

_____

_____

45. Remarks_____

_____

_____

_____

Form 2 (cont.)

under supervision, a questionnaire specially prepared for them. Moreover, if the pupils are relatively mature, certain questions, such as those pertaining to interests and to educational and vocational plans, should be answered by the pupils themselves.

If the questionnaire is carefully planned and specific directions are given for answering the questions, experience has shown that it can be filled out in home rooms or guidance rooms with satisfactory accuracy. There should be either an oral or a written introductory statement explaining the purpose of the questionnaire to the pupils and enlisting their cooperation. A clear and diplomatic statement of the purpose of the questionnaire is important, for some of the pupils may feel that certain questions tend to encroach upon their privacy. They will be more likely to answer the questions willingly and honestly if they know that the information will be treated confidentially by the counselors and will be used to help the pupils themselves as individuals.

The guidance department in each school should formulate its pupil questionnaire to fit its own situation. A questionnaire which was prepared by a guidance chairman to obtain background information from the pupils in one high school is shown in Form 2. It was filled out in the guidance groups under the supervision of the counselors and was filed in the pupil's cumulative folder which was kept by his counselor.

If the school has individual cumulative record cards to which information from the pupil questionnaires is transferred, it is desirable to employ a questionnaire the items of which will closely parallel the items on the cumulative record form and will be keyed to them. An excellent illustration of this kind of questionnaire and of a carefully prepared procedure for having it filled out was developed at the Plainfield High School, under the direction of Dr. Galen Jones, formerly principal of that high school, and Miss Adria Galbraith, who is in charge of testing and records.[5]

A visible file adaptation of the American Council cumulative record folder is used at Plainfield. The questionnaire parallels the cumulative record form item for item.[6] Early in each year the questionnaire is given to all the pupils in their home rooms. Approximately two home room periods of thirty-eight minutes are required for the completion of all three sections. Both the general directions and the questionnaire itself are reproduced[7] in full on the remaining pages of this chapter.

---

[5] Various other school systems have developed thorough pupil questionnaires. Among the better ones which have come to the attention of the writer are a *General Inventory for High School Pupils* devised by Ralph P. Gallagher, supervisor of guidance in the Elizabeth, New Jersey, Public Schools, and the *Student Information* blanks prepared by the Cincinnati Public Schools Division of Counseling Services, of which Mary P. Corre is supervisor.

[6] See Form 11 for an illustration of the cumulative record folder used at Plainfield.

[7] Reprinted with the permission of Plainfield High School, Plainfield, New Jersey.

DIRECTIONS FOR MAKING ENTRIES

Part A 1

Item A 1. Name

The pupil should record his full name, being careful to get the correct spelling of each portion of the name; real names instead of nicknames; and names in full instead of initials. If a pupil regularly goes by a nickname instead of his real name (for example, the nickname Jack instead of John, his real name), the nickname should be written in parenthesis at the side of his real name.

Item A 1. Place of birth

Check to certify that the name of the city (township or borough) has been entered.

Item A 4. Telephone

This is the home telephone number. In cases where the home is without telephone, instruct the pupil to enter the information, "No telephone."

Item A 6 1. General health

The general statement as to health is to be answered in the following terms: excellent, good, fair, or poor.

Item A 10. Help with school-work

If there is anyone at home who can help the pupil, he is to state who that person is, whether mother, father, older brother, older sister, etc.

Part A 2

Item A 13. Occupation

If possible, the student should name a specific occupation; if not, the general type of work he prefers and for which he feels himself qualified, as "commercial," "industrial," "professional," etc.

Item A 14. Leaving school

A pupil intending to remain until graduation should write "At graduation"; pupils leaving before then should state when they intend to leave.

Item A 17. Self-support

To be answered "Completely," "In part," or "Not at all."

Item A 24. Occupation of father

Great care should be taken to state the occupation of the father. The entry should be an answer to the question, "What is your father's work?" or "Just what does he do?" Guard against the pupil's tendency to conceal the real nature of the father's occupation by giving a general name for it, such as "Laborer," or "Factory-worker."

Item A 24. Father's Business Address

The business address should include the name of the firm for which the father works as well as the address.

Item A 25. Mother's Business Address

See Item A 24, if mother works outside the home.

Item A 26. Guardian's Business Address

See Item A 24.

Form 3.

Items B 9, 10, 11, 12. Emphasize that these are extra-curricular activities.

Item B 16. Summers

Pupils are requested to answer this in some detail. The following questions are suggested:

a. What special things did you do this summer? Did you have any unusual experiences?

b. Did you take any trips this summer? If so, where?

c. Did you attend a summer camp or participate in special outdoor activities, such as camping, etc.?

d. Did you read any unusual books?

Specific information is wanted, as: "At camp," with the name of the camp, its location, and the length of time spent there; "Traveling," stating where and length of time; "Working," stating where, type of work, and length of time; "Summer School," stating where, subjects taken, and length of time spent.

Form 3 (cont.)

THE PUPIL QUESTIONNAIRE

To be of most assistance to you in planning your way through school, each one of your teachers would like to have a talk with you about your ambitions, interests, and activities. Since most pupils carry four subjects, this would mean at least four interviews. It would, of course, be ideal if some arrangement could be made whereby you could meet with all your teachers at one time; such an arrangement would conserve your time and theirs. But this is scarcely feasible when almost two thousand pupils are involved.

The following questionnaire represents an attempt to find a substitute for an interview at which you and all your teachers talk over your plans. We expect that you will give your fullest cooperation in answering these questions and by so doing help us in our endeavors to help you.

NAME_____

HOME ROOM_____ _____

DATE_____

Part A 1

Name_____
    Last   First   Middle

A 1. Where were you born?_____
           City and State, or City and Foreign Country

A 1. How old were you on your last birthday?_____

A 1. When is your birthday?_____
        Month   Day

A 3. Address_____

A 4. Telephone_____

A 1. Of what church are you a member?_____

A 6. Physical record:

 1. What is the condition of your general health?_____

 2. Do you suffer from headaches?_____Other pains?_____

 3. Have you ever had any trouble with your eyes?_____

 4. Have glasses been recommended for you?_____

 5. Do you wear glasses?_____

Form 3 (cont.)

6. Have you ever had trouble in hearing?-------------------------------

7. Do you have heart trouble?---

8. Have you any other physical defects?---------------------------------

9. What are they?---

10. Have you ever had an illness which kept you out of school for a month

or more?----------------When?--------------------------

What was the illness?---

11. Have you a speech defect?---------What is it?------------------------.

12. How many days have you been absent from school this year because of

ill health?---------What ailments caused these absences?------------

----

A 10. Study:
1. Do you take home books to study each night?------------------------

2. How long do you study at home each night?------------------------

3. In what room at home do you study?---------------------------------

4. Do you study within hearing of the radio?--------------------------

Is the light good?--

Do others study with you?--------Who?--------------------------

5. Is there anyone at home who can help you with your school-work—as

father, mother, older brother, or sister?--------------------------

6. What lesson takes the most time?---------------------------------

7. How many times each month do you go to the movies?--------------

8. Do you attend the movies on school nights?------------------------

A 12. What school subjects do you like most?------------------------------

----

Why?--

What school subjects do you dislike most?. ----------------------------

----

Form 3 (cont.)

Why?---

----

3. Do you play a musical instrument?--------What?---------------------

4. Do you intend to try for any of the school teams or join any of the school

    organizations?---------What?--

5. What is your particular hobby or interest?--------------------------

6. How do you spend your spare time? (Answer fully)-------------------

    ----

Part A 2

A 13. Have you decided what you want to do to earn a living?----------------

What?---

In what other occupations are you interested?-------------------------

----

A 14. When do you intend to leave school?------------------------------

Is this because you have to help the family, or because you wish to do so?

Do you expect to attend an institution of higher learning after you graduate

from high school?---------Name and type of school?-------------------

----

Whom have you consulted regarding your preparation for this school?

A 17. Do you support yourself completely or in part?----------------------

A 24. Father's name?---

Is his health good?--

Birthplace?---
                        (City and State, or City and Foreign Country)

Nationality?--

Form 3 (cont.)

Arrived in U. S. A. in what year?_____

Occupation?_____Business firm?_____

Address (Business)_____

Telephone (Business)_____

Died (date)_____

A 25. Mother's name?_____

Is her health good?_____

Birthplace?_____
(City and State, or City and Foreign Country)

Nationality?_____

Arrived in U. S. A. in what year?_____

Occupation?_____

Address_____

Telephone_____

Died (date)_____

A 26. Step-parent or guardian's name?_____

Is (his, her) health good?_____

Birthplace?_____
(City and State, or City and Foreign Country)

Nationality?_____

Arrived in U. S. A. in what year?_____

Occupation?_____

Address_____

Telephone_____

A 27. Older brothers (Names and Ages):_____

_____

A 28. Younger brothers (Names and Ages):_____

_____

A 29. Older sisters (Names and Ages):_____

_____

A 30. Younger sisters (Names and Ages):_____

_____

Form 3 (cont.)

A 31, 32, 33.	Years in Grammar Sch.	Years in High School	Years in College	College (Name)
Father (Guardian)				
Mother (Guardian)				
Brother				
"				
"				
"				
"				
"				
Sister				
"				
"				
"				
"				

A 38. What language or languages were spoken in your home:

    1. Before you were 10 years old?_____

    2. After you were 10 years old?_____

Part B

B 6. What school offices have you held?

1942–43	1943–44

B 7. Unusual experiences:

    1. What prizes, medals, or honors have you won?_____

_____

Form 3 (cont.)

2. What poem, letter, or article have you written that has been published?

----

3. Have you built or made anything unusual (a boat, a cabin, an engine, etc.)?

----

4. Have you appeared on a radio broadcast program?_____

   Have you ever given a musical recital?_____

5. What foreign countries have you visited?_____

   _____When?_____

6. Other unusual experiences not listed above_____

B 8. Of what school clubs have you been a member?

1942–43	1943–44

Of what other clubs have you been a member?

B 9, 10, 11, 12. Time spent in *extra-curricular* activities.

1942–43	1943–44
Athletic	
Hrs. a wk.	
Non-Athletic	
Hrs. a wk.	

Form 3 (cont.)

B 13. What work do you perform daily or weekly in your home?_____

_____

Have you a job outside your home?_____

What kind of work is it?_____

Where do you work?_____

How many hours do you work each day?_____Each week?_____

How late do you work at night?_____

B 14. List all jobs you have held for the past two years:

	1943	1944
Type		
Duration		
Weekly Pay		
Hrs. a wk.		

B 16. Describe in some detail how you have spent your summers:

1943

_____

_____

_____

_____

1944

_____

_____

_____

Form 3 (cont.)

CHAPTER IV

Appraisal of Aptitudes for Guidance Purposes

LET US TURN FROM QUESTIONNAIRES AND INTERVIEWS TO MORE OBJECTIVE PROCEDURES for collecting information for guidance. These procedures include tests, rating scales, and other devices for measurement and evaluation. Tests may be divided into three broad classes: aptitude tests, achievement tests, and tests of personal qualities. The present chapter will deal with the first group, tests of aptitude. No attempt will be made in this chapter to provide a complete coverage of all aptitude tests in the manner of a book on tests and measurements, but it will present a point of view concerning the measurement of aptitudes and a discussion of certain selected instruments which experience and observation have shown to be useful in a guidance program.[1]

WHAT IS APTITUDE? [2]

Aptitude is a condition, a quality, or a set of qualities in an individual which is indicative of the probable extent to which he will be able to acquire under suitable training, some knowledge, skill, or composite of knowledge and skill, such as ability to contribute to art or music, mechanical ability, mathematical ability, or ability to read and speak a foreign language. Aptitude is a present condition which is indicative of an individual's potentialities for the future.

Laymen, and sometimes teachers and counselors, give evidence of a misconception which causes them to regard aptitude as almost entirely inborn, and

[1] For an up-to-date, thorough, and not too highly technical treatment of all aspects of testing discussed in this and subsequent chapters, see H. H. Remmers and N. L. Gage, *Educational Measurement and Evaluation*. New York: Harper & Brothers, 1943. Pp. ix + 580.

[2] For a brief but excellent treatment of the theory of aptitude, see Walter VanDyke Bingham, *Aptitudes and Aptitude Testing*, Chapters II and III. New York: Harper & Brothers, 1937. Pp. ix + 390.

aptitude tests as measures of innate characteristics. It should be clearly understood that aptitude tests measure a complex of innate tendencies and the influence of training, and that there is no way of separating the influences of heredity and environment in the test results. From a theoretical point of view this situation may be cause for regret, but in the practical work of counseling there is no need for a separation of the influences of innate tendencies and experience on the basis of the person's present aptitude. In fact, if the counselor were able to make the separation on a valid basis, he probably would not know what to do with his data in his personnel work with the individual. He needs the total picture of present aptitude, regardless of the influences which have created that aptitude, but he also needs to be aware that when he is thinking in terms of aptitude he is dealing with something that is only partly inborn and that is constantly being modified to some extent by the day to day experience of the individual pupil.

There are three important assumptions concerning aptitudes which are justified by general observation and research, and which are among the basic tenets of a program of guidance which lays any claim to being scientific. The first assumption is that few, if any, individuals have equally strong aptitudes in all directions. If one were able to make a perfectly valid and reliable measurement of any individual's aptitudes and were to graph the results, the resulting curve would consist of peaks and valleys. Almost every normal individual learns some activities easily, others with a moderate amount of effort, and still others only, if at all, with extremely long and arduous application.

A second assumption is that individuals differ from one another in every aptitude they possess regardless of whether broad aptitudes or very specific aptitudes are being considered. Moreover, a certain type of curve has commonly been used to express these differences. The hypothesis has been widely accepted by theorists and research workers in psychology that on numerous measurable characteristics individuals tend to distribute themselves according to the normal or bell-shaped curve. According to this hypothesis, most individuals tend to be grouped very close to the median or average, and the number thins out rapidly on each side of the average. The normal curve is the basis of a large proportion of all educational and psychological measurement and research, notwithstanding the fact that some psychologists and experts in measurement hold that there are many characteristics to which it is not applicable.

Counselors need not be highly conversant with error theory in which the normal curve hypothesis finds its most advanced application, but they should be aware that the normal curve and the standard deviation along the base line under the normal curve are the bases of nearly all systems of converted or derived or standard scores in terms of which the results of the newer objective tests are very frequently expressed. Figure 2 may be helpful in visualizing the

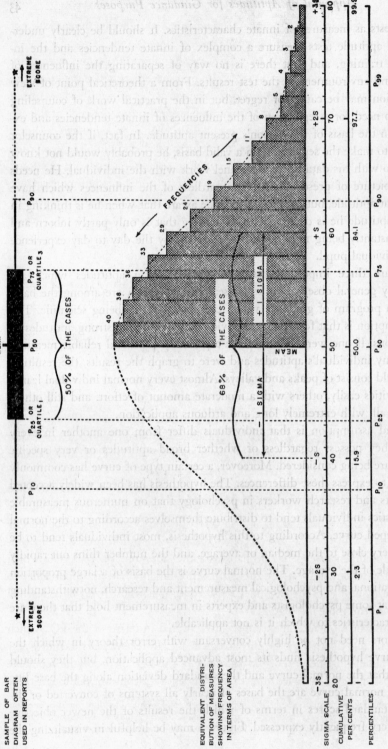

FIGURE 2. Explanation of the Sigma Scale in Relation to a Typical Distribution. Fifty per cent of the cases lie between P₂₅ and P₇₅. Approximately 68 per cent lie between ± 1.0 sigma from the mean. Approximately 2 per cent of the measures lie above + 2 sigmas, and approximately 2 per cent below − 2 sigmas, from the mean. (Reproduced with the permission of the Carnegie Foundation for the Advancement of Teaching.)

normal curve and in clarifying the relationship between the sigma scale, or standard deviation scale, and the normal curve.

The third hypothesis is that differences among individuals and within individuals tend to persist within limits. They are fairly, although not completely, stable. An individual who is definitely superior in a certain kind of aptitude at the age of six will, as a rule, be above average in that kind of aptitude at the age of sixteen or twenty-six. Patterns of aptitudes do change to some extent, but a complete reversal in aptitudes within the life span of an individual is practically unknown, if pathological cases or cases involving severe accidents are ruled out. If it were not for the fairly persistent character of aptitude, a long-time guidance program would be a waste of time and might actually be harmful to many individuals.

KINDS OF APTITUDE TESTS

Aptitude tests may be divided into two broad classes, known as *tests of general aptitude* and *tests of aptitude in specific fields*. General aptitude tests are designed to measure a wide range of aptitudes, particularly those important in school work. Tests of aptitude in specific fields include tests of musical aptitude, art aptitude, mechanical aptitude, clerical aptitude, and so forth.

APTITUDE AND INTELLIGENCE

Tests of general scholastic aptitude have long been known as intelligence tests. There is now a tendency to favor the terms "academic aptitude test" or "scholastic aptitude test" rather than "intelligence test," because to many people "intelligence test" implies a measure of native ability.

Intelligence is generally understood to be "ability to learn" or "ability to solve new problems." Tests of intelligence usually have not been composed wholly or even mainly of new problems, for it is very difficult to improvise problems or situations that will be new to everyone. The more common procedure in constructing intelligence tests has been to base the questions on materials which everyone for whom the test is designed has presumably had an opportunity to learn. The assumption is that under these conditions, those who have learned the most are the most intelligent.

The results of most intelligence tests are reported in terms of the I.Q., which is the mental age divided by the chronological age. In recent years a controversy nas raged about the question of the constancy of the I.Q.[3] Probably no reputable psychologist has ever believed that the I.Q. is entirely constant, although there

[3] For a comprehensive summary of the points of view and of the literature on this question, see *Intelligence: Its Nature and Nurture.* National Society for the Study of Education, Yearbook 39, Parts I and II. Bloomington, Illinois: Public School Publishing Company, 1940.

has been a popular belief in its constancy. The I.Q. continues to be a useful concept provided one remembers that it is influenced to some extent by schooling and by other environmental factors, and that I.Q.'s obtained from different tests may not be directly comparable.

It should be pointed out that aside from the question of the constancy of the I.Q., there is a theoretical objection to the use of mental ages and I.Q.'s for purposes of expressing the test results of persons who are above average and are mentally mature. This group would of course include many students in college, and even a considerable number in the last two years of the secondary school. The limitations to the use of mental ages and intelligence quotients in connection with tests given to these students have been stated clearly by Thurstone and Thurstone, as follows:

The intelligence quotient is, by definition, the ratio of the mental age to the chronological age. The mental age of a test performance is the chronological age for which the test performance is the average. It follows from this definition that mental ages and intelligence quotients are indeterminate for the upper half of the adult population. If a person scores above the average for adults in a psychological examination, then there exists no age for which his score is the average. College students can be assumed to score above the average for the adult population of the country and, consequently, they cannot be assigned any mental ages or intelligence quotients. This is not a debatable question. It is a question of very simple and straightforward logic.

Intelligence quotients are assigned to the upper half of the adult population by changing the definition of mental age. For example, a mental age of 15 or 18 does not mean the average test performance of people of that age. Such mental ages are arbitrary designations of what the test author may choose to call superior adult performance.[4]

While it must be admitted that the I.Q.'s obtained for the more mature and the brighter pupils are not true intelligence quotients according to the strict meaning of the term, their use at the secondary school level may still be defended if, through serving as indices of brightness, they help teachers and counselors in the instruction and guidance of the pupils.

TESTS OF GENERAL ACADEMIC APTITUDE

Tests Yielding One Mental Age and Intelligence Quotient. As already indicated, the oldest and best-known type of intelligence or academic aptitude test is the kind which provides a single score which is translated into a mental age, which is in turn divided by a chronological age to find an I.Q. The Terman-

[4] L. L. Thurstone and Thelma Gwinn Thurstone. *Psychological Examinations, 1941 Norms.* Washington, D. C.: American Council on Education Studies, VI (May 1942) p. 2.

Merrill revision of the Stanford-Binet Scale[5] is usually regarded as the best single measure of intelligence or academic aptitude, and it is highly desirable for a guidance department to have some member of its staff trained to administer, score, and interpret the results of this examination. However, since it is an individual test, few schools have the time and clerical assistance to use this test with all pupils. In the usual school situation it should be reserved for the testing of special and doubtful cases, and it will be necessary to resort to group tests for the measurement of the academic aptitude of the entire school population.

There are several group tests of this type which have about equal merit. Two of the simplest and most widely used intelligence tests are the Otis Self-Administering Test of Mental Ability and the Otis Quick-Scoring Mental Ability Test. The second test is a revision of the first one and probably it should be preferred, since it includes a few more items, covers a wider range of grades, and is more easily scored, particularly if machine-scoring services are available.

The Kuhlmann-Anderson Tests, which consist of a series of overlapping batteries extending from the kindergarten to the adult level, are in some respects preferable to the Otis tests, for they represent a somewhat better balance of verbal, numerical, and spatial material, and the fact that there is a different battery for each grade probably results in better adjustment of the test items to the age level of the pupils. These tests must be carefully administered, however, because each booklet contains a large number of subtests, each of which has short time limits. The scoring procedure is also somewhat more difficult and time-consuming than that required by most group intelligence tests.

Other well-constructed and widely used tests of general scholastic aptitude are the Henmon-Nelson Tests of Mental Ability; the Pintner General Ability Tests, Verbal Series; the Terman-McNemar Test of Mental Ability; and the Ohio State University Psychological Test. The Terman-McNemar Test of Mental Ability is a revision of the well-known Terman Group Test of Mental Ability.

Two-Axis Tests. While tests yielding one mental age and intelligence quotient probably continue to be more extensively employed than any other tests of academic aptitude, there is a growing tendency among guidance specialists to prefer scholastic aptitude tests which are to some extent diagnostic. For example, information concerning a pupil's aptitude in terms of language and non-language factors is definitely helpful in both educational and vocational guidance. The California Test of Mental Maturity represents an attempt to meet the need for this type of instrument. This test is available in a short form, requiring approximately one class period, and in a long form, calling for two

---

[5] Detailed information concerning all the tests listed in this section is given in the annotated list in the last part of the chapter.

periods of working time. It provides mental ages and I.Q.'s for language factors, non-language factors, and total mental factors, as well as a more detailed profile which is intended to be diagnostic.

Observation and research have indicated that two kinds of aptitude are related to success in a variety of school subjects and vocations. These are verbal or linguistic aptitude, and numerical or quantitative aptitude. The American Council Psychological Examination yields an L-score or score for linguistic ability, a Q-score or score for quantitative ability, and a total score, as well as scores on certain subtests within the linguistic and quantitative areas. There is a High School Edition for Grades 9 to 12 and a College Freshman Edition.

The Secondary Education Board Junior Scholastic Aptitude Test provides for the measurement of verbal aptitude and numerical aptitude in Grades 7, 8, and 9. It is used as a basis of entrance, placement, and guidance in a large number of the independent schools. The Scholastic Aptitude Test of the College Entrance Examination Board, which is primarily a college placement test for high school seniors, also gives a verbal total and a mathematical total.

Tests Yielding Several Aptitude Scores. In recent years, the perfection of factor analysis techniques and concomitant theoretical considerations have led to the development of two new mental tests which are longer and more highly diagnostic than the others and which may ultimately be much more serviceable in guidance. The Chicago Tests of Primary Mental Abilities, published in 1941, are a revision of the Thurstone Tests for Primary Mental Abilities first published in 1938. They are the result of several years of intensive work in factor analysis. They provide fairly independent measures of six mental factors.

The Yale Educational Aptitude Tests, prepared by Dr. A. B. Crawford, are an extensive battery including seven tests, each in a separate booklet. They are designed to measure verbal comprehension, artificial language, verbal reasoning, quantitative reasoning, mathematical aptitude, spatial visualizing, and mechanical ingenuity.

There is need for much research with these newer tests that are designed to make diagnostic measurements of mental functions. Their guidance possibilities are great, but as yet so little research has been done with the results that it is impossible for even the specialists in measurement to say just what the various scores mean or how they may be used in the practical job of counseling pupils. Counselors and teachers may use the scores experimentally, but until further studies are available, predictions based on them must be made cautiously.

Tests of Aptitude in Special Fields

General academic aptitude tests have important implications for appraisal of aptitude in special fields. In fact, if we had extensive and detailed knowledge of the relationship of the various scores on the Chicago Primary Mental Abilities Tests or the Yale Educational Aptitude Tests to success in different special fields, we would have an excellent basis for differential prediction and guidance. It is not too much to expect that such tests will some day largely supersede the aptitude tests designed for individual fields, except perhaps in such a highly specialized area as music. For the present, however, aptitude tests designed for specific fields should have a place in a guidance program, although, on the whole, such tests are less satisfactory for their purposes than general academic aptitude tests are for the purposes for which they are designed.

One reason why tests of aptitude in specific fields are not highly satisfactory is that they are designed according to different patterns and standardized on widely different populations. Thus, there is no adequate basis of comparison between the results of the tests in separate areas, and it is often difficult for a counselor to decide in which of several areas an individual possesses the greatest aptitude even when a variety of test scores is available.

The appraisal of aptitude in special fields can be made on a fairly broad basis or it can be highly specific. One can, for example, test individuals for mechanical aptitude or for any one of the hundreds of occupations within the field of mechanics. For placement of workers in jobs, industrial establishments can well use tests of the latter type, but for purposes of a long-term guidance program, such tests would be almost worthless. Even if valid tests for all occupations were available, no guidance department could give more than a few of them to any individual and the problem of selecting the most appropriate ones would involve a large element of subjective judgment concerning the aptitude of the individual concerned. Moreover, the occupations for which many of the tests were designed would include closely similar abilities, and thus the correlation would be too high for the tests to be of much use in differential guidance. Consequently, if a guidance department is going to employ tests of specific aptitudes, it needs to select and use a relatively small number of tests covering fairly broad functions. The guidance department should be acquainted with the administration, scoring, and interpretation of one or more tests in the fields of art, music, scientific aptitude, manual and mechanical aptitude, clerical aptitude, and perhaps aptitude for certain school subjects, such as algebra, geometry, and foreign languages.

Art. Three of the better-known art tests are the Knauber Art Ability Test, the McAdory Art Test, and the Meier-Seashore Art Judgment Test. The first test is, as the name indicates, designed to measure ability in art, and it appears to be quite difficult for the beginner. The other two tests are planned to measure judgment of artistic production. The reviews in Buros' *1940 Mental Measurements Yearbook* (8:145–148)[6] seem to be slightly more favorable to the Meier-

---

[6] The numbers in the parenthesis refer to the numbered items in the list of references at the end of the chapter. Item numbers are shown in italic type; page numbers in ordinary type.

Seashore test than to the McAdory test. The McAdory test, however, covers a wider range of grades.

Music Aptitude. The Seashore Measures of Musical Talent have long been one of the standard procedures for the appraisal of aptitude for music. The revised edition was published in 1939. The fact that some special equipment is required and that it is not practicable to test a large number of pupils simultaneously has prevented the use of these measures in some schools. The Kwalwasser Test of Musical Information and Appreciation and the Kwalwasser-Ruch Test of Musical Accomplishment are paper and pencil tests of the group type.

Scientific Aptitude. Aptitude for scientific work may be inferred to some extent from general academic aptitude tests which provide a basis for diagnosis, such as the Yale aptitude tests or the Chicago Tests of Primary Mental Abilities. One of the few tests designed specially for the measurement of aptitude for science is the Stanford Scientific Aptitude Test, by D. L. Zyve. The use of this test is confined to the high school and college levels.

Tests of Manual and Mechanical Aptitude. Some of the tests of manual and mechanical skill are individual tests which are administered through the use of special equipment. Among the tests of this type are the Tweezer Dexterity Test and the Wiggly Block Test, designed by Johnson O'Connor, and the Minnesota Manual Dexterity Test. Such tests are appropriate for use with special cases which are being studied intensively, but the general measurement program for guidance purposes will make more use of paper and pencil tests which can be administered to groups of pupils. The MacQuarrie Test for Mechanical Ability, the Stenquist Mechanical Aptitude Test, and the Detroit Mechanical Aptitudes Examination are among the more frequently used group tests in this field. Two somewhat newer tests are the Revised Minnesota Paper Form Board Test, which is primarily a test of space perception, and the Bennett Mechanical Comprehension Test. Data in the files of the Educational Records Bureau indicate that the Minnesota test and the Bennett test measure aspects of mechanical aptitude which are fairly independent of one another (*51*). The correlation between the scores on these two tests was found to be about .4. It would seem, therefore, that the Revised Minnesota test and the Bennett test might be used to supplement one another in the same program. The correspondence between scores on these tests, or any other tests of mechanical aptitude, and success in mechanical work probably varies considerably with the kind of job. It would seem desirable to administer more than one type of mechanical aptitude test and to keep a record of the value of the scores in predicting success in different employment situations.

Clerical Aptitude. The Minnesota Vocational Test for Clerical Workers is a rather simple test based on number checking and name checking, but because of the extensive norms now available, it is one of the most useful tests in this area. The Cardall-Gilbert Test of Clerical Competence is a newer test which yields a broader sampling of qualities believed important in clerical work, but as yet there is little objective information on the value of the test for predicting success in clerical work.

Aptitude for Professions. Various tests have been devised to measure aptitude for different professions. In the field of medicine the Moss Scholastic Aptitude Tests for Medical Students (26) have been used extensively and have been the subject of numerous studies. One of the earliest instruments designed for the measurement of legal aptitude was a Law Aptitude Examination by Ferguson and Stoddard. The Yale Legal Aptitude Test, a more recent examination in this field, has been discussed in an article by Crawford and Gorham (9). The National Teacher Examinations (31) explore both the aptitude and the achievement of candidates for teaching positions.

An especially comprehensive and vigorous attack upon the measurement of the aptitude and achievement of engineering students has been made by the Measurement and Guidance Project in Engineering Education under the sponsorship of the Carnegie Foundation for the Advancement of Teaching and the engineering societies. A battery of objective tests, known as The Pre-Engineering Inventory, has been constructed to measure abilities prerequisite to success in the engineering curriculum and is being used by a large number of colleges of engineering. The battery contains tests in general verbal ability, technical verbal ability, ability to comprehend scientific materials, ability to do quantitative thinking, ability to comprehend mechanical principles, spatial visualizing ability, and ability to comprehend social science materials. The entire program has been described and the first results have been reported by the director of the project, Kenneth W. Vaughn (52, 53).

Aptitude for School Subjects. More attention seems to have been given to the measurement of aptitude for mathematics and for foreign languages than for any of the other school subjects. For the appraisal of aptitude for mathematics, there are the Iowa Algebra Aptitude Test, the Iowa Plane Geometry Aptitude Test, the Lee Test of Algebra Ability, the Lee Test of Geometric Aptitude, the Orleans Algebra Prognosis Test, and the Orleans Geometry Prognosis Test. Two rather widely used tests of foreign language aptitude are the Luria-Orleans Modern Language Prognosis Test and the Symonds Foreign Language Prognosis Test.

While the small amount of research data available for the various tests of aptitude for school work indicates that the scores on these tests are significantly correlated with success in the subjects for which the tests are designed, a limiting factor in all these tests is that each one is an independent unit and it is difficult to make valid comparisons from one test to another and thus to predict relative success in the different subjects which a pupil might choose to study. From this standpoint, tests of aptitude for school subjects are less satisfactory than achievement tests which are part of a comprehensive battery, such as the Cooperative tests, and which yield derived scores of the type known as Scaled Scores, thus rendering comparability among the different tests possible. Moreover, it has not yet been established by research that the results of tests designed to measure aptitude in specific subjects or fields have significantly greater relationship to success in those areas than do the results of tests of general academic aptitude.

On the whole, tests designed to show aptitude for specific aspects of school work may play a useful role in a guidance program, but it is a less important role than that taken by tests of general academic aptitude and by achievement tests.

The point will bear emphasis that tests of general academic aptitude, tests of specific aptitude, and achievement tests have many elements in common and that all three types have values for prediction in specific fields. In their use of all types of tests, counselors should constantly be on guard against the "jingle fallacy," or the tendency to apply different names to what in reality may be the same thing.

ANNOTATED LIST OF APTITUDE TESTS

In the annotations of the tests in this list, an attempt is made to provide evidence concerning the reliability and validity of the tests if such data are available. Correlation coefficients reported in this way should be regarded as indicative of the worth of the tests only in general terms. Space limitations render it inadvisable to try to report in detail the technique used in finding the correlations or the grade range involved, both of which are likely to have an important effect upon the magnitude of the correlation coefficients.

American Council on Education Psychological Examination, by L. L. Thurstone and Thelma Gwinn Thurstone. Washington, D. C.: American Council on Education, 1924–1944. College edition, $0.07 per copy, specimen set, $0.35; high school edition, $0.05 per copy, specimen set, $0.25; answer sheets, $0.02 each, either edition.

  College Edition. A new form of this test has been issued annually since 1924. The editions since 1938 have included a number-series section in addition to parts similar to the forms in the earlier tests. In the 1940 to 1944 editions the scores on the number-series, arithmetic, and figure analogies subtests are combined to form a *quantitative* subtotal; those on the completion, same-opposite, and verbal analogies sections are added to obtain a *linguistic* subtotal. These editions are administered with separate answer sheets which may be scored either manually with a stencil or mechanically. Up to and including the 1937 edition, the test called for one hour of working time; in the more recent editions, the testing time is 38 minutes, but about an hour is required for the entire examination, including practice tests. The examination is widely used with college freshmen. More than 70,000 freshmen in 373 colleges took the 1941 edition. Since 1932 the college edition has been used in Grades IX–XII of the independent schools participating in the Educational Records Bureau testing program, and independent-school norms are available. Norms for college freshmen are published annually by the American Council on Education. The test does not yield an I.Q., but the Educational Records Bureau has a procedure for deriving an I.Q. indirectly through equating it with the Otis test. Various studies indicate that split-half reliabilities of total score are .95 to .97. Reliability of Q-score, 1940 hand-scoring edition, .94; machine-scoring edition, .96; reliability of L-score, 1940 hand-scoring edition, .95; machine-scoring edition, .95. Extensive correlation data for scores of independent-school pupils on the 1938 edition were published in an article by Seder (35). For bibliography of studies of the test, see Buros (8:199–200). Also see annual reports prepared each year by the authors of the test and published by the American Council on Education.

High School Edition. Editions published annually 1933–1936, 1938–1942, and 1944. The test has four parts: completion, arithmetic, analogies, and opposites. Earlier editions were issued in a hand-scoring edition only; recent editions may be scored either by hand or by machine. Linguistic subtotal (or L-score), consisting of completion and same-opposite, and quantitative subtotal (or Q-score), consisting of arithmetic reasoning and analogies, as well as the usual part and total scores are available in current editions. Working time for older editions, 60 minutes; for later editions, 35 minutes, but directions and practice exercises will extend the time to a full class period. Gross-score percentile norms based on the scores of more than 30,000 pupils in Grades IX–XII of 218 high schools are available for the 1933 edition. The number of cases in the norms for the more recent editions is somewhat smaller. There are no independent-school norms for the high school edition.

California Test of Mental Maturity, by Elizabeth T. Sullivan, Willis W. Clark, and Ernest W. Tiegs. Los Angeles: California Test Bureau, 1936–1939. $1.40 per 25 copies of the regular edition, which requires approximately two class periods for administration; $0.90 per 25 copies of the short form, which can be administered within one class period; $0.02 per machine-scorable answer sheet; $0.25 per specimen set of any one edition at any one level.

One of the newer intelligence tests in which an attempt is made to secure a diagnostic measurement of mental functions. Includes four main parts—memory, spatial relationships, reasoning, and vocabulary, each of which contains a number of subtests. Yields three intelligence quotients—an I.Q. for language factors and an I.Q. for non-language factors, as well as the usual type of I.Q. based on total scores. Five levels: Kindergarten–Grade I; Grades I–III; Grades IV–VIII; Grades VII–X; Grade IX–adults. Reliability of regular edition, advanced battery, as reported by authors: total mental factors, .96; language factors, .95; non-language factors, .94. Reliability reported in a study in *Journal of Educational Research* (48) using the scores of ninth-grade boys in an independent school: total mental factors, .92; language factors, .91; non-language factors, .86. The following data are taken from the same study: correlation of total mental factors with American Council Psychological Examination, .73 ± .04; correlation of total mental factors with Kuhlmann-Anderson I.Q., .81 ± .04; correlation of language I.Q. with Iowa Silent Reading, .69 ± .04, with Traxler Silent Reading, .75 ± .03; correlation of non-language I.Q. with Iowa Silent Reading, .36 ± .07, with Traxler Silent Reading, .36 ± .07. The rather high correlation of the language I.Q. and the low correlation of the non-language I.Q. with silent reading suggest that this test may be useful in the study of reading disability cases. References: Tiegs (*44*); Traxler (*48*); Buros (*7, 8*).

Chicago Tests of Primary Mental Abilities, by L. L. Thurstone and Thelma Gwinn Thurstone, with the cooperation of the Bureau of Child Study of the Chicago Public Schools. Washington, D. C.: American Council on Education, 1941. For information on prices, write to the Washington office of the American Council on Education. Also distributed by Science Research Associates, 228 South Wabash Avenue, Chicago, Illinois.

A new and promising contribution to mental measurement, based on several years of intensive work in factor analysis. The first tests to eventuate from Thurstone's research in factor analysis were the *Tests for Primary Mental Abilities,* prepared mainly for high school and college students. That battery is now out of print. The *Chicago Tests of Primary Mental Abilities* are a similar, but easier battery, designed for ages 11 to 17. They include six test booklets and five instruction booklets, as well as separate answer sheets for machine scoring. The tests are intended to be administered on six successive school days, using about one forty-minute class period each day. Yield scores for six factors: Number N, Verbal Meaning V, Space S, Word Fluency W, Induction or Reasoning R, and Rote Memory M. Results are reported by means of an individual profile based on percentile rank for age. The authors report split-half reliabilities for factors N, V, S, R, and M in Grades VI, VIII, X, and XII. They range as follows: N, .96–.98; V, .95–.97; S, .96–.98; R, .96–.97; M, .63–.82. Reliabilities cannot be determined for the Word Fluency tests by the split-half method. Intercorrelations of factors range from .13 to .59. Also a single-booklet edition, working time two hours, published in 1943, and a single-booklet battery for kindergarten and Grade I, published in 1945. Reference: Thurstone and Thurstone (*43*).

Henmon-Nelson Tests of Mental Ability, High School Examination, by V. A. C. Henmon and M. J. Nelson. Boston: Houghton Mifflin Company, 1929; $0.81 per 25 tests.

Contains 90 multiple-choice items including both linguistic and quantitative material. Working time, 30 minutes. Scoring is rapid, as this is one of the tests in the Clapp-Young Self-Marking Series. Responses are scored on a separate answer sheet rather than on the test booklet. Designed for Grades VII–XII. Yields raw score, mental age, and I.Q. Three forms. Authors report that reliability for tenth-grade pupils, as indicated by correlation between Forms A and B, is .90 ± .01. Split-half reliabilities range from .88 for Grade VII to .90 for Grade X. Correlation of Henmon-Nelson I.Q.'s with I.Q.'s obtained from the Stanford Revision of the Binet-Simon Scale, .84 ± .01. Reference: Henmon and Nelson (*13*).

Junior Scholastic Aptitude Test, by the Bureau of Research (A. L. Lincoln, Chairman), Secondary Education Board, Milton, Massachusetts. Distributed and scored by the Educational Records Bureau, 437 West 59th Street, New York City. $1.00 per individual for test materials and scoring service.

An especially valuable test for placement and guidance in Grades VII, VIII, and IX. Based on extensive experimentation carried on since 1935 by the Bureau of Research of the Secondary Education Board. Present forms are DR, ER, and FR. Provides separate scores for verbal aptitude and numerical aptitude. No total score. mental age, or I.Q. Results are expressed in terms of percentiles derived from independent-school population. Administration time, 81 minutes. Reliability: correlation of alternate forms: verbal score, .87; numerical score, .82; Spearman-Brown odd-even reliability: verbal score, .97; numerical score, .95; median correlation between verbal and numerical scores, .59. This test is not scored locally. All materials, used and unused, must be returned to the Educational Records Bureau, which scores the test and makes a typewritten report of the results. Half of the income from scoring goes to the Secondary Education Board to maintain a continuous program of research directed toward the improvement of the test. References: Traxler (*50*) and Townsend (*47*).

Kuhlmann-Anderson Intelligence Tests, by F. Kuhlmann and Rose G. Anderson. Minneapolis: Educational Test Bureau, 1940 (Fifth edition). $1.25 per 25 tests; instructional manual, $0.40; specimen set, $0.50.

The Kuhlmann-Anderson tests consist of nine overlapping batteries, covering the age range from Grade I to adult. The highest battery, Grades IX–Maturity, is suitable for use in the high school. This battery includes ten short tests made up chiefly of linguistic and numerical items. Yields mental age and I.Q. Norms for Fifth Edition published in 1940 and revised in 1942. Working time varies from about half an hour to an hour depending on the level. More time is required for administration of test to younger children than to older ones. One form. The authors do not report reliability coefficients. Some unpublished correlation coefficients for the Kuhlmann-Anderson Test and the Otis Self-Administering Test of Mental Ability administered a year apart are in the Educational Records Bureau files. Correlations range from .66 ± .05 to .80 ± .03. *References:* Kuhlmann (*17*), Kuhlmann and Anderson (*18*), and Traxler (*49*).

Ohio State University Psychological Test, Form 22, by Herbert A. Toops. Columbus: Ohio State University, 1937. Test blanks with inserted answer pad, 10 cents each; additional answer pads, 6 cents each.

A group test of ability to think, requiring about two hours of working time. The latest form, 22, is the result of experimentation carried on since 1919. Includes three subtests, same-opposites, analogies, and paragraph comprehension. The test booklets may be used repeatedly, since the subject indicates his responses by punching holes in appropriate squares on an answer pad. A hidden key between the leaves of the answer pad eliminates the necessity of scoring the test in the usual way. The scorer merely counts the number of squares correctly punched out on the answer key. Can also be administered with answer sheets for machine scoring. Designed for secondary schools and colleges. There are public school norms for Grades IX–XIII; also independent-school norms for an earlier form, 15, for Grades IX–XII. Reliability, resulting from four separate studies in which one form was correlated with another, .90, .91, .88, and .91. Reference: Toops (45).

Otis Quick-Scoring Mental Ability Tests, by Arthur S. Otis. Yonkers: World Book Company, 1938. Alpha Test, Grades I–IV, Forms A and B, $1.25 per package of 25; Beta Test, Grades IV–IX, Forms A and B, $0.95 per 25, Forms Cm and Dm, $1.05 per 25; Gamma Test, high schools and colleges, Forms Am and Bm, $1.05 per 25, Forms C and D, $0.95 per 25; specimen set, Alpha, $0.25, Beta or Gamma, $0.20.

One of the newer tests that is very easily and quickly administered and scored. Yields an I.Q. that is closely comparable with the I.Q. secured with the older Otis Self-Administering Test of Mental Ability; in fact, the Quick-Scoring test is a revision of the Self-Administering test. Contains 80 multiple-response items. Working time, 30 minutes, except Alpha, 20 minutes. The test may be scored with a stencil and is also adapted for machine scoring through the use of special answer sheets. The Alpha test has two forms; the Beta test, four; and the Gamma test, four. The author reports that the average correlation between the Gamma test and the Otis Self-Administering Higher Examination is .86.

Otis Self-Administering Test of Mental Ability, by Arthur S. Otis. Yonkers: World Book Company, 1922. Intermediate Examination, Grades IV–IX; Higher Examination, Grades IX–XII and college. $0.90 per package of 25; specimen set, $0.30.

One of the most widely used group intelligence tests. Administration and scoring are very simple. Provides mental age and I.Q.; the latter is found by the deviation method instead of the M.A./C.A. Consists of 75 items, most of which are verbal, although there is some numerical and spatial material in the test. Working time, 30 minutes; can also be administered with a 20-minute time limit. Four forms, A to D. Publisher reports reliability coefficients of .95 for Intermediate Examination, and .92 for Higher Examination.

Pintner General Ability Tests: Verbal Series, by Rudolph Pintner, Bess V. Cunningham, and Walter N. Durost. Yonkers: World Book Company, 1939. Pintner-Cunningham Primary Test, Kindergarten–Grade II, $1.25 per 25, specimen set, $0.20; Pintner-Durost Elementary Test, Grades II–IV,

Scale 1, $1.50 per 25, Scale 2, $1.35 per 25, specimen set, $0.35; Pintner Intermediate Test, Grades IV–IX, $1.40 per 25, specimen set, $0.30; Pintner Advanced Test, Grade IX and above, $1.40 per 25, specimen set, $0.30.

Four levels, two forms. One of the newer batteries of mental tests, apparently carefully constructed and standardized on large population. Results are expressed in terms of standard scores, mental ages, and I.Q.'s. Time for administering varies from approximately 25 minutes, for primary battery, to 55 minutes, for advanced test. Split-half reliability according to publisher's catalog, .90 to .97. Correlations between these tests and seven other tests range from .71 for Revised Stanford-Binet Scale to .87 for Otis Group Intelligence Scale.

Revised Stanford-Binet Scale, by Lewis M. Terman and Maud A. Merrill. Boston: Houghton Mifflin Company, 1937. $2.20 per 25 booklets; box of supplementary materials, $9.00; Directions for Administering, $1.45.

A revision of the most widely used individual intelligence scale. May be used from age two to superior adult level. Should be administered, scored, and interpreted only by persons trained in the use of this particular scale. The main concepts in Binet's original scale and the first Stanford revision have been conserved in this revision, but important innovations have been made. The newer revision contains two forms instead of one, covers a wider range, is more accurately standardized, provides a more extensive sampling of abilities, and is less verbal than the older scale. One important feature in the late revision is a correction in the chronological ages used in finding the intelligence quotients between the ages of thirteen and sixteen. The results of the test may be expressed in mental ages, I.Q.'s, or standard scores. The authors report that the reliability values range from .98 for subjects below 70 I.Q. to approximately .90 for subjects above 130 I.Q. The authors also found reliability coefficients for the twenty-one age groups, using subjects who were within four weeks of a birthday or half-birthday. The coefficients ranged from .85 to .95 with a median of .91. Terman and Merrill's book, *Measuring Intelligence* (*42*), includes a very complete manual of directions for the test. This book, which costs $2.60, should be in the possession of anyone who plans to administer the test. See Buros *1940 Mental Measurements Yearbook,* pages 242–244, for extensive bibliography of studies of 1916 and 1937 revisions (*8*). Reference: McNemar (*23*).

Terman-McNemar Test of Mental Ability, by Lewis M. Terman and Quinn McNemar. Yonkers: World Book Company, 1941. $1.35 per package of 25; specimen set, $0.25.

Revision of *Terman Group Test of Mental Ability.* Two forms, adapted for machine scoring. Grades VII–XII. Includes subtests on information, synonyms, logical selection, classification, analogies, opposites, and best answer. I.Q.'s based on deviation method similar to Otis. Working time, 40 minutes. Reliability based on inter-form correlation is .96 according to publisher's data.

Yale Educational Aptitude Tests, by A. B. Crawford. New Haven, Connecticut: Department of Personnel Study, Yale University, 1939. Distributed and scored by Educational Records Bureau, 437 West 59th Street, New York City. $5.00 per individual for test materials and complete service.

These tests, like the Chicago Tests of Primary Mental Abilities, comprise a uniform battery designed to measure differential capacities. They are the result of a decade of systematic experimentation. Consist of seven booklets, each requiring 45 minutes of testing time. They are labeled Verbal Comprehension, Artificial Language (Linguistic Facility), Verbal (Syllogistic) Reasoning, Quantitative (Scientific) Reasoning, Mathematical Aptitude, Spatial (Three-Dimensional) Visualizing, and Mechanical Ingenuity. Split-half reliabilities of the separate tests, .92 to .98. The author reports that several hundred correlations between test scores and appropriate criteria of subsequent achievement range from .45 to .65. All materials for this test must be obtained from the Educational Records Bureau and returned to the Bureau after the tests have been given. The report of the results is made in the form of a diagnostic profile. A portion of the income from services is used for further research on these tests.

ART

Knauber Art Ability Test, by Alma Jordan Knauber. Cincinnati, Ohio: The Author, 3331 Arrow Avenue, 1932–1935. $0.10 per test; $1.00 per manual; $0.15 per sample test; $1.10 per specimen set.

A production test using semi-objective scoring. One form, Grades VII–XVI and adults. The test is not timed, but it requires about three hours. Author reports reliability of .95 by split-half technique, but this correlation is based on scores of only 83 students. Reference: *Knauber (16)*.

McAdory Art Test, by Margaret McAdory. New York: Bureau of Publications, Teachers College, Columbia University, 1929. $15.75 per folio of 72 plates; $0.40 per 25 record sheets.

A test of aesthetic judgment, consisting of 72 plates, each of which has four variations of the same theme to be ranked in order of merit. Usually administered individually, but it may be given to an entire class of as many as 30 students, if the plates are displayed along a rack. Norms for ages 10 to 19 and over, and Grades III to XII are limited to New York City population. Non-timed; about 90 minutes is needed to give the test. Low correlation with Meier-Seashore tests. References: McAdory (22); Siceloff and Woodyard (37).

Meier-Seashore Art Judgment Test, by N. C. Meier and C. E. Seashore. Iowa City, Iowa: Bureau of Educational Research and Service, 1929–1930. $0.75 per book of test pictures; $0.10 per examiner's manual; $2.00 per 100 record sheets; $0.90 per specimen set.

A test of aesthetic judgment containing 125 pairs of pictures. Each pair consists of a picture created by a great artist and the same picture altered to reduce its artistic merit. The score is based on the number of unaltered masterpieces chosen by the subject as better. One form, suitable for use in Grade VII and above and with adults. No time limit; administration usually requires 45 to 50 minutes. References: Meier (*25*) and Seashore (*33*).

Tests in Fundamental Abilities of Visual Arts, by Alfred S. Lewerenz. Los Angeles, California: California Test Bureau, 1927. $7.00 per color chart; $0.35 per manual; $0.50 per specimen set; Part I, $2.40 per 100; Part II, $2.40 per 100; Part III, $3.60 per 100.

This test is designed to measure the art abilities developed in the public schools. A battery of nine tests arranged in three parts, as follows: Part I, Recognition of Proportion, Originality of Line; Part II, Observation of Light and Shade, Knowledge of Subject Matter Vocabulary, Visual Memory of Proportion; Part III, Analysis of Problems in Cylindrical Perspective, Analysis of Problems in Parallel Perspective, Analysis of Problems in Angular Perspective, Recognition of Color. One form suitable for Grades III–XII. Working time 30 to 35 minutes for each part. Author reports reliability of .87 based on 100 cases in Grades III–IX and correlation of .40 with marks in art classes. Reference: Lewerenz (*21*).

MUSIC

Seashore Measures of Musical Talent, Revised Edition, by Carl E. Seashore, Don Lewis, and Joseph G. Saetveit. Camden, New Jersey: RCA Manufacturing Co., Inc., 1919–39. $9.00 per album of six records including manual and 200 test blanks; $1.50 per record; $0.50 per manual; $0.40 per 200 test blanks.

One of the best-known of all aptitude tests. Consists of two series of three double-faced phonograph records. Designed to measure sense of pitch, sense of intensity, sense of time, tonal memory, sense of rhythm, and sense of timbre. Records are played to the subjects who enter their answers on special blanks. Grades V–XVI and adults. Series A is for the testing of unselected groups in general surveys; Series B is for the testing of musicians and prospective or actual students of music. Reference: Saetveit, Lewis, and Seashore (*32*); also extensive bibliography in Buros (*8*:155–156).

Kwalwasser Test of Musical Information and Appreciation, by Jacob Kwalwasser. University of Iowa, Iowa City, Iowa: Bureau of Educational Research and Service, 1927. $0.05 per copy.

A group test dealing with knowledge of composers—their nationality, compositions, types of composition—artists, instruments and production of tones on them, and of musical structure and form in general. Testing time is 40 minutes. Percentile norms based on scores of high school and college students in music appreciation courses are given. Reliability, .70 to .72. Reference: Semeonoff (*36*).

Kwalwasser-Ruch Test of Musical Accomplishment, by Jacob Kwalwasser and G. M. Ruch. University of Iowa, Iowa City, Iowa: Bureau of Educational Research and Service, 1924. $0.06 per copy.

A group test designed to measure achievement of pupils in a typical public school music course in the elementary and high school grades. It includes knowledge of musical symbols and terms, recognition of syllable names, detection of pitch errors and time errors in a familiar melody, recognition of pitch names, time and key signature, note and rest values, and recognition of familiar melodies from notation. Testing time is 40 minutes. The split-half reliability of the total score is quoted as .97; reliability of subtests, .70 to .97. Norms are based on scores of 5,414 pupils in Grades IV to XII and are given by deciles. Reference: Kwalwasser (*19*).

SCIENCE

Stanford Scientific Aptitude Test, by D. L. Zyve. Stanford University, California: Stanford University Press, 1930. Test booklets, $0.25 each; $4.00 per 25; $14.50 per 100; Explanatory Booklet, $0.25; Scoring Key, $0.25.

A two-hour test for senior high school and college students. Developed to measure eleven components of scientific aptitude. Speed of work is not important since most persons finish within the two-hour period. Norms based on scores of 323 college students. References: Zyve (*54*), and Benton and Perry (*5*).

MECHANICAL APTITUDE

Bennett Mechanical Comprehension Test, by George K. Bennett. New York: Psychological Corporation, 1940. Booklets and answer sheets, $3.00 per 25; additional answer sheets, $0.60 per 25; specimen set, $0.25.

Presents in pictorial form sixty mechanical situations, each of which is accompanied by three responses, one of which correctly identifies the situation. Designed to measure an understanding of the operation of physical principles. For high school boys and adults. Two forms, AA and BB. Form BB is about 12 points more difficult than Form AA. Not timed; usually requires about half an hour. Machine-scorable. Norms for boys in Grades IX–XII, engineering freshmen, and adult candidates for technical courses and positions. Author reports split-half reliability of .84 for ninth-grade boys. Correlation with American Council Psychological Examination, .37. Reference: Bennett and Cruikshank (*4:37–38*).

Detroit Mechanical Aptitudes Examinations, by Harry J. Baker and Alex C. Crockett. Bloomington, Illinois: Public School Publishing Company, 1928. $0.04 per copy; $3.00 per 100; sample set (either boy's or girl's test), $0.15.

This group test is provided in two forms, one for boys, which involves mechanical devices and vocabulary used by carpenters, machinists, and so forth, and one for girls, which involves mechanical devices and vocabulary used in the household. Three types of material are included: tool knowledge, a type of motor skill, and visual acuity. Age and grade norms are furnished in the manual of directions. The test retest reliability, with an interval of two weeks, for the boy's form was .76 and for the girl's form, with an interval of one week, .87. The correlation with intelligence is .30 to .50. Evidences of validity include a correlation of .64 between teachers' ratings of mechanical aptitude and test scores and the large difference found between scores of seniors in an academic high school and scores of seniors in a vocational high school. Reference: Baker (*3*).

MacQuarrie Test for Mechanical Ability, by T. W. MacQuarrie. Los Angeles: California Test Bureau, 1925. $1.75 per 25 tests; specimen set, $0.25.

Test measures mechanical ability in terms of ability at tracing, tapping, dotting, copying, location, pursuit, and spatial perception. A group test. Norms are given on a seven-point scale, "very low," the lowest 7 per cent, to "very high," the highest 7 per cent, for every year group from ten to twenty. Reliability of the test is quoted as .90. Testing time is 15 minutes. Reference: Stein (*38*).

Revised Minnesota Paper Form Board Test, by Rensis Likert and William Quasha. Chicago: Science Research Associates, 1941. $0.04 each; specimen set, $0.10.

Designed to measure ability to visualize and mentally manipulate geometric forms and objects in space, which is one aspect of success in mechanical and engineering occupations. Two forms, series AA and BB. Working time, 20 minutes. Norms are available for educational groups in elementary school, high school, and college, and for several occupational groups. Correlation with Otis Self-Administering Test of Mental Ability, .40; American Council Psychological Examination, 1940 High School Edition, .42; Bennett Mechanical Comprehension Test, .39. Reference: Quasha and Likert (*28*).

Stenquist Mechanical Aptitude Tests, by J. L. Stenquist. Yonkers: World Book Company, 1921. Price of either Test I or Test II, $1.40 per 25 tests; specimen set, $0.35.

Tests measure mechanical aptitude by problems presented in pictures. In Test I the pupil is required to determine which of five pictures of common mechanical objects belongs with which of five others. There are thirty-eight of these sets of exercises, and testing time is 45 minutes. Test II has three exercises, the first involving matching of pictures as in Test I, and the second and third involving answering questions about six machines and a collection of pulleys and mechanical levers. Test II requires 50 minutes of testing time. Norms are in terms of T-scores, based on the standard deviation of ability among unselected twelve-year-old children. Percentile ranks by age groups from eleven to fifteen are also given. Tests I and II correlate to the extent of .68. The reliability of Test I, found by correlating the first half with the second, is reported as .79, and the reliability of Test II is reported as .65. That the ability measured by these tests is relatively independent of general intelligence is indicated by a correlation of .21 between this test and the average of six intelligence tests for seventh- and eighth-grade boys. Validity coefficients as measured by correlation with teachers' ratings of mechanical aptitude are about .67, and as measured by the Stenquist Assembling Tests, which involve actually putting together locks, traps, bells, and so forth, are about .67. Reference: Stenquist (*39*).

CLERICAL APTITUDE

Cardall-Gilbert Test of Clerical Competence, by Alfred J. Cardall and Jane Gilbert. Chicago: Science Research Associates, 1944. $2.50 per 25 copies; specimen set, $0.25.

Designed to measure aptitude for various clerical occupations. Contains four parts: checking (numbers), checking (names), classification of verbal material, and classification of numerical material. Percentile norms based on scores of clerical workers and pupils in junior and senior high schools are available. Working time is 23 minutes. Authors report reliability coefficients of .90 to .98 for the parts and reliability of .99 for the total score on basis of application of Kuder-Richardson formula to scores of clerical workers.

Minnesota Vocational Test for Clerical Workers, arranged by Dorothy M. Andrew, under the direction of Donald G. Paterson and Howard P. Longstaff. New York: Psychological Corporation, 1933. $3.50 per 100 copies; scoring key, $0.25.

There is a long form and a short form of this test. The short form consists of the first half of the long form. Each half has two parts. The first part consists of 200 pairs of numbers; the second part contains 200 pairs of names. Each pair is separated by a line. A check mark is to be made on the line if the two numbers or two names of a pair are exactly the same; no mark is to be made if they are different. The working time for the long form is 28 minutes; that for the short form is 15 minutes. Separate norms are available for adult men and women. In general, women excel men on this test. Reference: Andrew (2).

MATHEMATICS

Iowa Algebra Aptitude Test, by Harry A. Greene and Alva H. Piper. Iowa City, Iowa: Bureau of Educational Research and Service, State University of Iowa, 1931. $1.00 per 25; manual, $0.15; specimen set, $0.20.

Designed to predict achievement in first-year algebra. One form for use in Grade IX. Forty-five minutes administering time. Percentile norms established on 223 cases. More information is needed on the validity and reliability of the test.

Lee Test of Algebra Ability, by J. Murray Lee. Bloomington, Illinois: Public School Publishing Company, 1930. $1.00 per 25 booklets; manual, $0.15; specimen set, $0.20.

Planned to indicate the algebra ability of pupils who have not studied algebra. One form consisting of four subtests: arithmetic problems, analogies, number series, and formulas. Working time, 25 minutes. Correlation with later algebra achievement was .71 according to one study by the author of the test. Reliability estimated by the split-half method is given as .93. Reference: Torgerson and Aamodt (46).

Orleans Algebra Prognosis Test, by Joseph B. Orleans and Jacob S. Orleans. Yonkers: World Book Company, 1928-32. $1.60 per 25 booklets; specimen set, $0.20.

Planned as a measure of the ability of pupils in Grades VII–IX to learn algebra. Contains eleven simple lessons on principles and skills in learning algebra with a test on each lesson. One form requiring 81 minutes of working time. No available data on reliability or validity. Reference: Orleans (*27*).

Iowa Plane Geometry Aptitude Test, by Harry A. Greene and Harold W. Bruce. Iowa City, Iowa: Bureau of Educational Research and Service, State University of Iowa, 1935. $0.90 per 25; specimen set, $0.15.

A prognosis test for high school pupils who have studied no geometry. Four parts: Reading Geometry Content, Algebraic Computation, Algebraic and Arithmetical Reasoning, Visualization. One form; working time, 44 minutes. The authors report a Spearman-Brown reliability coefficient of .901, which is probably somewhat too high for the present basis of administering the test, because a longer time limit was used when the study was made. The authors also report a correlation of .705 with a test of achievement in geometry and one of .592 with first- and second-semester grades. Percentile norms based on 413 pupils enrolled in public school plane geometry classes are available.

Lee Test of Geometric Aptitude, by Doris M. Lee and J. Murray Lee. Los Angeles: California Test Bureau, 1931. $0.75 per 25; specimen set, $0.15.

Designed to measure the aptitude for geometry of high school pupils who have not studied the subject. Four parts, including a total of 50 items of the recall type. One form requiring 31 minutes of working time. Split-half reliability of .811 is reported. Percentile norms based on 450 cases are available. Also there is a critical score for the test which may have some guidance value. Reference: Lee and Lee (*20*).

Orleans Geometry Prognosis Test, by Joseph B. Orleans and J. S. Orleans. Yonkers: World Book Company, 1929. $2.00 per 25 tests; specimen set, $0.20.

A test for the prediction of geometry ability of pupils who have not studied the subject. Similar in purposes and general form to *Orleans Algebra Prognosis Test.* Contains nine brief lessons, each followed by a short test. One form requiring 70 minutes of working time. No data on reliability and very little on validity. No norms have been provided. In spite of these limitations, it seems to be one of the better tests of its kind. Reference: Orleans (*27*).

FOREIGN LANGUAGE

Foreign Language Prognosis Test, by Percival M. Symonds. New York: Bureau of Publications, Teachers College, Columbia University, 1930. $8.00 per 100; specimen set, $0.30.

A test designed to predict success in learning a foreign language. Prediction may be better for classes taught by grammar-translation method than by less formal procedures. Two forms for use in Grade VIII or IX. Working time, 44 minutes. Correlations of .60 and .61 are reported between prognosis test scores and achievement test scores. Reference: Symonds (*41*).

Luria-Orleans Modern Language Prognosis Test, by Max A. Luria and Jacob
S. Orleans. Yonkers: World Book Company, 1928–30. $1.40 per 25; speci-
men set, $0.20.

This test purports to measure the ability of pupils to learn French, Spanish, or
Italian. One form for use in Grades VII–XIII. Working time, 76 minutes. Some
time ago, the authors obtained a correlation of .68 between prognosis test scores
and scores on an achievement test. Kaulfers (*15*) reported correlations between
prognosis test scores and achievement test scores in Spanish at end of first semester
as .35 for an eighth-grade group and .51 for a ninth-grade group. He found correlations of .43 and .52, respectively, between the prognosis test scores and teachers'
marks in Spanish. He appropriately pointed out that these correlations were rather
low. No norms are available, for this type of test cannot readily be standardized.

REFERENCES

1. Anderson, Roy N. "Review of Clerical Tests (1929–42)," *Occupations,* XXI
   (May 1943), 654–660.
2. Andrew, D. M. *An Analysis of the Minnesota Vocational Test for Clerical
   Workers.* Unpublished Doctor's thesis, University of Minnesota, 1935.
3. Baker, Harry J. "A Mechanical Aptitudes Test," *Detroit Educational Bulletin,*
   XII (January 1929), 5–6.
4. Bennett, George K., and Cruikshank, Ruth M. *A Summary of Manual and
   Mechanical Ability Tests.* New York: Psychological Corporation, 1942. Pp.
   75. Mimeographed.
5. Benton, Arthur L., and Perry, James D. "A Study of the Predictive Value of
   the Stanford Scientific Aptitude Test (Zyve)," *Journal of Psychology,* X (October 1940), 309–312.
6. Bingham, Walter V. *Aptitudes and Aptitude Testing.* New York: Harper &
   Brothers, 1937. Pp. ix + 390.
7. Buros, Oscar K. *The Nineteen Thirty-Eight Mental Measurements Yearbook.*
   New Brunswick, New Jersey: Rutgers University Press, 1938. Pp. xiv + 415.
8. Buros, Oscar K. *The Nineteen Forty Mental Measurements Yearbook.* Highland Park, New Jersey: The Mental Measurements Yearbook, 1941. Pp. xxiii +
   674.
9. Crawford, A. B., and Gorham, T. J. "The Yale Legal Aptitude Test," *Yale
   Law Journal,* XLIX (May 1940), 1237–1240.
10. Crissy, William J. E., and Wantman, M. L. "Measurement Aspects of the Na-
    tional Clerical Ability Testing Program," *Educational and Psychological Meas-
    urement,* II (January 1942), 37–46.
11. Ferguson, M. L., and Stoddard, G. D. *Law Aptitude Examination.* St. Paul,
    Minnesota: West Publishing Company, 1926.
12. Ghiselli, Edwin E. "A Comparison of the Minnesota Vocational Test for Cleri-
    cal Workers with the General Clerical Battery of the United States Employment
    Service," *Journal of Applied Psychology,* XXVI (February 1942), 75–80.

13. Henmon, V. A. C., and Nelson, M. J. "The Measurement of Intelligence," *Educational Progress Bulletin,* XIII, No. 2 (September 1937), 1–21. Boston: Houghton Mifflin Company.

14. Hull, Clark L. *Aptitude Testing.* Yonkers, New York: World Book Company, 1928. Pp. xiv + 535.

15. Kaulfers, Walter Vincent. *The Forecasting Efficiency of Current Bases for Prognosis in Junior High School Beginning Spanish.* Unpublished Doctor's thesis, Stanford University, 1933. Pp. 381.

16. Knauber, Alma Jordan. "The Construction and Standardization of the Knauber Art Tests," *Education,* LVI (November 1935), 165–170.

17. Kuhlmann, F. "The Kuhlmann-Anderson Intelligence Tests Compared with Several Others," *Journal of Applied Psychology,* XII (1928), 545–594.

18. Kuhlmann, F., and Anderson, Rose G. *Kuhlmann-Anderson Intelligence Tests: Instruction Manual.* Minneapolis: Educational Test Bureau, 1927 and 1940. Pp. vii + 131.

19. Kwalwasser, Jacob. *Tests and Measurements in Music,* pp. 65–73, 107–137. Boston: C. C. Birchard and Company, 1927. Pp. xiii + 146.

20. Lee, J. Murray, and Lee, Doris May. "The Construction of a Test of Geometric Aptitude," *Mathematics Teacher,* XXV (April 1932), 193–203.

21. Lewerenz, Alfred S. "Predicting Ability in Art," *Journal of Educational Psychology,* XX (December 1929), 702–704.

22. McAdory, Margaret. *The Construction and Validation of an Art Test.* Teachers College Contributions to Education, No. 383. New York: Bureau of Publications, Teachers College, Columbia University, 1929. Pp. 35.

23. McNemar, Quinn. *The Revision of the Stanford-Binet Scale.* Boston: Houghton Mifflin Company, 1942. Pp. 185.

24. Marshall, Mortimer V. "A Study of the Stanford Scientific Aptitude Test," *Occupations,* XX (March 1942), 433–434.

25. Meier, Norman Charles. *Aesthetic Judgment as a Measure of Art Talent.* University of Iowa Studies, Vol. 1, No. 19; Series on Aims and Progress of Research. Iowa City, Iowa: University of Iowa, August, 1926. Pp. 30.

26. Moss, F. A. "Scholastic Aptitude Tests for Medical Students," *Journal of the Association of American Medical Colleges,* VI (January 1931). (Also Annual Reports of the Committee on Aptitude Tests for Medical Students in volumes of this journal, 1936– .)

27. Orleans, Joseph B. "A Study of Prognosis of Probable Success in Algebra and in Geometry," *Mathematics Teacher,* XXVII (April–May 1934), 165–180, 225–246.

28. Quasha, W. H., and Likert, R. "The Revised Minnesota Paper Form Board Test," *Journal of Educational Psychology,* XXVIII (March 1937), 197–204.

29. Remmers, H. H., and Gage, N. L. *Educational Measurement and Evaluation.* New York: Harper & Brothers, 1943. Pp. ix + 580.

30. Richardson, H. D. "Discovering Aptitude for the Modern Languages," *Modern Language Journal,* XVIII (December 1933), 160–170.

31. Ryans, David G. "The Professional Examination of Teaching Candidates: A Report of the First Annual Administration of the National Teacher Examinations," *School and Society,* LII (October 5, 1940), 273–284.

32. Saetveit, Joseph G.; Lewis, Don; and Seashore, Carl E. "Revision of the Seashore Measures of Musical Talent," *University of Iowa Studies, Series on Aims and Progress of Research,* No. 65. Iowa City, Iowa: University of Iowa, 1940. Pp. 62.

33. Seashore, Carl E. "Meier-Seashore Art Judgment Test," *Science,* LXIX (April 5, 1929), 380.

34. Seashore, Carl E. *The Psychology of Musical Talent.* New York: Silver, Burdett Company, 1919. Pp. xvi + 288.

35. Seder, Margaret. "The Reliability and Validity of the American Council Psychological Examination, 1938 Edition," *Journal of Educational Research,* XXXIV (October 1940), 90–101.

36. Semeonoff, Boris. "A New Approach to the Testing of Musical Ability," *British Journal of Psychology,* XXX (April 1940), 326–340.

37. Siceloff, Margaret McAdory, and Woodyard, Ella. *Validation and Standardization of the McAdory Art Test.* New York: Bureau of Publications, Teachers College, Columbia University, 1933. Pp. 33.

38. Stein, M. L. "A Trial with Criteria of the MacQuarrie Test of Mechanical Ability," *Journal of Applied Psychology,* XI (October 1927), 391–393.

39. Stenquist, J. L. "The Case for the Low IQ," *Journal of Educational Research,* IV (November 1921), 241–254.

40. Stoddard, George D. *The Meaning of Intelligence.* New York: The Macmillan Company, 1943. Pp. ix + 504.

41. Symonds, Percival M. "A Foreign Language Prognosis Test," *Teachers College Record,* XXXI (March 1930), 540–556.

42. Terman, Lewis M., and Merrill, Maud A. *Measuring Intelligence.* Boston: Houghton Mifflin Company, 1936. Pp. x + 319.

43. Thurstone, L. L., and Thurstone, Thelma Gwinn. *Manual, Scoring and Interpretation: The Chicago Tests of Primary Mental Abilities, Ages 11 to 17.* Washington, D. C.: American Council on Education, 1941. Pp. 36.

44. Tiegs, Ernest W. "Breaking Down the IQ," *Progressive Education,* XIII (December 1936), 603–605.

45. Toops, H. A. *A Catechism on a Statewide Testing and Guidance Program.* Columbus, Ohio: Ohio State University. Mimeographed.

46. Torgerson, T. L., and Aamodt, Geneva P. "The Validity of Certain Prognostic Tests in Predicting Algebraic Ability," *Journal of Experimental Education,* I (March 1933), 277–279.

47. Townsend, Agatha. "The Use of Results from the Junior Scholastic Aptitude Test," *1943 Fall Testing Program in Independent Schools and Supplementary Studies.* Educational Records Bulletin, No. 39. New York: Educational Records Bureau, January 1944. Pp. xii + 48.

48. Traxler, Arthur E. "A Study of the California Test of Mental Maturity: Ad-

vanced Battery," *Journal of Educational Research*, XXXII (January 1939), 329–335.

49. Traxler, Arthur E. "IQ's Obtained on the New Edition of the Kuhlmann-Anderson Tests and on the Binet Scale," *Elementary School Journal*, XLI (April 1941), 614–617.

50. Traxler, Arthur E. "A Study of the Junior Scholastic Aptitude Test," *Journal of Educational Research*, XXXV (September 1941), 16–27.

51. Traxler, Arthur E. "Correlations Between 'Mechanical Aptitude' and 'Mechanical Comprehension' Scores," *Occupations*, XXII (October 1943), 42–43.

52. Vaughn, K. W. "The Measurement and Guidance Project in Engineering Education," *Journal of Engineering Education*, XXXIV (March 1944), 516–520.

53. Vaughn, K. W. "The Pre-Engineering Inventory," *Journal of Engineering Education*, XXXIV (April 1944), 615–625.

54. Zyve, D. L. "A Test of Scientific Aptitude," *Journal of Educational Psychology*, XVIII (November 1927), 525–546.

CHAPTER V

Evaluation of Achievement in a Guidance Program

ACHIEVEMENT IS PROBABLY, WITH THE EXCEPTION OF GENERAL SCHOLASTIC APTITUDE, the most important type of appraisal for a guidance program. Scores on achievement tests are excellent bases for the prediction of the future educational success of individuals in the subjects covered by the tests, afford very helpful clues for purposes of vocational guidance, and are significantly correlated with aptitude and with interests. Thus, tests of achievement help to provide information concerning the general academic aptitude and the functioning interests of each individual, and probably should form the core of the systematic testing program of every school which hopes to do a thorough and objective job of guidance.

ACHIEVEMENT TEST BATTERIES FOR THE ELEMENTARY SCHOOL

The general achievement tests for the elementary school may be divided into two types: tests in which one battery is intended to serve throughout practically the whole range of the elementary school grades, and tests consisting of overlapping batteries for different grade levels. The Modern School Achievement Tests, designed for Grades 2–9, illustrate the first type. Three well-known achievement tests—the Stanford, the Metropolitan, and the Progressive—represent the second type. The Stanford test consists of three batteries—Elementary, Intermediate, and Advanced; the Metropolitan, of five—Primary I, Primary II, Primary III, Intermediate, and Advanced; and the Progressive, of four—Primary, Elementary, Intermediate, and Advanced. In general, the one-battery type tends not to be well suited to the lowest and highest grades that it is designed to serve. There is evidence, on the other hand, that the equating between the batteries of some of the existing achievement tests of the overlapping-battery type is open to criticism.

The Progressive Achievement Tests not only cover the elementary school but also include a battery for the secondary school. These tests provide for more detailed diagnosis than the other achievement tests, but they do not include as broad a range of subjects. The tests in the Progressive batteries are confined to reading, arithmetic, and language usage, while those in the other achievement tests named cover nearly all the elementary school subjects. The Progressive test has three forms, except in the Advanced Battery, for which there are two forms; the Stanford test, five; the Metropolitan test, five (three at the Elementary level); and the Modern School Achievement Test, two.

SECONDARY SCHOOL ACHIEVEMENT TESTS

The achievement tests for secondary school use are so numerous that an entire book would be required for even a brief statement about each one. The two fields of social studies and natural science alone account for about 500 published tests. Many of these tests, however, are so carelessly constructed and so inferior that they are worthy of no serious consideration. It is safe to say that there is no high school subject for which more than half a dozen really good, standardized, objective tests are available.

Within the past decade, one series of tests has almost taken command of objective achievement testing in the secondary school and college, namely, the extensive series of Cooperative tests produced by the Cooperative Test Service of the American Council on Education under a grant from the General Education Board. The broad purposes of the Cooperative Test Service are to help coordinate testing and guidance in America and to cooperate with institutions and individuals interested in adjusting educational procedures to the needs of pupils. These purposes have been fostered through the construction of a series of comparable forms of a wide variety of achievement tests. Under the direction of Ben D. Wood and with the assistance of many subject-matter and testing specialists, the Cooperative Test Service issued new forms of tests annually from 1932 to 1941 in nearly all academic subjects. The war necessitated temporary curtailment in the construction of tests for school use.

The earlier forms of nearly all the Cooperative tests were ninety minutes in length. After five ninety-minute forms had been made for most subjects, the Cooperative Test Service began, in 1937, to produce a series of forty-minute tests that could be administered within the ordinary class period. Several forms of the forty-minute tests are now available for nearly all the secondary school subjects. It was found that by careful selection of the items, tests with reliabilities not greatly lower than those of the ninety-minute tests could be produced.

An important innovation in connection with the Cooperative tests has been the development of a procedure for translating the raw scores into uniform and stable units known as Scaled Scores. This Scaled Score system, which was devised by Colonel John C. Flanagan, formerly Associate Director of the Cooperative Test Service, incorporates the concept of the norm in each individual score and makes possible the comparison of scores on tests in different fields as well as direct comparability between the results of different forms of the same test. The Scaled Score concept has been explained in a bulletin published by the Cooperative Test Service (*15*) and in a bulletin of the Educational Records Bureau (*6*).

The recent forms of nearly all the Cooperative tests are completely objective and are adapted to scoring with the electrical test scoring machine of the International Business Machines Corporation as well as to hand scoring. The earlier forms of many of these tests are also entirely objective, and while special machine answer sheets are not available for them, they can be scored mechanically through the use of standard answer sheets.

While the annotated list of achievement tests in this chapter consists mainly of the Cooperative tests, several other tests are included. This is true especially of the field of reading, in which several useful tests are available.

No school should be satisfied to depend entirely on the tests in this list or any other list of standardized tests. Every school needs to supplement objective tests with essay tests and others of its own construction and in line with its own objectives. All schools, too, should be alert to the possibilities for the measurement of some of the less tangible objectives of secondary education through the use of tests similar to those which were developed in the Eight-Year Study of the Progressive Education Association, or by means of essay examinations and semi-objective tests such as those exemplified in the work of John M. Stalnaker (*27*) of the College Entrance Examination Board. The tests prepared under the auspices of the United States Armed Forces Institute should also be considered carefully, for they are destined to play an important part in the guidance of the men returning to college and to vocations from the Armed Services. A brief discussion of the Armed Forces Institute Tests appears in the appendix.

ANNOTATED LIST OF READING TESTS

Chicago Reading Tests, by Max D. Engelhart and Thelma Gwinn Thurstone. Milwaukee: E. M. Hale and Company, 1939. $1.00 per 25 tests; specimen set of any one test, $0.25.

Four booklets: Test A for Grades I and II; Test B for Grades II, III, and IV; Test C for Grades IV, V, and VI; and Test D for Grades VI, VII, and VIII. Three forms each consisting of several parts covering word meaning, rate, and various aspects of comprehension. The time for the tests varies from 31 minutes for Test A to 45 minutes for Test C. The scores may be interpreted in terms of grade equivalents. The authors' reliability coefficients for the total comprehension score range from .85 to .99. Reliability data for the parts of the test apparently are not available. Reference: Engelhart and Thurstone (*13*).

Cooperative Reading Comprehension Test, by Frederick B. Davis and others. New York: Cooperative Test Service, 1940–1943.   10 to 99 copies, $0.06; 100 or more copies, $0.055 each; specimen set, $0.25.

Four forms: Q, R, S, and T. These tests are part of the Cooperative English Test but are also printed in separate booklets. Two levels: C1 for junior and senior high schools, and C2 for upper high school grades and colleges. Each level contains two parts: vocabulary and paragraph reading. Provides scores for vocabulary, speed of comprehension, level of comprehension, and total score. The level score is obtained by means of a repeating-scale technique, which eliminates the influence of speed of reading on the results. Working time, 40 minutes. Public school and independent-school percentile norms are available. According to the publisher, the reliability of the total reading score is .94 to .95. Reliabilities reported for the parts vary from .75 to .92. In a study at the Educational Records Bureau, the median of the intercorrelations among the three scores yielded by the test was .671. A factor analysis of the test was made by Davis. Reference: Davis (*3*).

Durrell-Sullivan Reading Capacity and Achievement Tests, by Donald D. Durrell and Helen Blair Sullivan.   Yonkers, New York: World Book Company, 1938.   Primary Test (both Capacity and Achievement), $1.75 per 25; specimen set, $0.45.   Reading Capacity Test, Intermediate, $1.30 per 25; specimen set, $0.35.   Reading Achievement Test, Intermediate, $1.45 per 25 tests; specimen set, $0.40.

Designed to provide evidence concerning whether the reading achievement of an individual pupil is up to his reading capacity. One form consisting of two levels: an Intermediate Test for Grades III to VI, and a Primary Test for Grades II to IV. There are two sections, Reading Capacity and Reading Achievement, at each level. Each section contains a word meaning part and a paragraph meaning part. The Reading Achievement Test includes a spelling test and a written recall test which may be used at the option of the teacher. From 30 to 40 minutes are required for each booklet. Reliabilities according to the publisher are: reading capacity score, .89 to .94; reading achievement score, .94 to .96. No reliability data are available for the subtests.

Gates Basic Reading Tests, by Arthur I. Gates.   Grade III (second half) through Grade VIII.   New York: Bureau of Publications, Teachers College, Columbia University, 1942. $2.30 per 100 for each form of each type; specimen set, $0.30.

There are four forms of this test, each of which consists of four booklets designed to measure the following types of reading ability: Type A, Reading to Appreciate the General Significance of a Paragraph; time, 6 to 8 minutes. Type B, Reading to Predict the Outcome of Given Events; time, 8 to 10 minutes. Type C, Reading to Understand Precise Directions; time, 8 to 10 minutes. Type D, Reading to Note Details; time, 8 to 10 minutes. Norms are provided for each testing time.

These tests are a revision of the Gates Silent Reading Tests which have been in use since 1926. The range of the reliability coefficients reported by the author is as follows: Type A, .83 to .93; Type B, .80 to .94; Type C, .76 to .94; Type D, .88 to .96. The intercorrelations of the four types range from .72 to .92.

Iowa Silent Reading Tests, New Edition (Revised), Elementary Test, by H. A. Greene and V. H. Kelley. Yonkers, New York: World Book Company, 1939. Revised, 1943. $1.45 per 25 tests; specimen set, $0.35.

A new revision of the older form published in 1933. Subtests include rate, comprehension, directed reading, word meaning, paragraph comprehension, sentence meaning, and location of information, which consists of alphabetizing and the use of index. Four forms, Am, Bm, Cm, and Dm, yielding comparable results. Working time, 49 minutes. Raw scores are converted to standard scores, thus providing a profile in graphic form. The authors' reliabilities for the subtests found by means of the Spearman-Brown formula, range from .605 for sentence meaning, to .939 for alphabetizing. The reliability of the median standard score is reported as .93. The Educational Records Bureau has independent-school norms for Form Cm.

Iowa Silent Reading Tests, New Edition (Revised), Advanced Test, by H. A. Greene, A. N. Jorgensen, and V. H. Kelley. Yonkers, New York: World Book Company, 1939; revised, 1943. $1.80 per 25 tests; specimen set, $0.40.

These tests, which consist of four forms, Am, Bm, Cm, and Dm, are similar to the elementary tests just described. There are nine subtests: rate, comprehension, directed reading, poetry comprehension, word meaning, sentence meaning, paragraph comprehension, and location of information, including use of index and selection of key words. Raw scores may be changed into standard scores and arranged in the form of a graphic profile. The score on the test as a whole is the median score, or middle one of the nine part scores when they are arranged in order of size. Working time, 45 minutes. According to authors' manual, Spearman-Brown reliabilities of parts range from .683 for poetry comprehension, to .871 for word meaning. Reliability of median standard score, .918. Adapted for machine scoring. Independent-school norms for Form Cm may be obtained from the Educational Records Bureau.

Nelson-Denny Reading Test, by M. J. Nelson and E. C. Denny. Boston: Houghton Mifflin Company, 1929. $1.80 per 25, including 25 tests and 25 answer booklets; $0.81 per 25 extra answer booklets.

This test provides two scores, one for vocabulary and one for the understanding of paragraphs. The vocabulary test consists of 100 words and the paragraph test contains nine selections with four questions on each one. Time limit: vocabulary test, 10 minutes; paragraph test, 20 minutes. Two forms. Responses are recorded on an answer sheet and scoring is facilitated through the use of the Clapp-Young Self-Marking carbon paper device. Public school norms for each grade from Grade IX through college. Independent-school norms available at the Educational Records

Bureau for Grades IX–XII. Author's reliability, found by correlating scores made on Form A and Form B by college freshmen, .91 ± .01.

Pressey Reading Tests, by S. L. Pressey.   Columbus, Ohio: Ohio State Department of Education, 1934. $0.03 per booklet.

Three booklets: (1) Reading Speed and Comprehension, a test of rate and comprehension in continuous reading; (2) General Reading Test, comprising subtests for paragraph meaning, general vocabulary, and outlining; and (3) Special Reading Test, including technical vocabulary of English grammar, foreign words, phrases, and abbreviations, the use of the dictionary, and graphs and maps. Time required for (1) reading speed, 5 minutes, comprehension, not timed; for (2) and (3), 60 minutes each. One form. Grade 12.

Progressive Reading Tests, by Ernest W. Tiegs and Willis W. Clark. Los Angeles, California: California Test Bureau, 1934–1939. Primary Test, Grades I–III; Elementary Test, Grades III–VI; Intermediate Test, Grades VII–IX; Advanced Test, Grades IX–XIII. $0.90 per 25; specimen set of any one level, $0.25; machine-scorable answer sheets, $0.02 each.

These reading tests are a part of the corresponding batteries of the Progressive Achievement Tests, but are also printed in separate booklets. The Advanced Battery contains two forms and each of the other three batteries has three forms. In the machine-scoring edition, two forms are available for the Elementary, Intermediate, and Advanced Tests. There are two main divisions, reading vocabulary and reading comprehension, each of which is subdivided into several parts. A graphic profile for each pupil may be drawn on the cover page of the booklet or on the answer sheet. Reliabilities of reading vocabulary and reading comprehension are close to .90 according to manual of directions. Reliabilities of subtests are probably not very high. The test does not have definite time limits, as it is intended to measure power rather than speed. There are public school norms for Grades I–XIII. Independent-school norms for Grades I–XII are available at the Educational Records Bureau.

Sangren-Woody Reading Test, by Paul V. Sangren and Clifford Woody. Yonkers, New York: World Book Company, 1927. $1.40 per 25; specimen set, $0.20.

Two forms, A and B, for use in Grades IV through VIII. Seven parts, including word meaning, rate, fact material, total meaning, central thought, following directions, and organization. Total working time, 27 minutes. There are public school grade norms for each part and for the total score. Independent-school norms for Grades IV to VI have been prepared by the Educational Records Bureau. Reliability coefficients reported by publisher range from .777 for fact material, to .919 for organization. Reference: Sangren (24).

Shank Tests of Reading Comprehension, by Spencer Shank. Cincinnati: C. A. Gregory Company, 1929. Test I, Grades III–VI; Test II, Grades VII–IX;

Test III, Grades X–XII. $1.00 per 25 or $0.05 per copy; manual, $0.30; specimen set, any one form, $0.10; three tests, $0.30.

There are three forms of the test at each of the three levels. Each form contains ten paragraphs. Each paragraph in Test I is followed by questions representing six different types. Seven kinds of questions follow the various paragraphs in Tests II and III. Working time, 20 minutes. End-of-semester public school norms: Test I, Grades III–VII; Test II, Grades VI–X; Test III, Grades X–college. Educational Records Bureau has independent-school norms: Test I, Grades V–VI; Test II, Grades VII–IX; Test III, Grades X–XII. Author's reliability, for total score: Test I, .90; Test II, .90; Test III, .90. Diagnosis can be made by means of a chart, but this procedure is rather involved. No norms and no reliabilities have been reported for different types of questions.

Traxler Reading Tests, by Arthur E. Traxler. Silent Reading Test, Grades VII–X; High School Reading Test, Grades X–XII. Bloomington, Illinois: Public School Publishing Company, 1934 to 1942. $1.50 per 25; sample set, $0.30.

The Silent Reading Test contains three parts: reading rate and story comprehension, word meaning, and paragraph comprehension. Working time, 46 minutes. Forms 1, 2, 3, and 4, the last two of which are adapted for machine scoring. The High School Reading Test contains two parts: reading rate and story comprehension, and main ideas in paragraphs. Working time, 45 minutes. Two forms. Public school percentiles for part scores and total scores are available for both tests. Independent-school percentile norms for Grades VI to IX, inclusive, have been prepared for the lower test at the Educational Records Bureau. Reliability of Silent Reading Test, based on correlations of two forms of the test administered to pupils at a single grade level: average reliability of part scores, .80; of total score, .92. Average reliability of part scores in High School Reading Test, .81; estimated reliability of total score, .93. Reference: Traxler (29).

Van Wagenen Reading Scales, by M. J. Van Wagenen. Minneapolis: Educational Test Bureau, 1938. $1.00 per 25 tests; specimen set, $0.25.

Four scales published in separate booklets, entitled "Reading Scales in Science," "Reading Scales in Biology," "Reading Scales in History," and "Reading Scales in Literature." Each test consists of a series of paragraphs, each followed by several statements. The pupil is required to indicate the statements containing ideas which are in the paragraph or can be derived from it. Sufficient time is allowed for all students to finish. Grades VII–XII. Two forms, A and B. The raw scores on these scales are changed to derived measures known as C-scores. These scales are similar to the Van Wagenen Reading Scales published in 1921 by the Public School Publishing Company.

Van Wagenen-Dvorak Diagnostic Examination of Silent Reading Abilities, by M. J. Van Wagenen and August Dvorak. Minneapolis: Educational Test Bureau, 1939. Examination booklet, $2.00 per 25; separate answer sheet,

$0.0125; rate of comprehension test with profile and answer sheet, $0.75 per 25; specimen set, $0.50.

A relatively long reading test designed for diagnostic purposes. Three levels: Intermediate Division for Grades IV and V, Junior Division for Grades VI to IX, and Senior Division for Grades X to XII and college. Each division contains three parts, the first of which is printed in a four-page booklet and the second and third of which are printed together in a booklet of 16 pages. The latter booklet is designed for use with a machine-scorable answer sheet. The test is planned to measure rate of comprehension, ability to perceive relationships, vocabulary (words in context), vocabulary (isolated words), range of general information, grasping general thought, retention of clearly stated details, interpretation of content, integration of dispersed ideas, and drawing inferences from content. Raw scores are converted into C-scores, which presumably provide comparability among the parts. The test also yields a reading level score and a reading index somewhat similar to the I.Q. No reliability data are reported in the manual of directions. Rather low reliabilities were obtained in a study at the Educational Records Bureau as reported in Educational Records Bulletin No. 31. The Spearman-Brown reliabilities were as follows: Junior Division, range of correlations for nine parts, .471 to .924; median correlation, .758; Senior Division, range of nine correlations, .431 to .787; median, .689.

ANNOTATED LIST OF GENERAL ACHIEVEMENT TESTS—ELEMENTARY SCHOOL

Iowa Every-Pupil Tests of Basic Skills, by H. F. Spitzer, Ernest Horn, Maude McBroom, H. A. Greene, and E. F. Lindquist. Boston: Houghton Mifflin Company, 1940, 1941, 1942, and 1943. Test A, Silent Reading Comprehension; Test B, Work-Study Skills; Test C, Basic Language Skills; Test D, Basic Arithmetic Skills. Elementary battery for Grades III–V, $1.25 per 25 booklets of any test; complete battery, $4.00; Advanced battery for Grades VI–VIII, $1.35 per 25 booklets of any test; complete battery, $4.25.

Four forms, L, M, N, and O, issued by the present publishers. Other forms to be published periodically. Several forms of the advanced battery were previously published annually over a period of several years by the Bureau of Educational Research and Service, University of Iowa. The skills measured by these tests, which are published in separate booklets, are as follows:

Test A: Elementary battery—reading comprehension and vocabulary; Advanced battery—paragraph comprehension, details, organization, total meaning, total reading comprehension, and vocabulary.

Test B: Elementary battery—map reading, use of references, use of index, use of dictionary, and alphabetization; Advanced battery—comprehension of maps, references, use of index, use of dictionary, and reading graphs, charts, and tables.

Test C: Elementary battery—punctuation, capitalization, usage, spelling, and sentence sense; advanced battery similar to the elementary battery with omission of test of sentence sense.

Test D: Elementary battery, Part I, vocabulary and fundamental knowledge; Part II, computational skill in whole numbers, fractions, and decimals; Part III, solution of problems. Advanced battery similar to elementary battery except for Part II which includes whole numbers, fractions, percentage, decimals, and denominate numbers.

Working time: Elementary battery: Test A, 44 minutes; Test B, 44 minutes; Test C, 51 minutes; Test D, 60 minutes; Advanced battery: Test A, 67 minutes; Test B, 78 minutes; Test C, 70 minutes; Test D, 80 minutes.

Results may be graphed to show profile of strengths and weaknesses. There is an extensive manual for administration and interpretation. No reliability or validity data are given in the manual.

Metropolitan Achievement Tests (Revised), by Richard D. Allen, Harold H. Bixler, William L. Connor, Frederick B. Graham, and Gertrude H. Hildreth. Yonkers, New York: World Book Company, 1932–1940. Primary I battery for Grade I, $1.30 per 25 tests; specimen set, $0.25; Primary II battery for Grade II, $1.40 for 25 tests; specimen set, $0.25; Primary III battery for Grade III, $1.75 for 25 tests; specimen set, $0.30. Intermediate battery for Grades IV, V, and VI: complete, $2.40 for 25 tests; specimen set, $0.35; partial, $1.80 for 25 tests; specimen set, $0.30. Advanced battery for Grades VII and VIII: complete, $2.40 for 25 tests; specimen set, $0.35; partial, $1.80 for 25 tests; specimen set, $0.30.

Primary I battery tests word and phrase recognition, word meaning, and numbers; administering time, 60 minutes.

Primary II battery tests reading, vocabulary, arithmetic fundamentals, arithmetic problems, and spelling; administering time, 70 minutes.

Primary III battery tests reading, vocabulary, arithmetic fundamentals, arithmetic problems, language, and spelling; administering time, 95 minutes.

Intermediate complete battery tests reading, vocabulary, arithmetic fundamentals, arithmetic problems, English, literature, history, geography, and spelling; administering time, 3 hours and 40 minutes. Literature, history, and geography are omitted from the partial battery, for which the administering time is 2 hours and 40 minutes.

Advanced battery contains the same kinds of tests as intermediate battery. Administering time is 4 hours for complete advanced battery and 2 hours and 40 minutes for partial battery.

Each of the primary batteries is available in three forms: A, B, and C; the intermediate and advanced batteries may be obtained in five forms: A, B, C, D, and E. Results are expressed in standard scores and public school grade equivalents, which may be graphed to form a profile of strengths and weaknesses in the different subjects. Independent-school percentile norms for all batteries are available at the Educational Records Bureau. A new revision of the tests is being prepared.

The reading and arithmetic tests may be obtained in separate booklets at the primary, intermediate, and advanced levels.

Modern School Achievement Tests, by Arthur I. Gates, Paul R. Mort, Percival M. Symonds, Ralph B. Spence, Gerald S. Craig, De Forest Stull, Roy Hatch, Amy I. Shaw, and Laura B. Krieger. New York: Bureau of Publications, Teachers College, Columbia University, 1931. Complete battery $8.20 per 100; short form: Skill Subjects test booklet, $5.70 per 100; specimen set, $0.20 for complete battery or short form.

One battery, two forms, designed to test reading comprehension, reading speed, arithmetic computation, arithmetic reasoning, spelling, health knowledge, language usage, history and civics, geography, and elementary science. Testing time, 176 minutes divided into four sittings. Raw scores are translated into age and grade norms and may be graphed in profile form. According to manual of directions, range of reliability of individual tests for a single grade is .67 to .96 with most of reliabilities over .85; reliability of entire battery is .94 to .97.

Progressive Achievement Tests, by Ernest W. Tiegs and Willis W. Clark. Los Angeles: California Test Bureau, 1933–1938. Primary battery for Grades I–III, $1.10 per 25 tests; specimen set, $0.25; Elementary battery for Grades IV–VI, $1.40 per 25 tests; specimen set, $0.25; Intermediate battery for Grades VII–IX, $1.40 for 25 tests; specimen set, $0.25; Advanced battery for Grades IX–XIII, $1.75 per 25 tests; specimen set, $0.25.

The Primary, Elementary, and Intermediate batteries exist in three forms: A, B, and C; the Advanced battery is available in two forms: A and B. There are five main tests in each battery: reading vocabulary, reading comprehension, arithmetic reasoning, arithmetic fundamentals, and language. Within the five tests, there is a total of nineteen subtests. The results are translated into age-grade scores and percentiles. A diagnostic profile may be prepared for each pupil. There are percentiles for independent-school pupils at the Educational Records Bureau. Time limits are approximately as follows: Primary battery, 90 minutes; Elementary battery, 120 minutes; Intermediate battery, 150 minutes; Advanced battery, 150 minutes. Reliability at single grade level as reported by publishers: Primary battery, total score, .96; range for five tests, .84 to .93; Elementary battery, total, .97; range for five tests, .88 to .96; Intermediate battery, total, .97; range for five tests, .89 to .95; Advanced battery, total, .98; range for five tests, .88 to .93. Reliabilities of subtests not given but probably considerably lower. The reading, arithmetic, and language tests are available in separate booklets as well as in single booklet covering entire battery.

Stanford Achievement Tests, by Truman L. Kelley, Giles M. Ruch, and Lewis M. Terman. Yonkers, New York: World Book Company, 1941. Primary battery for Grades II and III, $1.20 per 25 tests; specimen set, $0.25; Intermediate complete battery for Grades IV–VI, $2.40 for 25 tests; specimen set,

$0.45; partial battery, $1.80 per 25 tests; specimen set, $0.35; Advanced complete battery, $2.40 per 25 tests; specimen set, $0.45; partial battery, $1.80 per 25 tests; specimen set, $0.35.

Primary battery tests paragraph meaning, word meaning, spelling, arithmetic reasoning, and arithmetic computation; working time about 50 minutes.

Intermediate and Advanced complete batteries test paragraph meaning, word meaning, language usage, arithmetic reasoning, arithmetic computation, litera-ture, social studies I, social studies II, elementary science, and spelling; working time about 150 minutes.

The Intermediate and Advanced partial batteries include paragraph meaning, word meaning, language usage, arithmetic reasoning, arithmetic computation, and spelling; working time about 110 minutes.

These tests are a revision of the New Stanford tests, Forms V, W, X, Y, and Z. There are five forms in the new series, D, E, F, G, and H. Raw scores are changed to equated scores which render the different parts comparable. The scores may be graphed in a profile form and the corresponding age and grade equiva-lents identified. The Educational Records Bureau has independent-school per-centile norms for the Stanford test.

ANNOTATED LIST OF ACHIEVEMENT TESTS—SECONDARY SCHOOL AND JUNIOR COLLEGE

English

Barrett-Ryan-Schrammel English Test, by E. R. Barrett, Teresa M. Ryan, and H. E. Schrammel. Yonkers, New York: World Book Company, 1938. Booklets, $1.25 per 25; specimen set, $0.25; machine-scorable answer sheets, $0.70 per 25.

Three parts testing sentence structure and diction, grammatical forms, and punctuation. Designed for Grades IX–XII. Working time, 40 minutes. Scoring is completely objective; planned for use with answer sheet to be scored with a stencil or with special answer sheet for machine scoring. Percentile norms are available for Grades IX–XII and college freshmen. Three forms. The authors re-port total-score reliability coefficients of .88 and .89 for correlations of comparable forms and corrected odd-even correlations of .91 to .94. They also report corre-lations of .73 and .75 between total scores and final semester marks in English composition at the college level.

Cooperative English Test, by Geraldine Spaulding, Frederick B. Davis, Harold V. King, Miriam May, and W. W. Cook. New York: Cooperative Test Service, 1940–1943. Test A, Mechanics of Expression, Grades VII–XII; Test B1, Effectiveness of Expression, Grades VII–XII; Test B2, Effectiveness of Expression, Grades XI, XII, and college; Test C1, Reading Comprehen-sion, Grades VII–XII; Test C2, Reading Comprehension, Grades XI, XII, and college.   Each part, 10 to 99 copies, $0.06 per copy; 100 or more copies,

$0.055 per copy; specimen set, $0.25; machine-scorable answer sheets, $0.015 per copy; single booklet including all three parts, 10 to 99 copies, $0.13 per copy; 100 or more copies, $0.12; specimen set, $0.30; machine-scorable answer sheets, $0.035 per copy.

Published at two levels—a lower level for junior and senior high schools, and a higher level for superior students in Grades XI and XII and for college. Test A, Mechanics of Expression, is the same at both levels. The three parts are available either separately or printed together in a single-booklet edition at each level. Four comparable forms: Q, R, S, and T. Working time, 40 minutes for each part. May be scored either manually or by machine. Scaled Scores and public high school and college norms are available. The Educational Records Bureau has independent-school norms on all four forms. Widely used by schools and colleges throughout the country. Reference: Educational Records Bureau (8).

Cooperative English Test, by Sterling A. Leonard, M. H. Willing, V. A. C. Henmon, M. F. Carpenter, E. F. Lindquist, W. W. Cook, D. G. Paterson, F. S. Beers, and Geraldine Spaulding.   New York: Cooperative Test Service, 1937–1939.   10 to 99 copies, $0.07 per copy; 100 or more copies, $0.065 per copy; specimen set, $0.25; machine-scorable answer sheets, $0.02 per copy.

This test consists of three parts and provides separate scores for usage, spelling, and vocabulary, as well as a total score. Three hand-scoring forms: 1937, O, and P; two machine-scoring forms: Om and Pm. Working time, 80 minutes for the hand-scoring edition and 70 minutes for the machine-scoring edition. Public school norms are available on all forms of this English test for Grades VII to XII. Most public schools, however, find it better suited for Grades IX and upward than for Grades VII and VIII. Independent-school norms for Grades VIII to XII are also available. In addition, there are norms for all years in college. Scaled Scores corresponding to raw scores are shown on the scoring keys; also standard errors of measurement. The corrected odd-even reliability of the total score of Form 1937 is reported as .99 for total score and .96 for each of the part scores.[1] The reliability of Form O is reported as .98 for the total score; .95 for usage; .97 for spelling; and .95 for vocabulary. The validity of the tests is indicated by a correlation of .71 between test scores on an earlier form, known as Form 1934, Series 1, and school marks in English for pupils in public high schools of the State of New York (2). The same correlation, .71, was found for English test scores and school marks of boys in independent secondary schools; when intelligence as measured by the American Council Psychological Examination was held constant, the partial correlation was .50 (5, 30). Correlation of English scores with marks in college freshman English, .48. ± .03. Earlier forms of the Cooperative English Test, Series 1 and Series 2, were published as Forms 1932, 1933, 1934, 1935, and 1936. Limited supplies of certain forms are still available from the publisher.

---

[1] Unless otherwise indicated, the reliability coefficients reported for the Cooperative tests are corrected for a standard deviation of ten Scaled Scores.

Cooperative Literary Acquaintance Test, by Rosa Lee Walston and Edward E. Cureton. New York: Cooperative Test Service, 1938–1941. 10 to 99 copies, $0.06 per copy; 100 or more copies, $0.055; specimen set, $0.25; machine-scorable answer sheets, $0.015 per copy.

Tests acquaintance with English and foreign literature. Makes no direct attempt to measure appreciation. Wide range of difficulty of items makes it suitable for both secondary school and college classes. Four forms available: Forms O, P, Q, and R, each requiring 40 minutes of testing time. Forms Q and R are divided into three parts to measure: I, Pre-Renaissance and Foreign Literature; II, English and American Literature; III, Modern English and American Literature. All forms adapted for machine scoring. There are Scaled Scores, and public school independent-school, and college percentile norms for all forms. The odd-even reliability of Form O is reported as .94 (2).

Cooperative Literary Comprehension Test, by M. F. Carpenter and E. F. Lindquist. New York: Cooperative Test Service, 1938–1940. 10 to 99 copies, $0.06 per copy; 100 or more copies, $0.055; specimen set, $0.25; machine-scorable answer sheets, $0.015 per copy.

Measures understanding of conventional modes of literary expression, such as figures of speech, puns, symbolism, and historical and classical allusions, and ability to discern general mood of selection. Short unfamiliar passages of prose and poetry are presented, followed by multiple-choice questions on them. Test is suitable for upper secondary school and college classes as measuring device and teaching aid. Three forms available: Forms O, P, and Q, each requiring 40 minutes of testing time. This test provides separate scores for speed of comprehension and level of comprehension. Scaled Scores, and public school, independent-school, and college percentile norms are available for all forms. The odd-even reliability of Form O is reported as .97 (2). The correlation between the speed and level scores on Form O has been reported in two studies. Flanagan found a correlation of .77 for entering college freshmen (*14*). In a study reported in Educational Records Bulletin No. 24, the average correlation between the speed and level scores of high school students is given as .92 (*7*).

Cooperative Literary Comprehension and Appreciation Test, by Hyman Eigerman, Mary Willis, and Frederick B. Davis. New York: Cooperative Test Service, 1941 and 1943. 10 to 99 tests, $0.06 per copy; 100 or more tests, $0.055 per copy; specimen set, $0.25; machine-scorable answer sheets, $0.015.

Designed to measure the student's ability to get the meaning of literary materials and to appreciate their emotional, aesthetic, and rhythmical qualities. Two forms: R and T. Working time, 40 minutes. Yields one over-all Scaled Score. Grades X–XII and college. Percentile norms for public high schools, colleges, and independent secondary schools.

Inglis Tests of English Vocabulary, by Alexander Inglis. Boston: Ginn and Company, 1924. $1.16 per 30.

One of the older tests, but still used extensively for measuring vocabulary power. Consists of 150 multiple-choice items. No time limit. Four comparable forms. Based on a sampling of the field covered by the intelligent reader's general vocabulary. Norms for Grades IX–XII, college freshmen, and college graduates. Reliability resulting from correlations between the different forms, .90. Reference: Inglis (*18*).

There is a lower extension of the Inglis tests for Grades VI–X, by Chester M. Downing. $0.92 per 30 copies.

Michigan Vocabulary Profile Test, by Edward B. Greene.   Yonkers, New York: World Book Company, 1939. $1.70 per 25; machine-scorable answer sheets, $0.03 per copy; specimen set, $0.30.

One of the few vocabulary tests that is long enough to yield reliable diagnostic scores. Contains 240 multiple-choice items covering eight fields: human relations, commerce, government, physical science, biological science, mathematics, fine arts, and sports. Two forms: Am and Bm. No time limit; about 40–60 minutes required for administration. Norms are available for Grades IX–XII and each year of college. Author reports that correlations between the subdivisions of the two forms range from .87 to .94, with a median of .91. Vocabulary profiles for various groups have been identified. Reference: Greene (*16*).

Lincoln Diagnostic Spelling Test, by A. L. Lincoln.   New York: Educational Records Bureau, 1941–1944. $0.04 per copy; specimen set, $0.10.

Contains 100 words arranged in cycles to cover ten aspects of spelling ability. Four forms for use at junior and senior high school levels. Words chosen from Lester's *A Spelling Review* and Simmons and Bixler's *The Standard High School Spelling Scale*. Diagnosis is based largely on words representing common spelling rules. Independent-school percentile norms are available. Spearman-Brown split-half reliability: Grade 10, .930; Grade 11, .925. Reference: Townsend (*28*).

Foreign Languages

American Council on Education French Reading Test, by F. D. Cheydleur, V. A. C. Henmon, and M. J. Walker.   New York: Cooperative Test Service, 1937–1939.   10 to 99 copies, $0.06; 100 or more copies, $0.055; specimen set, $0.25.

Test prepared by Committee on Modern Languages to measure reading ability in French. Two sections, one on vocabulary and one on comprehension. Useful with students who have had one year or more of college study or its equivalent; also valuable for measurement of reading ability of advanced French students in secondary schools. Percentile norms are supplied for high school and college groups. No Scaled Scores. Testing time, 40 minutes. Three forms, A, B, and C, are available.

Cooperative French Tests, Revised Series, by Jacob Greenberg, Geraldine Spaulding, and Paule Vaillant.   New York: Cooperative Test Service,

1937–1941. 10 to 99 copies, $0.06; 100 or more copies, $0.055; specimen set, $0.25; machine-scorable answer sheet, $0.015.

Measures reading, vocabulary, and grammar, and yields separate scores for each of these three sections as well as a total score. Five available forms: N, O, P, Q, and R. Working time, 40 minutes. The tests are published in two levels— one for students who have had four or more semesters of French and one for pupils with less than that amount. These tests are designated, respectively, as the advanced and elementary forms. The Scaled Scores on all forms, elementary and advanced, are directly comparable. Public school, independent-school, and college percentile norms are available for all forms. Before the 40-minute forms were published, a series of 90-minute tests, known as Forms 1933, 1934, 1935, 1936, and 1937, was issued. Limited supplies of some of these tests are obtainable. Corrected odd-even reliability of the total score is reported as .98 for both the junior and advanced tests, Form 1935; .93 for the elementary test, Form O; and .97 for the advanced test, Form O. The test-retest correlations for the 1935 and 1936 forms, given one year apart, are .67 for pupils with one year of training at the time of the first test and .88 for pupils with two years of training at the time of the first test (2). Median correlations between total scores and school marks for boys in independent secondary schools, .70; with intelligence held constant, the correlation is .59 (5, 30). In a study using pupils in public high schools of New York State, the relation of test scores to school marks was found to be .68 and of test scores to Regents' examination, .78 (2). These correlations are for total scores.

Cooperative French Test, Form S, by Geraldine Spaulding, Laura Towne, and Sarah Wolfson Lorge. New York: Cooperative Test Service, 1942. 10 to 99 copies, $0.07; 100 or more copies, $0.065; specimen set, $0.25; machine-scorable answer sheet, $0.02.

Consists of three parts: comprehension, grammar, and civilization. One form. Two levels: lower, for first two years of high school or first year of college French; higher, for students with more than two years of high school French or more than one year of college French. Working time, 80 minutes. Part I, Comprehension, is also published as a separate 40-minute test. Scaled Scores and percentile norms for public high schools, independent secondary schools, and colleges. According to one study, median correlation of total scores with marks in French is .5 to .6 (10).

American Council on Education German Reading Test, by E. P. Appelt and V. A. C. Henmon. New York: Cooperative Test Service, 1937–1938. 10 to 99 copies, $0.06; 100 or more copies, $0.055; specimen set, $0.25.

Test prepared by Committee on Modern Languages to measure reading ability in German. Two sections, measuring vocabulary and comprehension. Most useful for students who have had one year or more of college study or its equivalent, but also suitable for measurement of reading ability of advanced German students in secondary schools. Working time, 50 minutes. Percentile norms are supplied on high school and college groups. No Scaled Scores. Two forms, A and B, are available.

Cooperative German Tests, Revised Series, by Miriam V. Hespelt, E. Herman Hespelt, Geraldine Spaulding, Emma Popper, Alice Miller, and Lucy M. Will. New York: Cooperative Test Service, 1937–1940. 10 to 99 copies, $0.06; 100 or more copies, $0.055; specimen set, $0.25; machine-scorable answer sheet, $0.015.

Provides scores for reading, vocabulary, and grammar, and also a total score. The test is available on two levels—an advanced level for students who have had four or more semesters of German, and an elementary level for pupils with less than that amount. Four forms of advanced test: N, O, P, and Q; and three forms of elementary test: N, O, and P. The Scaled Scores on all forms are directly comparable. Working time, 40 minutes. Public school, independent-school, and college percentile norms are available. Before the 40-minute forms were published, a series of 90-minute tests—known as Forms 1933, 1934, 1935, 1936, and 1937—was issued. Limited supplies of some of these tests are available. According to the publisher, the corrected odd-even reliability of the advanced test, Form 1935, was .98 and of the junior test, .96. The reliability of Form O is given as .95 for the advanced form and .96 for the elementary form (2). The median correlation between total scores on the 1934 form and the school marks of independent-school boys was .65; with intelligence held constant, the relation was .56 (5, 30). A study made in 1933 by Moser at the University of Minnesota showed a correlation of .69 between German test scores and grades in German 3 and 4 (2).

Cooperative Latin Tests, Revised Series, by George A. Land. New York: Cooperative Test Service, 1937–1941. Booklets, 10 to 99 copies, $0.06; 100 or more copies, $0.055; specimen set, $0.25; machine-scorable answer sheet, $0.015.

Measures reading, vocabulary, and grammar, and also provides a total score. Five available forms: N, O, P, Q, and R. There are two levels—an elementary level for pupils who have had three semesters or less of Latin, and an advanced level for those with more than that amount. Working time, 40 minutes. Public school, independent-school, and college percentile norms are available. The Scaled Scores on all forms are directly comparable. Before the 40-minute forms were published, a series of 90-minute tests—known as Forms 1933, 1934, 1935, 1936, and 1937— was issued. Limited supplies of some of these tests are available. The corrected odd-even reliability of Form 1935 is reported as .96 for total score. For Form O, the coefficient is .96 for the elementary test and .94 for the advanced test. The 1935 form correlates with the 1936 form, when the tests are given a year apart to students who have had two years of training at the time of the first testing, to the extent of .64 (2). A median correlation of .76 was found between the test scores measured by the American Council Psychological Examination was held constant, and school marks of independent-school boys; when the effect of intelligence as the relation was .65 (5, 30). With public high school students of New York, the correlation between school marks and test scores was .81 and between test scores and Regents' examinations, .71 (2). All these coefficients are based on total scores.

Cooperative Latin Test, Form S, by Harold V. King and Geraldine Spaulding. New York: Cooperative Test Service, 1942. 10 to 99 copies, $0.07; 100 or more copies, $0.065; specimen set, $0.25; machine-scorable answer sheet, $0.02.

In this form of the Cooperative Latin Test, there are three parts: comprehension, grammar, and civilization. Consists of two levels—lower, for first two years of high school or first year of college Latin; higher, for students with more than two years of high school Latin or more than one year of the subject in college. Working time, 80 minutes. Part I, Comprehension, is also published as a separate 40-minute test. Scaled Scores and percentile norms for public high schools, independent secondary schools, and colleges. One study indicated that median correlation of total scores with marks in Latin is about .6 (10).

Cooperative Spanish Tests, Revised Series, by E. Herman Hespelt, Robert H. Williams, Geraldine Spaulding, and Jacob Greenberg. New York: Cooperative Test Service, 1937–1940. Booklets, 10 to 99 copies, $0.06; 100 or more copies, $0.055; specimen set, $0.25; machine-scorable answer sheet, $0.015.

Test consists of three parts—reading, vocabulary, and grammar—and also a total score. The test is published in two levels—an elementary level for pupils who have had three semesters or less of Spanish, and an advanced level for those who have had more than that amount. There are three forms of the elementary test: N, O, and P; and four forms of the advanced test: N, O, P, and Q. Working time, 40 minutes. The Scaled Scores on all forms are directly comparable. Public school, independent-school, and college percentile norms are available for the Scaled Scores. Before the 40-minute forms were published, a series of 90-minute tests—known as Forms 1933, 1934, 1935, 1936, and 1937—was issued. Limited supplies of some of these tests are available; they are not machine-scorable. The reliability of these tests, computed by the method of odd versus even items, was .98 for the advanced test, Form 1935, and .95 for the junior test. For Form O, the reliability of the advanced test is reported as .96 and of the elementary test, .93. All of these figures are based on total scores. Reliabilities of the various sections are given in the *Booklet of Norms* (2).

MATHEMATICS

Cooperative Elementary Algebra Test, Revised Series, by John A. Long, L. P. Siceloff, and Leone E. Chesire. New York: Cooperative Test Service, 1937–1942. Booklets, 10 to 99 copies, $0.06; 100 or more copies, $0.055; specimen set, $0.25; machine-scorable answer sheet, $0.015.

Tests basic skills and principles in elementary algebra up to and including quadratics. Seven 40-minute forms: N, O, P, Q, R, S, and T. There are both public school and independent-school percentile norms for all these forms. Standard errors of measurement, as well as Scaled Scores, are reported on scoring keys. Limited supply of 90-minute forms also available. The 90-minute tests, which are not machine-scorable, include Forms 1933, 1934, 1935, 1936, and 1937. Odd-even reliability based on standard group: Form 1935, .94; Form O, .92 (2). Median correlation with school marks in algebra is reported as .73 for boys in independent secondary schools; with intelligence constant, the relationship is .67 (5, 30). For students in New York high schools, the correlation between the test and school marks in algebra is .81 and between the tests and Regents' examinations, .71 for Form 1934 (2).

Cooperative Intermediate Algebra Test, Revised Series, by John A. Long, L. P. Siceloff, and Leone E. Cheshire. New York: Cooperative Test Service, 1938–1943. Booklets, 10 to 99 copies, $0.06; 100 or more copies, $0.055; specimen set, $0.25; machine-scorable answer sheet, $0.015.

This test is similar to the elementary algebra test but includes materials of the typical second course in algebra, quadratics, and beyond. Six 40-minute machine-scorable forms: O, P, Q, R, S, and T. Public school and independent-school percentile norms. Scaled Scores and standard errors of measurement are given on the scoring keys. Limited supply of 90-minute hand-scorable forms also available. The 90-minute tests include Forms 1933, 1934, 1935, 1936, and 1937. Odd-even reliability: Form 1935, .97; Form O, .93 (2). Median correlation between test scores and school marks in intermediate algebra is .90 for boys in independent secondary schools; when intelligence is held constant, the correlation is .82 (5, 30). For public school pupils in New York, the correlation between test scores and school marks is .60 and between test scores and Regents' examinations, .38 (2).

Cooperative Plane Geometry Test, Revised Series, by John A. Long, L. P. Siceloff, Emma Spaney, and Margaret P. Martin. New York: Cooperative Test Service, 1937–1943. Booklets, 10 to 99 copies, $0.06; 100 or more copies, $0.055; specimen set, $0.25; machine-scorable answer sheet, $0.015.

Measures fundamentals of a first course in geometry. Emphasizes logical reasoning and comprehensive understanding of geometric concepts. Does not require formal proofs of theorems. Seven machine-scorable 40-minute forms available: N, O, P, Q, R, S, and T. There are public school and independent-school percentile norms. Limited supply of 90-minute hand-scorable forms also available, including Forms 1933, 1934, 1935, 1936, and 1937. Standard errors of measurement as well as Scaled Scores are reported on the scoring keys. Odd-even reliability based on a standard group: Form 1935, .93; Form O, .89 (2). Correlation with school marks in plane geometry: .78 based on independent schools for boys (5) and .75 based on New York public school pupils (2). When intelligence is held constant, the first of the two preceding correlations becomes .69 (30). The correlation between test scores and Regents' examinations is .55 (2).

Cooperative Solid Geometry Test, Revised Series, by H. T. Lundholm, John A. Long, and L. P. Siceloff. New York: Cooperative Test Service, 1938 and

1939. Booklets, 10 to 99 copies, $0.06; 100 or more copies, $0.055; specimen set, $0.25; machine-scorable answer sheet, $0.015.

Emphasizes general ability to apply specific skills and information to appropriate problems in three-dimensional space. Two forms, O and P; each requires 40 minutes of working time. Public school and independent-school percentile norms are available. Scaled Scores and standard errors of measurement are shown on scoring keys. Three earlier forms—1933, 1934, and 1935—call for 90 minutes of administering time and are not machine-scorable. Reliability computed by the method of odd versus even items is .92 for Form 1933 and .90 for Form O (2). Median correlation between test scores and school marks in solid geometry is .58 based on independent secondary schools for boys; with intelligence constant, the relationship is .49 (5, 30).

Cooperative Trigonometry Test, Revised Series, by John A. Long and L. P. Siceloff. New York: Cooperative Test Service, 1938 and 1939. Booklets, 10 to 99 copies, $0.06; 100 or more copies, $0.055; specimen set, $0.25; machine-scorable answer sheet, $0.015.

Samples conventions, facts, and relationships included in a typical course in plane trigonometry and is appropriate as a measure of final achievement or as a placement test for courses requiring trigonometry as a prerequisite. Two machine-scorable, 40-minute forms, O and P. Public school and independent-school percentile norms are available. Scaled Scores and standard errors of measurement are shown on scoring keys. Limited supply of 90-minute forms available, including Forms 1933, 1934, 1935, 1936, and 1937. The odd-even reliability of Form 1933 is .96 and of Form O, .92 (2). Correlation between test scores and marks in trigonometry based on independent secondary schools for boys is .73; with intelligence constant, the relationship is .71 (5, 30).

Cooperative Mathematics Test for Grades 7, 8, and 9, by Alice H. Darnell, John C. Flanagan, Stevenson W. Fletcher, and Rose E. Lutz. New York: Cooperative Test Service, 1938–1941. Booklets, 10 to 99 copies, $0.07; 100 or more copies, $0.065; specimen set, $0.25; machine-scorable answer sheet, $0.015.

Includes skills, terms and concepts, applications, and appreciation. For use in a junior high school mathematics course. Requires 80 minutes working time. The scope and content of the examination are based on a survey of the objectives of mathematics courses in member schools of the Educational Records Bureau. Constructed by a subcommittee appointed by the Tests and Measurements Committee of the Bureau. Three forms: P, Q, and RO. Reliabilities (odd-even method) based on scores of 154 pupils in Grade VIII: total score, .94 (S.D., 16.6); Part I, Skills, .88 (S.D., 6.4); Part II, Facts, Terms, and Concepts, .69 (S.D., 4.3); Part III, Applications, .81 (S.D., 4.9); Part IV, Appreciation, .81 (S.D., 4.2). Intercorrelations: $r_{12} = .57 \pm .04$; $r_{13} = .71 \pm .03$; $r_{14} = .55 \pm .04$; $r_{23} = .59 \pm .04$; $r_{24} = .64 \pm .03$; $r_{34} = .56 \pm .04$. Reference: Seder (25).

Cooperative General Mathematics Test for High School Classes, Revised Series, by H. T. Lundholm and L. P. Siceloff. New York: Cooperative Test Service, 1937 and 1938. Booklets, 10 to 99 copies, $0.06; 100 or more copies, $0.055; specimen set, $0.25; machine-scorable answer sheet, $0.015.

Purpose of this test is to afford accurate classification and to measure growth. It samples materials from all mathematics courses usually taught in secondary schools. Suitable for high school students who have had three or four years of mathematics, or entering college freshmen. Covers interpretation of graphs, use of algebraic symbols, functional relations, geometric relations in two- and three-dimensional space and trigonometric relations. Two machine-scorable forms, N and O, each requiring 40 minutes of working time. Differential percentile norms and Scaled Scores based on pupils who have studied three years of mathematics (in the ninth, tenth, and eleventh grades) accompany scoring keys. This test has five earlier 90-minute forms, known as Forms 1933, 1934, 1935, 1936, and 1937. Limited supplies of some of these forms are available. The odd-even reliability of Form 1935 is reported as .93 and of Form O, as .91. The test re-test reliability with one year elapsing between tests, the pupils being in tenth grade for the first testing and eleventh for the second, is .74 (2).

Cooperative Test in Secondary School Mathematics (Higher Level), Form S, by Margaret P. Martin, William Mollenkopf, Radcliffe W. Bristol, William S. Litterick, and Carroll G. Ross. New York: Cooperative Test Service, 1942. 10 to 99 copies, $0.07; 100 or more copies, $0.065; specimen set, $0.25; machine-scorable answer sheet, $0.015.

One form, planned to cover the mathematics taught in Grades X, XI, and XII. Includes plane geometry, intermediate and higher algebra, solid geometry, and trigonometry. Emphasizes items calling for ability to do sustained mathematical thinking. No Scaled Scores or public school norms. Independent-school percentile norms are available at the Educational Records Bureau. Median correlation between test scores and school marks in mathematics is .66 based on nine independent-school classes (*10*).

Reavis-Breslich Diagnostic Tests in the Fundamental Operations of Arithmetic and in Problem Solving, by W. C. Reavis and E. R. Breslich. Chicago: Laidlaw Brothers. $0.04 per copy.

These tests in ten sections cover the four fundamental operations with whole numbers and fractions, placing the decimal point in multiplication and division problems, and arithmetical problems with and without numbers. Testing time is 28 minutes. Two forms, designed for use in Grades VII through XII. Public school norms for Grades V–XII. The Educational Records Bureau has independent-school percentile norms for Grades VII–XII. Included in this list as a suggestion for secondary schools that need a brief, yet fairly diagnostic, test of arithmetic fundamentals. Reference: Educational Records Bureau (*11*).

SCIENCE

Cooperative General Science Test, Revised Series, by O. E. Underhill and S. R. Powers. New York: Cooperative Test Service, 1937–1940. Booklets, 10 to 99 copies, $0.065; 100 or more copies, $0.055; specimen set, $0.25; machine-scorable answer sheet, $0.015.

This test is comprehensive and is designed to cover a wide enough area to be useful with groups whose instructional backgrounds vary widely. Questions are of multiple-choice and matching types and in some cases involve understanding of diagrams and identifications of objects in sketches. Nine forms issued. Four machine-scorable 40-minute forms: N, O, P, and Q. Public school and independent-school percentile norms are available. Scaled Scores and standard errors of measurement are provided on the scoring keys. Five 90-minute forms—1933, 1934, 1935, 1936, and 1937—were published earlier. Form 1937 is the only one of these which is machine-scorable. Limited supplies of some of the forms are still available. Reliability, based on odd versus even items, with a standard group is .88 for Form 1933 and .89 for Form O (2). Median correlation between test scores and school marks of pupils in independent secondary schools for boys is .63 (5). With intelligence, as measured by the American Council Psychological Examination, held constant, the correlation is .43 (30).

Cooperative Biology Test, Revised Series, by F. L. Fitzpatrick and S. R. Powers. New York: Cooperative Test Service, 1937–1942. Booklets, 10 to 99 copies, $0.06; 100 or more copies, $0.055; specimen set, $0.25; machine-scorable answer sheet, $0.015.

Measures factual knowledge of biology and, indirectly, scientific attitude and ability of the student to apply his information to the solution of problems. Test can be used as a basis for classification in advanced courses as well as a measure of achievement in biology. Items are mainly of three types: multiple-choice, matching, and labeling of drawings. Five 40-minute machine-scorable forms: N, O, P, Q, and S. The last form was constructed with the cooperation of a committee appointed by the Educational Records Bureau. There are both public school and independent-school norms. Scaled Scores and standard errors of measurement are shown on the scoring keys. Five 90-minute forms—1933, 1934, 1935, 1936, and 1937—were published earlier. Limited supplies of some of these tests are available. These forms are not machine-scorable. The odd-even reliability of Form 1935 is quoted as .94 and of Form O, as .94 (2). Median correlation between test scores and school marks made in biology by pupils in independent schools for boys is .58 (5). With intelligence, as measured by the American Council Psychological Examination, held constant, the median correlation is .46 (30).

Cooperative Biology Test, Educational Records Bureau Edition, by Thomas F. Morrison, Virginia F. Babcock, Donald H. Miller, and Robert H. Woodworth. New York: Cooperative Test Service, 1941–1943. $0.07 per copy.

Devised by the Committee on Biology Tests of the Educational Records Bureau. Based on the objectives and curricula of college preparatory schools. Three forms—ERB–R, ERB–S, and ERB–T—each requiring 40 minutes of working time. Hand-scored. Independent-school percentile norms are available. No Scaled Scores or public school norms. Median of correlations between test scores and biology marks in eight independent schools is .654 (9).

Cooperative Chemistry Test, Revised Series, by Victor H. Noll and S. R. Powers. New York: Cooperative Test Service, 1937–1942. Booklets, 10 to 99 copies, $0.06; 100 or more copies, $0.055; specimen set, $0.25; machine-scorable answer sheet, $0.015.

The test covers fundamental facts and principles basic to the understanding of chemistry. Includes also applications of chemical principles to daily life and chemical problems dealing with weight and volume, density, molarity, and so on. Range of difficulty is wide enough to make test useful with high school pupils or with students in first course in college chemistry. Five 40-minute machine-scorable forms: N, O, P, Q, and S. The last form was constructed with the cooperation of a committee appointed by the Educational Records Bureau. There are both public school and independent-school percentile norms. Scaled Scores and standard errors of measurement are given on the scoring keys. Five 90-minute forms—1933, 1934, 1935, 1936, and 1937—were released before the revised series was published. Limited supplies of some of these forms may be obtained. They are not machine-scorable. Odd-even reliability as reported for Form 1935 is .97 and for Form O, .92 (2). Median correlation between test scores and school marks in independent secondary schools for boys is reported as .78 (5). When intelligence is held constant, the relation is .64 (30). The correlation for public high school pupils in the State of New York between test scores and school marks in chemistry is .75 and between test scores and Regents' examinations, .63 (2).

Cooperative Chemistry Test, Educational Records Bureau Edition, by Charles L. Bickel, W. Gordon Brown, Robert N. Hilkert, C. S. Hitchcock, and H. H. Loomis. New York: Cooperative Test Service, 1941–1943. $0.07 per copy.

Devised by the Committee on Chemistry Tests of the Educational Records Bureau. Based on the objectives and curricula of college preparatory schools. Three forms—ERB–R, ERB–S, and ERB–T—each requiring 80 minutes of working time. Hand-scored. Independent-school percentile norms are available. No Scaled Scores or public school norms. Median of correlations between test scores and chemistry marks in eight independent schools is .680 (9).

Cooperative Physics Test, Revised Series, by H. W. Farwell. New York: Cooperative Test Service, 1937–1942. Booklets, 10 to 99 copies, $0.06; 100 or more copies, $0.055; specimen set, $0.25; machine-scorable answer sheet, $0.015.

This test attempts to measure knowledge of and ability to think in terms of the subject matter of a typical high school physics course. Suitable for use at end of first and second semesters of the high school course or as a pretest for college physics. Five 40-minute, machine-scorable, forms: N, O, P, Q, and S. The last form was constructed with the cooperation of a committee appointed by the Educational Records Bureau. Public school and independent-school percentile norms are available. Standard errors of measurement, as well as Scaled Scores, are given on the scoring keys. Five 90-minute forms—1933, 1934, 1935, 1936, and 1937—were released before the revised series was published. Limited supplies of some of these forms may be obtained. These forms are not machine-scorable. Reliability, odd versus even items, is reported as .97 for Form 1935 and .92 for Form O (2). The median correlation between school marks and test scores for independent secondary schools for boys was reported as .73 (5); when intelligence as measured by the American Council Psychological Examination was held constant, the relation was found to be .67 (30). Another indication of the validity of the test is contained in the correlation between school marks and test scores, and between Regents' examinations and test scores, for students in public high schools in New York State. The former is .68 and the latter, .71 (2).

Cooperative Physics Test, Educational Records Bureau Edition, by Russell S. Bartlett, Lester D. Beers, Winston M. Gottschalk, Roberta G. Poland, and Alan T. Waterman. New York: Cooperative Test Service, 1941–1943. $0.07 per copy.

Devised by the Committee on Physics Tests of the Educational Records Bureau. Based on the objectives and curricula of college preparatory schools. Three forms— ERB–R, ERB–S, ERB–T—each requiring 80 minutes of working time. Hand-scored. Independent-school percentile norms are available. No Scaled Scores or public school norms. Median of correlations between test scores and school physics marks in seven independent schools is .688 (9).

Cooperative Science Test for Grades 7, 8, and 9, by John G. Zimmerman, Richard E. Watson, and Carl A. Pearson. New York: Cooperative Test Service, 1941 and 1942. 10 to 99 copies, $0.07; 100 or more copies, $0.065; specimen set, $0.25; machine-scorable answer sheet, $0.015.

Consists of two 80-minute forms, R and S, each divided into three parts: (1) Facts, Skills, and Applications; (2) Terms and Concepts; and (3) Comprehension and Interpretation. Designed to measure knowledge of elementary scientific principles and understanding of natural phenomena of the physical world. Suitable for Grades VII, VIII, and IX. Scaled Scores, and public school and independent-school percentile norms are available.

SOCIAL STUDIES

Cooperative American History Test, Revised Series, by H. R. Anderson, Harry Berg, E. F. Lindquist, Mary Willis, and Charlotte W. Croon. New York: Cooperative Test Service, 1937–1943. 10 to 99 copies, $0.065; 100 or more copies, $0.055; specimen set, $0.25; machine-scorable answer sheet, $0.015.

This examination emphasizes reasoned understanding of the information, ideas, relationships, and generalizations presented in a secondary school course, and the ability to use these facts and ideas in the interpretation of historical movements, institutions, and practices. The examination measures three types of information: first, the breadth of the student's acquaintance with historical personages, and the understanding of historical and geographical terms; second, the student's time perspective of history in general, although specific dates are not required; and third, the student's historical judgment of causes and results of certain events. The test appears in seven 40-minute, machine-scorable, forms: N, O, P, Q, R, S, and T. Five 90-minute forms were published earlier: Forms 1933, 1934, 1935, 1936, and 1937. Limited supplies of some of these forms are available. They are scored by hand. Public school and independent-school percentile norms are available. The reliability of Form 1935 is given as .93, and that for Form O is given as .87 (2). Median correlation between scores on Form 1934 and school marks of independent-school boys is .75 (5); median partial correlation coefficient of .69 with school marks when intelligence scores were held constant (30). Correlation of Form T scores with marks in American history in two independent schools, .565 and .588 (12).

Cooperative Ancient History Test, by H. R. Anderson, E. F. Lindquist, Wallace Taylor, and Charlotte W. Croon. New York: Cooperative Test Service, 1933–1939. Booklets, 90-minute forms, $0.07; 40-minute forms, $0.06; discount for 100 or more copies; specimen set, $0.25; machine-scorable answer sheet for 40-minute forms, $0.015.

This test measures the evaluation and understanding of the fundamental movements and institutions as well as of personages, locations, and specific events important for an understanding of the major social problems in ancient times which are also significant for the present. Forms 1933, 1934, 1935, 1936, and 1937 require 90 minutes and are each sixteen pages long. The corrected odd-even reliability of Form 1935 is given as .94. Forms O and P are 40-minute, eight-page revised forms of the 90-minute tests and are comparable to them in difficulty. Forms O and P are adapted to the scoring machine. The reliability of this test is reported as .93 (2). Median correlation of scores on Form 1934 and school marks of independent-school boys is .59; partial correlation with intelligence constant, .40 (5, 30).

Cooperative English History Test, by H. R. Anderson and E. F. Lindquist. New York: Cooperative Test Service, 1933–1935. Booklets, 10 to 99 copies, $0.07; 100 or more copies, $0.065; specimen set, $0.25.

Designed chiefly for a specialized course in English history, but the authors suggest it may also be used as one element in a testing program in European history. The test consists of three parts, each separately timed and dealing, respectively, with: historical personages, and historical and geographical terms; dates and events; and historical judgment. The test requires 90 minutes and is sixteen pages long. It is not machine-scorable. Forms 1933, 1934, and 1935 are available. All the questions are either the matching or the multiple-choice type. No Scaled Scores are available for this test. The reliability coefficient for Form 1933 is given as .93 (2) Correlation between this test and school marks is .78; with intelligence scores held constant, the correlation is .62 (5, 30). This test and the modern European history test are in need of revision to bring them up to date.

Cooperative Medieval History Test, by H. R. Anderson and E. F. Lindquist. New York: Cooperative Test Service, 1933–1935. Booklets, 10 to 99 copies, $0.07; 100 or more copies, $0.065; specimen set, $0.25.

The emphasis in this examination is upon the significant implications and inter-relations of the facts tested, rather than upon information alone. The content of the examination is wide in its range, and parallels the objectives of a broadly conceived course in medieval history. Covers period from the barbarian invasions through the Renaissance. The examination is published in three comparable forms —Forms 1933, 1934, and 1935—but no Scaled Scores are available. Each form requires 90 minutes and is sixteen pages long. The questions are of the multiple-choice and matching types. The test is not machine-scorable. The reliability coefficient for the 1933 form is given as .94 (2).

Cooperative Modern European History Test, by H. R. Anderson, Wallace Taylor, E. F. Lindquist, Mary Willis, and Charlotte W. Croon. New York: Cooperative Test Service, 1937–1940. Booklets, 10 to 99 copies, $0.07; 100 or more copies, $0.055; specimen set, $0.25; machine-scorable answer sheet, $0.015.

This test is designed to measure a pupil's ability to relate various personages, historical and geographical terms, dates, and events to the fundamental movements and institutions of modern Europe. Covers period from beginning of Renaissance to beginning of World War II. Four 40-minute, machine-scorable forms: N, O, P, and Q. Five 90-minute forms—1933, 1934, 1935, 1936, and 1937—were published before the revised series. These forms are not machine-scorable. There are percentile norms for both public schools and independent schools. The reliabilities of the tests are given as .94 for Form 1935 and .91 for Form O (2). Median correlation between scores on Form 1934 and school marks of independent-school boys is .66; with intelligence held constant, the correlation is .46 (5, 30).

Cooperative Test of Social Studies Abilities, by J. Wayne Wrightstone. New York: Cooperative Test Service, 1936 and 1940. Booklets, 10 to 99 copies, $0.07; 100 or more copies, $0.065; specimen set, $0.25.

Designed to determine the extent to which students have acquired the skills basic to effective work in the social studies. The various parts of the test measure the ability to (1) obtain facts from tables, graphs, charts, and diagrams; (2) to organize facts by relating given statements to various topics and by making brief outlines; (3) to interpret facts by drawing conclusions from given data; and (4) to apply generalizations by checking the reasons certain generalizations can be made. There are two forms, Experimental Form 1936 and Experimental Form Q. The former requires 90 minutes of working time, the latter 80 minutes. For Form 1936, there are tentative public school percentile norms for Grades IX to XII; for Form Q, independent-school percentile norms are available for Grades IX to XII. Spearman-Brown reliability of total score at twelfth-grade level is .972; reliability of parts, .830 to .966. Reference: Selover (*26*).

Cooperative Economics Test, by H. R. Anderson, J. E. Partington, and Mary Willis. New York: Cooperative Test Service, 1939 and 1942. Booklets, 10 to 99 copies, $0.06; 100 or more copies, $0.055; specimen set, $0.25; machine-scorable answer sheet, $0.015.

Designed to measure a student's understanding of the basic concepts of economic life. Two 40-minute forms, P and S. No Scaled Scores. Percentile norms for high school and college classes in economics are available for Form P. There are tentative independent-school norms for both forms.

American Council Civics and Government Test, by Robert D. Leigh, Joseph D. McGoldrick, Peter H. Odegard, and Ben D. Wood. Yonkers, New York: World Book Company, 1929. $1.65 per 25 tests; specimen set, $0.25.

A 90-minute objective examination prepared by a committee of the American Council on Education for reliable and valid measures of achievement in civics and government. The test is published in two forms, Form A and Form B. The forms are comparable and each consists of four parts: Part I is made up of 108 true-false statements; Part II is a test of thirteen matching questions where five items in one group are to be paired with five of eight items in a second group; Part III consists of twenty-four multiple-choice questions with five or more alternatives; and Part IV consists of twenty-five one-word completion statements. The reliability as estimated by the Spearman-Brown formula for Form A is .88. Percentile norms based upon rather small groups of high school pupils and entering college students are given for Form A of the test. Validity of the examination is secured by a careful selection of the items used with a wide range of content.

GENERAL ACHIEVEMENT AND GENERAL CULTURE

Cooperative General Achievement Tests: Test I, A Test of General Proficiency in the Field of Social Studies, by Mary Willis and Charlotte W. Croon; Test II, A Test of General Proficiency in the Field of Natural Science, by Charlotte W. Croon, Carl A. Pearson, Mary Willis, Alexander Calandra, Richard E. Watson, and John G. Zimmerman; and Test III, A Test of General Proficiency in the Field of Mathematics, by Emma Spaney, Margaret Martin, and Charlotte W. Croon. New York: Cooperative Test Service, 1941–1943. Booklets, 10 to 99 copies, each test, $0.07; 100 or more copies, $0.065; specimen set, $0.25; machine-scorable answer sheet, $0.015.

Three separate booklets, each requiring 40 minutes of working time. Each test contains two parts. The first measures knowledge of terms and concepts needed for an understanding of the field for which the test is designed; the second tests the student's ability to read, comprehend, and interpret typical materials in the field. These tests do not measure knowledge of facts and topical content in the three fields. Grades X–XII and college freshmen. Scaled Scores and percentile norms for high school pupils and entering college freshmen are available. Three forms: QR, S, and T.

Cooperative General Culture Test, by Mary Willis, Margaret Martin, Carl A. Pearson, Carl Blose, William Mollenkopf, Agatha Townsend, and John G. Zimmerman. New York: Cooperative Test Service, 1933–1944. Booklets, 10 to 99 copies, $0.13; 100 or more copies, $0.12; specimen set, $0.30; machine-scorable answer sheet, $0.035.

Planned to measure the student's general cultural background without regard to course boundaries. Working time, three hours distributed among six 30-minute sections as follows: Current Social Problems, History and Social Studies, Literature, Science, Fine Arts, and Mathematics. Designed for college students, but may also be used with college preparatory seniors near the end of their secondary school course. Twelve forms have been constructed: Forms 1933, 1934, 1935, 1936, 1937, O, P, Q, R, S, T, and U. The last eight are machine-scorable. Only the last four are currently carried in stock by the publisher. There are college percentile norms for part and total scores.

BUSINESS SUBJECTS

National Clerical Ability Tests, by the Joint Committee on Tests of the National Office Management Association and National Council of Business Education. 16 Lawrence Hall, Kirkland Street, Cambridge, Massachusetts: Joint Committee on Tests. 25 or more copies, $0.20 per copy; $0.50 per sample copy (Series 1939); $1.55 per set of sample copies of all National Clerical Ability Tests (Series 1939).

A comprehensive series of tests designed to form the basis of a thorough program of measurement in the field of business education. The test battery includes Bookkeeping Ability Test, 180 minutes; Dictating Machine Transcription Test, 60 minutes; Filing Test, 120 minutes; Fundamental Test, 120 minutes; General Information Test, 40 minutes; Key-Driven Calculating Machine Ability Test, 120 minutes; Stenographic Ability Test, 180 minutes; Typing Ability Test, 120 minutes.

Elwell-Fowlkes Bookkeeping Test, by Fayette H. Elwell and John Guy Fowlkes. Yonkers, New York: World Book Company, 1929. $1.40 per 25; specimen set, $0.30.

Designed for measurement of achievement in bookkeeping. There is a test to be used at the end of the first semester, known as Test 1, and a test for use at the end of the second semester, called Test 2. Each test covers general theory, journalizing, classification, adjusting and closing the ledger, and statements. Two equivalent forms, A and B, for each test. Working time, 50 minutes. According to the authors' data, the reliability of Test 1 is .82 and that of Test 2 is .87.

Thompson Business Practice Test, by James M. Thompson. Yonkers, New York: World Book Company, 1937. $1.65 per 25; specimen set, $0.25.

A test of achievement in general business practice courses in junior and senior high schools. Two equivalent forms, A and B. Administering time, 80 minutes, in two sittings of 40 minutes each. Author's data indicate that reliability coefficients range from .94 to .97.

Turse-Durost Shorthand Achievement Test, by Paul L. Turse and Walter N. Durost. Yonkers, New York: World Book Company, 1941. $1.10 per 25; specimen set, $0.20.

An objective test of shorthand achievement. Includes language, shorthand principles, and shorthand penmanship. Two forms—A, which is published, and B, which is to be issued later. Working time for first year students, 50 minutes. Percentile norms for each of first and second years. Split-half reliabilities, .93 and .94, as reported by authors.

REFERENCES

1. Allen, Richard D. *Self-Measurement Projects in Group Guidance.* New York: Inor Publishing Company, 1934. Pp. xviii + 274.
2. Cooperative Test Service. *A Booklet of Norms,* pp. 10–14. New York: Cooperative Test Service, 1938. Pp. 85.
3. Davis, Frederick B. "Fundamental Factors of Comprehension in Reading," *Psychometrika,* IX (September 1944), 185–197.
4. Eckert, Ruth E. "Realism in Higher Education," *Educational Record,* XIX (January 1938), 86–104.
5. Educational Records Bureau. "Comparable Tests and School Marks," *1936 Fall Testing Program in Independent Schools and Supplementary Studies,* pp. 83–111. Educational Records Bulletin No. 19. New York: Educational Records Bureau, January 1937. Pp. x + 111.
6. Educational Records Bureau. "The Interpretation and Use of Scaled Scores," *The 1937 Achievement Testing Program of the Educational Records Bureau,* pp. 13–36. Educational Records Bulletin No. 20. New York: Educational Records Bureau, June 1937. Pp. xi + 134 + 14 charts.
7. Educational Records Bureau. "The Relation Between Speed and Level of Literary Comprehension," *1938 Achievement Testing Program in Independent Schools,* pp. 51–56. Educational Records Bulletin No. 24. New York: Educational Records Bureau, June 1938. Pp. xi + 59 + 13 charts.
8. Educational Records Bureau. "The Cooperative English Test, Form Q: Correlations with School Marks and Intercorrelations," *1940 Achievement Testing Program in Independent Schools and Supplementary Studies,* pp. 43–56. Educational Records Bulletin No. 30. New York: Educational Records Bureau, June 1940. Pp. xi + 76 + 13 charts.
9. Educational Records Bureau. "Some Data on the Difficulty and Validity of the

Cooperative Tests in Biology, Chemistry, and Physics, Forms ERB–R," *1941 Achievement Testing Program in Independent Schools and Supplementary Studies,* pp. 64–68. Educational Records Bulletin No. 33. New York: Educational Records Bureau, June 1941. Pp. x + 76 + 10 charts.

10. Educational Records Bureau. "Some Data on the Results of the Cooperative Tests in French, Latin, and Secondary School Mathematics," *1942 Achievement Testing Program in Independent Schools and Supplementary Studies,* pp. 55–59. Educational Records Bulletin No. 36. New York: Educational Records Bureau, June 1942. Pp. xiii + 59.

11. Educational Records Bureau. "The Reliability and Validity of the Reavis-Breslich Arithmetic Tests," *1942 Fall Testing Program in Independent Schools and Supplementary Studies,* pp. 44–50. Educational Records Bulletin No. 37. New York: Educational Records Bureau, January 1943. Pp. xiii + 50.

12. Educational Records Bureau. "Some Data on the Cooperative American History Test," *1943 Achievement Testing Program in Independent Schools and Supplementary Studies,* pp. 46–48. Educational Records Bulletin No. 38. New York: Educational Records Bureau, June 1943. Pp. xiii + 53.

13. Engelhart, Max D., and Thurstone, Thelma Gwinn. "The Chicago Reading Tests," *Chicago Schools Journal,* XX (November–December, 1938), 74–81.

14. Flanagan, John C. "A New Type of Reading Test for Secondary School and College Students Which Provides Separate Scores for Speed of Comprehension and Level of Comprehension," *Practical Values of Educational Research: Official Report of the American Educational Research Association, 1938,* pp. 195–199.

15. Flanagan, John C. *The Cooperative Achievement Tests: A Bulletin Reporting the Basic Principles and Procedures Used in the Development of Their System of Scaled Scores.* New York: Cooperation Test Service of the American Council on Education, December 1939. Pp. v + 41.

16. Greene, Edward B. "Vocabulary Profiles of Groups in Training," *Journal of Educational Research,* XXXIII (April 1940), 569–575.

17. Hawkes, Herbert E.; Lindquist, E. F.; and Mann, C. R. *The Construction and Use of Achievement Examinations.* Boston: Houghton Mifflin Company, 1936. Pp. xii + 497.

18. Inglis, Alexander. "A Vocabulary Test for High School and College Students," *English Leaflet,* XXIII (October 1923), 1–13.

19. Keys, Noel. *The Improvement of Measurement through Cumulative Testing.* Teachers College Contributions to Education No. 321. New York: Bureau of Publications, Teachers College, Columbia University, 1928. Pp. viii + 81.

20. Learned, William S., and Wood, Ben D. *The Student and His Knowledge.* Bulletin No. 29. New York: Carnegie Foundation for the Advancement of Teaching, 1938. Pp. xx + 313.

21. Lindquist, E. F. "The Technique of Constructing Tests in Relation to Various Uses of Test Results," *Educational Measurement and Guidance,* pp. 113–135. Washington, D. C.: American Council on Education, 1933.

22. McConn, C. M. "Examinations Old and New: Their Uses and Abuses," *Educational Record,* XVI (October 1935), 1–37.

23. Remmers, H. H., and Gage, N. L. *Educational Measurement and Evaluation.* New York: Harper & Brothers, 1943. Pp. ix + 580.

24. Sangren, Paul V. *The Measurement of Achievement in Silent Reading.* Kalamazoo, Michigan: The Author, 1927.

25. Seder, Margaret. "An Experimental Study of a New Mathematics Test for Grades 7, 8, and 9," *Mathematics Teacher,* XXXII (October 1939), 259–264.

26. Selover, Margaret Seder. "Some Data on the Reliability and Validity of the Cooperative Test of Social Studies Abilities," *1941 Fall Testing Program in Independent Schools and Supplementary Studies,* pp. 41–43. Educational Records Bulletin No. 35. New York: Educational Records Bureau, January 1942. Pp. xiv + 57.

27. Stalnaker, John M. "Essay Examinations Reliably Read," *School and Society,* XLVI (1937), 671–672.

28. Townsend, Agatha. "A Study of the Lincoln Diagnostic Spelling Test," *1943 Achievement Testing Program in Independent Schools and Supplementary Studies,* pp. 49–53. Educational Records Bulletin No. 38. New York: Educational Records Bureau, June 1943. Pp. xiii + 53.

29. Traxler, Arthur E. *The Measurement and Improvement of Silent Reading at the Junior-High-School Level.* Doctor's thesis. Chicago: Department of Education, University of Chicago, 1932. Pp. vii + 217.

30. Traxler, Arthur E. "Correlation of Achievement Scores and School Marks," *School Review,* XLV (December 1937), 198–201.

31. Traxler, Arthur E. "Comparison of Scores on the Revised Edition and the Older Edition of the Stanford Achievement Test," *Elementary School Journal* XLII (April 1942), 616–620.

32. Tyler, Ralph W. *Constructing Achievement Examinations.* Columbus: Ohio State University, 1934. Pp. vi + 102.

33. Wood, Ben D. "The Need for Comparable Measurements in Individualized Education," *Educational Record,* Supplement No. 12 (January 1939), 14–31.

34. Wrightstone, J. Wayne. "Correlations among Tests of High School Subjects," *School Review,* XLIII (March 1935), 776–780.

CHAPTER VI

Appraisal of Personal Qualities—Tests [1]

ACCURATE, OBJECTIVE INFORMATION IN REGARD TO APTITUDE AND ACHIEVEMENT, SUCH as may be obtained from the tests listed in Chapters IV and V, is very important in a guidance program, but it fills in only part of the picture for each individual pupil. Most teachers and guidance officers are aware that personality factors are fully as important in a pupil's academic and out-of-school adjustment as are those more easily measured factors of intelligence and achievement. There is an increasing demand for valid and reliable records of personality development to assist the school in its guidance program.

There are two broad approaches to the evaluation of personal qualities. One of these is by means of tests, while the other is by means of more informal procedures involving anecdotal records, ratings, descriptions of behavior, and projective techniques. Under ideal conditions anecdotal records, rating devices, and behavior descriptions undoubtedly have more to offer to a guidance program than do personality tests which for the most part are still definitely experimental. The more informal devices are, however, much more time-consuming than tests, and it is probable that for some time to come many schools which are establishing guidance programs will not be able to employ informal evaluative procedures on a school-wide basis until a long and thorough program of teacher education in guidance philosophy has taken place. In the meantime, personality tests furnish almost the only available means of systematically collecting helpful, although admittedly inadequate and imperfect, information in this important area.

---

[1] A more extensive discussion of this topic is contained in the author's *The Use of Tests and Rating Devices in the Appraisal of Personality.* Educational Records Bulletin No. 23 (Revised). New York: Educational Records Bureau, November 1942.

Extent of Attempts To Measure Personality

Notwithstanding the nebulousness of this field, there have been numerous attempts, within the last quarter of the century, to devise instruments for the appraisal of personality. In 1932 Maller (75) published a bibliography of some 300 character and personality tests. Hildreth's *A Bibliography of Mental Tests and Rating Scales* (54) published in 1933 and revised in 1939, contains 402 titles dealing with character and personality. Buros' bibliographies (16, 17, 18, 19) added 81 tests in the field of character and personality, attitudes and opinions, and social adjustment. A fair estimate of the number of published tests and inventories loosely classifiable under the heading of personality is close to 500. It is probable that the number of unpublished tests and devices for rating personality is even greater.

There are so many inferior instruments purporting to measure personality that busy teachers and counselors cannot find sufficient time to inspect all of them in order to find the few tests that hold out some promise of serving a practical purpose. The main purpose of this chapter is to provide a simple, nontechnical discussion of personality measurement and a carefully selected list of tests for counselors who may contemplate the use of personality tests but who do not have time to survey the whole field in order to select those best suited to their own needs.

Definition of Personality

One obstacle to the measurement of personality is that there is not general agreement on a definition of personality, or on the number and nature of the traits of which it is composed. In fact, there is difference of opinion in regard to the existence of personality traits. Some authorities insist that the immediate situation largely determines behavior, and consequently personality, which in an individual may change markedly as conditions vary. It is observed, for example, that a boy may be repressed and submissive in the classroom but very expressive and dominant on the playground, or that a pupil may be honest where money is concerned but dishonest when taking a test. Conclusions of this kind were reached in the Character Education Inquiry (46, 47, 48), the most extensive study of personality ever conducted.

If it is true that personality is determined by the immediate situation, its adequate measurement becomes an almost impossible task, for innumerable tests will be required in order to obtain an adequate sampling. Even if the tests were available, it would seem that measurement in this broad field would be of doubtful value, because the personality of a given individual from this point of view would be too unstable ever to be described accurately.

If we accept, however, the more common assumption that personality is a more or less definite entity made up largely of a number of generalized traits, the fact that there is difficulty in defining it and lack of agreement concerning its components should not be an insuperable obstacle to measurement. A similar situation exists with respect to intelligence, yet tests in that field have been in general use for years and have shown their worth in a guidance program.

For purposes of this discussion, personality will be defined as the sum total of an individual's behavior in social situations. Behavior includes not only overt acts but inward feeling tone produced by the situation as interpreted by the individual through introspection. It is necessary to include the inward reaction, since the great majority of personality tests proceed by attempting to obtain from the subject statements about how he feels in various situations.

Tests of intelligence and tests of achievement in certain fields, as, for example, reading and English, provide much evidence about personality, since intelligence and such abilities as reading and English affect an individual's behavior in a social situation. Mental ability has long been recognized as one of the components of personality. A test of intelligence should, without doubt, be a part of a comprehensive inquiry into the personality of a given individual. But functioning in relationship with intelligence and with the more specialized skills or abilities, is a whole complex of attributes which have thus far not been analyzed with precision but which undoubtedly play a basic role in adjustment.

The term "personality tests" is sometimes used as practically synonymous with character tests; tests of attitude and interest fall outside the scope of the term. As used in the present discussion, the term is more inclusive, and certain tests of interests and social attitudes will be included in this chapter.

Most personality tests are designed to yield a quantitative statement of personality in the form of a score or a division on a scale. These scores will be useful only if they make possible a better *description* of personality. It is valid, reliable, and meaningful *description* of personality that counselors need in guidance. Before introducing a new test for measuring personality, a school will do well to try it out experimentally with a few pupils to see whether or not it contributes to the description of the personality of the individual pupil.

Survey of Procedures for Appraising Personality

Tests of personality may be divided into two general classes, global and atomistic. In the first class of instruments of appraisal, personality as a whole is studied qualitatively and intensively by means of projective techniques, while in the latter class an attempt is made to analyze personality into its component parts. The majority of the recent personality tests have emphasized the atomistic approach, but there are a few noteworthy tests of the global type.

Free association method. Among the more important tests of personality as a whole are the free association tests. A well-known test of this kind is the Kent-Rosanoff Free Association Test. This test was published in 1910 in a monograph by Kent and Rosanoff (57) on free association among the insane. The test has been used quite often by research workers in the field of personality but it has seldom been employed in a school guidance program, probably because it is difficult to interpret a score on a free association test of this type. It has been found useful, however, as a counseling instrument in special cases.

At the present time, the Rorschach Ink Blot Test (92) is attracting more attention than any other free association test. The research bibliography related to this test is probably more extensive than that for any other personality test. In 1935 Hertz (51) compiled a bibliography of 152 titles dealing with the Rorschach test and many new articles on the test have been published each year since that date. The uniqueness of the test is no doubt partly responsible for the widespread interest in it. The stimuli, as the name indicates, are a series of ink blots which are presented visually to the subject with a request that he state what each blot suggests to him. The ink blots were chosen with great care some twenty-five years ago by Hermann Rorschach, a Swiss psychiatrist and psychoanalyst, who had studied the technique for several years. Beck (7) and Klopfer (58) are among the leading authorities in the United States on the interpretation and use of the Rorschach test. Some psychologists seem convinced that it is one of the most promising tests of personality now available for clinical use. However, it is seldom used by school personnel workers, for a long period of training and experience is needed by one who attempts to interpret the responses. In fact, it is probably correct to say that the test definitely should not be used in a counseling situation unless someone who can qualify as a Rorschach specialist is available to study and interpret the responses of the subject.

Disguised and Partially Disguised Personality Tests. Most personality inventories are not tests in the usual sense of the term. They do not try out the individual to determine what he is able to do in a given situation. They are standardized questionnaires which ask the subject how he reacts or feels in various situations. The responses of the individual are useful if he does not know the most desirable answer or if he is entirely sincere and honest in his responses. The validity of the test depends largely upon the truthfulness of the responses. It has been shown that it is possible to influence the scores on such a test significantly by instructing the persons taking it to mark the test in such a way that they will get a desirable score.

Since the validity of personality tests whose purpose is not disguised depends so largely upon the veracity of the responses, the value of such instruments for certain types of testing is greatly curtailed. The usefulness of this type of test for employment purposes, for example, or for testing candidates for entrance to college is limited. There is a need for personality tests whose purpose is not immediately evident to the subject. Thus far, relatively few such tests have been devised.

The largest group of tests which are thoroughly disguised are those developed in connection with the Character Education Inquiry, but because of the fact that they reproduce life situations, many of those employed in that inquiry are too elaborate for school use. Maller has utilized a technique similar to that employed in the Character Education Inquiry in devising a group test of honesty in school work known as the Self-Marking Test. He reports reliability coefficients above .90 for this test.

Probably the most noteworthy example of a well-disguised personality test that may be used in schools is the Downey Will-Temperament Test. This test was devised by June E. Downey (27) as a result of her interest in graphology as a means of expressing personality. The test is dependent entirely upon the subject's responses in situations involving handwriting, and it seems clear that the purpose of nearly all the subtests is well hidden from the subject. Unfortunately, however, the numerous studies of the reliability and validity of the Downey test have yielded discouraging results. Very few of the coefficients of reliability or validity appearing in the rather extensive literature concerned with this test are high enough to satisfy the criteria for a test that is to be used in individual diagnosis. In the hands of persons thoroughly acquainted with its limitations, the Downey test has occasionally been a useful laboratory tool, but at present the test is not practicable for general school use.

The Pressey X–O Tests (87) illustrate a technique in which the purposes of the examination are partially disguised. Lists of words are presented to the subject and he is required to cross out those which are distasteful to him. In general, it is probable that persons will tend to respond more truthfully in the situation presented by this test than in the situation set up by tests which ask the subject rather intimate questions about his reactions. Studies indicate that the Pressey X–O Tests are about as reliable as most other personality tests. The Pressey Interest-Attitude Tests, published in 1933 by the Psychological Corporation, contain many items selected from the Pressey X–O Tests.

Adjustment Questionnaires and Psychoneurotic Inventories. Although there are obvious limitations to the questionnaire method, personality measurement in recent years has tended to move in the direction of the standardized questionnaire or self-inventory. There are so many tests of this type that only a small proportion of them can be included in the present discussion.

The Woodworth Personal Data Sheet is the oldest and one of the best-known of the controlled-answer questionnaires. Woodworth based a series of questions calling for "yes" and "no" answers on symptoms that had been mentioned in studies of psychoneurotics. This questionnaire has been adapted by Woodworth and Mathews for use with children.

Many of the questions in Woodworth's sheet appear in modified form in more recent questionnaires. The Colgate Personal Inventory Rating Scales, developed by Laird (*62*), are a modification of the controlled-answer instrument. Instead of using questions that could be answered by "yes" or "no," Laird made use of a graphic rating scale on which the subject indicated his response by placing a cross at the appropriate place between the two extremes. In recent years the graphic rating scale has been utilized in many published and unpublished questionnaires.

In 1928 G. W. and F. H. Allport published the Allport Ascendance-Submission Scale, or the A–S Reaction Study (*3*). This scale, which contains 35 multiple-choice questions for women and 33 for men, has been used in a variety of studies.

About 1930 the Thurstones (*114*) developed an extensive Personality Schedule based on a large number of earlier questionnaires, one of which was Woodworth's sheet. The published form of the personality schedule was standardized on University of Chicago freshmen.

The best-known and doubtless the most widely used controlled-answer questionnaire for adolescents and adults is the Bernreuter Personality Inventory (*13*). The research bibliography on this inventory is already extensive. The inventory consists of 125 questions selected from Laird's C2 Test of Introversion-Extroversion, Allport's A–S Reaction Study, Thurstone's Neurotic Inventory, and an earlier test for self-sufficiency by Bernreuter. The unique contribution made by Bernreuter is that whereas the tests on which it is based furnish only a single measure of adjustment, Bernreuter scored his test with four different scales, thus making available measures of neurotic tendency, self-sufficiency, introversion-extroversion, and ascendance-submission. In 1934 Flanagan (*34*), using Hotelling's factor-analysis method, added two more scales for scoring the Bernreuter inventory. Flanagan tentatively called his scales self-confidence and sociability. The reliability of the Bernreuter scales compares favorably with that of many intelligence and achievement tests, but their validity, like the validity of nearly all personality tests, has not been established.

The Bell Adjustment Inventory (*9*), a test which is in form similar to the Bernreuter, was published in 1934. By means of a much simpler scoring procedure than that used by Bernreuter, Bell secures measures which he has called home adjustment, health adjustment, social adjustment, and emotional adjustment. The test is designed for use in high school and college. The few studies of it that have been made suggest that it is one of the better inventories in this field. The adult form of this inventory, published in 1938, has a fifth scale, occupational adjustment.

Bell has also published The School Inventory, which purports to make possible a quick, yet reliable, quantitative statement of the school adjustment of senior high school pupils.

Another test of the questionnaire type published in 1934 is the Nebraska Personality Inventory (*43*). This inventory, like the two scales which Flanagan added to the Bernreuter inventory, is a product of the application of factor analysis to the study of personality. The authors, J. P. Guilford and Ruth B. Guilford, identified five factors, three of which are included in the inventory. The traits are designated by the letters S, E, and M, which stand, respectively, for social introversion, emotionality, and masculinity.

Among the adjustment inventories published within the last few years, two which are already being quite widely used are the Washburne Social Adjustment Inventory (*127*) and the Adams-Lepley Personal Audit (*1*). The former yields scores for truthfulness, sympathy, alienation, purpose, impulse-judgment, control, happiness, and wishes; the latter inventory includes sociability, suggestibility, tendency to rationalize, tendency to anxiety, tendency to personal intolerance, flexibility or docility of attitudes, susceptibility to annoyance, tendency to excessive sexual emotionality and conflict, and tendency to think or worry about unsolved problems.

The majority of the personality inventories are designed for use among senior high school and college students and adults. Several inventories have been devised, however, for use in the elementary school and junior high school. One of these is the Brown Personality Inventory for Children (*15*) which is designed for ages 9 to 14. The questions included in this inventory were obtained by canvassing the literature about nervous children and making a list of symptoms. Another test which includes some of the younger age groups and which has been used in various schools is the Link Inventory of Activities and Interests (*65*), also known as the PQ Test because it yields a P.Q., or personality quotient, which is presumed to be roughly comparable to the I.Q. derived from certain mental tests. The test is suitable for children and young people between the ages of 10 and 20.

Another recent inventory for elementary and junior high school pupils is Aspects of Personality by Pintner, Loftus, Forlano, and Alster (*84*). This inventory, published in 1938 for Grades 4 to 9, inclusive, is designed to measure ascendance-submission, introversion-extroversion, and emotionality. Rogers' Test of Personality Adjustment (*91*) is for a somewhat similar range, including ages 9 to 13. It provides scores for personal inferiority, social inferiority, family relationships, and daydreaming.

Among the newer personality tests, there is one battery which is designed to cover all levels from Grade 1 to adult. This is the California Test of Personality prepared by Thorpe, Clark, and Tiegs (*115*). The tests in this series, which were published from 1939 to 1942, provide a profile of scores on component tests grouped under self-adjustment and social adjustment.

Attitude Tests and Scales. Chave (*21*) has defined attitude as a complex of feelings, desires, fears, convictions, prejudices, or other tendencies that have given a set, or readiness to act, to a person because of varied experiences. In recent years there have been many attempts to study attitudes, most of which have not been very successful. Two series of attitude scales, however, one by Thurstone and the other by Remmers, deserve careful consideration.

An extensive set of Scales for the Measurement of Social Attitudes (*113*) has been devised by Thurstone and his associates at the University of Chicago. Thurstone has made two important contributions to the measurement of attitudes. In the first place he has restricted the field which each instrument is designed to measure. In contrast to some test makers who apparently believe that attitude is a very broad and general aspect of personality, Thurstone has said that attitude is affect for or against a psychological object. In accordance with this definition, his social attitudes scales deal with attitude toward individual social institutions, such as the church, the Constitution, communism, and war. This approach lends definiteness to the measurement of attitudes, but at the same time it requires a large number of scales in order to provide comprehensive measurement in this field.

Thurstone's second contribution to the measurement of attitudes is the technique he has developed for the construction of attitude scales. This technique is more elaborate than that used in most of the other investigations of attitudes. The first step in the procedure is the collection of statements about a given social institution from many different sources. The second step is the sorting, by a large number of judges, of the statements into several piles with respect to degree of favorableness toward the institution. The third step is the selection of about twenty statements ranging from extreme favorableness to extreme unfavorableness toward the institution, and the assignment of scale values to these statements. This is done by a statistical procedure based on the sorting by the judges. In scoring, the scale value of each statement with which the subject agrees is noted and a score is assigned which corresponds to the median scale value. Available data indicate that most of the Thurstone scales are fairly reliable.

Remmers (*88, 89*) has edited a series of Attitude Scales, the purpose of which is somewhat similar to that of the Thurstone scales. Remmers' method of constructing his scales resembles Thurstone's method in that it utilizes the principle that equally-often-observed differences are equal. The main difference in methods is that whereas each of Thurstone's scales is designed to measure attitude toward one definite social institution, an attempt is made in Remmers' scales to measure attitude toward a large group or class of objects, such as attitude toward any school subject or attitude toward any vocation. The scales constructed by Remmers and his students may be used throughout the junior and senior high school and college.

Interest Inventories. Interests, like attitudes, are extremely difficult to measure with precision, but several useful instruments in this area have been devised. The Allport-Vernon Study of Values (5) is among the better-known scales for measuring dominant interests. This scale is aimed at the measurement of six basic interests of personality: theoretical, economic, aesthetic, social, political, and religious. This classification is based upon a scheme of ideal types proposed by Eduard Spranger, a German psychologist.

Because of their importance in guidance, vocational interests have no doubt been studied more intensively than any other type of interest. The Strong Vocational Interest Blanks (*107*) are probably the most widely used interest questionnaires at the present time. The Strong blank requires the subject to indicate whether he likes or dislikes various occupations, amusements, school subjects, types of people, and so forth. The men's blank is scored for thirty-five occupations and the women's blank for eighteen. Scales yielding scores for a number of groups of occupations are also available for the men's blank. Young and Estabrooks (*138*) have provided a studiousness scale for the men's blank.

The Strong blank was standardized on the basis of the actual interests of persons in the occupations for which the scale was developed. It was designed primarily for use with college students and adults, and it seldom should be used below the junior year in high school. The reliability of the scales averages about .85.

The greatest obstacle to the wider use of the Strong blank is the difficulty of its scoring. Since the blank must be scored separately with the scale for each occupation, hours are required to score by hand a single blank. Both the men's and the women's blanks, however, may be scored by special International Business Machines equipment, and the men's blank has also been set up for scoring on the International Test Scoring Machine. Machine-scoring is the only practicable method to use with the Strong blank.

Somewhat simpler scoring procedures are used in connection with the Specific Interest Inventory, by Stewart and Brainard, and two relatively new vocational interest inventories designed for high school and college students, the Vocational Interest Inventory by Glen U. Cleeton and the Vocational Inventory by Curtis G. Gentry. None of these inventories have been the subject of nearly as much research as the Strong blank, but they may be used experimentally.

One of the most promising testing procedures applied in the field of interest is the paired-comparison technique, exemplified in a doctor's dissertation by Weedon (*129*). The basis of this technique consists in preparing "preference" items in which each interest to be investigated is paired with every other interest, all stated in terms of behavior. Individuals are then asked to indicate which one of each pair they prefer to do, and the responses are treated statistically. This technique has not been used thus far on a wide scale, but one application of it is found in Kuder's Preference Record (*61*), published in 1939 and revised in 1942. The Preference Record, which provides scores in nine broad areas, is among the more carefully constructed and useful instruments for the appraisal of interests.

The Dunlap Academic Preference Blank (*30*) is a relatively new instrument designed to measure interest in subject-matter fields at the junior high school level. It utilizes the multiple-scoring technique. Another inventory which has implications for educational as well as vocational guidance is the Garretson-Symonds Interest Questionnaire for High School Students (*40*).

VALIDITY AND RELIABILITY

Although there have been many studies of personality tests, the validity of the various tests in this field has not been established. It is very difficult to determine the validity of personality tests because there is no satisfactory criterion with which to correlate the test scores. The ratings of judges are a common criterion in studies of validity, but judges' ratings are not highly reliable, even when the characteristic to be rated is well understood by the judges. When the trait is intangible and difficult to get clearly in mind, still less confidence can be placed in the ratings. The fact that scores on personality tests usually do not correlate highly with judges' ratings is by no means conclusive evidence that the tests fail to measure the traits which they are intended to measure.

The reliability coefficients for most personality tests are between .70 and .90. Personality tests thus tend to be as reliable as many of the widely used intelligence and achievement tests. Few, if any, however, have consistently shown reliability as high as the most reliable tests of mental ability or achievement. The most dependable intelligence tests and achievement tests have reliability coefficients as high as .95 to .98. Few reliability coefficients that high have thus far been reported for personality tests.

USES OF RESULTS OF PERSONALITY TESTS

It is apparent that most personality tests are reliable enough for group studies. If these tests may be assumed to be reasonably valid, then counselors may draw conclusions concerning the trend of the traits measured in guidance groups and can plan group treatment accordingly.

Most of the personality tests, however, are not reliable enough to be very satisfactory for use in individual diagnosis. Individual scores on personality tests can contribute materially, nevertheless, to the guidance program of the school. Two important uses of these tests are (1) to stimulate the pupils to evaluate critically their own personality characteristics, and (2) to serve as a point of departure in conferences between counselors and individual pupils. Personality tests are also helpful in locating pupils who are poorly adjusted and unhappy, and who need guidance in making emotional and personal adjustment. Tests are sometimes more successful in discovering such cases than observational or interview procedures, since many maladjusted pupils are so repressed that they give little outward evidence of poor adjustment. If scores on personality tests indicate that there are such cases in the school, a wise counselor will not accept the results unreservedly but will verify them by means of careful observation and well-planned personal interviews with the pupils.

For the purpose of records of growth, anecdotal records and behavior descriptions seem preferable to existing personality tests. Some of the rating scales in which the categories are carefully defined and explained in very concrete terms likewise may provide more valuable records than most of the personality tests. These types of appraisal will be discussed in the next chapter.

Selected and Annotated List of Personality Tests

The thirty-two personality tests and inventories included in this section have been selected from a possible list of more than four hundred. It is believed that they are among the more useful instruments of their respective types, although there is no intention of recommending them to the exclusion of all other personality tests.

Various ways of classifying tests and inventories for measuring character and personality have been suggested by different authors. The following ninefold classification is used in the present discussion: I, records of uncontrolled observations; II, rating devices; III, behavior descriptions; IV, self-inventories; V, tests utilizing life situations; VI, paper and pencil tests of broad traits; VII, scales for specific traits or attitudes; VIII, free association tests; IX, laboratory techniques.

The first three classes include devices to be discussed in the next chapter. The last class is omitted because such instruments can be used in few schools due to the elaborateness of the equipment required. Classes IV to VIII, inclusive, are represented in this list. The Roman numeral in parentheses following each title indicates the classification of the test or inventory.

Adams, Clifford R., and Lepley, William M. *The Personal Audit.*[2] Chicago: Science Research Associates, 1941. Form S, test and profile sheet, $0.10; Form L, $0.15 each; specimen set S, $0.25; specimen set L, $0.35. (IV)

___

[2] It will be observed that the aptitude tests and achievement tests in the two preceding chapters were listed with the name of the test first, followed by the name of the author, while in this list of

A personality inventory, designed for use with high school and college students and adults. Includes the following areas: (1) sociability, extroversion; (2) suggestibility, a tendency to agree with authority; (3) tendency to rationalize, a tendency to make alibis and excuses; (4) tendency to anxiety, a tendency to excess emotionality; (5) tendency to personal intolerance; (6) flexibility or docility of attitudes; (7) susceptibility to annoyance, a tendency to irritability; (8) tendency to excessive sexual emotionality and conflicts; and (9) tendency to think, possibly worry, about unsolved problems. Two forms—*S* consisting of first six parts, and *L* consisting of all nine parts. Tentative norms for high school boys, high school girls, college men, college women, and men in industry. More adequate norms are being prepared. Spearman-Brown reliability of all parts, .90 or above; intercorrelations of parts tend to be low according to manual of directions. Reference: Adams (*1*).

Allport, Gordon W., and Allport, Floyd H. *The A–S Reaction Study*. Boston: Houghton Mifflin Company, 1928. $1.80 for 25. (IV)

A self-inventory, the purpose of which is to discover the extent to which a person is disposed to dominate or be dominated by his fellows. A variety of situations is verbally presented and the subject selects for each situation that one of several possible responses which most nearly characterizes his customary behavior. No time limit; 30 minutes usually sufficient. Standardized on college classes but could probably be used in high school. A form for men and a form for women. Tentative norms for each sex are given in the manual. Reliability, .74 to .78. Validity, as indicated by correlation with ratings, .29 to .79. Manger (*76*) compared test scores with group ratings and self-ratings and concluded that self-interest influences the scores to a considerable extent. Wang (*126*) found that a shorter form consisting of 30 of the 41 questions was practically as good as the whole test, since correlation on these 30 questions with total score was .97. Beckman (*8*) revised the items; developed tentative norms. Copies of revision available from Psychological Corporation. Schultz and Roslow (*98*) criticized the business revision on the basis of the wide range and rectangular distribution of the scores and described a restandardization that yielded a more nearly normal distribution. Ruggles and Allport (*94*) reported a revision of the test for women and found the reliability through the application of the Spearman-Brown formula to be .90 ± .04. Reference for additional information about the test: Bender (*10*).

Allport, Gordon W., and Vernon, Philip E. *A Study of Values*. Boston: Houghton Mifflin Company, 1931. $1.80 per 25. (VI)

---

personality tests the author's name precedes that of the test. There is a logical reason for this apparent lack of consistency. Many of the aptitude tests and achievement tests are identified with a certain series or battery, e.g., the American Council Psychological Examination, the Cooperative Plane Geometry Test, and so forth. Most of the personality tests, on the other hand, are customarily identified by the name of the author, although the author's name is not a part of the title of some of them—for instance, the Adams-Lepley Personal Audit, the Bernreuter Personality Inventory, and the Kuder Preference Record. For this reason, it was thought that the tests annotated in the book could be found more readily if the aptitude tests and achievement tests were listed according to the name of the test, and if the personality tests were listed alphabetically by names of the authors.

A scale for measuring the dominant interests of personality according to Spranger's classification of six ideal types: theoretical, economic, aesthetic, social, political, and religious. Contains two parts arranged in a single booklet. In all there are forty-five items, which call for a total of 120 responses—twenty for each value. The blank is self-administering and may be filled out within a period of 20 minutes. The score sheet provides for showing graphically the scores of an individual on the six values. Percentile norms for adults and undergraduates. One form. The following statistical data have been reported by the authors: Average split-half reliability of the separate values, .65. Religious and aesthetic values the most reliable; social value the least reliable. Reliability of the test as a whole, .72. Theoretical validity is square root of consistency, or .85. Empirical validity, based on correlation of scores with criterion made up of five external and one self-rating: theoretical, .40; economic, .57; aesthetic, .57; social, .06; political, .44; religious, .69; total, .532. Theoretical agreement between test and ratings corrected for attenuation is .826, a figure close to theoretical validity. The test has also been validated by finding the scores for certain groups and noting the extent to which the results agree with what one would reasonably expect. Whitely (*131*) studied the constancy of scores of college students on the Allport-Vernon test. The mean scores on the scales agreed closely from year to year and, with the exception of the religious scale, were in close agreement with the norms. The correlations ranged from .38 to .78. Reference: Allport and Vernon (*5*).

Bell, H. M. *The Adjustment Inventory*. Stanford University, California: Stanford University Press, 1934. $1.75 per 25; sample set, $0.15. (IV)

Measures home adjustment, health adjustment, social adjustment, and emotional adjustment. Consists of series of questions to which pupil responds by encircling *yes, no* or *?*. One form, intended for use in Grades IX–XVI. No time limit; can be completed in about 25 minutes. Scoring time, 3 minutes. Norms for high school boys and girls and college men and women are given separately in the manual. Tyler (*124*) used scores of students in Sacramento Junior College in studying reliability. Average of reliability coefficients reported by him for the four descriptive classifications is .81; reliability of total adjustment score, about .90. Concluded that studies of the inventory made thus far at Sacramento point toward wide usefulness for the instrument. Turney and Fee (*122*) reported a study of the use of the Bell Adjustment Inventory in high school guidance. They found reliability coefficients of .74 to .85 for the descriptive classifications and .82 for the total score. Correlations of scores on the inventory with average ratings of fifteen judges were low, ranging from .18 to .42. Traxler (*117*) obtained somewhat similar reliability and validity data in a study based on the scores of high school pupils. Pedersen (*82*) studied validity of inventory on basis of scores and ratings of freshman girls in University of Rochester. Found evidence of validity of home adjustment, health adjustment, and social adjustment, but not of emotional adjustment. An adult form of this inventory was published in 1938. It is scored with an occupational adjustment scale in addition to the four scales used with the other inventory. Odd-even coefficients of reliability predicted with the Spearman-

Brown formula range from .81 to .94. Reference for further information about the test: Bell (9).

Bell, H. M. *The School Inventory.* Stanford University, California: Stanford University Press, 1936. $1.00 per 25; sample set, $0.10. (IV)

One of the newer inventories for use in investigating pupils' attitudes toward their school. Designed for senior high school pupils who have attended the school in which the test is given for at least three months. Contains seventy-six questions which are to be answered by encircling *yes, no,* or *?.* Pupils who make high scores tend to be poorly adjusted to the school. The test is practically self-administering. No time limit; most students can complete it within 15 minutes. Scoring time about one minute. There are tentative norms for high school students. The author reports a reliability coefficient of .94 ± .004, based on the scores of 242 high school freshmen, sophomores, juniors, and seniors. Traxler (*117*) found a reliability of .917 for this inventory; he also obtained a correlation of .536 ± .083 between scores on the inventory and the pooled opinions of judges.

Bernreuter, Robert G. *The Personality Inventory.* Stanford University, California: Stanford University Press, 1931, 1935. $1.75 per 25; sample set, $0.25. (IV)

Measures neurotic tendency, self-sufficiency, introversion-extroversion, dominance-submisson, confidence, and sociability. The last two scales were added by Flanagan. Consists of series of questions to which pupil responds by encircling *yes, no,* or *?.* No time limit; requires about 30 minutes. Scoring is complicated; if many blanks are to be scored, it is economical to have the work done by machine scoring at a statistical bureau, such as the one at Columbia University. One form, for high school and college students. Percentile norms for high school and college students, and for men and women, accompany each scale.

The Bernreuter test has been the subject of many studies. Series of articles by Lorge (*67, 68, 69*), together with Flanagan's (*35*) reply to Lorge's second article, probably constitute best appraisal to date. Conclusion to be drawn from Lorge's articles is that Bernreuter's scales lack trait consistency and trait independence; conclusion to be drawn from Lorge's and Flanagan's articles is that Flanagan's scales are independent and show internal consistency. Average reliability of the six scales is about .85. Lorge has insisted that this reliability is not high enough for individual diagnosis and prognosis. Flanagan has pointed out that with a reliability coefficient of .85, about 70 per cent of the subjects would be rated correctly and nearly 100 per cent with an error of but one step on a five-point scale. Both writers agree that validity of the scales has not been established. Bernreuter (*12*) attempted to validate his four scales by correlation with criterion made up from scores on Thurstone's Neurotic Inventory, the Allports' A–S Reaction Study, and Laird's C2 Introversion-Extroversion Test. Secured coefficients which varied from .84 to approximately 1.00. The research literature concerned with this test is so extensive that it is impossible to summarize even the main findings in this annotation. A summary of 147 articles dealing with the Bernreuter has recently been made by Super (*108*). Reference for further information about the test: Bernreuter (*13*).

Brown, Fred. *Personality Inventory for Children.* New York: Psychological Corporation, 1935. $2.00 per hundred; sample set, $0.15. (IV)

A psychoneurotic inventory applicable to younger children. Consists of eighty questions about behavior and feeling to which the pupil responds with *yes* or *no*. One form for Grades IV–IX or ages 9–14. Yields a total score indicating personality adjustment. Items may be grouped as follows and a score found for each group: home, school, physical symptoms, insecurity, irritability. No time limit; requires about 15 minutes. Decile norms for total score, ages 9–14 combined. Author reports reliability coefficient of .896 ± .007. States that test scores are not significantly correlated with socio-economic status, chronological age, or intelligence. Reference: Brown (*15*).

Character Education Inquiry. *Tests of Honesty.* New York: Association Press, 1930. Price of Tests varies from $1.25 per 20 to $2.50 per 20. (V and VI)

Four tests among a long series of C. E. I. tests: (1) Attitudes S. A. Test, (2) Self-Scoring Intelligence and Achievement Tests, (3) Self-Scoring Speed Tests, and (4) Coordination Tests. The Attitudes S. A. Test is a test of attitudes in reference to honesty; consists of two forms, and is not timed. Tentative norms are available. The Self-Scoring Intelligence and Achievement Tests measure deception. They require two hours on two days. The Self-Scoring Speed Tests also measure deception through putting temptation in the way of the pupils; they require 40 minutes for administration. The Coordination Tests measure honest or dishonest reactions; testing time, 40 minutes. All tests are for Grades V–VIII. Reference: Hartshorne and May (*46*).

Cleeton, Glen U. *Vocational Interest Inventory.* Bloomington, Illinois: McKnight & McKnight, 1937. Blanks, 10 cents each; $4.50 per 100; Manual of Directions, $0.25. (IV)

Two forms, one for vocational interests of men and one for vocational interests of women. Designed for use in Grades IX–XII and in college. Can also be used with adults. Each blank contains nine occupational groups and a tenth section on social adjustment. Scoring is very easy in comparison with that of the Strong blank and other vocational interest tests. Reliability coefficients reported by the author are relatively high, .822 to .910. Congdon (*24*) found the inventory valuable in counseling freshmen and senior students in the Colorado State College of Education. Reference: Cleeton (*23*).

Cowan, E. A. *Cowan Adolescent Personality Schedule* (Revision No. 2). Wichita, Kansas: Wichita Child Research Laboratory, 1938. $2.00 per 25; $7.50 per 100. (IV)

Designed to measure maladjustment in nine fields: fears, family emotional maladjustments, maladjustment to family authority, inferiorities, maladjustment to non-family authority, maladjustment to responsibility, escapes, neurotic symptoms, compensations. The scores in these areas may be compared with a normal profile. Standardized on about twelve hundred children, twelve to eighteen years of age. Reference: Brigden (*14*).

Darley, John G., and McNamara, Walter J. *Minnesota Personality Scale.* New York: Psychological Corporation, 1941. Booklets, $2.00 per 25; $6.00 per 100; answer sheet, $0.75 per 25; $2.50 per 100; specimen set either form, $0.50. (IV)

Designed to measure morale, social adjustment, family relations, emotionality, and economic conservatism. Forms for men and women. Adapted for machine-scoring. Same answer sheet used for both forms. Grades XI and XII and college. Reference: Darley and McNamara (*26*).

Dunlap, Jack W. *Dunlap Academic Preference Blank.* Yonkers, New York: World Book Company, 1937. $1.00 per 25 booklets; scoring keys, $0.70 per set of 10. (IV)

Two forms, A and B, designed to measure interest in subject matter fields of the curriculum of Grades VII, VIII, and IX. Scored with ten keys to yield objective measures in literature, geography, word meaning, paragraph meaning, language usage, arithmetic, history, general achievement, mental ability, and intellectual alertness. No definite time limit. Working time, about ten minutes. Correlations between forms A and B range from .56 to .85. Validity as indicated by correlation with scores on achievement tests is reported as fairly high. Reference: Sharkey and Dunlap (*101*).

Garretson, Oliver K., and Symonds, Percival M. *Interest Questionnaire for High School Students.* New York: Bureau of Publications, Teachers College, Columbia University, 1931. $3.45 per 100; specimen set, $0.35; manual and keys, $0.30. (IV)

Designed to provide a measure of the inclination of pupils entering high school toward the academic, commercial, and technical curricula. Allows for an expression of attitudes toward 234 items distributed through occupations, activities, school subjects, positions, etc. Uses like-indifferent-dislike type of response. Standardized on boys in high schools of New York City. The questionnaire is scored for each pupil with three different keys to secure a measure of academic interest, commercial interest, and technical interest. Split-half reliability: academic preference, .861; commercial preference, .925; technical preference, .953. Validity of questionnaire was studied by computation of bi-serial r between the scores in one curriculum and the scores in the other curricula. The authors concluded that "by means of the questionnaire one can predict with greater exactness the curriculum a boy will choose than it is possible to predict his success in the curriculum of his choice by means of an intelligence test." Reference: Garretson (*40*).

Gentry, Curtis G. *Vocational Inventory*. Minneapolis: Educational Test Bureau, 1940. Inventory and individual score tabulation sheet, $0.10; individual analysis report, $0.05; set of accessories, including manual and keys, $0.25. (IV)

Contains 384 questions related to occupations and fifty related to personality. Vocational questions yield scores in eight occupational groups: social service, literary pursuits, law and government, business, artistic pursuits, mechanical designing, mechanical construction, and scientific pursuits. Specific vocations which the subject may consider within each group are listed. Personality test is scored for introversion-extroversion. Secondary school and college. In a recent study of this inventory, Froehlich concluded that the test needs to be more carefully standardized and evaluated (*38*).

Guilford, J. P., and Guilford, Ruth B. *The Nebraska Personality Inventory*. J. P. Guilford, University of Nebraska, Lincoln, Nebraska, 1934. $4.00 per 100 copies; $2.50 per 50 copies, with scoring keys and norms. (IV)

One of the few personality tests now available which has been set up by the use of factor-analysis techniques. Measures factors S, E, and M, which designate, respectively, social introversion, emotionality, and masculinity. The test contains 100 questions which are to be answered by *yes, no,* or *?*. The test is apparently planned for college students and adults, but it could probably be used satisfactorily in the senior high school. Decile norms have been reported for college sophomores. The authors report reliability coefficients within the following ranges: S-factor, .85–.93; E-factor, .86–.92; M-factor, .54–.74. In regard to validity, they state that "since primary factors are being measured, the validity coefficient is the index of reliability, or the square root of the reliability coefficient in each case." Reference: Guilford and Guilford (*43*).

Kent, Grace H., and Rosanoff, A. J. *Kent-Rosanoff Association Tests*. Chicago: C. H. Stoelting Company, 1910. $2.50 per 100. (VIII)

Consists of 100 stimulus words. Examiner pronounces each word aloud to the subject and he responds with the first word that he associates with the stimulus word. Authors have reported frequency of response to each word for 1000 individuals. Number of atypical responses is taken as a measure of psychopathic tendencies. Manual for the test is contained in Rosanoff's *Manual of Psychiatry*. No significant correlation with neurotic scale of Bernreuter according to a study by Laslett and Bennett (*63*). Data on reliability not available. Reference: Kent and Rosanoff (*57*).

Kuder, G. Frederic. *Preference Record*. Chicago, Illinois: Science Research Associates, 1942. Test booklets, $0.30 each; answer pads, $0.05 each; profile sheets, $0.38 per 25; specimen set, $0.50. Form BB, published by Science Research Associates is a revision of the form first published by the author in 1939. (IV)

Consists of 168 items each listing three activities. Subject indicates which activity he likes most and which one he likes least. Scoring procedure yields a profile of preference scores in nine areas as follows: mechanical, persuasive, computational, scientific, literary, musical, artistic, social service, and clerical. Designed for high school and college students and adults. Administered without time limit. Test booklet is used with separate answer sheets, one for hand scoring, one for machine scoring, and one for self scoring. Reliability coefficients of scores in seven areas reported by Kuder on basis of method that is highly correlated with Spearman-Brown procedure: scientific, .87; computational, .85; musical, .98; artistic, .90; literary, .90; social service, .84; persuasive, .90. Retest reliabilities reported by Traxler and McCall (118) are in fairly close agreement with Kuder's data. Correlations of the Kuder record with the Strong blank and various other measures have been reported by Triggs and others (*119, 120, 135*). Reference: Kuder (*61*).

Link, H. C. *Inventory of Activities and Interests* (The P.Q. Tests). New York: Psychological Corporation, 1936; revised, 1938. $0.06 each; $5.00 per 100; specimen set, $0.25. (IV)

The purpose of the test is to measure social initiative, self-determination, economic self-determination, adjustment to opposite sex, and introversion-extroversion. A weighted combination of the scores on these traits gives a score from which a personality quotient (P.Q.) is derived. Ages, 10–20. Separate forms for boys and girls. No time limit; 30 minutes usually sufficient. Reliability as reported by the author: introversion-extroversion, .87; self-determination, .88; social initiative, .82; sex adjustment, .78; economic self-determination, .70. In a study of results of the test administered to high school pupils at Mooseheart, Illinois, Thomson (*112*) found that pupils with high P.Q.'s had a slight advantage in academic competition and that there was no statistical evidence to indicate that low P.Q.'s are associated with problem behavior. Through the use of special scoring strips and two Veeder counters, Gibbons (*41*) reduced the scoring time for the P.Q. test from 20 to 8 minutes. Drake, Roslow, and Bennett (*28*) correlated scores of high school pupils on each scale of the inventory with ratings by associates. Most of the correlation coefficients were between .40 and .60. Reference: Link (*65*).

Loofbourow, Graham C., and Keys, Noel. *Personal Index*. Minneapolis: Educational Test Bureau, 1933. $1.00 per 25; specimen set, $0.25. (IV and VI)

Designed to discover attitudes indicative of problem behavior. Has four parts as follows: (1) false vocabulary for measuring deception, (2) social attitudes, (3) virtues, and (4) adjustment questionnaire. One form for boys, Grades VII–IX. No time limit; 40 minutes usually ample. Percentile norms are available. Reliability, .84 to .95. Validity correlations with behavior ratings, .57 to .66. Riggs and Joyal (*90*) reported a study in which biserial correlations were computed between the scores of junior high school boys and groups of "best" and "worst" boys in the school as selected by the boys' adviser. The correlations were .58 and .45 for two selections made at different times. The authors of the article recognized the possibility that the criterion itself was low in validity. Reference: Loofbourow and Keys (*66*).

Maller, J. B.   *Self-Marking Test*.   New York: Bureau of Publications, Teachers College, Columbia University, 1930. $2.50 per 20; specimen set, $0.40.   (V)

A group test of honesty in school work. Contains eleven subtests, each of which includes some items so difficult that no pupil can answer them correctly. The pupils score their own tests. A pupil's deception score is the number of very difficult items for which he has accepted credit. Two forms. Grades V–X. Norms based on scores of pupils in Grades VII and VIII. Reliability, .92.

Pintner, Rudolph; Loftus, John J.; Forlano, George; and Alster, Benjamin.   *Aspects of Personality*.   Yonkers, New York: World Book Company, 1938. $1.30 per 25; specimen set, $0.20.   (IV)

A psychoneurotic inventory for Grades IV–IX. Consists of three sections containing a total of 114 statements such as "I have a lot of nerve"; "I like to read before the class"; "I feel tired most of the time"; etc. Pupil is instructed to indicate after each statement whether he feels the "same" or "different." The sections purport to measure ascendance-submission, introversion-extroversion, and emotionality. Separate percentile norms for boys and for girls in Grades IV, V, and VI; and Grades VII, VIII, and IX. Average split-half reliability: ascendance-submission, .731; introversion-extroversion, .613; emotionality, .855. Average retest reliability for four administrations of the test to 100 pupils in Grade V: ascendance-submission, .71; introversion-extroversion, .70; emotionality, .72. Pintner and Forlano (*85*) validated the test on the basis of the outstanding characteristics of the pupils as reported by their teachers. Concluded that the technique afforded a rough measure of the validity of the test. In another study, Pintner and Forlano (*84*) investigated the stability of scores and particular item responses on the inventory. Intercorrelations between scores on four separate administrations of the test at intervals of two weeks varied from .61 to .83. This inventory may serve somewhat the same purpose in the elementary school that the Bernreuter, Nebraska, and other personality inventories serve at more advanced levels.

Pressey, S. L., and Pressey, L. C.   *Pressey X–O Tests*.   Chicago: C. H. Stoelting Company, 1920. $1.00 per 25.   (IV)

Developed for use in studying sex and individual differences, affective and moral judgment, and emotional makeup; also for use in dealing with delinquents, neurotics, or other atypical individuals. Next to the Kent-Rosanoff test, the oldest and one of the most widely used tests included in this bibliography. Lists of words are presented to the subject and he crosses out those which are distasteful to him. The test provides a score for "affectivity," of the number of items to which the individual reacted, and one for "idiosyncracy," or the difference between the items to which the subject reacted and those to which the standard group responded. The specific responses are more useful than the score. Reliability, with 48-hour interval between two administrations of the test, is, according to McGeoch and

Whitely (*74*), as follows: affectivity scores, .820 to .867; idiosyncracy scores, .426 to .770; classification scheme in Test I (disgust, sex, fear, self-feeling), .767 to .899; classification scheme in Test II (paranoid, neurotic, shut-in, melancholic), .737 to .869. The test has been revised recently to permit scoring for emotional age. Reference: Pressey (*87*).

Remmers, H. H. *Attitude Scales.* Lafayette, Indiana: Division of Educational Reference, Purdue University, 1934–1936. $0.015 per test. (VII)

A series of separate, brief scales for measuring attitude toward the following: any homemaking project, any institution, any national or racial group, any practice, any school subject, any teacher, any vocation, any play, any proposed social action, any selection of poetry, any disciplinary procedure; also a high school attitude scale, a scale for measuring attitude toward teaching, and a scale for measuring individual and group "morale." The technique of construction resembles that employed by Thurstone, but the scales are designed to serve broader purposes than the Thurstone scales. Grades VII–XVI. Average reliability of scale for measuring attitude toward high school, one form, .74; two forms combined, .85. References: Remmers, Brandenberg, and Gillespie (*88*), and Remmers and Silance (*89*).

Rogers, Carl R. *A Test of Personality Adjustment.* New York: Association Press, 1931. $1.75 per 20 with manual; specimen set, $0.40. (IV)

The purpose of this test is to measure the extent to which a child is satisfactorily adjusted toward his fellows, his family, and himself. It yields four diagnostic scores: personal inferiority, social inferiority, family relationships, and daydreaming. Two forms: boys and girls. Ages 9–13. Norms based on study of fifty-two "problem" children and eighty-four "normal" children. Reliability, .72. Reference: Rogers (*91*).

Rorschach, Herman. *Rorschach Psychodiagnostik.* Chicago: C. H. Stoelting Company; also New York: Psychological Corporation. 10 cards containing ink blots, $4.50; 4-page folder with space for recording and summarizing responses, $1.50 per 25. (VIII)

A series of 10 ink blots selected by Rorschach from a much larger group of ink blots for their value in diagnosing emotional disorders. The test is administered individually. The subject is directed to look at each blot and state what it seems to be or what it suggests to him. Free range of responses permitted. Standards have been developed for evaluating responses. Results are reputed to provide information about emotional stability, originality of thinking, adaptability, and other traits, all of which are studied in terms of the whole personality. Literature relating to this test is very extensive, but there have been few attempts to evaluate the test. Reliability has been studied infrequently. Vernon (*125*), using split-half method, found reliability of most of the categories unsatisfactory. Hertz (*50*) revised certain steps in the procedure to insure standardized conditions and studied reliability by split-half method; found standardization of procedure had raised reliability considerably. All the correlation coefficients were above .70 and most of them were above .80. Benjamin and Ebaugh (*11*) criticized statistical studies of reliability and validity of the Rorschach test and presented results indicating that its diagnostic validity was high. Hertz and Rubenstein (*52*) and Piotrowski (*86*) reported "blind analyses" which were likewise favorable to the diagnostic validity of the test. Present data on the test not comparable because of differences in techniques of administration. Scoring is subjective and interpretation calls for considerable background in psychology and much training in the use of the test. Klopfer has recently contributed much to the interpretation of the test. Klopfer and Davidson (*59*) have published a 4-page record blank including instructions. It is claimed for the test that it will show the general intellectual level of the subject while at the same time exploring his emotional traits. References: Rorschach (*92*) (no English translation); Hertz (*50, 51*); Beck (*7*); Klopfer (*58*).

Stewart, Francis J., and Brainard, Paul P. *Specific Interest Inventory.* New York: Psychological Corporation, 1932. 8 cents each, $7.00 per 100; sample set, $0.25 any one form. (IV)

An inventory of tendencies which are regarded as essential to vocations. Four forms; men, women, boys, and girls. Forms W and G contain the following grouping of items: artistic, commercial, creative imagination, emotional expression, esthetic, experimental, leadership, literary, manual, mathematics, mechanical, musical, observations, order, outdoor, physical, scientific, social, study, and vocal expression. The divisions in Forms M and B are as follows: physical, mechanical, outdoor, vocal expression, drawing, leadership, social, order, literary, mathematics, esthetic, scientific, fine manual, commercial, skilled manual, music, study, experiment, observation, and creative imagination. Each division has five items, each beginning with the phrase "How do you like." The answers are to be indicated in one of five categories ranging from "dislike very much" to "like very much." A procedure is outlined for getting a rank in interests from one to twenty according to the above divisions and for discovering vocational trends from the rank in interest groups. The average time used in filling out the inventory is 30 minutes. Forms B and G, ages 10–16; Forms M and W, over 16 years of age. For inventories given to a group of junior high school pupils in November and again in May, the authors report in the manual of instructions that correlations of the subtotals of the twenty groups ranged from .13 to .94 with an average of .68. No separate studies of the test available.

Strong, Edward K., Jr. *Vocational Interest Blanks.* Stanford University, California: Stanford University Press, 1930, 1933: revised, 1938. Blanks, $2.00 per 25; scoring scales, $1.00 each; answer sheets, $2.25 per 100; sample set, $0.15. (IV)

An inventory of vocational interest rather than personality; included in this bibliography because information about vocational interests is useful in the study of personality. The purpose is not to test interest in vocations, but to discover the extent to which an individual's interests agree with those of persons in various occupational groups. Designed for adults and college students, and probably should not be used below the junior or senior year of high school. There is a form for persons who have been out of school several years and a form for students. Separate blanks for men and women. The men's blank is scored for thirty-five occupations and the women's, eighteen. The blank is scored separately for each occupation. The men's blank is also scored for several occupational groups. In addition, three special scales—occupational level, masculinity-femininity, and interest maturity—are available for use by trained counselors. Scoring is laborious if done by hand. Certain statistical bureaus, as the Statistical Bureau at Columbia University, are equipped for scoring of both blanks with Hollerith tabulating equipment. If separate answer sheets are used, the men's blank may now be scored for all scales on the International Test Scoring Machine. The women's blank has not yet been adapted for scoring with this machine. Raw scores for various occupations are translated into letter ratings: A, B+, B, B—, C+, and C. Average reliability, .80 to .85. Separate scoring scale required for each vocation. Segel and Brintle (*100*) studied the relation of occupational interest scores to achievement test results and marks of college students. Concluded that interest blanks designed for use in vocational guidance may also be used in educational guidance. However, the relationship of the scores with the college marks was quite low. Dwyer (*31*) carried on a factor analysis of nineteen occupational scales of the Strong blank for men and found four factors. The best indication of these four traits was given by the occupational scales for physicist, journalist, minister, and life insurance salesman. A study by Seder (*99*) based on the scores of women physicians and life insurance saleswomen indicated that the interests of men and women engaged in the same occupation tend to be similar and suggested that separate occupational scales for the two sexes were not needed. Sarbin and Anderson (*97*) found that adults who complain of occupational dissatisfaction tend to show Strong interest patterns which do not agree with their occupations. Young and Estabrooks (*138*) added a studiousness scale for scoring the Strong blank. Scale is sold for $1.00 by the Stanford University Press. Williamson (*132, 133*) found that the correlation between scores on the studiousness scale and the marks of university freshmen was only .20. Peterson and Dunlap (*83*) have proposed a simplified scoring procedure for the Strong blank for men, which, according to their data and data reported by Kogan and Gehlmann (*60*) and Lester and Traxler (*64*), yield results that are highly correlated with the scores obtained by means of the weights assigned by Strong. Reference: Strong (*106, 107*).

Thorpe, L. P.; Clark, W. W.; and Tiegs, E. W. *California Test of Personality.* Los Angeles: California Test Bureau, 1939. $1.00 per 25 of any series; specimen set, $0.25. (IV)

An extensive battery consisting of five levels: primary series, Grades I–III; elementary series, Grades IV–IX; intermediate series, Grades VII–X; secondary series, Grades IX–XIV; adult series, Grades VII–adults. Planned to measure personal adjustment and social adjustment at all levels. Within each main part there are several subtests, the results of which may be graphed in the form of a profile. Spearman-Brown split-half reliability of the entire scale reported as .933 for the elementary battery and .931 for the secondary battery. Adapted for machine scoring. Reference: Tiegs, Clark, and Thorpe (*115*).

Thurstone, L. L. *Scales for the Measurement of Social Attitudes*. Chicago: University of Chicago Press, 1930. 1 package of 25, any one form, $0.65; 2 to 4 packages, each $0.55; 5 to 9 packages, each $0.45; 10 to 19 packages, each $0.40; 20 or more packages, each $0.30. (VII)

Scales designed by Thurstone and his associates for measuring attitude toward a variety of social institutions. At least thirty-five scales have been prepared, including, among others, scales for the measurement of attitude toward the church, war, the Negro, prohibition, communism, treatment of criminals, unions, public office, patriotism, the Constitution of the United States, the social position of women, immigration, birth control, God, the Chinese, the Germans, Sunday observance, law, censorship, the Bible, evolution, capital punishment, and the economic position of women. Some of these are now out of print. Each scale consists of about twenty statements. The subject checks those with which he agrees. The score is the average of the scale values of the statements checked. Each scale was carefully constructed according to a definite technique, involving a statistical treatment of the independent judgments of a large number of judges. The scales were standardized on college students, but some of them can probably be used in high school to advantage. Two forms, A and B. Reliability varies; about .80 for some of the scales. Miller (*77*) criticized the Peterson-Thurstone War-Attitude Scale because he found that the average person checked items ranging over 7.2 scale units while the entire range of the scale itself was only 10.8 units. Traxler (*116*) questioned the validity of the Droba-Thurstone Attitude-toward-War Scale when used with high school pupils for a similar reason. Lorge (*70, 71*) studied the reliability of scores resulting from four different ways of scoring the Thurstone attitude scales. The highest correlations between alternate forms were obtained with the median check score, which is the regular method used in scoring the scales. Criticisms of the Thurstone technique of scale construction have been published by Ojemann (*81*) and by Tuttle (*123*). Reference: Thurstone and Chave (*113*).

Thurstone, L. L., and Thurstone, Thelma G. *Personality Schedule*. Chicago: University of Chicago Press, 1929. $1.25 per 25. (IV)

A questionnaire designed to obtain an index of neurotic tendency. Contains a series of questions to which subject responds with *yes, no,* or *?*. One form suitable for high school, college, and adult use. Standardized on 694 University of Chicago freshmen. Neprash (*79*) found reliability coefficients of .84, .91, and .74, for intervals of two, four, and eight weeks, respectively. Willoughby (*134*), after presenting a study of the Thurstone scale, suggested an abbreviated scale of twenty-five items and five choices, for which he found a reliability of .83. Reference: Thurstone and Thurstone (*114*).

Washburne, J. N. *Washburne Social Adjustment Inventory* (Thaspic edition). Yonkers, New York: World Book Company, 1940. $1.40 per 25; specimen set, $0.20. (IV)

A group test of social adjustment, consisting of 123 items, some of which call for more than one response. Most of the questions are to be answered by writing *yes,* or *no* on a line preceding each question. The scoring key indicates the questions that attempt to get at the same trait or complex, thus providing for a grouping of the questions according to "elements." The aspects of personality for which scores are obtained by means of this inventory are truthfulness, sympathy, alienation, purpose, impulse-judgment, control, happiness, and wishes. One form suitable for all ages above Grade VIII. Calls for 30–40 minutes of working time. Reliability coefficients reported in the manual are as follows: truthfulness, .73 ± .03; alienation, .81 ± .02; happiness, .85 ± .02; wish, .88 ± –.02; total adjustment score, .92 ± .01. Reliabilities are not available for the other elements. It is reported that the correlation with intelligence and chronological age is negligible and that the correlations between test elements are also slight. Reference: Washburne (*127*).

Woodworth, R. S., and Mathews, E. *Personal Data Sheet*. Chicago: C. H. Stoelting Company, 1924. $1.25 per 25 copies. (IV)

A questionnaire for obtaining a measurement of the general emotionality and nervous and mental stability of pre-adolescent and adolescent children. One form. Ages 9–18 years. Norms based on unselected group of 1034 cases. Flemming and Flemming (*36*) compared scores made by children on the test with ratings of emotional balance made for the children by teachers two years earlier. Found no relation between the tests of emotional stability and the teachers' estimates of emotional balance. The time interval between the ratings and the test is a limitation of the study. Wrightstone (*137*) found the Woodworth-Mathews sheet fairly valid for diagnosing certain personality disorders of children.

REFERENCES

1. Adams, Clifford R. "A New Measure of Personality," *Journal of Applied Psychology,* XXV (April 1941), 141–151.
2. Adkins, Dorothy C., and Kuder, G. Frederic. "The Relation of Primary Mental Abilities to Activity Preferences," *Psychometrika,* V (December 1940), 251–262.
3. Allport, Gordon W. "A Test of Ascendance-Submission," *Journal of Abnormal and Social Psychology,* XXVI (October–December 1931), 231–248.
4. Allport, Gordon W. *Personality: A Psychological Interpretation.* New York: Henry Holt and Company, 1937. Pp. xiv + 588.
5. Allport, Gordon W., and Vernon, P. E. "A Test of Personality Values," *Journal of Abnormal and Social Psychology,* XXVI (October–December 1931), 231–248.

6. Baxter, Edna Dorothy. "Baxter Group Test of Child Personality (Abstract)," *Psychological Bulletin,* XXXVI (October 1939), 629–630.

7. Beck, Samuel J. *Introduction to the Rorschach Method.* The American Orthopsychiatric Association, 1937. Pp. xv + 278.

8. Beckman, R. O. "Ascendance–Submission Test—Revised," *Personnel Journal,* XI (April 1933), 387–392.

9. Bell, H. M. *The Theory and Practice of Student Counseling, with Special Reference to the Adjustment Inventory.* Stanford University, California: Stanford University Press, 1935. Pp. 138.

10. Bender, I. E. "Ascendance–Submission in Relation to Certain Other Factors in Personality," *Journal of Abnormal and Social Psychology,* XXIII (1928), 137–143.

11. Benjamin, John O., and Ebaugh, Franklin G. "The Diagnostic Validity of the Rorschach Test," *American Journal of Psychiatry,* XCIV (March 1938), 1163–1178.

12. Bernreuter, Robert G. "Validity of the Personality Inventory," *Personnel Journal,* XI (April 1933), 383–386.

13. Bernreuter, Robert G. "The Theory and Construction of the Personality Inventory," *Journal of Social Psychology,* IV (November 1933), 387–405.

14. Brigden, R. L. "The Cowan Adolescent Personality Schedule: Its Function in Psychological Diagnosis," *American Journal of Medical Jurisprudence,* II (1939), 97–99.

15. Brown, Fred. "A Psychoneurotic Inventory for Children between Nine and Fourteen Years of Age," *Journal of Applied Psychology,* XVIII (August 1934), 566–577.

16. Buros, Oscar K. *Educational, Psychological, and Personality Tests of 1933, 1934, and 1935.* New Brunswick, New Jersey: School of Education, Rutgers University, 1936. Pp. 83.

17. Buros, Oscar K. *Educational, Psychological, and Personality Tests of 1936.* New Brunswick, New Jersey: School of Education, Rutgers University, 1937. Pp. 141.

18. Buros, Oscar K. *The Nineteen Thirty Eight Mental Measurements Yearbook.* New Brunswick, New Jersey: Rutgers University, 1938. Pp. xiv + 415.

19. Buros, Oscar K. *The Nineteen Forty Mental Measurements Yearbook.* Highland Park, New Jersey: The Mental Measurements Yearbook, 1941. Pp. xxiii + 674.

20. Carter, Harold D., and Jones, Mary Cover. "Vocational Attitude Patterns in High-School Students," *Journal of Educational Psychology,* XXIX (May 1938), 321–334.

21. Chave, E. J. *Personality Development in Children.* Chicago: University of Chicago Press, 1937. Pp. xiii + 354.

22. Chave, E. J. "A New Type Scale for Measuring Attitudes," *Religious Education,* XXIII (1938), 364.

23. Cleeton, Glen U. "An Analysis of Women's Vocational Interests," *Report of the Twelfth Annual Meeting,* American College Personnel Association, 1935.

24. Congdon, Nora A. "A Study of Cleeton's Vocational Interest Inventory," *Occupations,* XVIII (February 1940), 347–352.

25. Corey, Stephen M. "Measuring Attitudes in the Classroom," *Elementary School Journal,* XLIII (April 1943), 457–461.

26. Darley, John G., and McNamara, Walter J. "Factor Analysis in the Establishment of New Personality Tests," *Journal of Educational Psychology,* XXXI (May 1940), 321–334.

27. Downey, June E. *The Will-Temperament and Its Testing.* Yonkers, New York: World Book Company, 1923. Pp. v + 339.

28. Drake, Margaret J.; Roslow, Sidney; and Bennett, George K. "The Relationship of Self-Rating and Classmate-Rating on Personality Tests," *Journal of Experimental Education,* VII (March 1939), 210–213.

29. Droba, D. D. "Methods for Measuring Attitudes," *Psychological Bulletin,* XXIX (May 1932), 309–323.

30. Dunlap, Jack W., and Kroll, Abraham. "Observations on the Methodology in Attitude Scales," *Journal of Social Psychology,* X (November 1939), 475–487.

31. Dwyer, Paul S. "An Analysis of Nineteen Occupational Scores on the Strong Vocational Interest Test Given to 418 Students Entering the Michigan Medical School during the Years 1928, 1929, and 1930," *Journal of Applied Psychology,* XXII (February 1938), 8–16.

32. Ferguson, Leonard W. "A Study of the Likert Technique of Attitude Scale Construction," *Journal of Social Psychology,* XIII (February 1941), 51–57.

33. Fisher, Vivian E., and Watson, Robert I. "An Inventory of Affective Tolerance," *Journal of Psychology,* XII (October 1941), 149–157.

34. Flanagan, John C. *Factor Analysis in the Study of Personality.* Stanford University, California: Stanford University Press, 1935. Pp. x + 103.

35. Flanagan, John C. Technical Aspects of Multi-Trait Tests," *Journal of Educational Psychology,* XXVI (1935), 641–651.

36. Flemming, E. G., and Flemming, C. W. "The Validity of the Mathews Revision of the Woodworth Personal Data Questionnaire," *Journal of Abnormal and Social Psychology,* XXIII (January–February 1939), 500–506.

37. Frank, Lawrence K.; Hertz, Marguerite R.; Krugman, Morris; Munroe, Ruth; Piotrowski, Z. A.; Beck, Samuel; Klopfer, Bruno; and Harrower-Erickson, M. R. "The Rorschach Method," *Journal of Consulting Psychology,* VII (March–April 1943), 63–126.

38. Froehlich, Clifford. "A Study of the Gentry Vocational Interest Inventory," *Educational and Psychological Measurement,* II (January 1942), 75–82.

39. Fryer, Douglas. *The Measurement of Interests.* Henry Holt and Company, 1931. Pp. xxxvi + 488.

40. Garretson, Oliver K. *Relationship between Expressed Preferences and Curricular Activities of Ninth Grade Boys.* New York: Bureau of Publications, Teachers College, Columbia University, 1930. Pp. 77.

41. Gibbons, Charles C. "A Short Scoring Method for the Link P.Q. Test," *Journal of Applied Psychology,* XXII (December 1938), 653–656.

42. Giffen, Lowell L. "An Improved Method for Scoring the Pressey X–O Test," *Journal of Applied Psychology,* XXVI (December 1942), 841–845.

43. Guilford, J. P., and Guilford, Ruth B. "Personality Factors S, E, and M, and Their Measurement," *Journal of Psychology,* II (1936), 109–127.

44. Guilford, J. P., and Guilford, Ruth B. "Personality Factors D, R, T, and A," *Journal of Abnormal and Social Psychology,* XXXIV (January 1939), 21–36.

45. Guilford, J. P., and Guilford, Ruth B. "Personality Factors N and GD," *Journal of Abnormal and Social Psychology,* XXXIV (April 1939), 239–248.

46. Hartshorne, Hugh, and May, Mark. *Studies in Deceit.* New York: The Macmillan Company, 1928. Pp. xxi + 414 and viii + 306.

47. Hartshorne, Hugh; May, Mark; and Maller, J. B. *Studies in Service and Self-Control.* New York: The Macmillan Company, 1929. Pp. xxv + 559.

48. Hartshorne, Hugh; May, Mark; and Shuttleworth, F. K. *Studies in the Organization of Character.* New York: The Macmillan Company, 1930. Pp. xxv + 503.

49. Hathaway, Starke R., and McKinley, John C. *The Minnesota Multiphasic Personality Inventory,* Revised edition. Minneapolis: University of Minnesota Press, 1943.

50. Hertz, Marguerite R. "The Reliability of the Rorschach Ink Blot Test," *Journal of Applied Psychology,* XVIII (1934), 461–477.

51. Hertz, Marguerite R. "The Rorschach Ink Blot Test: Historical Summary," *Psychological Bulletin,* XXXII (1935), 33–66.

52. Hertz, Marguerite R., and Rubenstein, Boris B. "A Comparison of Three 'Blind' Rorschach Analyses," *American Journal of Orthopsychiatry,* IX (April 1939), 295–314.

53. Hildreth, Gertrude. "An Interest Inventory for High School Personnel Work," *Journal of Educational Research,* XXVII (September 1933), 11–19.

54. Hildreth, Gertrude. *A Bibliography of Mental Tests and Rating Scales.* New York: Psychological Corporation, 1933 (Revised, 1939). Pp. 295.

55. Humm, Doncaster G.; Storment, Robert C.; and Iorns, Martin E. "Combination Scores for the Humm-Wadsworth Temperament Scale," *Journal of Psychology,* VII (1939), 227–253.

56. Hunsicker, A. L. "The Nash-Hunsicker Personality Scale," *Psychological Bulletin,* XXXVIII (October 1941), 705 (Abstract).

57. Kent, Grace H., and Rosanoff, A. J. *A Study of Association in Insanity.* Baltimore: Lord Baltimore Press, 1910. Pp. 142.

58. Klopfer, B. "Theory and Technique of Rorschach Interpretation," *Rorschach Research Exchange,* III (1939), 152–194.

59. Klopfer, B., and Davidson, H. H. *Record Blank for the Rorschach Method of Personality Diagnosis.* New York: Rorschach Institute, Inc., 1939.

60. Kogan, Leonard O., and Gehlmann, Frederick. "Validation of the Simplified Method for Scoring the Strong Vocational Interest Blank for Men," *Journal of Educational Psychology,* XXXIII (April 1942), 317–320.

61. Kuder, G. F. "The Stability of Preference Items," *Journal of Social Psychology,* XI (1939), 41–50.

62. Laird, D. A. "Detecting Abnormal Behavior," *Journal of Abnormal and Social Psychology*, XX (1925), 128–134.

63. Laslett, H. R., and Bennett, Elizabeth. "A Comparison of Scores on Two Measures of Personality," *Journal of Abnormal and Social Psychology*, XXVIII (March 1934), 459–461.

64. Lester, Helene, and Traxler, Arthur E. "Simplified Method for Scoring the Strong Vocational Interest Blank Applied to a Secondary School Group," *Journal of Educational Psychology*, XXXIII (November 1942), 628–631.

65. Link, H. C. "A Test of Five Personality Traits of Adolescence," *Journal of Applied Psychology*, XX (October 1936), 527–534.

66. Loofbourow, Graham C., and Keys, Noel. "A Group Test of Problem Behavior Tendencies in Junior High School Boys," *Journal of Educational Psychology*, XXIV (December 1933), 641–653.

67. Lorge, Irving. "Personality Traits by Fiat. I. The Analysis of Total Trait Scores and Keys by the Bernreuter Personality Inventory," *Journal of Educational Psychology*, XXVI (April 1935), 273–278.

68. Lorge, Irving. "Personality Traits by Fiat. II. The Consistency of the Bernreuter Personality Inventory by the Bernreuter and by the Flanagan Keys," *Journal of Educational Psychology*, XXVI (September 1935), 427–434.

69. Lorge, Irving. "Personality Traits by Fiat. II. A Correction," *Journal of Educational Psychology*, XXVI (December 1935), 652–654.

70. Lorge, Irving. "The Thurstone Attitude Scales: I. Reliabilty and Consistency of Rejection and Acceptance," *Journal of Social Psychology*, X (May 1939), 187–198.

71. Lorge, Irving. "The Thurstone Attitude Scales: II. Reliability and Consistency of Younger and Older Intellectual Peers," *Journal of Social Psychology*, X (May 1939), 199–208.

72. Lurie, W. A. "Study of Spranger's Value-Types by the Method of Factor Analysis," *Journal of Social Psychology*, VIII (February 1937), 17–37.

73. McCall, William A., and Herring, John P. *My Personality Growth Book for Junior and Senior High Schools, Colleges, and Adult Groups.* New York: Bureau of Publications, Teachers College, Columbia University, 1941.

74. McGeoch, J. A., and Whitely, P. "Reliability of Pressey X–O Tests for Investigating the Emotions," *Pedagogical Seminary*, XXXIV (June 1927), 255–270.

75. Maller, J. B. *Character and Personality Tests.* New York: Bureau of Publications, Teachers College, Columbia University, 1932. Pp. 53.

76. Manger, C. W. "The Effect of Self-Interest on Scores Made on the Allport Test for Measuring Ascendance-Submission," *Psychological Clinic*, XXI (1933), 268–270.

77. Miller, Lawrence W. "A Critical Analysis of the Peterson-Thurstone War Attitude Scale," *Journal of Educational Psychology*, XXV (December 1934), 662–668.

78. Murray, Henry A., and the workers at the Harvard Psychological Clinic.

Explorations in Personality. New York: Oxford University Press, 1938. Pp. xiv + 761.

79. Neprash, J. A. "The Reliability of Questions in the Thurstone Personality Schedule," *Journal of Social Psychology,* VII (May 1936), 239–244.

80. Neymann, C. A., and Kohlstedt, K. D. "A New Diagnostic Test for Introversion-Extroversion," *Journal of Abnormal and Social Psychology,* XXIII (1929), 482–487.

81. Ojemann, R. H. "A Revised Method for the Measurement of Attitude," *University of Iowa Studies in Child Welfare,* XVII (1939), 5–18.

82. Pedersen, Ruth A. "Validity of the Bell Adjustment Inventory When Applied to College Women," *Journal of Psychology,* IX (January 1940), 227–236.

83. Peterson, Bertha M., and Dunlap, Jack W. "A Simplified Method for Scoring the Strong Vocational Interest Blank," *Journal of Consulting Psychology,* V (November–December 1941), 269–274.

84. Pintner, Rudolph, and Forlano, George. "Four Retests of a Personality Inventory," *Journal of Educational Psychology,* XXIX (February 1938), 93–100.

85. Pintner, Rudolph, and Forlano, George. "Validation of Personality Tests by Outstanding Characteristics of Pupils," *Journal of Educational Psychology,* XXX (January 1939), 25–32.

86. Piotrowski, Z. A. "A Rorschach Blind Analysis of a Compulsive Neurotic," *Kwartalnik Psychologiczny,* XI (1939), 231–264.

87. Pressey, S. L. "A Group Scale for Investigating the Emotions," *Journal of Abnormal Psychology and Social Psychology,* XVI (April 1921), 55–64.

88. Remmers, H. H.; Brandenberg, G. C.; and Gillespie, F. H. "Measuring Attitude toward the High School," *Journal of Experimental Education,* II (September 1933), 60–64.

89. Remmers, H. H., and Silance, E. B. "Generalized Attitude Scales," *Journal of Psychology,* V (August 1934), 298–312.

90. Riggs, Winifred C., and Joyal, A. E. "A Validation of the Loofbourow-Keys Personal Index of Problem Behavior in Junior High Schools," *Journal of Educational Psychology,* XXIX (March 1938), 194–201.

91. Rogers, Carl R. *Measuring Personality Adjustment in Children 9 to 13 Years of Age.* New York: Bureau of Publications, Teachers College, Columbia University, 1931. Pp. 98.

92. Rorschach, Hermann. *Psychodiagnostik: Methodik und Ergebnisse eines Wahrnehmungs-diagnostischen Experiments.* Berne: E. Birchner, 1921. Pp. 174.

93. Rothney, J. W. M. "Interests of Public Secondary School Boys," *Journal of Educational Psychology,* XXVIII (November 1937), 561–594.

94. Ruggles, Richard, and Allport, Gordon W. "Recent Applications of the A–S Reaction Study," *Journal of Abnormal and Social Psychology,* XXXIV (October 1939), 518–528.

95. Ryans, David G. "A Tentative Statement of the Relation of Persistence Test Scores to Certain Personality Traits as Measured by the Bernreuter Personality

Inventory," *Pedagogical Seminary and Journal of Genetic Psychology,* LIV (March 1939), 229–234.

96. St. Clair, Walter F., and Seegers, J. Conrad. "Certain Aspects of the Validity of the Bernreuter Personality Inventory," *Journal of Educational Psychology,* XXVIII (October 1937), 530–540.

97. Sarbin, Theodore R., and Anderson, Hedwin C. "A Preliminary Study of the Relations of Measured Interest Patterns and Occupational Dissatisfaction," *Educational and Psychological Measurement,* XX (January 1942), 23–36.

98. Schultz, Richard S., and Roslow, Sidney. "Restandardization of the A–S Reaction Study as a Personnel Form," *Journal of Applied Psychology,* XXII (December 1938), 554–557.

99. Seder, Margaret. "Vocational Interests of Professional Women, Parts I and II," *Journal of Applied Psychology,* XXIV (April and June 1940), 130–143, 265–272.

100. Segel, David, and Brintle, S. L. "The Relation of Occupational Interest Scores as Measured by the Strong Interest Blank to Achievement Test Results and College Marks in Certain College Groups," *Journal of Educational Research,* XXVII (February 1934), 442–445.

101. Sharkey, Vincent J., and Dunlap, Jack W. "Study of the Reliability and Validity of the Academic Preference Blank," *Journal of Educational Psychology,* XXXI (February 1940), 103–110.

102. Sherman, Mandel. "Theories and Measurement of Attitudes," *Child Development,* III (March 1932), 15–28.

103. Sims, Verner M. *Manual of Directions for the Sims Score Card for Socio-Economic Status.* Bloomington, Illinois: Public School Publishing Company, 1927. Pp. 12.

104. Spencer, Douglas. *Fulcra of Conflict: A New Approach to Personality Measurement.* Yonkers, New York: World Book Company, 1938. Pp. 306.

105. Stagner, Ross. *Psychology of Personality.* New York: McGraw-Hill Book Company, 1937. Pp. xi + 465.

106. Strong, Edward K., Jr. *Change of Interests with Age.* Stanford University, California: Stanford University Press, 1931. Pp. xix + 235.

107. Strong, Edward K., Jr. *Vocational Interests of Men and Women.* Stanford University, California: Stanford University Press, 1943. Pp. xxix + 746.

108. Super, Donald E. "The Bernreuter Personality Inventory: A Review of Research," *Psychological Bulletin,* XXXIX (February 1942), 94–125.

109. Sweet, Lennig. *Personal Attitudes Test for Younger Boys.* New York: Bureau of Publications, Teachers College, Columbia University, 1929. Pp. 58.

110. Swineford, Frances. "The Measurement of a Personality Trait," *Journal of Educational Psychology,* XXIX (April 1938), 295–300.

111. Symonds, P. M. *Diagnosing Personality and Conduct.* New York: D. Appleton-Century Company, 1931. Pp. xvi + 602.

112. Thomson, William A. "An Evaluation of the P.Q. (Personality Quotient) Test," *Character and Personality,* VI (June 1938), 274–292.

113. Thurstone, L. L., and Chave, E. J. *The Measurement of Attitude.* Chicago: University of Chicago Press, 1929. Pp. xii + 96.

114. Thurstone, L. L., and Thurstone, Thelma G. "A Neurotic Inventory," *Journal of Social Psychology,* I (February 1930), 1–29.

115. Tiegs, Ernest W.; Clark, Willis W.; and Thorpe, Louis P. "The California Test of Personality," *Journal of Educational Research,* XXXV (October 1941), 102–108.

116. Traxler, Arthur E. "Evaluation of Scores of High School Pupils on Droba-Thurstone Attitude-toward-War Scale," *Journal of Educational Psychology,* XXVI (November 1935), 616–622.

117. Traxler, Arthur E. "The Reliability of the Bell Inventories and Their Correlation with Teacher Judgment," *Journal of Applied Psychology,* XXV (December 1941), 672–678.

118. Traxler, Arthur E., and McCall, William C. "Some Data on the Kuder Preference Record," *Educational and Psychological Measurement,* I (July 1941), 253–268.

119. Triggs, Frances O. "A Study of the Relation of Kuder Preference Record Scores to Various Other Measures," *Educational and Psychological Measurement,* III (Winter 1943), 341–354.

120. Triggs, Frances O. "A Further Comparison of Interest Measurement by the Kuder Preference Record and the Strong Vocational Interest Blank for Men," *Journal of Educational Research,* XXXVII (March 1944), 538–544.

121. Tubbs, William R. "A Study of the Inter-relationships between the Adams-Lepley Personal Audit and the Bernreuter Personality Inventory," *Journal of Applied Psychology,* XXVI (June 1942), 338–351.

122. Turney, Austin H., and Fee, Mary. "An Attempt to Use the Bell Adjustment Inventory for High School Guidance," *School Review,* XLIV (March 1936), 193–198.

123. Tuttle, Harold S. "Selective Applications of the Thurstone Test," *Journal of Educational Research,* XXXIII (May 1940), 705–709.

124. Tyler, H. T. "Evaluating the Bell Adjustment Inventory," *Junior College Journal,* VI (April 1936), 353–357.

125. Vernon, P. E. "The Significance of the Rorschach Test," *British Journal of Medical Psychology,* XV (1935), 199–217.

126. Wang, C. K. A. "The Internal Consistency of the Allports' A–S Test," *Journal of Abnormal and Social Psychology,* XXVI (July–September 1931), 154–161.

127. Washburne, J. N. "A Test of Social Adjustment," *Journal of Applied Psychology,* XIX (April 1935), 123–144.

128. Watson, Robert I., and Fisher, Vivian E. "An Inventory of Affective Potency," *Journal of Psychology,* XII (October 1941), 139–148.

129. Weedon, Vivian F. "Technique for Determining Interest," *Educational Research Bulletin,* XIII (November–December 1934), 191–197, 231–234.

130. Whitely, Paul L. "A Study of the Allport-Vernon Test for Social Values," *Journal of Abnormal and Social Psychology,* XXVIII (April–June 1933), 6–13.

131. Whitely, Paul L. "The Constancy of Personal Values," *Journal of Abnormal and Social Psychology,* XXXIII (July 1938), 405–408.

132. Williamson, E. G. "An Analysis of the Young-Estabrooks Studiousness Scale," *Journal of Applied Psychology,* XXI (June 1937), 260–264.

133. Williamson, E. G. "A Further Analysis of the Young-Estabrooks Studiousness Scale," *Journal of Applied Psychology,* XXII (February 1938), 105.

134. Willoughby, Raymond R. "Some Properties of the Thurstone Personality Schedule and a Suggested Revision," *Journal of Social Psychology,* III (November 1932), 401–423.

135. Wittenborn, J. R.; Triggs, Frances O.; and Feder, Daniel D. "A Comparison of Interest Measurement by the Kuder Preference Record and the Strong Vocational Interest Blanks for Men and Women," *Educational and Psychological Measurement,* III (Autumn 1943), 239–257.

136. Wolfle, Dael. "Factor Analysis in the Study of Personality," *Journal of Abnormal and Social Psychology,* XXXVII (July 1942), 393–397.

137. Wrightstone, J. Wayne. "Validity of the Woodworth-Mathews Personal Data Sheet for Diagnosing Certain Personality Disorders," *Journal of Educational Psychology,* XXV (1934), 39–44.

138. Young, C. W., and Estabrooks, G. H. "Report of the Young-Estabrooks Studiousness Scale for Use with the Strong Vocational Interest Blank for Men," *Journal of Educational Psychology,* XXVIII (March 1937), 176–187.

139. Zubin, Joseph. "The Determination of Response Patterns in Personality Adjustment Inventories," *Journal of Educational Psychology,* XXVIII (September 1937), 401–413.

CHAPTER VII

Appraisal of Personal Qualities—
Rating Scales, Anecdotal Records,
and Behavior Descriptions

RATING SCALES

THE INSTRUMENTS FOR THE APPRAISAL OF PERSONAL QUALITIES DISCUSSED IN Chapter VI were based on the reaction of the individual to a series of questions or situations. Closely related to the self-inventories which formed an important part of that chapter are the behavior rating scales in which the rating of the pupil is done by counselors, teachers, parents, or others, rather than by the pupil himself.

A limitation to the use of rating scales is that unless the rater is well acquainted with the individual being rated or has perfected a technique for getting reliable information from persons who do know the subject intimately, the ratings will probably be low in validity. On the other hand, persons are less likely to be biased in their judgments concerning others than in their estimates of themselves, and it has been demonstrated that the reliability and validity of ratings can be increased by combining those secured from several judges concerning the same individual.

There are several well-known scales for rating behavior, among which are the Haggerty-Olson-Wickman Behavior Rating Schedules (*19*), A Scale for Evaluating the School Behavior of Children Ten to Fifteen, by Hayes (*11*), and the Winnetka Scale for Rating School Behavior and Attitudes (*32, 34*). The last scale was devised for the rating of pupils from the nursery school through the sixth grade with respect to the five general headings of cooperation, social consciousness, emotional security, leadership, and responsibility. A somewhat similar form was prepared for use in the high school (*33*).

One advantage of rating scales over questionnaires is that they may be used with children who are too young to read questionnaires or to evaluate their own reactions. Marston (*18*) has published an instrument entitled Introversion-

Extroversion in Young Children which may be used in rating traits of children between two and six years of age. The Merrill-Palmer School has published nine Personality Rating schedules for young children (25).

The number of rating scales devised especially for pupils above the elementary school level is not large. Rulon and others have published the BEC Personality Rating Schedule, which is for use in rating pupils in Grade VII and above. Ratings are obtained in eight areas: mental alertness, initiative, dependability, cooperativeness, judgment, personal impression, courtesy, and health. This schedule, and Schedule B of the Haggerty-Olson-Wickman blank, are graphic rating scales. In this type of scale the pupil is rated with respect to a certain characteristic by placing a check mark at an appropriate place on a continuous line. The rater indicates where he thinks the individual falls between the two extremes of behavior of that particular type. Descriptive statements are sometimes printed below portions of the scale to help define the thinking of the rater. Test technicians tend to prefer the graphic rating scale to other types.

One difficulty with the usual procedure of using rating scales is that the ratings are frequently subject to "halo effect"; that is, the rating assigned to the pupil on one trait often influences the rating which is assigned to him on the next trait. Halo effect can be reduced by having the rater judge all the individuals in the group on a single trait, then rate all the individuals on the next trait, and so forth. Some of the newer rating scales now provide for the use of the latter procedure. Among these is the Teacher's Rating Scales for Pupil Adjustment, by Freeman and Kawin. The Progressive Education Association Behavior Description plan, which is described near the end of this chapter, also makes use of this procedure.

ANECDOTAL RECORDS [1]

Within the last fifteen years, some schools have begun to use a device for the appraisal of personality known as the anecdotal record. This record, as the name implies, involves the setting down of an anecdote concerning some aspect of pupil behavior which seems significant to the observer. There is no standardized technique for the making and utilizing of anecdotal records, but there are many points of similarity in the plans described by different writers.

Records of this kind were discussed in a report entitled "Personnel Methods," a supplement to the *Educational Record* published in 1928 by the American Council on Education, but these records were called descriptions of personality.

---

[1] Anecdotal records and behavior descriptions are discussed in this chapter rather than in the chapters on personnel records because their main purpose is the securing of evaluative data instead of the organizing and relating of different types of evaluations. They are comparable to test papers in that they constitute primary sources of data and not secondary sources as do most other kinds of personnel records.

The term anecdotal record apparently originated at the Rochester Athenaeum and Mechanics Institute [2] (22), which has been a leading institution in the use of such records.

Wood (35), Tyler (31), and others have directed the attention of schools to anecdotal records, and experimentation with this type of appraisal was encouraged in several schools through the Eight-Year Study of the Progressive Education Association.

Among the various definitions of the anecdotal record, the following are especially significant:

The anecdotal record is a specialized form of incidental observation. It is a description of the child's conduct and personality in terms of frequent brief, concrete observations of the pupil made and recorded by the teacher. [Strang (30:84–86).]

An anecdotal record is a report of a significant episode in the life of a student. [Raths (23).]

Anecdotes are descriptive accounts of episodes or occurrences in the daily life of the student. [Brown and Martin (6).]

Here used, the anecdotal record is a simple statement of an incident deemed by the observer to be significant with respect to a given pupil. [Zahn (36).]

. . . descriptions of actual behavior taking place in situations noted by the instructor, in contrast with rating scales which provide records only of the summary interpretation of the behavior observed. [Tyler (31).]

As used there [the Rochester Athenaeum and Mechanics Institute], the anecdote is a record of some significant item of conduct, a record of an episode in the life of the student; a word picture of the student in action; the teacher's best effort at taking a word snapshot at the moment of the incident; any narrative of events in which the student takes such part as to reveal something which may be significant about his personality. [Randall (22).]

CHARACTERISTICS OF A GOOD ANECDOTE

The natural tendency of an untrained observer when reporting an incident is to mix facts and opinion, but this is not desirable. Objectivity is the essence of a good anecdote.

One who is just beginning to experiment with anecdotes may be helped if he draws an analogy between the writing of anecdotes and good news reporting. A newspaper contains both news items and editorial opinion, but as a rule these are carefully separated. The function of the anecdotal writer, like the function of the news writer, is to report the facts accurately, objectively, and dispassionately.

The following is an anecdote from an untrained observer:

In study hall today, George showed his great desire to get attention, particularly from girls, by whispering and clowning for the benefit of everyone about him when-

[2] Now the Rochester Institute of Technology.

ever he thought the teacher's attention was elsewhere. He seems to be a born trouble-maker who will be a bad influence in this school. I think the principal and his counselor should call him in and take strong action before it is too late.

The phrases "showed his great desire to get attention," "born trouble-maker," and "bad influence in this school" are matters of opinion that have no place in a report of the incident itself. An objective report of what took place would read approximately as follows:

Incident. In study hall today, George whispered frequently and created a disturbance by various antics which attracted the attention of the pupils sitting near him.

This is a brief, clear statement of what took place. Some authorities on this method would limit the anecdotal record to a report of the incident, but most of them agree that it is sometimes desirable to add an interpretation, if it is clearly separated from the incident. The interpretation can well be placed in a separate paragraph or column carefully labeled thus:

Interpretation. George seems to be a boy who wants much attention from other pupils, particularly girls. He manages to get some of the attention he craves, but his classmates seem more annoyed and disgusted than amused.

Occasionally a recommendation is also helpful, provided it is separated from both incident and interpretation. It can be placed in a separate short paragraph, as follows:

Recommendation. It would be advisable for George's counselor to find an opportunity to talk with him about his relations with the other students and the school generally, and to make suggestions which will improve the boy's adjustment before he becomes a serious problem case.

An important advantage in separating the interpretation and the recommendation from the report of what was observed is that persons interested in obtaining an impartial appraisal of the pupil by summarizing many different anecdotes can deal with the incidents and entirely ignore the subjective parts of the record. This procedure will keep the points of view of different teachers from influencing the conclusions.

It may be felt that the mere report of an incident without interpretation is of such slight importance that it can be of little value in helping a counselor to understand a pupil. This opinion is no doubt justified if a single anecdote is considered alone, but ordinarily anecdotes are not used in that way. The anecdotal method is essentially cumulative in nature. While a single incident may not be at all typical of the behavior of the pupil concerned, the assembling and studying of many anecdotes, together with the other information the school has recorded about a pupil, presents a pattern of individual personality that is most helpful in a counseling program.

Steps in an Anecdotal Record Plan

Procedures for the introduction, preparation, and use of anecdotal records have not been standardized, and it would not be desirable to standardize them, but it appears that certain steps are needed when records of this kind are being introduced into a school regardless of modifications to meet the local situation.

Enlisting Cooperation. At the outset, the entire faculty of the school should be given an understanding of what is involved in the anecdotal record plan, and willingness to cooperate in trying out the method should be created. Counselors, as a rule, tend to favor the plan, for they can see possibilities of immediate and direct help from it in connection with their work, whereas some of the teachers may at first be unable to see the value of these records and may feel that they are just an addition to the load they are already carrying. It is the teachers, however, whose attitudes and cooperation are most essential to the success of the plan, for they have a better opportunity to observe pupil behavior than do the other members of the study. The success of the plan depends largely upon them, for they write the great majority of the anecdotes.

The introduction of anecdotal records should begin with the development within the faculty of the ideal of individualized education. The anecdotal method rests on an interest in individual boys and girls, a grasp of the concept of individual differences, a conviction that the development of each pupil is more important than the teaching of subject matter, and a knowledge that teaching effectiveness increases in proportion to one's acquaintance with the individuals composing the class. Until the faculty has reached a point in their thinking where they believe that the study of pupils is at least as important as the teaching of their subject, they are not ready to participate wholeheartedly in the preparation of anecdotal records. Schools whose staff members have already reached that point should find these records an easy and logical next step.

Deciding How Much Should Be Expected of Observers. When a faculty has decided to try out the anecdotal method, the next step is to arrive at an understanding of what shall be expected of those who are to write the anecdotes. This step involves two dangers. The first is that too much will be attempted and that the staff will become discouraged because so much time is required. The second is that after it has been agreed that anecdotal records are a promising approach to the investigation of pupil personality, the whole matter will be left to the individual whim of each teacher. The probable net result will be that the plan will resolve itself into an expression of good intentions with little or no tangible result. It seems desirable to decide on some reasonable minimum number of anecdotes which each teacher will write each week. It is not easy to say just what constitutes a "reasonable minimum number." Probably the best plan in deciding what can reasonably be expected of observers in a given school is to set aside an experimental week in which each teacher will prepare as many anecdotes as possible, after which a meeting can be held to study the anecdotes and to find out how many of them various teachers have written. This procedure will be advantageous both for showing the number of anecdotes that teachers should be able to write and for obtaining criticism on those which have been prepared.

Another plan is to choose certain aspects of behavior, such as cooperation or punctuality, and to ask all the teachers to observe the pupils and write anecdotes concerned with these particular kinds of behavior. A plan of this kind for limiting the scope of the project has the advantage of focusing the attention of the teachers on a few traits. This helps to keep them from becoming over-whelmed and discouraged in the very beginning by the size of the under-taking.

It may be feared that the writing of anecdotes will become routinized and per-functory if teachers are asked to submit a certain minimum number. Some per-sons will insist that teachers should be requested to write anecdotes only when they observe behavior that they feel is worth recording. The danger here is that some teachers will not be led to observe the pupils carefully and that they may record only striking behavior that may not be at all typical of the pupil. Be-havior is a continuing process, and it is probable that during any class hour every pupil in the group exhibits behavior that brings out his personal qualities in a significant way, if only the observer is alert and sees the behavior and grasps its implications.

Preparing Forms. The anecdotal record does not require elaborate forms. In fact, two or three simple ones are usually sufficient. There must be, first of all, forms for the original record to be made by the teacher or other observer. Each faculty member should be supplied with these.

The form for the original record may be placed on a small card, a half-sheet, or an ordinary letter-size sheet. When a card or a half-sheet is used, it is assumed that there will be only one anecdote on each form, while the full-size sheet may serve for the writing of several anecdotes about the same pupil.

A form which, it is believed, should prove adequate in most classroom situa-tions is shown in Form 4. The same four columns can be ruled on the back, if desired. If this is done, five or six anecdotes can frequently be entered on one sheet. The date and the place should be given in connection with each anecdote. The behavior observed should be stated clearly, concisely, and objectively under *incident*. Both interpretation and recommendation can be entered in separate paragraphs under *comment*. It should be understood that there is no neces-sity for writing anything under *comment* unless the observer feels that a com-ment will help the counselor understand the incident. The name of the ob-server should be signed at the bottom of each anecdotal record page.

If a letter-size record sheet of this kind is adopted for classroom use, it may

ANECDOTAL RECORD

Student_____Class_____

Date	Place	Incident	Comment

Observer_____

Form 4.

be desirable to supplement it with some small cards, particularly if the members of the staff are encouraged to write anecdotes concerning behavior outside class.

Pupil_____Date_____

Class_____Place_____

ANECDOTE

Observer_____

Form 5.

Cards similar to the one illustrated in Form 5 are easily carried and are convenient for the making of quick notes when there is an occasion to do so.

A third form that some schools may use is one for organizing and summarizing periodically the anecdotes from the various staff members. Other schools may avoid the use of a secondary-entry form of this type through a system of filing the original records. A form for summarizing anecdotes periodically is suggested in Form 6.

The anecdotes should be arranged in chronological order in the periodic summary. The name of the staff member reporting the anecdote should be entered under *observer*. Under *anecdote,* a brief statement of each incident, ordinarily without interpretation or recommendation, will be transferred from the original record.

At the end of each year, the periodic summary sheets may be used in preparing an annual summary for the cumulative record. The annual summary may take one of several different forms, depending on the nature of the cumulative record employed in the local school. These will be discussed later.

Obtaining the Original Records. It is seldom convenient for a teacher to write an anecdote at the moment the incident takes place. Many incidents that

PERIODIC ANECDOTAL RECORD SUMMARY

Pupil_____Grade_____

From_____To_____

Date	Place	Observer	Anecdote

Form 6.

should be recorded occur during class discussion or immediately before or after class, when a multitude of different things is claiming the attention of the teacher. If the teacher stopped to record significant behavior as it took place, the continuity of the work of the class would be interrupted and in the minds of the pupils undesirable importance would be attached to the preparation of anecdotes. At most, the teacher can find time merely to jot down the name of the pupil, with perhaps a phrase to call the incident to mind later.

In order to be successful in preparing anecdotes, teachers must learn to observe the behavior of individuals accurately, to remember what took place, and to make a record of each incident later when they are free to give their entire attention to the writing of the anecdotes. It is advisable for each teacher to set aside a certain period toward the end of each day—perhaps fifteen to thirty minutes—for the preparation of anecdotes concerning all the significant behavior incidents they have observed earlier in the day.

One who is engaged in the making of anecdotal records should check occasionally to see how the anecdotes are distributed among the various pupils. It may be found that there are many anecdotes for some pupils and very few or none at all for others. If this proves to be true, attention should consciously be directed toward those quiet members of the group whose behavior is so inconspicuous that their individuality has previously failed to impress itself upon the observer. It would be inadvisable to attempt to prepare the same number of anecdotes for all pupils, but it seems fair to assume that in the course of a semester a teacher should be able to write several anecdotes for every pupil in his classes.

Central Filing. Anecdotes concerning any individual take on added meaning when those written by different observers over a period of time are brought together and compared. It is highly desirable, therefore, that a system be worked out in each school whereby the anecdotal records for each pupil are collected in one place at regular intervals, so that they may be studied in relation to one another. If certain teachers wish to retain in their own files a record of the anecdotes they prepare, they can easily make carbon copies when writing the originals.

In schools that have well-established counseling systems, the anecdotes for each pupil will naturally be sent to the office of his counselor, where they will be utilized in conferences (although usually not shown to the pupil) and filed in individual folders. In other schools, the home-room teachers will be the logical persons to receive the anecdotes. In small schools where the principal is the chief guidance officer, the anecdotes will probably be filed in his office. Anecdotal records should be filed in the office of that functionary who will make the most use of them in guidance.

The frequency with which the anecdotes are collected should be determined by the local situation. In some schools they are brought together at the end of each week, whereas in other schools they are collected at longer intervals.

Summarization. Even though it is time-consuming, a carefully developed procedure for summarizing anecdotes is highly desirable. When the school reaches the point where the teachers have been trained in the writing of anecdotes and have accepted the preparation of them as one of their responsibilities, it is in the organization and summarization of the anecdotal material that the system is most likely to break down. If all teachers conscientiously turn in several anecdotes each day, the wealth of the material obtained may overwhelm those responsible for summarizing it, since a great many anecdotes will be collected for nearly every pupil in the school within the course of a year. At the Rochester Athenaeum and Mechanics Institute, for example, the average number of anecdotes reported for 520 students during the first semester of the school year 1934-1935 was forty-six (22). At this rate, ninety-two anecdotes for each student would be obtained in one school year. It is no small task to go through so much material for even one student, to discover trends in personality development, and to reduce all that material to a brief, usable statement for the cumulative record.

If there is sufficient staff time available for the making of periodic summaries, perhaps once a month, on blanks similar to the one shown in Form 6, the task of summarizing at the end of the year should be greatly simplified. If the periodic summary consists merely of a chronological arrangement of "boiled-down" statements of the behavior incidents collected from the various staff members concerning each pupil, it can probably be entrusted to intelligent clerical workers. The annual summary, however, which involves interpretation and a statement of trends and growth to be entered on the cumulative record, is no clerical task. It calls for the best knowledge and thinking that are available for this work. Ordinarily, the annual summary should be prepared by the counselor, or better still, by a committee consisting of the counselor, the pupil's teachers, and the psychologist.

If it is the custom in the school to obtain a checking of certain personality traits of each pupil on a rating scale, or if a behavior-description form is employed, the annual summary of the anecdotal material may readily be made to conform to the rating scale or the behavior description. This point will be discussed at greater length in another section of this chapter.

LIMITATIONS AND CAUTIONS IN THE PREPARATION OF ANECDOTES

Several limitations and dangers are inherent in anecdotal records, although these can be minimized by observing certain cautions. A number of these have already been suggested, but a more formal listing of them may be helpful.

1. It is apparent, of course, that an anecdotal record can be valuable only if the original observation is accurate and correctly recorded; otherwise, it may be worse than useless. Court records provide ample evidence that reports of observation are often faulty. Frequently, persons do not see what they think they see nor hear what they think they hear. In the school situation, there is especial danger that some observations will be faulty, for in conducting a class a teacher may be able to give only partial attention to a behavior incident and still keep the discussion moving. Great care must therefore be observed. The first rule in the writing of an anecdote is to make sure that the report of behavior is correct. It is far better to omit an anecdote entirely than to turn it in if there is a possibility that it may be incorrect in any detail.

2. Many persons find it extremely difficult to write with complete objectivity, but practice will do a great deal to overcome the tendency to intersperse the report of behavior with statements of opinion. A report of an incident should be as cold and impartial as an X-ray photograph. If the teacher must "let himself go" in describing the incident, he can do so under *comments,* where his remarks will not be prejudicial.

3. A pernicious but fortunately rare use of anecdotal records is their employment for the defense of the person making the report. The central purpose of every anecdotal record is to help the entire school staff to obtain better understanding of a given student. Such a record should never be written to explain or justify action on the part of the teacher. Needless to say, if a behavior incident has created an emotional reaction in a teacher, he should not attempt to prepare an anecdote about it.

4. It is evident that there is danger in lifting a behavior incident out of the social setting in which it occurred and in reporting it in isolation. This is true especially when under the stimulus of group sentiment and action a pupil may behave in a way that is not typical of him. Observers should remember that a brief description of the background against which an action took place is often essential in the reporting.

5. At best, only a small proportion of the total number of significant behavior incidents for any pupil will find its way into anecdotal records. One who is summarizing and interpreting anecdotal records should guard against a tendency to accept a small number of anecdotes as valid evidence of the total picture. The danger at this point will be minimized as more and more anecdotal material is accumulated.

6. Some persons fear that anecdotes, through preserving a record of unfortunate behavior incidents on the part of certain pupils, may prejudice their success long afterward, when the behavior is no longer typical of them. There is ground for this fear if the school carelessly allows the anecdotes to fall into the hands of irresponsible persons. The original records should be regarded as confidential material for which the counselor, or other person entrusted with the care of them, is personally and professionally responsible. On the other hand, the annual summary of the anecdotes, since it does not report specific incidents but is a general

statement of development, is no more confidential than the rest of the cumulative record.

7. It cannot be emphasized too strongly that the adoption of a system of anecdotal records is no small commitment and that it will add inevitably to the load of the entire school, particularly the counselors and the clerical staff. A definite and workable plan for handling the additional clerical work and for summarizing the anecdotes should be developed before the writing of anecdotes is undertaken.

8. It is obvious that the indications in the anecdotal records should be studied and an attempt made to improve the adjustment of the pupils when the anecdotes show that better adjustment is needed. In this connection, however, a caution should be observed. As Zahn (*36*) has pointed out, ordinarily adjustment is a long-term process. There is some danger that anecdotal records will throw the need for the better adjustment of certain pupils into such high relief that too marked an effort will be made to short-cut the adjustment process. Counselors should remember that personality adaptations frequently involve the formation of new sets of habits and that time is required for this.

9. Undesirable behavior, because of its nuisance aspect, is likely to make a stronger impression on teachers than desirable behavior. There is some danger, therefore, that the total effect of anecdotal records will be negative rather than positive. The staff members of a school should train themselves to observe and record evidences of growth even more diligently than they note retarded personality development.

10. Occasionally teachers will observe incidents that are not at all typical of the behavior of the pupil concerned. Sometimes these may be of such a character that they should be recorded, but ordinarily it is desirable to "select those illustrations of conduct which are consistent with the personality of the student as you have observed and understood it" (*22*).

Values and Uses of Anecdotal Records

Various uses and values of anecdotal records have been mentioned in preceding sections of this chapter. According to the writers of published articles on the subject, the following are especially noteworthy.[3]

1. Anecdotal records provide a variety of descriptions concerning the unconstrained behavior of pupils in diverse situations and thus contribute to an understanding of the core or basic personality pattern of each individual and of the changes in pattern.

2. They substitute specific and exact descriptions of personality for vague generalizations.

3. They direct the attention of teachers away from subject matter and class groups and toward individual pupils.

4. They stimulate teachers to use records and to contribute to them.

[3] For additional information concerning values and uses of anecdotal records, see especially Brown and Martin (*6*), Charters (*7*), Randall (*22*), Raths (*23*), Wood (*35*), and Zahn (*36*).

5. They relieve individual teachers of the responsibility of making trait ratings, and provide a basis for composite ratings. Moreover, they provide a continuous record, whereas trait ratings are usually made only at certain points in a pupil's school experience.

6. They encourage teacher interest in and understanding of the larger school problems that are indicated by an accumulation of anecdotes.

7. They provide the information which the counselor needs to control the conferences with individual pupils. An appropriate starting point for each conference can be found in the data, and the discussion can be kept close to the pupil's needs.

8. They provide data for pupils to use in self-appraisal. Whereas in some cases the anecdotes should not be shown to the pupils, each pupil can profitably study the indications in many of the anecdotes about him in order to decide what he needs to do to improve.

9. Personal relationships between the pupil and the counselor are improved by these records, for they show the pupil that the counselor is acquainted with his problems.

10. Anecdotal records aid in the formulation of individual help programs and encourage active pupil participation in remedial work.

11. They show needs for the formation of better work and study habits and also provide encouraging evidence of growth in these respects.

12. Curriculum construction, modification, and emphasis may be improved through reference to the whole volume of anecdotal record material collected by a school. The anecdotes indicate where there should be general presentation of material in character development to satisfy the needs of the whole school community.

13. An appropriate summary of anecdotes is valuable for forwarding with a pupil when he is promoted to another school.

14. Anecdotal records may be used by new members of the staff in acquainting themselves with the student body.

15. The qualitative statements contained in these records supplement and assist in the interpretation of quantitative data.

16. Collections of anecdotal records may provide the necessary validating evidence for various evaluative instruments. For instance, when the results of the Bernreuter Personality Inventory indicate that certain pupils are high in dominance and others are low, the anecdotal record material for these pupils may be analyzed to find out whether or not the Bernreuter scores agree with the observations of behavior.

17. Anecdotal records aid in clinical service. When pupils are referred to clinical workers for special study of their problems, there is a great advantage in having these records available for these highly trained workers to interpret. In this connection, Charters (7) makes the following significant observation concerning the anecdotal records of the Rochester Athenaeum and Mechanics Institute: "How penetrating the accumulated emphasis of these anecdotes is was put to a test recently when a psychiatrist came to the faculty for information about a student of the class of 1933 who had been brought to him as a mild case for

observation. As he and the supervisor exchanged impressions, it appeared that the psychiatrist had uncovered no characteristics that were not already recorded among the anecdotes."

SAMPLE ANECDOTES

The following anecdotes, consisting of reports from four different teachers about the same pupil, show clearly a need for counseling to bring about better adjustment (*15*:197).

Teacher 1. Objective Description: John was late and was told to go to the dean's office for an entrance pass to class. He did not return all period. Another pupil who was late was sent to the same office for a pass, and when he returned was questioned as to the whereabouts of John. The second pupil reported he had not seen him at the dean's office.

Comment: On first writing this anecdote the observer thought that John resented being sent to the dean's office and to show this had cut class. However, the next day it was learned that he had gone to the nurse complaining of illness. To the observer, it represents a shifting of responsibility.

Teacher 2. Objective Description: John became angry when the assignment was longer than he thought it should have been. He said, "I'm not goin' to do that work."

I told him to do what he thought best about it. The next day the assignment was done.

Comment: I believe that John is subject to sudden outbursts of temper. During these times it is useless to talk to him because he seems to expect an argument. I have observed this several times and, after almost every such experience, he does the thing he knows is right, even though he has opposed it.

Teacher 3. Objective Description: Donald, when talking with me, stood beside John's desk. Upon taking his seat, John said, "Donald has the top of my pen." This Donald denied. John insisted, telling him to look in his pocket. There it was found.

Donald immediately handed it to John, saying to me, "He put it there himself. He's always trying to get others in bad."

Comment: I knew John put the top of his pen in Donald's pocket. I have observed that he is very anxious to have attention from boys in the Leaders' Club. He is a member, but does not seem to be entirely taken into the group. Hence his attempts at attention.

Teacher 4. Objective Description: I asked John to sit up front near my desk because he kept annoying his neighbors, even after two warnings.

Comment: John seldom seems to have any work to do, and delights in annoying his neighbors.

The next series of anecdotes, written by an English teacher about a backward pupil, provide encouraging evidence of improvement (*15*:198–199).

English Teacher. Objective Description: Tom informed me before class that he had finished his library book, *The Story of David Livingstone,* which I helped him select last Friday.

Comment: Tom has the lowest score of any freshman on the Iowa test. He usually labors through a book, if he finishes it at all.

This book he liked very much, and I was proud of this achievement—a book read in one weekend.

English Teacher. Objective Description: Tom answered "Unprepared" when the chairman of the Book Club announced him on the program. I asked to see him after school.

Comment: I knew Tom had a book which he had told me he liked. I asked him whether he had read it all. He said he had, but that he couldn't pronounce the names, and he couldn't make a story out of it for the class. I asked why he had not come for help before our meeting. He said he did not think about doing that.

After more questioning, I came to the conclusion that he would have to get even simpler material. He asked me to find another book for him. There are very few books in the library within his capacity, and they are usually out of circulation.

English Teacher. Objective Description: I sent for Tom before school to give him the library book he requested me to choose for him. He promised to "look it over" and to let me know in class whether he wished to keep it.

By afternoon he informed me he had read 103 pages!

"This is interesting," he volunteered.

Comment: That he had finished 103 pages amazed me. Of course, I praised him, and told him of a sequel to the same book.

I have never known the Silver Chief books to fail in their appeal to freshman boys who are very low in their reading ability. We need more books of this caliber.

English Teacher. Objective Description: Before class Tom stopped at my desk to tell me that the librarian had promised to let him know when the sequel to Silver Chief was available.

"Have you finished this one already?" I asked.

He grinned. "Yes, I have."

Comment: This is the same book that started another boy on his reading "career." I wish we had more books with such a universal appeal for non-readers.

English Teacher. Objective Description: Tom was responsible for an oral assignment today. When called upon, Tom shook his head and said he was unprepared.

I asked him to come after school for a talk with me.

English Teacher. Objective Description: Tom is one of my poorest readers, so I wondered at first whether the assignment had been too difficult, but Tom said he knew his assignment without any notes even. Sitting beside my desk, he told his story. I asked him to tell it again, and suggested several improvements. He did it better. I asked him to do it a third time, so that he was thoroughly familiar with it. Then I asked him to go to the rear of the room, and tell his story to me.

"I don't want to do that," he said.

Comment: This is the real difficulty.

English Teacher. Objective Description: Tom was prepared today with his oral report, which he gave without apparent nervousness. It was short, but a real achievement, nevertheless.

Note how the following series of anecdotes present a picture of personality development.[4]

Date	Observer	Anecdotal Record
Sept.	Supervisor	Dorothy's stunt in the Retailing Party was highly original. Her attitude was abrupt and superior. The other girls avoided her.
Nov.	Teacher 9	She monopolized the entire group discussion today.
Dec.	Teacher 8	She told me in conference that the other students do not like her. I tried to explain that it would be desirable to be a little less aggressive and to avoid giving the appearance of feeling superior. She said little in reply and I do not know whether or not I got the idea across.
Jan.	Teacher 7	Dorothy came to me for advice on overcoming characteristics which make students dislike her. She took a difficult assignment in color and design which involved doing a costume analysis and prescription for a classmate who seemed antagonistic to her. She is doing a good job with it.
March	Teacher 7	She gave the other students opportunity to discuss and to work out their share of group assignments.
April	Teacher 7	Several students have told me that they feel she is not so much self-centered as ambitious. They said that she was gaining the cooperation and confidence of nearly all her classmates.
May	Teacher 8	In the sorority, Dorothy has become the person (next to the president) to whom people turn for suggestions, assistance, and leadership. This is true of those who first resented her.

A summary statement for this student's cumulative record might read as follows:

At the beginning of the year, Dorothy's manner was so aggressive, self-centered, and superior that she was very unpopular with the other students. She became aware of her shortcomings and tried, with the help of some of her teachers, to change her behavior. She was so successful that she won the cooperation and confidence of her fellow students, and at the end of the year she was regarded as a leader by her group.

[4] Adapted from Wood (*35*).

RELATION OF ANECDOTAL RECORDS TO PERSONALITY RATINGS AND BEHAVIOR DESCRIPTIONS

Anecdotal records, when properly prepared, provide rather highly objective information which need not replace rating or behavior description plans already established in a school but which may be used as a valuable supplement to established procedures. If a school is using a personality rating scale, the teachers and counselors should be encouraged to keep in mind the traits which are emphasized in the scale and to try to prepare anecdotes which will throw light on these traits. If the American Council on Education Personality Rating Scale is used, for example, there will be special interest in anecdotes that are applicable to the following areas: (1) appearance and manner, (2) industry, (3) ability to control others, (4) emotional control, and (5) distribution of time and energy (5). In such cases, the scale may appropriately be utilized in making annual summaries of the anecdotes.

Some schools, particularly certain progressive ones, are now basing the appraisal of the personality of their pupils on the Behavior-Description plan devised by the Reports and Records Committee of the Eight-Year Study of the Progressive Education Association (29). This plan is designed to secure and record in permanent form judgments of behavior with respect to the traits which the committee decided, after extensive study, were important. It consists of a "behavior-description" filing and transfer card in the form of a folder, a sheet to be used by the teacher in making a report on the pupils, and a "trait-study" manual containing complete directions. The traits included are responsibility-dependability, creativeness and imagination, influence, inquiring mind, open-mindedness, power and habit of analysis, social concern, emotional responsiveness, serious purpose, social adaptability, work habits, physical energy, assurance, self-reliance, and emotional control. A series of descriptive statements is given in connection with each trait and the teacher indicates the one which describes the pupil best. The trait-rating sheets are sent by the teachers to the records office, where the judgments concerning each pupil are transferred to the individual record folders by clerical service. Space is provided on the pupil's folder for recording the judgments of all his teachers from Grade 7 through Grade 12.[5]

The front and back of the experimental edition of the Behavior-Description folder, filled out with a sample record, are shown in Forms 7A and 7B.

As Wood has pointed out, there is no conflict between anecdotal records and behavior descriptions; on the contrary, these plans are supplementary. Anecdotes provide the basic material for behavior descriptions, and there is little doubt that the validity and efficiency of the behavior-description plan is en-

[5] Copies of the Behavior-Description forms may be obtained from the American Education Fellowship, 289 Fourth Avenue, New York 10, N. Y.

hanced when there is a wealth of anecdotal material available for reference.

Two other scales that are essentially devices for obtaining behavior description under standardized conditions are worthy of mention at this point. The first of these is the Detroit Scale for the Diagnosis of Behavior Problems, by Baker and Traphagen. An indispensable adjunct to this scale is an exceptionally complete manual in the form of a book entitled *The Diagnosis and Treatment of Behavior Problem Children* (*1*).

The other instrument is the Vineland Social Maturity Scale, by Edgar A. Doll (*8, 9*). The technique for using the scale has been carefully outlined in a comprehensive manual. A unique feature of this blank is that it yields an age scale and an S.Q., or social quotient, roughly analogous to the I.Q. The scale may be applied to subjects from birth to thirty years of age.

ANNOTATED LIST OF RATING SCALES AND BEHAVIOR DESCRIPTION FORMS

The following is a selected list of rating scales and behavior description blanks. The Roman numerals in parentheses in connection with the citation of each scale are based on the nine-fold classification of devices for appraising personality as given in Chapter VI. The Roman numeral II refers to rating devices, the numeral III to behavior descriptions.

American Council on Education Personality Rating Scale. Washington, D.C.: American Council on Education, 1928; revisions A and B, 1929. 1 cent each. (II)

Revision A is a graphic scale which provides for the rating of five traits: (1) appearance and manner, (2) industry, (3) ability to control others, (4) emotional control, and (5) distribution of time and energy. Below each scale the rater is requested to record instances that support his judgment. Revision B is not graphic, but is filled out by checking one of six alternatives. Designed primarily for college freshmen. Reliability of the average of three raters against the average of three other raters, using 107 freshmen as subjects, was .77. Scale A is now out of print. Reference: Bradshaw (*5*).

Baker, Harry J., and Traphagen, Virginia. *Detroit Scale for the Diagnosis of Behavior Problems.* New York: The Macmillan Company, 1935. 12 cents per case record blank. (III)

A behavior description scale consisting of sixty-six items which are considered significant in the diagnosis of behavior problems. These are grouped as follows: health and physical factors, personal habits and recreational factors, personality and social factors, parental and physical factors of the home, and home atmosphere and school factors. Baker and Traphagen's book, *The Diagnosis and Treatment of Behavior Problem Children,* serves as a manual for administration and a guide for interpretation. All items are scored according to a five-point plan and the scores are added to obtain a total score. Detailed instructions for recording and scoring are given in the book. Data relative to reliability and validity of the scale are reported by the authors in their book. Reliabilities of the total score by the split-half method for three groups are .884, .904, and .964, respectively. Reference: Baker and Traphagen (*1*).

Doll, Edgar A. *The Vineland Social Maturity Scale,* Experimental Form B. Vineland, New Jersey: Department of Research, The Training School at Vineland, 1936. Record blanks, $3.00 per 100; manuals, 25 cents each. (III)

A social maturity scale standardized for normal subjects from birth to 30 years. A behavior description form rather than a rating scale. Judgments are recorded by the examiner after interviewing in detail either some one well acquainted with the subject, or the subject himself. The author warns that at least as much care should be used in mastering the technique as is given to acquiring technique of the Binet scale. The present Vineland scale consists of 117 items aranged in order of difficulty and also grouped by year values. Examples: Year 0–1, balances head, grasps objects within reach; Year 7–8, tells time to quarter hour, disavows literal Santa Claus; Year 25, systematizes own work, shares community responsibility. Yields a raw score, an age score, and an S.Q., which is the subject's age score divided by his life age. A plus score is given for habitual behavior, a minus for absence of behavior, and a ± for occasional behavior. The scale has been used as a developmental measure for normal subjects and also for various types of socially handicapped subjects. Reference: Doll (*8, 9*).

Freeman, Frank N., and Kawin, Ethel. *Teacher's Rating Scales for Pupil Adjustment.* Chicago: University of Chicago Press, 1937. 1 to 9 copies, 25 cents each; 10 to 24 copies, 20 cents each; 25 to 99 copies, 15 cents each; 100 or more copies, 10 cents each. Additional copies of the individual pupil graphs are 25 cents per package of 25. Now out of print. (II)

These scales provide for rating the adjustment of each pupil under five general categories: intellectual characteristics, work and study habits, emotional adjustment, social adjustment, and scholastic adjustment. The scales are so arranged that they provide a behavior analysis both of the class and of the individual pupil. They consist of a booklet and an individual pupil graph. The booklet contains complete instructions for teachers, detailed explanations of the categories, and spaces for recording the names and ratings of forty pupils with respect to each category. A five-step scale is used with 1 as high and 5 as low. All pupils are rated in connection with one scale before the next one is taken up, and the booklet is so arranged that when the teacher turns to the next scale she does not see her ratings on the preceding one. It is probable that this procedure reduces "halo effect." Space is also provided in the booklet for summarizing the ratings assigned to the different pupils. The ratings for the various pupils may be transferred to individual pupil graphs. The blank for the pupil graph also has space for recording information concerning handedness, special abilities, special disabilities, special interests, and special aversions, and the reverse side of the blank is reserved for anecdotal records. The scales are suitable for use from the kindergarten through the junior college.

Haggerty, M. E.; Olson, W. C.; and Wickman, E. K. *Haggerty-Olson-Wickman Behavior Rating Schedules.* Yonkers, New York: World Book Company, 1930. $1.00 per 25; specimen set, $0.15. (II)

Designed for the study of behavior problems and problem tendencies in children. Two schedules, A and B. A is for behavior problems—the rater checks each item to indicate the relative frequency of occurrence of the behavior in the child being rated. Schedule B is a graphic rating scale for intellectual, physical, social, and emotional traits. One form only for elementary grades. No time limit, as it is a rating device. Reliability of Schedule B has been reported in various studies. Correlation coefficients vary from .56 to .92 in nursery, elementary, and high school populations. Correlation between Schedule A and Schedule B, .62. A more reliable measure can be obtained by averaging the ratings of several judges. Reference: Olson (*19*).

Hayes, Margaret. *Scale for Evaluating the School Behavior of Children Ten to Fifteen.* New York: Psychological Corporation, 1933. $1.25 per 25; sample set, 20 cents. (II and IV)

Consists of 100 statements about behavior arranged in eight groups as follows: relation to others generally, respect for rights of others, relation to teacher, relation to other pupils, initiative, health habits, general interests, scholarship and study habits. Intended primarily for use by teachers in rating pupils, but may also be used by pupils for self-rating. One form. Ages 10–15. No time limit; requires about 30 minutes working time. Percentile norms for each behavior group. Chart provided for graphing results. Author reports reliability of .94. Data indicate that the scale differentiates between desirable and undesirable personalities. Reference: Hayes (*11*).

Marston, L. R. *Introversion-Extroversion in Young Children.* Chicago: C. H. Stoelting Company, 1925. $1.00 per 25. (II)

Devised for the rating of introversion-extroversion traits of children between 2 and 6 years of age. Since this is a rating device, there is no time limit. One form. Powers (*21*) had six members of the staff of the Francis E. Willard School rate girls in the school and compared the results. She believes that the scale has a practical value since it yields ratings which indicate the course of remedial treatment. Reference: Marston (*18*).

Merrill-Palmer School *Personality Rating.* Detroit, Michigan: Merrill-Palmer School. 10 cents per set; 25 or more sets, 10 per cent discount; 100 or more sets, 20 per cent discount. (II)

Nine rating schedules for young children including compliance with routine, tendency to face reality, ascendance-submission, attractiveness of personality, physical attractiveness, independence of adult affection, respect for property rights, response to authority, sociability with other children. Standardized according to scaling procedure Thurstone used with his scales for the measurement of social attitudes. Reference: Roberts and Ball (*25*).

Progressive Education Association *Behavior Description*. Reports and Records Committee of the Progressive Education Association, 1938. Sample set, 50 cents; behavior description card, 10 cents; trait study manual, 40 cents; sheets to be used by teachers in reporting on pupils, 50 cents per 100. (III)

A plan, resulting from intensive work over an extended period of time by the Reports and Records Committee, designed to secure and record in permanent form judgments of teachers concerning traits believed to be important. Consists of a "behavior description" filing and transfer card in the form of a folder, a sheet to be used by the teacher in making a report on his pupils, and a "trait study" manual containing complete directions. The traits included are: responsibility-dependability, creativeness and imagination, influence, inquiring mind, openmindedness, power and habit of analysis, social concern, emotional responsiveness, serious purpose, social adaptability, work habits, physical energy, assurance, self-reliance, and emotional control. A series of descriptive statements is given in connection with each trait and the teacher indicates the one which describes the pupil best. Space is provided on the pupil's card for recording judgments of all his teachers from Grade VII through Grade XII. Reference: Manual for Behavior Description, Reports and Records Committee of the Commission on the Relation of School and College of Progressive Education Association (Eugene R. Smith, Chairman).

Rulon, P. J.; Nash, Elizabeth A.; Woodward, Grace L; and others. *B E C Personality Rating Schedule*. Cambridge, Mass.: Harvard University Press, 1936. 50 cents per 25 schedules. (II)

A graphic rating scale prepared under the direction of the Business Education Council which represents the National Office Management Association and the Eastern Commercial Teachers Association. One of the instruments used by the Business Education Council in the certification of certain students who have pursued studies in preparation for office work. The schedule contains eight principal scales, for each of which there are several sub-scales. The principal scales are mental alertness, initiative, dependability, cooperativeness, judgment, personal impression, courtesy, and health. The rating on each principal scale is computed by averaging the ratings on appropriate sub-scales. The average of the eight summary scales may also be recorded in a final summary scale. A ruled line with numbered divisions is provided for each sub-scale. The rater is assisted by appropriate descriptive statements below each of the five main divisions. Grades VII–XVI and adults. References: Rulon (*27*).

Van Alstyne, Dorothy, and the Winnetka Public School Faculty. *Winnetka Scale for Rating School Behavior and Attitudes*. Winnetka, Ill., 1935. 10 cents per copy; 2 cents per directions sheet. (II)

A form for obtaining ratings over a two-year period of the school behavior and attitudes of pupils with respect to the following classification: cooperation, social consciousness, emotional control, leadership, and responsibility. Thurstone's method of factor analysis used in setting up the categories. Ratings assigned at different periods may be combined at the end of the year and the composite ratings in each of the five characteristics shown graphically on a scale of one to ten. Nursery school through Grade VI. Reliability, based on ratings of same teachers at intervals of from two to eight weeks: complete scale, .87; main groupings, .72 to .82. Correlation with Haggerty-Olson-Wickman scale, .71. Reference: Van Alstyne (*32, 34*).

REFERENCES

1. Baker, Harry J., and Traphagen, Virginia. *The Diagnosis and Treatment of Behavior Problem Children.* New York: The Macmillan Co., 1935. Pp. xiv + 393.

2. Barr, A. S. "On the Use of Anecdotal Records," *Journal of Educational Research,* XXXIV (January 1941), 358–360.

3. Blatz, William E., and Bott, E. A. "Studies in Mental Hygiene of Children, I. Behavior of Public School Children: A Description of Method," *Pedagogical Seminary and Journal of Genetic Psychology,* XXXIV (December 1927), 552–582.

4. Bowes, Fern H. "The Anecdotal Behavior Record in Measuring Progress in Character," *Elementary School Journal,* XXXIX (February 1939), 431–435.

5. Bradshaw, F. F. "American Council on Education Rating Scale," *Archiues of Psychology,* CXIX (1930), 1–80.

6. Brown, Marion, and Martin, Vibella. "Anecdotal Records of Pupil Behavior," *California Journal of Secondary Education,* XIII (April 1938), 205–208.

7. Charters, W. W. "A Character Development Study," *Personnel Journal,* XII (August 1933), 119–123.

8. Doll, E. A. "The Vineland Social Maturity Scale," *Training School Bulletin,* XXXII (March, April, May, June 1935), 1–7, 25–32, 48–55, 68–74.

9. Doll, E. A. "Preliminary Standardization of the Vineland Social Maturity Scale," *American Journal of Orthopsychiatry,* VI (1936), 283–293.

10. Hamalainen, Arthur E. *An Appraisal of Anecdotal Records.* Teachers College Contributions to Education, No. 891. New York: Bureau of Publications, Teachers College, Columbia University, 1943. Pp. 87.

11. Hayes, Margaret. "A Scale for Evaluating Adolescent Personality," *Pedagogical Seminary and Journal of Genetic Psychology,* XLIV (March 1934), 206–222.

12. Jarvie, L. L. "Anecdotal Record as a Means of Understanding Students," *Institute for Administrative Officers of Higher Institutions Proceedings,* 1940, pp. 127–142.

13. Jarvie, L. L., and Ellingson, Mark. *Handbook on the Anecdotal Behavior Journal.* Chicago: University of Chicago Press, 1940. Pp. xii + 72.

14. Johnson, O. E. "Cumulative Anecdotal Records," *School Executive,* LXI (February 1942), 28–30.

15. Jones, Galen, and Galbraith, Adria. "An Experiment with Anecdotal Records," *Guidance in Public Secondary Schools,* Chapter XI. New York: Educational Records Bureau, 1939. Pp. xxv + 329.

16. Lloyd-Jones, Esther McD., and Smith, Margaret Ruth. *A Student Personnel Program for Higher Education,* Chapter XVI. New York: McGraw-Hill Book Company, Inc., 1938. Pp. x + 322.

17. McCormick, C. F. "Anecdotal Record in the Appraisal of Personality," *School and Society,* LIII (January 25, 1941), 126–127.

18. Marston, L. R. *The Emotions in Young Children.* University of Iowa Studies in Child Welfare, Vol. III, No. 3, 1925. Pp. 99.

19. Olson, W. C. "Utilization of the Haggerty-Olson-Wickman Behavior Rating Schedules," *Childhood Education,* IX (April 1933), 350–359.

20. Olson, W. C. "The Diagnosis and Treatment of Behavior Disorders of Children," *Educational Diagnosis,* pp. 363–397. Thirty-Fourth Yearbook of the National Society for the Study of Education, Chapter XVIII. Bloomington, Illinois: Public School Publishing Co., 1935. Pp. x + 563.

21. Powers, N. E. "An Application of the Marston Introversion-Extroversion Rating Scale," *Journal of Educational Psychology,* XIX (March 1928), 168–174.

22. Randall, J. A. "The Anecdotal Behavior Journal," *Progressive Education,* XIII (January 1936), 21–26.

23. Raths, Louis. *Anecdotal Records,* Bulletin No. 1 (September 1935). Progressive Education Association, Evaluation in the Eight-Year Study, Ohio State University, Columbus, Ohio. Mimeographed.

24. Report of Subcommittee on Personality Measurement (D. A. Robertson, Chairman). "Personnel Methods," *Educational Record,* Supplement No. 8 (July 1928), 53–68.

25. Roberts, Katherine E., and Ball, Rachel S. "A Study of Personality in Young Children by Means of a Series of Rating Scales," *Pedagogical Seminary and Journal of Genetic Psychology,* LII (March 1938), 79–149.

26. Rugg, Harold O. "Is the Rating of Human Character Practicable?" *Journal of Educational Psychology,* XII (November–December 1921), 425–438, 485–501; XIII (January–February 1922), 30–42, 81–93.

27. Rulon, P. J. "A Personality Rating Schedule," *Harvard Teachers Record* VI (February 1936), 46–53.

28. Smith, Eugene R. "Judging and Recording Pupil Characteristics," *Educational Record,* XV (January 1934), 87–105.

29. Smith, Eugene R.; Tyler, Ralph W.; and the Evaluation Staff. *Appraising and Recording Student Progress,* Chapter X. New York: Harper & Brothers, 1942. Pp. xxiii + 550.

30. Strang, Ruth. *Counseling Technics in College and Secondary School,* pp. 84–86. New York: Harper & Brothers, 1937. Pp. x + 159.

31. Tyler, Ralph W. "Techniques for Evaluating Behavior," *Educational Research Bulletin,* XIII (January 17, 1934), 1–11.

32. Van Alstyne, Dorothy. "A New Rating Scale for Behavior and Attitudes in

the Elementary School," *Journal of Educational Psychology*, XXVII (December 1936), 677–688.

33. Van Alstyne, Dorothy. "A Record for Describing Attitudes and Behavior in the High School," *Journal of Educational Research*, XXXV (December 1941), 276–286.

34. Van Alstyne, Dorothy; Hattwick, L. W.; and Totten, Helen. "New Scale for Rating School Behavior and Attitudes," *Elementary School Journal*, XXXV (October 1936), 115–121.

35. Wood, Ben D. "The Major Strategy of Guidance," *Educational Record*, XV (October 1934), 419–444.

36. Zahn, D. Willard. "Anecdotal Record in Relation to Character Development," *Education for Dynamic Citizenship*, pp. 294–300. Twenty-Fourth Annual Schoolmen's Week Proceedings. Philadelphia: University of Pennsylvania, School of Education, January 25, 1937.

CHAPTER VIII

Planning and Administering a Testing Program for Guidance Purposes

THE NEWER CONCEPT OF A PROGRAM OF INDIVIDUALIZED GUIDANCE AS CONTRASTED WITH the older practice of mass education is concentrating the attention of administrators, teachers, and counselors at all levels of the school on the need for a great variety of information about each individual pupil. In their efforts to obtain records of ability and achievement that have a high degree of objectivity and reliability, an increasing number of schools are introducing programs of measurement. Consequently many questions are being asked concerning how a test program should be planned and what kinds of tests should be used.

Tests for a school guidance program may be divided into two broad categories: those to be used systematically and those for special uses. The tests to be used systematically should be given at regular intervals in a program which is carefully planned in every detail and in which every normal pupil in the school participates fully. The tests for special uses should supplement the regular program and should be administered to individuals and groups as needs arise.

A systematic testing program ordinarily includes tests of three general types: (1) group intelligence tests or tests of academic aptitude; (2) tests of reading ability; and (3) tests of achievement in the subjects commonly included in the academic curriculum or, if the school is one in which subject-matter lines have been broken down, tests in the broad fields of the curriculum. There are so many tests of each type and so many new tests are produced each year that most schools, unless they happen to employ specialists in testing, find the choosing from among the available instruments a baffling problem. The following are among the more important guiding principles of test selection.

1. *First secure a statement of the school's objectives from the faculty of the school itself.* Then choose (or construct) tests that measure the progress of the pupils toward these objectives—or at least toward some of them, for it is improbable

that any test or combination of tests will include all the purposes that a school believes to be important.

2. *Choose tests that have been shown to be highly reliable.* A reliable test is one that measures consistently; that is, if the test is repeated or given in alternate forms, the results obtained are in close agreement. Try to find studies in which the reliabilities of the tests have been reported from several sources. Remember that split-half reliability coefficients are likely to be spuriously high if they involve a speed factor. Give preference to reliability coefficients which result from the administration of different forms of a test and which are based on cases taken from a single grade level rather than from a range of grades.

3. Other things being equal, *select tests for which several comparable forms are available.* This point is important in a regular testing program in order that practice effect may be minimized. The opportunities for systematic testing are even more favorable if a new form of the test is issued each year.

4. Other things being equal, *select tests for which adequate norms are available.* It is helpful to be able to compare the achievement of a given pupil with norms of national scope as well as with the local population. Private schools and public schools in residential districts of suburban communities usually find the independent-school norms prepared by the Educational Records Bureau of more value than norms for unselected public schools.

5. When a number of different achievement tests are being given to the same group of pupils, *it is helpful to select tests that are scaled on a common criterion group.* Obviously, if the raw scores are translated into derived scores that have the same meaning for all tests, comparisons of achievement in different subject fields will be greatly facilitated.

6. Other things being equal, *choose tests that can be scored objectively, rapidly, and inexpensively.* Objectivity of scoring is ordinarily a practical necessity from the standpoint both of reliability of scoring and of economy. Rapidity of scoring is highly desirable in order that the results may be used in guidance and instruction before interest has waned. Inexpensive scoring is usually essential since most budgets for testing are limited. In this connection every school should investigate the possibilities inherent in the electrical test-scoring machine of the International Business Machines Corporation.

A school which can afford to administer on a systematic basis only one test annually to all pupils will do well to select a group test of general academic aptitude, for a test of this kind naturally tends to be more highly correlated with academic achievement in general than tests whose functions are specialized. The present tendency among test specialists is to recommend tests that yield separate verbal and numerical scores in preference to tests that provide only a single total score, mental age, or I.Q.

Next to an intelligence test probably the test that has the most general usefulness is a silent reading test. Reading ability plays so large a part in academic success, particularly in the verbal subjects and in vocational adaptability, that in every guidance program the reading achievement of all pupils should be checked regularly. Moreover, many personality aberrations have their root in the failure of the child to learn to read and thus to make one of the most important of all adaptations to his social environment. A still further reason for measuring reading is that no conclusion concerning intelligence that is based on the usual group test of mental ability is really valid unless the reading ability of the pupil is known.

STEPS IN PLANNING AND CONDUCTING A TESTING PROGRAM

The values of measurement depend to a great extent on the care with which the testing program is planned and carried out. The responsibility for the testing program should be centered in a member of the school staff who will give patient attention to the planning of the entire program each year, who will faithfully administer every detail, and who will make it his business to see that the test records of every pupil are complete, unless there are extenuating circumstances which make it impossible for the pupil to take the tests. The following rules for administering a testing program have been found useful in actual practice:

1. Select the test carefully, preferably in cooperation with a faculty committee. If there is a state testing program in your state, consider carefully the tests recommended in connection with that program, for they are usually selected by experts in measurement and guidance. Take into account the tests recommended by an independent organization such as the Educational Records Bureau in connection with its fall and spring testing programs. The tests for those programs are chosen by a committee of teachers from member schools of the Bureau, working in cooperation with test specialists on the Bureau's staff.

2. Order the tests well in advance of the date on which they are to be used. Allow plenty of time to get all the materials in readiness before the day on which the tests are to start.

3. Plan *in detail* for the administration of the tests. Choose examiners and proctors with great care. If possible, use examiners who have had previous experience in giving the objective type of test. If inexperienced examiners must be used, they should be rehearsed beforehand. Remember that some very intelligent people are temperamentally unsuited to the exacting routine of administering a test. You may use such persons as proctors where tests are being given to larger groups, but they should not be placed in charge of the administration of a test.

4. Mimeograph an examination schedule and see that every person concerned receives a copy of it. The schedule should give the time and place of each test, indicate just where each class which is to take the test is to go, where the pupils who are not taking the test should be during that hour, what material the pupils will need when taking the test, and the name of the faculty member in charge at each examination.

5. Avoid overemphasis on the tests. Urge the teachers to have the pupils take them "in stride."

6. Give pupils who have never taken objective tests an opportunity to examine old tests of this kind. Better still, have them take a short practice test of the objective type.

7. Do not distribute the tests to the examiners before the day of the examination. Have packages containing the requisite numbers of test booklets made up and ready for the examiners when the date for the tests arrives.

8. Provide each examiner with a manual and a sample copy of the test several days before the examination and urge him to study the manual and to practice by taking the test himself. Most errors in the administration of tests are caused by the failure of the examiner to prepare sufficiently beforehand.

9. Provide each examiner and proctor with a written set of instructions outlining his duties during the examination.

10. When administering tests to large groups:

    a. Make arrangements so that there will be no interruptions or distractions during the testing period. Persons should not come into or go out of the room unless absolutely necessary.

    b. Seat the pupils in alternate chairs if possible.

    c. See that each proctor understands what is expected of him.

    d. Make announcements slowly and clearly in a voice that is loud enough to be heard throughout the room. Assume a businesslike and efficient attitude that will command attention, but do not be unnecessarily severe. Remember that some pupils become nervous when faced with an examination.

    e. Have proctors supply all pupils with booklets and pencils. Announce that the pupils are not to write on the booklets nor to open them until so instructed.

    f. Have the blanks on the front of the booklets filled out. Be sure to announce the date, how names are to be written, and other items that may need clarification. Spend sufficient time on this step to see that the information is given correctly by the pupils. Ages and birth dates are especially important on tests of academic aptitude.

    g. Hold faithfully to the exact wording of the printed directions unless there is an excellent reason for introducing a minor variation in them. The preparation of directions for a test is one aspect of test construction and standardization. The wording of the directions has been carefully thought out by the test author. Don't improvise or introduce short cuts. If you do, you may change the test results significantly.

    h. Time the examination with extreme care, using a watch which has a second hand and which has been checked for accuracy. It is advisable to have one of the proctors check your timing to be sure that no error occurs. In many tests accurate timing is the most important single feature of the entire procedure of administering them.

    i. Move about the room occasionally to see that all pupils are working on the right part of the examination, but do not stand gazing over a pupil's shoulder until he becomes self-conscious, and do not constantly move nervously from pupil to pupil.

   j. Stop the examination immediately when the time is up and collect the booklets.

11. As soon as a certain test has been given, have all examiners turn in their booklets promptly. Alphabetize and check the test papers against the class lists.

12. Except in cases of protracted illness, *see that all absentees make up the examination.* You will find this part of the testing program a great nuisance and you will feel that it is not worth the bother, but it is an unavoidable step, for complete data are essential if the results are to be used successfully in either teaching or guidance. Moreover, if the pupils once discover that absentees do not have to make up the tests, a few escapists will conveniently be ill every time an examination period arrives.

13. See that the tests are scored promptly. Report the results to the faculty in a form that they can use and provide them with an explanation of the meaning of the results.

14. Have the scores of each pupil entered on an individual cumulative record card and make this card available to both counselors and classroom teachers. The card may also be shown to the parents if the data are carefully explained in conference.

With regard to step number four in the foregoing list of suggestions, the following "General Directions Concerning Fall Testing Program" provide an appropriate illustration of the recommended procedure. These directions were distributed in mimeographed form to the students in the Hill School, Pottstown, Pennsylvania, in connection with the Fall, 1943 testing program in that school.

GENERAL DIRECTIONS CONCERNING FALL TESTING PROGRAM [1]

(Do not lose these sheets!)

1. There will be a General School Meeting on Thursday evening at 7:45 P.M. in Memorial Hall. All boys, *including day students,* must attend.

2. The tests start on Thursday evening and continue through Saturday noon. There will be no classes on Friday and Saturday.

3. Read carefully Page 2 in order to determine which tests you are to take.

4. Consult Page 3 for the schedule of these tests.

5. Consult the Common Room Bulletin Boards to find out the room in which you will take a given examination. *YOU WILL NOT HAVE ALL YOUR TESTS IN THE SAME ROOM.* Therefore, be sure to consult the Bulletin Board

---

[1] Prepared by Ralph C. Johnson, director of personnel study in The Hill School, Pottstown, Pennsylvania, and used with his permission.

before each test and PLEASE DO NOT WAIT UNTIL THE LAST MINUTE TO DO THIS.

6. Be in your seat in the examination room at least five minutes ahead of the scheduled examination time. EXAMINATIONS WILL START ON TIME! The tests are spaced close together and it is important that everyone be on time.

7. Be sure to have with you at each test a SUPPLY of well-sharpened pencils. Ink must not be used.

8. No one may leave the room until the end of each test. WAIT FOR DISMISSAL. You will need all the time allotted.

9. On each test you must indicate the name of the course you are taking in that subject, giving the exact full name. For example:

6F. Honor English	2F. English
6F. Special English	5F. Mathematics
4F. French A	5F. Geometry

et cetera

Be sure you know the name of your instructor and how to spell his name.

10. THE MOST IMPORTANT THING IN TAKING THE TESTS IS TO FOLLOW ALL DIRECTIONS VERY CAREFULLY. *Wise* guessing may improve your score. *Wild* guessing *will* lower it. Don't be a gambler!

The scores you receive on these tests will be recorded on your cumulative record card. Make yourself look as brilliant as possible!

WHICH EXAMINATION DO YOU TAKE? *This sheet tells you. Read it carefully.*

SOCIAL SCIENCE
Everybody in school *except 2nd Form.*

AMERICAN COUNCIL PSYCHOLOGICAL EXAMINATION
Everybody in school *except 2nd Form.*

KUHLMANN–ANDERSON TEST
2nd Form only.

IOWA SILENT READING TEST
Everybody in school *except 2nd Form.*

TRAXLER SILENT READING TEST
2nd Form only.

FRENCH (*advanced*)
Those taking 4F. French A., 5F., 6F., and Special French.

FRENCH (*elementary*)
Those taking 4F. French.

GERMAN
Those taking 4F., 5F., 6F., and Special German.

SPANISH

Those taking 4F. and 5F. Spanish.

MATHEMATICS

Gen. Achievement Math. . . . . .5F. Geom., 5F., and 6F. Math.

Mathematics, 7, 8, 9 . . . . .2F., 3F., 4F., Algebra & 4F. Math.

ENGLISH

Everybody in school.

LINCOLN SPELLING TEST

Everybody in school.

SCHEDULE OF TESTS—October 1943

Note: The starting time indicates the time that the examiner will start the examination. YOU MUST BE IN YOUR SEAT FIVE MINUTES BEFORE STARTING TIME.

BE SURE TO CONSULT:

1. Page 2—"Which Examinations do you take?"
2. The Common Room Seating Lists.

. . . .

THURSDAY, October 14.

7:45 P.M. General School Meeting in Memorial Hall.

8:15 P.M. Social Science Test.

FRIDAY, October 15.

9:00 A.M. American Council Psychological Examination.

Kuhlmann-Anderson Test.

10:45 A.M. All tests in Mathematics.

2:00 P.M. French, German, and Spanish Tests.

7:45 P.M. Iowa Silent Reading Test.

Traxler Silent Reading Test.

9:00 P.M. Lincoln Spelling Test.

SATURDAY, October 16

9:00 A.M. All English Tests.

AFTER YOU HAVE READ THIS SEE IF THERE ARE ANY CONFLICTS; IF SO, REPORT THEM TO MRS. MERWIN, PERSONNEL OFFICE, *BEFORE NOON ON THURSDAY.*

Test Information for Students [2]

Suggestions concerning the taking of objective tests which may be mimeographed on a single page and given to each pupil are contained in the following paragraphs:

[2] Adapted from a sheet prepared by Ralph D. Britton, The Loomis School, Windsor, Connecticut.

The purpose of this sheet is to inform you about the general nature of some tests you will take within the next few days. The purpose in giving them is to inform your teachers and counselors about your ability and your needs so that they can provide the best possible learning and guidance conditions for you.

Each test contains a large number of questions calling for very brief answers. For most of the questions, several answers are suggested and you will be asked to select the one which you think is right. You should not become discouraged if you find some questions which you are unable to answer, for you are not expected to answer all the questions. Some of the tests are used in several grades and, of course, the pupils in the lower grades are not expected to answer as many questions as those in the higher ones. It is almost impossible for even the most advanced student to obtain a perfect score.

It is advisable to answer some questions about which you are not entirely sure. If you think you know the answer, you should put it down, even though you are not certain, but you should not guess wildly on questions concerning which you are totally uninformed. In some tests in which a certain proportion of the wrong answers is subtracted from the correct answers, blind guessing may result in a large reduction in one's score.

There is no passing mark for these tests. Results will be expressed in percentiles which will show how you stand in comparison with other students in the same grade or class who take the same test in many different schools.

Since time is an important element, be sure to have at least two well-sharpened pencils and an eraser. Do not use ink because of the possibility of the pen running dry and the difficulty of erasing.

Some tests are to be given with special answer sheets so that they may be scored by means of an electrical machine. If you take one of these tests, you will be given a practice test to acquaint you with the way in which the answer sheets should be marked. The important thing to remember is to use *only* the special pencil which will be furnished you and to make heavy black marks.

Points to Keep in Mind When Taking the Test

1. *Listen carefully* to all instructions given by the examiner and follow them exactly.
2. You are not expected to answer *all* the questions but *answer as many as you can*.
3. Work as *rapidly* as you can, spending very little time puzzling over difficult questions. Return to the hard questions if you have time after you have gone through the test.
4. Guess only if you can do so *intelligently*. Don't guess if you know nothing about the question.
5. Go to the examination room with *two pencils* and an eraser. If a special pencil is given to you use it *only*.
6. Do not waste your spare time during the days on which the examinations are scheduled, but spend the time as constructively as you would during any school day.

NEED FOR PLAN OF USING TEST RESULTS

It cannot be emphasized too often that the administration of tests is merely a means to an end. The purpose of testing is to obtain data that can be used in improving the instruction, distribution, and adjustment of individual boys and girls. Too often persons in charge of testing programs feel that they have discharged their responsibility when reports of the results have been filed, and any use that is made of the results is left to the initiative of individual staff members.

Every school should have a carefully planned program for using the results of all tests given to the pupils. The first step in this program is to provide each counselor and teacher with a copy of the test results which are of special concern to that particular staff member. The second step is to record the results cumulatively on some meaningful and comparable basis, such as Scaled Scores or percentiles. The test scores should be merely one of several important parts of a comprehensive record form which covers several years and contains a digest of all pertinent information about each pupil. Along with the cumulative-record system there should go a vigorous and continuous program of educating the school staff in the interpretation and the use of the records. Test technicians, statisticians, psychologists, psychiatrists, and clinicians can well cooperate in training the school staff. The most important aspect of the training, however, is the daily experience that each staff member should have in using the data in solving the problems of his own pupils, until he habitually turns to objective records as his most useful tool in individualizing instruction and fulfilling his guidance function.

CHAPTER IX

Scoring, Organizing, and Reporting
Test Results

AS SUGGESTED IN THE PRECEDING CHAPTER, IF A TESTING PROGRAM IS TO BE OF ANY great value in the guidance work of a school, it is necessary that the tests be scored accurately and quickly and that the results be reported to the teachers in a form that they can and will use. Unless the whole program is carefully planned, there is danger that the scoring of the tests will be allowed to drag over a period of several weeks until the teachers have lost all interest in them. A still more serious danger is that of inaccuracy of scoring. Objective scoring with an answer key seems such an easy, mechanical procedure that novices in testing are likely to be entirely unaware of the difficulties involved. The work may be placed unknowingly in incompetent hands, for some otherwise intelligent and capable persons seem constitutionally not fitted for a mechanical task such as scoring papers. Sample checking of scoring frequently reveals a surprisingly high percentage of errors, some of which are serious enough to affect the standing of the pupil significantly.

In general, there are three ways of getting the scoring done after the tests have been administered—local hand scoring, local machine scoring, and scoring by a service agency. Let us consider briefly what is involved in each plan.

Local Hand Scoring. If the tests are to be scored at the local school, one of the first and most important questions concerns the personnel to be used in the scoring. Probably the most common, but certainly the least satisfactory procedure, is to have the teachers or counselors do the scoring. A teacher may be a good instructor but a very poor scorer.[1] Teachers as a group are probably no more efficient scorers than office clerks. Since the salaries of teachers and coun-

---

[1] Arthur E. Traxler. "A Note on the Accuracy of Teachers' Scoring of Semi-Objective Tests," *Journal of Educational Research*, XXXVII (November 1943), pp. 212–213.

selors are higher (or should be higher) than those of clerks, it is obviously poor economy to use them for scoring.

A more important reason for not assigning the scoring of objective tests to teachers is that this routine drudgery takes valuable time and energy that should be used in planning instruction and guidance. In answer to this statement, it is sometimes insisted by administrators that the scoring of tests is valuable experience for teachers because they believe that this work acquaints the teachers with the strengths and weaknesses of their pupils. This argument would have validity if a scorer of objective tests were obliged to read each question and evaluate each answer, but that is not the way efficient scoring is done. One compares a key with the answers of the pupils and checks the right and the wrong responses mechanically. It is true that the teacher could take the time to study each pupil's paper while correcting it, but this would not be scoring; it would be diagnosis. Diagnosis is a necessary step for the teacher to take, but it should not be confused with the scoring of the papers. It is reasonable to believe that both the diagnosis and the scoring will suffer if the teacher's attention is thus divided between two unrelated activities.

Although the use of teachers or counselors in scoring is not advised, it is realized that in some schools the instructional and counseling staff will continue to do this kind of work because no other services are available for it. When this is necessary, it is desirable to observe the following rules:

1. Make sure that each teacher understands just how the scoring is to be done.
2. Rescore the first few papers scored by each teacher and make suggestions for the elimination of errors as needed.
3. Thereafter, check the scoring of every fifth or sixth paper and the addition of part scores on all papers.
4. Completely rescore the test booklets marked by all teachers who average more than one scoring error a paper.

For objective hand scoring that is to be done locally, it is preferable to hire clerks who are specially selected for this purpose. They should be placed under a supervisor, who will carefully check their scoring and insist upon a high standard of accuracy and reasonable speed. The checking of counting and addition is more important than the checking of the scoring of individual items, since it is in counting and adding that large errors are usually made.

Local Machine Scoring. The most revolutionary development in the scoring of objective tests has been the production of the electrical, test-scoring machine of the International Business Machines Corporation. Some of the larger school systems have been using this time-saving machine for nearly ten years, but it is still a novelty to the staff members of most schools. Since it will probably have an increasing influence on objective testing during the next few years, it seems appropriate to discuss the machine at some length.

Although the scoring machine is a fairly recent invention, the idea of a mechanical device for scoring tests goes back several years. One of the first persons to suggest the feasibility of a machine of this kind was Dr. Ben D. Wood of Columbia University, who saw the need in connection with the great volume of test scoring required by the Pennsylvania study carried on by the Carnegie Foundation for the Advancement of Teaching. President Thomas J. Watson of the International Business Machines Corporation became interested in the idea and various procedures were tried out, but for a time no satisfactory plan was evolved. Finally, Reynold B. Johnson, a young science instructor, who later became an engineer in the laboratories of the International Business Machines Corporation, set up a model that became the basis of the present machine.

The scoring machine makes use of the elementary fact that a soft lead pencil will conduct an electric current. Instead of indicating his answers in the test booklet in the usual manner, the pupil records them on an answer sheet similar to the one shown in Figure 3.[2] Each side of the standard answer sheet provides for answers to 150 questions, with a maximum of five choices to each question. Instead of writing the number of his choice for each item in a designated place, as is done in the ordinary objective test, the pupil indicates it by penciling a heavy mark between the printed lines in the position which represents the number of his choice.

The scoring machine is so constructed that it contains 750 sensing units corresponding to the 750 possible choices on the answer sheet. Each sensing unit is connected in series with a high resistance coil which allows an infinitesimal but definite amount of electricity to flow through the unit when the connection is made by means of a pencil mark. After the test has been given, the machine is set by means of a master scoring key which divides the current into two circuits—one for the right responses and one for the wrong responses. The answer sheets are then dropped one by one through a slot in the machine and the score is read from an ammeter conveniently placed in front of the operator.

The great advantage of the scoring machine, of course, lies in the fact that it works with the speed of electricity and that it will score up to 150 five-choice items at once, or an even larger number of items having fewer choices. It has been found that an experienced operator can score as many as 500 tests an hour with no error of more than one point.

The scoring machine has been equipped with an item analysis unit which makes it possible to secure a graphic record of the number of right responses given by a class or other group to each item in the test as the tests are being scored. The advantages of this unit for research purposes and for diagnosis and reteaching are obvious.

The scoring machine can be set so that formulae for correcting for guessing,

[2] Reprinted by permission of the International Business Machines Corporation.

such as R—W in true-false tests, and R—W/4 in five-response tests, are applied automatically and the corrected score is shown on the meter.

A limitation to machine scoring, as far as the classroom use of the tests is concerned, is that although the machine shows the score of the pupil it does not mark each individual item. Therefore, if one wishes to note just what questions a given pupil has answered correctly, resort must be had to supplementary procedures such as a punched-out key that can be superimposed on the pupil's paper.

Another limitation is that all items must be phrased strictly in objective form, such as multiple-choice items and matching items. Some persons may try to force all tests into purely objective form even though their content may not be adapted for the objective type of item, although the distributors of the machine, as well as psychologists and test constructors, are taking the precaution of warning users that not all kinds of testing material are at present suitable for machine scoring.

The extent to which test publishers are recognizing the availability of the scoring machine, by making the changes that are necessary in order to set their tests up for machine scoring, varies considerably. The Cooperative Test Service has adapted practically all the Cooperative tests for machine scoring either with special answer sheets or standard sheets. The World Book Company has prepared special answer sheets for a large number of the tests it publishes and has provided special features to facilitate the alignment of the answer sheets with the test booklets. The California Test Bureau has adapted its more important tests for the scoring machine. Several other companies are publishing machine-scorable tests, and even the more conservative ones are making provision for the use of a few of their tests with standard answer sheets. Thus far the machine-scored tests for secondary schools and colleges are more numerous than those for elementary schools.

The hesitancy of some test authors to revise their tests for machine scoring is understandable in view of the fact that if the nature of the items is changed to make them purely objective, it is necessary to prepare new norms. The proper standardization of a test is a very tedious and expensive procedure. Moreover, if the score is based partly upon a speed factor, it is necessary to go to the additional trouble of equating the results of hand-scored booklets and machine-scored answer sheets, for the use of the answer sheet causes those taking the test to work at slower speed than they would if they marked their answers in the booklet.

Cost is an important aspect of machine scoring. The International Business Machines Corporation does not sell the scoring machine but rents it at a charge of four hundred eighty dollars a year, which includes servicing the machine. This amount would be a small item in the budget for testing in a large city

NAME OF TEST Biology   PART

GRADE OR CLASS 10   INSTRUCTOR Miss Clark

DATE OF BIRTH March 7, 1929   AGE 15   SEX M
M. OR F.

SCORES

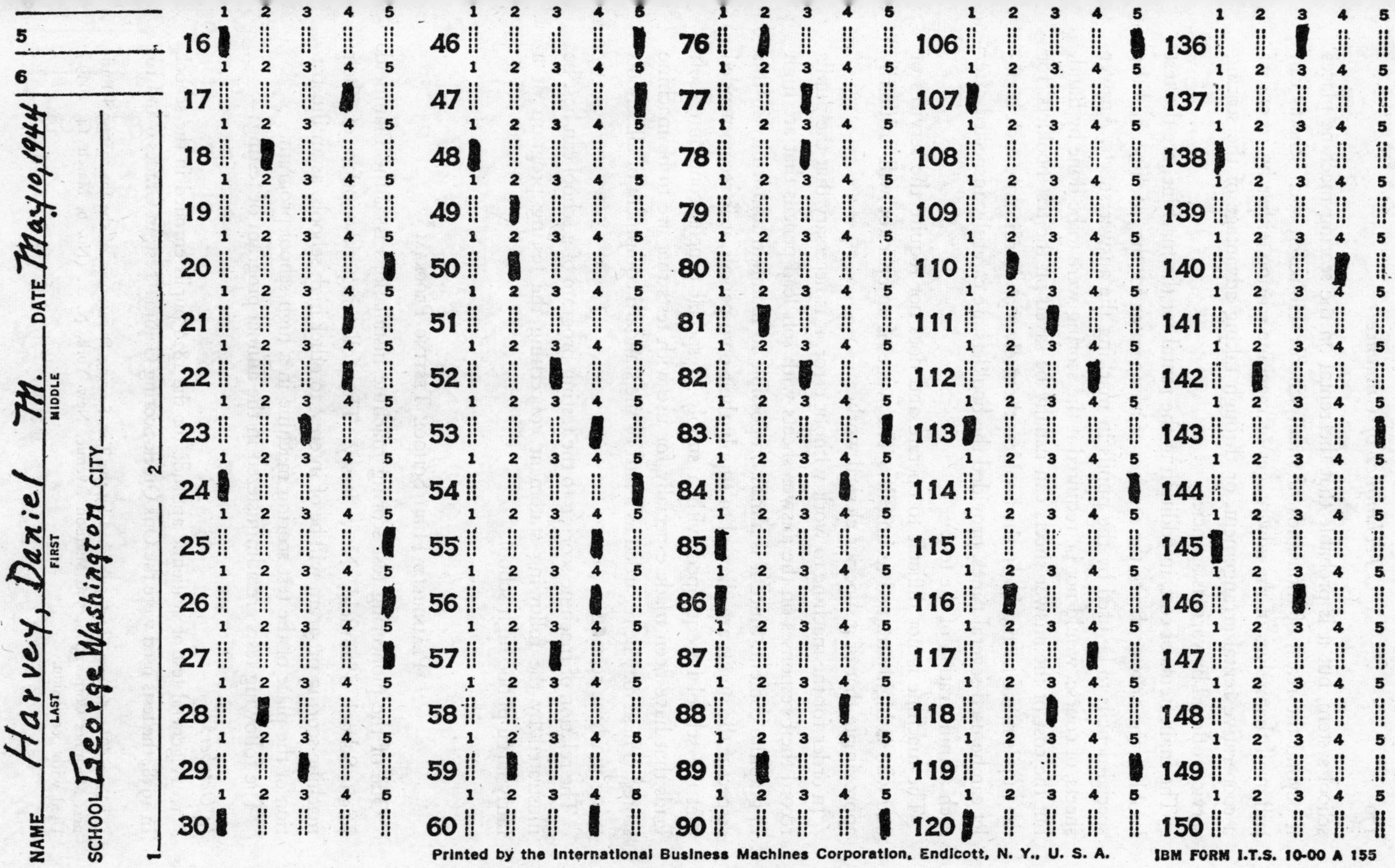

FIGURE 3. Answer Sheet for Test Scoring Machine. (Used with permission.)

school system, but it is probable that the rental on the scoring machine places it beyond the reach of thousands of small schools. However, such schools can still avail themselves of the advantages of machine scoring, either by means of a cooperative rental arrangement, or through taking advantage of the scoring services offered by various agencies.

The main items of cost, in addition to the rental for the machine, are the test booklets, the answer sheets, the services of an operator for the machine, and the special pencils to be used by the pupils in marking the answer sheets. Answer sheets, of course, would not be required if the scoring were to be done by hand, but the cost of the answer sheets can usually be saved on the test booklets, for the pupils make no marks on the booklets themselves and ordinarily each book-let can be used several times, provided the booklets are carefully inspected after each administration of the test.

The machine is not difficult to operate and does not require the services of one who is highly trained technically. The wage of an operator will ordinarily approximate that of a superior clerical worker.

In order for the machine to work without error, it is necessary that the pupils record their responses on the answer sheets with soft lead pencils that are high in graphite content. Since it is almost impossible to maintain uniformity in this respect if the pupils are allowed to supply their own pencils, it is recommended that the school be equipped with a supply of special pencils containing soft leads that have been made especially for use with tests that are to be machine scored. These may be regarded as a part of the standard equipment of all schools using machine scoring.

The relation of machine scoring to the testing program of a school can best be illustrated by the following statement concerning the testing program of a fairly large public high school.

PLAINFIELD HIGH SCHOOL TESTING PROGRAM [3]

One of the pioneering test scoring machine installations is at the Plainfield High School, Plainfield, New Jersey. The following description of their machine-scoring program will be of interest to other high schools, as an illustration of the place of the test scoring machine in a high school program.

The following tests are administered in the annual program of testing:

In October:

1. A general test of academic aptitude for the 1820 pupils enrolled in the school. In 1938, the tests used were the Otis Quick-Scoring Gamma Test, in Grades 9 and 10;

[3] From *The Answer Sheet,* published by the Test Scoring Department of the International Business Machines Corporation, 590 Madison Avenue, New York, N. Y. (No. 6, March 14, 1939.) Used with permission.

and the American Council Psychological Examination for College Freshmen, Form 1938, in Grades 11 and 12.

2. The Iowa Silent Reading Tests, in Grades 9 and 10; also the Traxler High School Reading Test in all grades.

In April:
1. Iowa Algebra Aptitude Test, in Grade 8.
2. Iowa Plane Geometry Aptitude Test, for all pupils electing Algebra 1.

In June:
Cooperative tests in the five academic areas for which these tests are prepared.

The essential program for 1937–1938 included 11,080 standardized tests administered, scored, reported, and recorded.

All tests now used in the annual program, with the exception of the Iowa tests, are machine-scored.

The machine is used not only for scoring the tests given in the annual testing programs, but also for scoring classroom quizzes, final examinations, etc., which are constructed by the teachers. Since October 1, 1938, twenty-nine objective tests constructed by teachers in the English, Science, History, and Commercial departments have been administered to a total of 4,256 pupils.

The Plainfield administration has noted the following benefits resulting from the elimination of the tedium of hand scoring:

1. By making test results almost instantly available, the machine has increased the efficiency of the testing program, and has decreased the probability of a loss of interest on the part of the teachers concerned, during the time required for hand scoring.

2. By making use of a standard answer sheet that is now carried in stock for objective tests which they prepare, teachers may have these tests scored by the office on the same day on which they are given, thus decreasing the clerical burden of classroom testing.

3. Since the test booklets are not marked in any way by the pupils, the tests purchased annually, formerly written off as current expenses, now become part of the school's permanent library of tests. At present this library contains about 18,000 tests, which may be administered at any time in the school year that the teacher feels it would be advisable, for checking progress or for diagnosis.

Scoring by a Service Agency. Many schools are now taking advantage of the scoring services provided by various agencies. This plan insures accuracy of scoring and statistical work and relieves the local school of a great deal of routine work. Both hand- and machine-scoring services are provided by various state bureaus and at least one organization of national scope, the Educational Records Bureau. A report of the scoring procedures used by the Educational Records Bureau may perhaps be suggestive to schools that are obliged to do their own scoring locally.

The Educational Records Bureau is a research and service agency for about 380 member institutions, most of which are independent, or private, elementary and secondary schools. It is a self-supporting organization. Its income is derived mainly from its services in connection with scoring and reporting the results of tests for the schools belonging to the Bureau. It does not construct tests, but through a committee composed of representatives from its member schools, it selects from the available tests those which seem best adapted to the needs of the whole group of schools taking part in the testing. A limited portion of the Bureau's scoring services is available to non-members, although it is expected that institutions using the services regularly will become members of the organization.

Two testing programs are conducted annually by the Bureau's member schools. The fall program consists of academic aptitude and reading tests, along with some achievement tests for placement and diagnosis. In the spring, a comprehensive achievement testing program is conducted in all academic subjects at the elementary and secondary school levels. Every member school is free to participate as little or as fully as desired in the testing programs. The schools obtain the tests with complete directions for giving them from the Bureau. The tests are administered by the schools themselves, usually within a specified period, although they are free to utilize the services of the Bureau at other times if they so desire. Some of the schools score their tests locally, but the majority return them for central scoring by the Bureau's staff at a per-test-per-pupil cost. Norms for independent schools are prepared from the results of the tests scored at the Bureau.

Most of the schools participating in the testing programs are independent schools whose enrollments, in comparison with those of public schools, are rather small. The teachers are able to do a considerable amount of diagnostic work with the test results provided the scored test booklets are returned. Hand scoring, therefore, is still used more extensively than machine scoring in connection with the independent-school tests.

During a testing program, the tests from as many as 150 schools may be returned to the Bureau almost simultaneously. The careful organization of all details of the scoring and reporting, therefore, is absolutely essential. During the testing season the scoring is set up in departments according to the nature of the different tests and about half of the Bureau's regular staff of twenty persons serve as supervisors of these departments. Most of the actual scoring work is done by part-time employees who have been carefully selected for this work.

Each applicant for a scoring position is given a scorer's test, in which a regular scoring situation is approximated as nearly as possible. Many copies of the same standardized test, filled out as if students had taken them, are available. The applicants, who frequently are tested in groups, are supplied with copies of the test and with scoring keys. They proceed to score the test according to a definite set of directions. Their scoring is then evaluated for both accuracy and speed.

Percentile norms for scoring are available on several hundred cases. Under normal employment conditions, only those whose percentiles are above 75, in both accuracy and speed, are considered for scoring positions.

Formerly an intelligence test was also administered to the applicants for scoring work, but this has been discontinued since it does not appear that the results of the usual verbal test of mental ability are very highly correlated with success in objective scoring. It is possible that some of the mental tests highly saturated with a perceptual factor would be more closely related to scoring ability.

A scorer is assigned to a certain department and usually works on one particular type of test. The work done in any department is always identified by the initials of scorers so that responsibility can be allocated definitely. The papers scored by new employees are always completely rescored. After a worker has satisfactorily demonstrated his accuracy, the rescoring is reduced to the checking of one paper in five, except in the case of certain very important tests. However, such operations as the counting of number of right answers, and the addition of part scores in tests containing several sections, are invariably done twice.

When the tests are received from the schools they go to the classification department where they are inspected for discrepancies and carefully separated into the proper groups as determined by number of years of study and other factors. The amount of time that will be needed for scoring is estimated and the report to the school is scheduled for a certain date.

As fast as the scoring of a certain type of test is completed, the test booklets are turned over to members of the staff whose responsibility it is to make distributions of the scores and to compute medians, quartiles, and any other statistical data that are needed. The booklets then go to the typists who type alphabetical class lists showing the scores of the various pupils. These lists are made in triplicate. When all distributions and lists have been made and the work has been checked, the various parts of the report are assembled and inspected by the chief scoring supervisor.

The assembled report, together with the school's statistical folders for preceding testing programs, is sent to the desk of another member of the staff, who is trained in psychological, measurement, and guidance techniques. He dictates an extensive letter in which the results are explained and interpreted in considerable detail for the school to which the report is going. This report is preliminary in nature, unless norms for independent schools based on an earlier testing program are available for the tests included in the report. At the end of the program, independent-school percentiles are computed on the basis of the scores from all participating schools, and a second report showing the percentile ratings of each individual pupil is sent to each school.

Almost the same general plan is followed in connection with the machine scoring that is done at the Bureau, except that all the actual scoring is done in a single department and one machine operator replaces several scorers. Operators usually work in shifts of about two hours' duration.

The scoring and reporting procedures of the Educational Records Bureau have been described in considerable detail because during the seventeen years that the Bureau has been rendering this type of service to its member schools, these procedures have proved sound, and it is believed that some of them could be followed in local scoring. Such a plan might readily be adopted with modifications in a uniform testing program involving all the schools in a city school system. Careful systematizing and supervision of the scoring work, together with a thorough plan for checking every important operation, insures the accuracy and speed which are the prime essentials of every testing program.

REPORTING PROCEDURES

In any testing program worthy of the name, it is imperative that the results be placed in the hands of the teachers and counselors as soon as possible. Too often a school will end its testing program with the scoring of the tests, apparently under the mistaken impression that the mere taking of the tests will bring about improvement.

The emphasis in reporting results of tests to the faculty should be on the scores of individuals rather than on group comparisons, although the achievement of groups may well receive some attention. An adequate summary report of the results of tests consists of at least two types of record: (*a*) distributions of scores by classes, together with medians and quartiles, or means and standard deviations; and (*b*) alphabetical class lists showing the part scores, total scores, and percentile ratings of individual pupils.

Lists and Distributions of Scores. In preparing class lists, it is desirable to show the scores made on the parts of the test, as well as the total score, if such part scores are of sufficient practical importance and reliability to be used as a basis for studying the pupils and for planning teaching procedures. Percentile ranks, standard scores, or other derived measures, as well as raw scores, should be shown on the lists. A sample class list is shown in Table 1.[4]

The preparation of distributions of scores is a straightforward, routine task that any accurate clerk can readily learn to do once he has been shown the elementary procedures involved. The purpose of a distribution is to indicate the number of pupils making scores at each level from highest to lowest, and thus to facilitate the study of both individuals and groups. In most tests, the range

---

[4] All names in the table are fictitious, but the data are the actual test results obtained by one class.

TABLE I. SCORES AND PERCENTILES OF A NINTH-GRADE CLASS ON THE COOPERATIVE ENGLISH TEST

School Century Day   City New York   State N.Y.

Grade 9   Date of Report April 28, 1944   Date Adm. April 7, 1944

Names of Pupils	Chron. Age	A Mech. of Expression		B₁ Effect. of Expression		C₁ Reading Comprehension					Total English	
		Sc. Sc.	%ile	Sc. Sc.	%ile	Vocab.	Speed	Level	Total	%ile	Sc. Sc.	%ile
1. Barton, Barbara A.	15–5	47	35	49	38	43	54	57	51	37	49	35
2. Bradley, John W.	15–3	48	40	53	53	49	46	49	48	24	50	38
3. Denton, Robert D.	14–6	47	35	58	68	57	54	59	57	65	54	57
4. Dickinson, Samuel J.	13–7	64	94	72	97	68	72	73	74	98	72	98
5. Duncan, George W.	14–1	52	59	61	77	59	55	62	59	73	58	72
6. Elkins, George H.	14–11	60	88	60	74	61	59	62	61	79	61	82
7. Fenton, Frederick B.	15–8	36	6	40	9	48	34	36	39	4	37	5
8. Frost, Virgil C.	15–1	54	68	64	84	52	46	40	46	18	55	61
9. Haynes, Julie A.	15–4	49	44	46	27	54	52	62	56	60	50	38
10. Hunt, Barbara A.	15–5	56	76	56	62	51	53	54	53	46	55	61
11. Kerr, Mary J.	14–11	58	82	64	84	54	53	57	55	54	60	79
12. Livingstone, Martin H.	14–11	50	48	62	80	47	51	51	50	32	54	57
13. McKean, Sarah A.	14–8	49	44	47	31	51	46	54	50	32	48	32
14. McNaughton, Jean	13–11	52	59	59	71	51	51	62	55	54	56	65
15. Prescott, Elsie	15–4	47	35	39	7	49	53	46	49	28	44	19
16. Royer, Laurence	14–3	59	85	60	74	52	58	61	57	75	59	76
17. Simpson, Martha F.	15–7	56	76	62	80	64	54	72	64	86	62	85
18. Smith, Marie A.	15–0	50	48	50	42	50	63	60	58	70	53	53
19. Swanson, John S.	14–8	57	79	62	80	55	68	66	64	86	62	85
20. Thompson, Carol E.	15–2	50	48	51	46	52	48	51	50	32	50	38
21. Warren, Gertrude W.	14–10	60	88	63	82	64	60	67	65	88	64	89
Class Median		52.5	62	59.5	73	53.0	53.8	59.0	55.5	57	55.3	62
E.R.B. Median		50.4	50	52.1	50	53.2	53.5	54.4	54.1	50	52.3	50

of scores is so great that it is not feasible to show every score in the distribution. The scores are therefore grouped thus:

Scores	Number of Pupils
85–89	2
80–84	5
75–79	4
70–74	6
65–69	3

etc

Sometimes only the bottom score in each interval is written and it is understood that the scores below the next higher one appearing in the table are to be recorded in the same interval. In this case, the illustration just given would appear as follows:

Scores	Number of Pupils
85	2
80	5
75	4
70	6
65	3

etc.

Ordinarily it is advisable to use a class size of 2, 5, or 10, if the whole range of the scores justifies the use of one of such class sizes, for the speed of making the distribution will be greater and the chance of mechanical error will be less than if some other size is employed, simply because we are accustomed to grouping numbers in that way. Occasionally, however, intervals of 3, 4, 7, or some other number will be preferable because of the range. As a rule, distributions containing from ten to twenty intervals are the most practicable. If

Score	Tally	F (Frequency)
18	I	1
17	II	2
16	I	1
15	III	3
14	I	1
13	III	3
12	IIII	4
11	IIII	4
10	III	3
9	II	2
8	II	2
7	II	2
6	I	1
5		0
4	I	1
3		0
2	I	1

N = 31

less than ten intervals are used, the grouping is likely to be too coarse; if more than twenty are employed, the central tendency of the group may be obscured, although this is not always the case.

In making a distribution, of course, one must first tally the scores in the proper intervals and then count the tally marks in order to find the number of scores at each interval. Let us assume, for instance, that the following numbers represent the scores of a class of thirty-one pupils on an arithmetic test containing twenty problems: 13, 10, 8, 15, 11, 12, 9, 11, 14, 9, 7, 18, 10, 13, 11, 6, 12, 17, 15, 2, 8, 15, 12, 17, 11, 13, 7, 4, 16, 12, and 10. A distribution of the scores in intervals with a class size of one is shown on page 176. For a group of about thirty pupils, this simple procedure requires only two or three minutes.

If distributions are prepared for the part scores as well as the total scores yielded by a test, it is helpful to report all of them on the same sheet, particularly if the raw scores have been translated into derived scores that are comparable one part to another. Distributions of the Scaled Scores made by a class of twenty-one ninth-grade pupils in an independent school on the Cooperative English Test are shown in Table 2. The class is the same one that furnished the scores for the list given in Table 1.

The Scaled Scores, in intervals of 2, are shown along the left-hand margin. The dotted lines across the distribution columns indicate the independent-school medians for Grades 7–12, and the broken lines show the public school medians. The median scores of the class in question are shown graphically by the short horizontal lines, and the interquartile range (the range from the 25th to the 75th percentile) of each distribution is marked off by the vertical line. The medians, quartiles, and ranges of the distributions are also stated numerically near the bottom of the page.

It is apparent that the median total English score of this ninth-grade class, 55.3, is almost identical with the independent-school median for Grade 10. The range of total scores is wide; the lowest score is considerably below the independent-school median for Grade 7 and is close to the public school norm for Grade 8. The highest score, on the other hand, is more than ten Scaled-Score units above the independent-school median for the twelfth grade.

A study of the distributions of part scores shows that the class, as a group, tends to be a little higher in effectiveness of expression than in mechanics of expression and reading comprehension. The median mechanics score, although it is a little lower than the reading comprehension median in terms of Scaled Scores, is approximately equivalent to the reading median in comparison with independent-school achievement. Both medians are a little below the independent-school medians for Grade 10, but above the medians for Grade 9.

The distributions in Table 2 could be analyzed in much more detail, but perhaps enough has been said to show that considerable helpful information

TABLE 2. DISTRIBUTIONS OF SCALED SCORES OF A NINTH-GRADE CLASS ON THE COOPERATIVE ENGLISH TEST

COOPERATIVE ENGLISH TESTS. FORM R

School Park Country Day   Grade 9   Date April 29, 1943

Scaled Score	A: MECHANICS OF EXPRESSION	B1: EFFECTIVENESS OF EXPRESSION	C1: READING. COMPREHENSION	TOTAL A+B+C
80				
78				
76				
74				
72		1	1	1
70				
68				
66				
64	1	2	3 (Gr.12)	1
62		4 (Gr.12)		2 (Gr.12)
60	2	3	1 (Gr.11)	2 (Gr.11)
58	2 (Gr.12)	2	2	1 (Gr.10)
56	3 (Gr.11)	1	3 (Gr.10)	4 (Gr.9)
54	1 (Gr.10)	1 (Gr.12)	2 (Gr.9)	1
52	2 (Gr.12)	1 (Gr.9)	1 (Gr.8)	3
50	3 (Gr.11, Gr.9)	2 (Gr.11)	4 (Gr.11)	2
48	3 (Gr.8)	1 (Gr.8)	2	
46	3 (Gr.11, Gr.10)	2 (Gr.10)	1 (Gr.10)	2
44			1 (Gr.7)	1
42	(Gr.9)	1 (Gr.7)	(Gr.9)	
40	(Gr.7)	(Gr.9)		
38	1 (Gr.8)	1 (Gr.8)	1 (Gr.8)	1
36	1			
34				
32				
30				
Total	21	21	21	21
Q3	57.8	62.9	59.8	60.8
Md	52.5	59.5	55.5	55.3
Q1	48.8	50.3	50.6	50.8
Range	36–64	39–72	39–74	37–72

about the achievement of a class may be derived from a careful study of a well-planned set of distributions.

Statistical Procedures Involved in Summarizing and Reporting the Results of Tests. The statistical procedures needed in summarizing and reporting test results are very simple. Any one with a knowledge of sixth-grade arithmetic should be able to master them without difficulty. The only skills necessary are those required for the finding of medians, quartiles, and percentiles. An understanding of how to find means and standard deviations from distributions is also helpful, but not absolutely essential. The whole thing should be kept very elementary if it is to be understood by all the teachers, for in certain fields there are many teachers who are allergic to anything mathematical, but who can perform important guidance functions if they are provided with data in terms which they find meaningful.

The median may be defined as the mid-point in a distribution. If the test scores of a class are arranged in order of magnitude and if there is an odd number of pupils in the class, the median is the middle score. In a class of thirty-three pupils, for example, the median is the seventeenth score from either end of the distribution. If there is an even number of pupils in the class, the median is the point halfway between the two scores nearest the middle. The finding of the median by counting is thus a very simple process.

When the scores are arranged in a distribution, however, a slightly different procedure must be used, particularly if the class size is greater than one. Let us consider the distribution of scores on the usage part of one of the earlier forms of the Cooperative English Test, as shown in Table 3. Here the class size is 2. The steps in finding the median for this distribution are as follows:

1. Divide the number of pupils by 2: $\frac{35}{2} = 17.5$.

2. Start at the bottom (or the top) of the distribution and add all the number of pupils in the different intervals until you reach the interval in which the median falls: $1 + 2 + 3 + 3 + 6 = 15$. The median must fall in the next interval for if the three cases in that interval were added, the total would be 18, whereas half of 35 is only 17.5.

3. The interval in which the median falls includes scores 56 and 57. It is probable that two of the cases in this interval have one of these scores and one has the other, but one cannot tell from the distribution exactly what the scores are. The fairest assumption, therefore, is that the cases are distributed equally throughout the interval. Following this assumption we can compute the median by a simple numerical process. We know that after adding the cases up to the lower limit of the interval we were 2.5 cases short of 17.5. There are three cases in the interval and, as already indicated, the class size is 2. To find the median,

TABLE 3. DISTRIBUTION OF SCORES ON USAGE PART OF
COOPERATIVE ENGLISH TEST

Scaled Score	Frequency
80	
78	
76	
74	1
72	1
70	3
68	1
66	2
64	1
62	1
60	4
58	3
56	3
54	6
52	3
50	3
48	2
46	1
44	
42	
40	
38	
36	
34	
32	
30	

$$N = 35$$

we merely multiply 2.5 by 2, divide the product by 3, and add it to the lower limit of the interval, thus:

$$2 \times 2.5 = 5$$

$$\frac{5}{3} = 1.7 \text{ (rounded to one decimal place)}$$

$$56.0 + 1.7 = 57.7 = \text{median}$$

Here we have assumed that the lower limit of the interval is 56.0 and that the interval runs from 56.0 to 57.9 +. From a statistical standpoint, a better assumption is that the limits of the interval are 55.5 to 57.4 +, but the reason for preferring this assumption requires a rather involved explanation which will not be taken up here. For most practical purposes, it is satisfactory to use as the lower limit of the interval the lowest whole number falling within the interval.

The whole procedure of finding the median is represented by the following formula:

$$Md = L.L. + \left(\frac{\frac{N}{2} - F\,up}{fmi}\right)h$$

Where Md = median

$\qquad L.L.$ = lower limit of interval in which median falls

$\qquad N$ = number of cases

$\qquad F\,up$ = frequency number up to the interval containing the median

$\qquad fmi$ = frequency of the interval containing the median

$\qquad h$ = size of class interval

The finding of Q1, and Q3, or the 25th and 75th percentiles, involves essentially the same steps as the computation of the median. The formulae are as follows:

$$Q1 = L.L. + \left(\frac{\frac{N}{4} - F\,up}{fqi}\right)h$$

$$Q3 = L.L. + \left(\frac{\frac{3N}{4} - F\,up}{fqi}\right)h$$

Let us refer again to the distribution of scores on the usage part of the Co-operative English Test.

$$Q1 = 52.0 + \left(\frac{8.75 - 6}{3}\right)2$$

$$= 52.0 + \left(\frac{2.75 \times 2}{3}\right)$$

$$= 52.0 + 1.8 = 53.8$$

$$Q3 = 64.0 + \left(\frac{26.25 - 26}{1}\right)2$$

$$= 64.0 + 0.5 = 64.5$$

It is somewhat easier to begin at the top of the distribution and work downward when computing Q3. If this is done, the equation becomes:

$$Q3 = U.L. - \left(\frac{\frac{N}{4} - F\,do}{fqi}\right)h$$

$$= 66.0 - \left(\frac{8.75 - 8}{1}\right)2$$

$$= 66.0 - 1.5 = 64.5$$

The two other measures of central tendency, in addition to the median, are the *mean* and the *mode*. The mode is the most frequent measure in a distribution. It is found by inspection. Where scores are grouped in intervals larger than one, the mode cannot be determined from the distribution, but the *modal interval* can be seen at a glance. For example, in the distribution of scores on the usage part of the Cooperative English Test, the modal interval is 54–55. If two intervals in different parts of the distribution have a greater frequency than any of the others, the distribution is said to be bimodal. The mode is not a very important measure of central tendency, but it is of some value for making a quick inventory.

The mean is simply the arithmetic average. Although it can be found from a distribution, most teachers interested in computing the mean score for a class will find it more convenient to do the work in the familiar way of adding the scores and dividing by the number of pupils, particularly if a calculating machine is available.

The last elementary statistical concept that usually is essential in the reporting of test results is the percentile rank, or percentile rating. Notwithstanding the criticism that is sometimes directed toward the statistical properties of percentiles, their simplicity has without doubt caused them to be more extensively used than any other procedure for interpreting test results.

All teachers and counselors, however far removed their own field may be from that of mathematics, can quickly grasp the idea that a pupil's percentile rating on a certain test shows the per cent of the pupils in a group that he equals or excels in score—or, even more simply but slightly less accurately stated, the per cent of pupils that are below him in score. It is, for example, very easy to explain to a teacher or counselor that Robert Denton's percentile for total English score, as given in Table 1, means that this boy's score on the Cooperative English Test, as a whole, is up to or above the scores of 57 per cent of the independent-school ninth-grade pupils who took the test. If the teacher understands further that the percentile ratings range from 1 to 100, and that 50 is the median or average, it should be clear to her that Robert's score is a little above the median for his grade.

The teacher should readily grasp the further idea that Robert's achievement in mechanics of expression is above that of about one-third of the independent-school ninth-grade group, whereas his achievement in effectiveness of expression and total comprehension surpasses that of approximately two-thirds of the pupils at the ninth-grade level.

Various procedures are used in computing local percentile ranks from a distribution of test scores. A graphic method is favored by some persons, but perhaps the simplest procedure is one which involves the following four steps:

1. Arrange the scores in a distribution that shows every score (class size of 1).
2. Find the cumulative frequency.
3. Find the reciprocal of the number of pupils in the group (divide 1 by the number of pupils).
4. Multiply each number in the cumulative frequency by the reciprocal.

By means of this procedure, the percentile ranks of the tops of the class intervals are found. It is usually not regarded as worthwhile to compute percentiles for groups containing less than a hundred cases, but the general procedure may be illustrated with a smaller group. For this purpose, we will use the arithmetic scores of the class of thirty-one pupils mentioned earlier in the chapter.

TABLE 4. PERCENTILES BASED ON DISTRIBUTION OF ARITHMETIC
SCORES OF ONE CLASS

Score	Frequency	Cumulative Frequency	Percentile
18	1	31	100
17	2	30	97
16	1	28	90
15	3	27	87
14	1	24	77
13	3	23	74
12	4	20	65
11	4	16	52
10	3	12	39
9	2	9	29
8	2	7	23
7	2	5	16
6	1	3	10
5	0	2	6
4	1	2	6
3	0	1	3
2	1	1	3
	31		

To find the cumulative frequency, simply add up from the bottom of the distribution and write the total frequency up to, and including, each interval.

Reciprocal of 31 = 1/31 = .032258

The cumulative frequency at each interval multiplied by .032258 gives the percentile rank of the score in that interval. For example, the cumulative frequency up to and including a score of 16 is 28. 28 $\times$ .032258 = .90. Therefore, the percentile rank of a score of 16 is 90.

When percentiles are found by this procedure, a percentile rating corresponding to a score shows the per cent of the scores in a distribution that are *equaled or exceeded* by that particular score.

The percentiles for all the scores on a test can be computed on a calculating machine in a very short time. It is advisable to type percentile tables for the scores on each test and to use these tables in entering the percentiles on the class lists that are to be sent to the teachers. All this applies, of course, to the computation of local percentiles and may not be necessary in the case of well-standardized tests for which national norms are available. Many test publishers and service agencies now supply complete percentile norms for defined groups on a variety of tests.

CHAPTER X

Use of Results of Objective Tests in Improving the Instructional and Counseling Program of the School

ADMINISTRATIVE AND SUPERVISORY USES OF TESTS

THE RESULTS OF TESTS MAY BE USED IN MANY DIFFERENT WAYS. SOME OF THE COMMON uses are mainly administrative and supervisory, rather than for purposes of diagnosis, instruction, or counseling. A detailed discussion of the administrative and supervisory uses of tests is outside the scope of this book but it will perhaps be desirable to enumerate and comment briefly upon some of them. Two types of uses which are closely related to the administration of the school will be discussed in Chapters XII and XIII. These are the uses of tests in permanent and cumulative school records of pupil progress, and in reports to parents.

Another administrative use of tests is in the classification, grouping, and placement of pupils. Tests are employed widely in the classification and placement of new pupils at levels conforming to their ability, and this kind of use will no doubt increase as the tendency to promote on the basis of time served is gradually abandoned. Tests form one of the main bases for the grouping or sectioning of classes studying the same subject in a given school.

A fourth administrative use of tests is in the modification of programs of study of individual pupils. Tests may sometimes show the inadvisability of trying to have individual pupils proceed beyond a certain level in a field of study. For example, a pupil with a percentile rating of 2 in mathematical aptitude can scarcely be expected to profit from the study of higher mathematics. In similar fashion, tests may show that a pupil has unusual ability in a certain field and may lead to the modification of his program to permit him to take advantage of that ability.

A fifth use of test results which has both administrative and supervisory relationships is the evaluation of methods and materials of instruction. A school may, for instance, wish to experiment with conventional and progressive methods in the teaching of social studies and to evaluate the results. Or, it may desire to compare the achievement obtained with different textbooks, or with a certain textbook as contrasted with extensive reading materials not confined to any one book. The cautious use of tests in these ways is legitimate provided all possible influences on the test results are carefully considered and weighed.

Tests may, in the sixth place, serve administrative and supervisory functions by forming an objective basis for suggestions concerning the instruction of individual pupils. For instance, a high school principal, through an analysis of the results of a reading test, may note that certain individuals are very low in general reading achievement and he may suggest to the English Department that the teachers consider what can be done to bring it up.

In addition to these commonly accepted uses of tests, some schools have occasionally employed the results of tests in ways that are of questionable value. For example, administrators and supervisors have sometimes used test results to rate the proficiency of their teachers. Unless all other factors which help to determine test scores are carefully controlled, such uses may result in marked injustice to individual teachers. Among the factors which influence test results are the chronological age of the pupils; their brightness and the number of years of schooling they have had; their individual rate of growth; the school, departmental, and course objectives; the content of the courses; the methods of instruction employed in the school; the effort put forth by the pupils both in their school work and in the taking of the tests; the amount of experience that the pupils have had in taking tests; and the psychological and physical conditions under which the tests were administered. Any one of these factors may have a more potent influence upon the results of the tests of a given class than the teaching ability of the instructor. For instance, in the instruction of an algebra class that has a median intelligence quotient of 90, it is doubtful if even an extremely able teacher could bring their median algebra test score up to the national average. Since it is practically impossible to control all the other factors in the usual school situation, the use of test results for rating teachers is seldom advisable. In fact, it is not too much to say that this is the most pernicious use of testing that is ever made in our schools and that it has done more than anything else to retard the legitimate uses of tests in the study of individuals.

Another common administrative use of test results is the comparison of median scores in the local school with norms that have been established by giving the tests in a large number of other schools. This is a defensible use, if the findings are interpreted with caution and understanding. It should be remembered that the failure of school averages to reach national averages may not indicate inferior instruction. It may be the result of somewhat lower scholastic aptitude in the local school than in the schools from which the norms were derived; it may indicate that the school has made new and valuable innovations in its curriculum that are not measured by the tests; or it may be due to any of several other factors. The school, therefore, should strive to determine in the light of local conditions the meaning of the deviation from norms rather than to assume that high or low average scores are indicative of superior or inferior work on the part of either teachers or pupils.

INSTRUCTIONAL USES OF TESTS

Main Uses of Test Results by the Teacher. In the meeting of individual and group needs and abilities, teachers may use test results in the following valuable ways: (1) discovering the scholastic aptitudes of the pupils and adapting instruction to their individual levels of aptitude; (2) knowing in detail the cumulative achievement record and the achievement status of each pupil, and guiding him in the development of all types of achievement in the school curriculum which are in line with his abilities; (3) discovering the exceptionally bright or high-achieving pupils and making special provision for them; and (4) diagnosing individual pupil weaknesses and abilities in the different subjects and giving remedial treatment based on the diagnosis.

It should be noted that there is a distinction between the use of test results as aids to instruction and the use of the tests themselves as goals of instruction. The uses just listed are those in which the findings resulting from tests become aids to instruction by enabling the teacher to analyze pupil achievement and to discover those aspects in which each pupil is superior and those points in which he needs special help. Such uses are unquestionably sound, for they lend definiteness and purposefulness to teaching. If, however, the content of the tests used in surveying or diagnosing achievement becomes in itself a teaching goal, the practice may be a hindrance to the development of a program of instruction based on a fundamental philosophy, and it will unquestionably tend to invalidate future measurements with the same or similar tests.

Principles Governing the Use of Objective Tests in Diagnosis and Instruction. When utilizing test results in diagnosing pupil difficulties and in planning special help to meet the needs indicated by the tests and other evidence, teachers and counselors would do well to keep the following points in mind:

1. *Test results are valuable in the degree to which constructive use is made of them in securing improved educational and vocational adjustment and distribution.* They are useful only if someone does some thinking about them and interprets the standing of individuals and groups with reference both to national or local norms and to the past performance and future plans of these same individuals and groups. If the school is going to realize the potential values of its testing program, it is practically imperative that someone who understands not only the fundamental philosophy or purposes of the school but also the basic philosophy of measurement and guidance, and who is acquainted with the

elementary statistical techniques utilized in educational measurement, and who understands the legitimate uses and limitations of individual tests, be assigned the major responsibility for the testing and guidance program and remedial work.

2. *As far as possible, tests should be employed which measure the achievement of the pupils with respect to the purposes of the individual school using the tests.* Since a considerable number of the objectives of most schools are implied rather than expressly stated, the testing program should rarely be restricted to the consciously emphasized local objectives of a school, but it is very important to know the status of the pupils and their rate of growth in relation to purposes which the school does have in mind and for which it is striving. No test, or combination of tests, will measure every attainment a school desires for its pupils, but through wise use of standardized and locally made tests most of its more important objectives can be evaluated.

3. *No test is infallible.* The best test ever made is not perfectly reliable—that is, if the test were repeated under identical conditions, it is highly improbable that every pupil would make exactly the same score he made before or would maintain precisely the same position in the group of pupils tested. Human nature is, moreover, variable, and an occasional pupil's test score may fail by a wide margin to reveal his true ability or achievement because of obscure psychological factors over which the examiner may have no control and of which he may be unaware. It is, therefore, highly important that a school, in making any major decision about the achievement of a pupil, utilize the results of more than one test of a particular kind, as well as all other available information. In selecting pupils for special remedial work in reading, for example, it is wise to use at least two, and preferably three or more, reading tests. An even better procedure is to test the various basic skills at yearly intervals and to keep a record of the results in comparable units. In this way not only status at any given time but extent and rate of growth over a period of several years can be found. This enables the school to discover readily and to analyze marked changes in the progress of any given pupil.

4. *Achievement in a particular subject nearly always bears a close functional relationship to general intelligence.* Dependable diagnostic work in any subject almost always calls for the use of a good test of mental ability along with the achievement test results. Other things being equal, an individual test, such as the Stanford-Binet Scale, is to be preferred, but if a school does not have the facilities for individual mental testing, such group tests as the Otis Self-Administering, the Kuhlmann-Anderson, and the American Council Psychological, which correlate highly with the Binet, may be used, preferably at intervals of one year or one semester.

5. *Intelligence tests involving language are not highly valid measuring in-*

struments for pupils who have language difficulties. For instance, if retarded readers are given a group test of mental ability calling for a considerable amount of reading, the results are ambiguous because it is uncertain whether low scores indicate low intelligence or undeveloped reading ability. It is evident, therefore, that conclusions about the mental ability of such pupils should be held in abeyance until the results have been checked by an individual mental test or a non-language intelligence test.

6. *Scores on all intelligence and achievement tests are influenced, to some extent, by practice.* In other words, the second time a pupil takes a test he will probably do a little better than he did the first time, merely because he will have had experience with the test and will be familiar with its general form. This will be true even though the content may be varied through the use of a different form of the test. Because of the effect of practice, a pupil to whom the tests are new is under a certain handicap in comparison with pupils to whom the tests are familiar, and a single low score by such a pupil should be regarded as inconclusive evidence that he is really inferior in the ability or skill measured by the test to the extent indicated by his score.

7. *The real cause of a disability may be far removed from the disability as revealed by a test.* A language handicap, for example, may be the result of lack of emotional balance rather than of low learning capacity. Hasty conclusions concerning the reasons for low scores should be avoided and the assembling and careful analysis of a variety of information about each pupil should be a regular practice. In some instances the advice of medical or psychiatric experts may be imperative for accurate and adequate diagnosis, but the collection of many facts about study habits and personality traits and the consideration of these facts in relation to scholastic performance can be done effectively by the school staff itself.

General Procedures in Diagnostic and Instructional Uses of Tests. Although methods of diagnosis and instruction naturally vary considerably from subject to subject, there are certain elements in the general procedure which are common to all tool subjects. Regardless of what he is teaching, the teacher who expects to diagnose the difficulties of his pupils and to provide suitable instruction to meet these difficulties will need to go through most of the steps suggested in the following paragraphs:

1. It is sometimes possible for an instructor to make an educational diagnosis with some degree of success without using any measuring instruments whatsoever, just as it is possible for a physician occasionally to diagnose correctly the ills of a patient without utilizing any of the instruments peculiar to his profession. Diagnostic work is unquestionably much more accurate, however, when its basis includes objective data. The first step, therefore, in diagnosis is *to give a suitable test to all the pupils.*

This first step is often cared for in the regular testing program of the school. If, for example, a school participates extensively in the testing programs of the Educational Records Bureau, it will in all probability administer at regular intervals at least one test in each of the basic tool subjects.

Achievement tests are often divided into two general types: *survey and diagnostic*. The main difference between these two types lies in the method of scoring. A survey test ordinarily results only in a total score, or at most, scores in a few of the larger, grosser features of a pupil's achievement in a subject, whereas a diagnostic test not only yields a total score but also shows achievement with respect to specific elements of the subject. These two types may be illustrated by reference to reading tests. The Thorndike-McCall Reading Scale is a survey test, since it provides only one score which represents a composite of reading skills; the Iowa Silent Reading Test, on the other hand, has apparent diagnostic features, for it yields scores in rate; comprehension; directed reading; poetry comprehension; the vocabularies of social science, natural science, mathematics, and English; sentence meaning; paragraph comprehension; and location of information, including use of the index and selection of key words.

Both survey tests and diagnostic tests have important functions in measurement. Survey tests are often used as the initial step to identify the pupils who need diagnosis; they can, in fact, be used in diagnosis if the teacher will take the trouble to tabulate and classify the kinds of errors made by individual pupils. Diagnostic tests are highly useful in locating specific weaknesses, especially when followed by interviews with pupils about the parts which gave them difficulty. Some schools use the procedure of giving a survey test in a subject and following it with a diagnostic test for the pupils who make low scores on the survey test. Other schools prefer to use diagnostic tests with all their pupils in the subjects in which such tests are readily available. Diagnostic tests usually take more time than survey tests. In a regular testing program conducted on an annual or semi-annual basis, it is ordinarily desirable to use some tests of each type, as the exclusive use of diagnostic tests would involve more time than most schools would wish to give to testing.

2. After the test data have been assembled in convenient form, the next step is *to study the data carefully* in relation to all available information from other sources. This often entails not only an inspection of the test scores but a careful perusal of the test papers as well. This step should be carried on by the teacher. Detailed diagnosis is excellent preparation for corrective and remedial teaching, for in this way the teacher acquires a familiarity with the difficulties of her pupils that she could get in probably no other manner.

Study of the data will probably reveal at least five groups of pupils: (1) a few pupils whose achievement is very high (percentile of 90 or better for their grade level) on all parts of the test and who may possibly be excused, after their cases have been carefully scrutinized, from some of the routine aspects of the class work in order that they may use their time to better advantage in the development of special abilities and interests; (2) pupils whose achievement is as high as can be expected in view of their scholastic aptitude and their cumulative record of achievement in the subject measured by the test, and who apparently need no other teaching than that which is provided in the regular developmental program of the school; (3) pupils whose achievement in the various aspects of the subject or skill is so uneven that they apparently need special help in certain phases but not in others; (4) pupils who are somewhat low in all parts of the test, but whose difficulties can probably be corrected by group teaching; and (5) pupils who are so seriously handicapped that their cases demand individual attention. The proportions of pupils falling into the different groups will of course vary with the school and with the subject. Some schools follow the practice of giving remedial training in reading and other tool subjects to the lowest one-fourth of their pupils, regardless of how they stand with respect to national norms.

The teacher in discovering the pupils who need remedial help should avoid by all means the naïve assumption that a given grade norm for a test is necessarily an acceptable standard of achievement for all pupils in the grade. A moment's consideration will show that, in fact, the norm may not be a suitable achievement standard for any of the pupils. It is, at best, an average score of a widely distributed school population of that grade level. If the pupils used in establishing the norm happen to be, in general, rather low in achievement, their average score will probably represent an achievement level that is by no means acceptable for schools in general. On the other hand, selection of superior pupils or differences in emphasis on various aspects of the curriculum may lead to the establishment of norms that are practically unattainable for pupils in certain schools.

Whether or not the grade norm for a test is a suitable standard for average pupils in the group, it is certainly not a desirable standard for exceptionally able pupils or pupils with limited aptitude. Superior pupils may justifiably be regarded as remedial cases if they fall as low as the norm in achievement, whereas some pupils of low ability should never be forced to try to reach the norm. Each pupil must be considered individually in the light of all the evidence at hand. In some subjects, the interests and life ambitions of the pupils must be taken into consideration when making decisions about remedial work. In selecting pupils for remedial work in the *tool* subjects, however, interests and professional or vocational aptitudes of individuals are not so important, for a certain minimum level of skill is required of every pupil in order that he may be able to function successfully in adult life.

In deciding on some of the doubtful cases, the teacher will find it very helpful, if time permits, to retest the pupils individually while she observes their methods of work and perhaps has them do certain sections of the test aloud. This method has been found particularly useful in diagnosing arithmetic difficulties (2). The teacher will also find it advantageous to check her diagnosis with the opinion of other teachers of the pupil and with teachers who have had the pupil in preceding years, if these can be secured. When cumulative records of the type recommended by the American Council on Education are kept, it will be much easier and more convenient to study the previous history of the pupil.

3. The third step in the diagnostic and instructional uses of tests is *to set up procedures for the teaching that is needed*. The procedures will, of course, vary greatly with the subject, but some features are similar in all subjects. The first two groups listed in the preceding step do not require special teaching. The pupils in the third group—those low in one or two aspects but up to acceptable achievement for their grade level in the others—may be taught individually or in small groups of pupils with like deficiencies, or they may be brought into the fourth group at appropriate points. The corrective teaching of the pupils in the fourth group can be mainly group instruction, but the individual needs of the pupils should not be neglected. It has usually been found that the most effective plan is to organize the group as a regular class which is an integral part of the curriculum, but if this is not feasible the group may be met at study periods or other convenient times. The instruction of the pupils in the fifth group will necessarily be organized for individual teaching or work in very small groups.

4. Before the instruction is begun, *the school should make sure that there is an adequate record of the achievement status of the pupils near the time the teaching is started,* so that their progress during the teaching may be measured accurately. Ordinarily the test, or tests, used as a basis of diagnosis will provide this record. If a considerable time elapses between the original measurement and the beginning of the remedial work (if, for example, a test in English usage administered in the spring forms the background for the setting-up of a remedial program in English the following autumn) it is probable that the pupils who were selected for the remedial teaching should be retested shortly before the beginning of the remedial program. Comparable forms of the test will be needed, of course, if this procedure is followed.

5. The next step is to launch the program of instruction according to a plan that is carefully thought out, yet flexible enough to be modified, if necessary, as the work progresses. A general rule in all remedial and corrective work is that *the teaching should be directed toward the specific difficulties experienced by the pupils*. This means that the diagnosis should be made as definite and detailed as possible. It also means that the teacher must keep the details of the

diagnosis in mind in her instruction. Since the needs of the pupils will vary, the work must be highly individualized. Teachers with limited experience in remedial teaching will find some of the better workbook material a distinct aid in individualizing instruction.[1]

Care should be taken to avoid goals that are really beyond the ability of the student. Continued driving, after the pupil has reached the limit of his ability, may be positively harmful. Remedial work must not be allowed to become disguised coercion.

In connection with the remedial teaching, the instructor should remember that environmental factors, both in and out of school, may contribute to the learning difficulties of the various pupils and should be alert to opportunities to discover and help relieve maladjustments of this kind. In other words, diagnosis is not something that is finished before instruction begins but is a continuing process.

The teacher should keep in mind, too, that the root of the difficulty of an individual pupil may be in a faulty mental attitude toward the school or toward the particular subject in which the remedial instruction is being given. Reading cases, for example, are sometimes of this sort. No real disability is involved, but the pupil is simply interested in other activities to the exclusion of reading and has, therefore, not developed facility in it. The remedy obviously lies in bringing about a changed attitude on the part of the learner.

Pupils of high mental ability who encounter learning difficulties and become remedial cases need a different type of instruction from pupils of low mental ability. Considerable repetition is needed in giving remedial instruction to dull pupils, whereas bright pupils may find repetition so deadening to their interest that they may make little or no improvement. Remedial instruction is most effective with pupils who are above average in intelligence if they are encouraged to make a self-diagnosis of their difficulties and to initiate their own attack under guidance on the solution of their learning problems. At all levels of ability, progress is more rapid if pupils have an opportunity to measure their status at regular intervals and to keep an individual cumulative record of growth.

6. It is desirable to test the pupils a few weeks after the beginning of the teaching with a comparable form of the test used before the teaching was undertaken in order to find out if the methods in use are producing results. If there are enough forms of the test, retesting at intervals is very helpful. It aids the teacher in planning her remedial program and enables her to release pupils who no longer need the training. Evidence of progress also encourages the pupils and spurs them on to greater effort. Even if a different test is used and national norms are not available, the relative positions of students can be determined and

---

[1] For lists of such material, see Educational Records Bulletin No. 18, *The Use of Test Results in Diagnosis and Instruction in the Tool Subjects*. New York: Educational Records Bureau, 1942 (Revised).

their response to training noted. *A form of the test originally used should be given, by all means, at the conclusion of the period of teaching, to measure gains.* It is only by careful measurement of progress made under different methods of teaching, that the various remedial methods can be properly evaluated. A test should also be administered several months later to measure the permanence of improvement and to find the pupils who still need special help.

7. When the results of the tests given at the conclusion of the group instruction have been analyzed, the pupils who are up to the goals originally set as desirable and possible should be released from further remedial training of this kind, but should probably be kept under observation for a time. Those who have made progress in relation to what may be expected but are still somewhat low will require further group instruction, perhaps at less frequent intervals and in certain special aspects. *The pupils who have failed to gain should be scheduled for intensive individual instruction.* Such instruction, in order to be successful, may require case study, diagnosis, and supervision of treatment by a psychologist.

The Use of the Results of Tests in Providing for Pupils of High Ability. If test scores indicate that the bright pupils have already mastered much of the work planned for a given grade, this fact should frequently lead to an enriched program for them. Another way of taking care of the needs of these pupils is to excuse them from aspects of the work in which they test very high in order that they may do advanced work in keeping with their interests and special abilities. A ninth-grade pupil who reached the 95th percentile for twelfth-grade pupils on the Mechanics of Expression part of the Cooperative English Test may be excused, for example, from formal participation in those activities of the English class designed to train pupils in correct usage, and may be permitted to give his time under guidance to more advanced work in English or to some other phase of his school program in which he had special interest and in which he had the capacity for independent study. Special promotions or other procedures for accelerating the rate of progress through school are also a way of taking care of pupils whose test records are exceptionally high. Procedures for acceleration were brought to the foreground in recent years because of the educational demands related to the war effort.

USE OF TEST RESULTS IN COUNSELING

The uses of test results in counseling are conditioned by the guidance functions which are carried on in each school. Although these vary considerably from one school to another, there are a number of activities which seem to be common to most guidance programs.

One function of guidance is to *identify weaknesses of individual pupils* and provide for long-time study and treatment. This function is related to those of diagnosis and instruction discussed in the preceding section but, considered as an aspect of guidance, it implies the follow-up of a pupil over a longer period than is usually possible in connection with the work of a single class.

Tests may be used effectively in this connection. For example, one can follow the case of a pupil who has a deficiency in mathematics and note year after year the changes in score and percentile rank that have resulted from different kinds of treatment. The prediction of the later success of the individual depends not alone on what his achievement is today but also on what it was last year and the year before, and the year before that. The prognosis for a pupil whose standing was low at high school entrance but who has managed to come up to average by the end of the secondary school may be better than that for the pupil who has maintained an average record throughout the secondary school grades.

A second function of guidance is to *discover special abilities* that should be developed. If there is sufficient variety in the tests used, one not infrequently finds that a pupil handicapped in the academic subjects has marked ability in some other area. Tests of clerical and mechanical ability, for instance, are valuable supplements to tests in the academic subjects. The discovery and development of exceptional ability is of great importance for the benefit of society generally as well as for that of the individual pupil.

A third function of guidance officers is to *confer with pupils* from time to time *about achievement.* Such conferences are much more meaningful if the counselor is able to present objective evidence to the pupils. There is no better way to encourage a hard-working pupil than to show him how much he has increased his test scores. Also, there is no more convincing evidence with which to arouse pupils who are not working up to capacity than to show them the decline in their percentile ratings or to compare their achievement test percentiles with their percentiles for academic aptitude. In the latter type of comparison, however, the counselor should be aware that, because of regression effect, a pupil with exceptionally high academic aptitude percentiles cannot be expected consistently to maintain quite as high percentiles in all aspects of achievement.

A fourth and closely related function of guidance counselors is to *confer with certain pupils about problems of adjustment.* For this purpose, the results of tests of personality, attitude, and interests may sometimes be used to advantage. The scores on such tests may not be reliable enough to be given much weight in the total record of the pupil, but the responses to specific items are very valuable in interviews. An individual's aptitude and achievement scores are also useful in interviews of this kind, and they should be scrutinized closely in cases of maladjustment that may grow out of inability to do the required work of certain classes.

A fifth function of personnel officers in a guidance program is *to confer with parents about the ability, achievement, growth, and school adjustment of their children.* Tests have potential values that few schools, even those with extensive guidance programs, have fully realized. Parents are naturally keenly interested in the test scores of their children and are usually glad to have an opportunity to study objective, impartial evidence concerning ability, achievement, and special aptitudes. One technique that is sometimes employed is to give a general explanation of the meaning of test records to groups of parents and to invite them to visit the office of the staff member in charge of testing for a more detailed explanation based on the records of their own child. A helpful report on this use of test results and other types of recorded material has been made available by Hilkert (*11*).

A sixth function of counselors is to *guide pupils into or away from certain courses* and thus to reduce failure through careful planning based on available evidence. A function similar to this one was mentioned earlier in this chapter in connection with administration, but it is as much a counseling function as an administrative one. Tests can be used extensively in this kind of guidance. Assume that a test yields just two scores, verbal and mathematical, and that a certain pupil has a high percentile rating in the former and a low percentile rating in the latter. These data provide some evidence for guiding the pupil into linguistic subjects and away from mathematical ones. Whereas the scores on one test alone cannot be used with perfect assurance as a basis for action, the piling up of evidence from several tests over a period of two or three years may be so strong that the guidance to be given a pupil in the choice of a field of specialization will be indicated beyond reasonable doubt.

A seventh guidance function is to *help pupils and parents make plans for the pupils' careers after graduation.* This includes advice concerning whether or not the pupil should attend college, assistance in selecting a suitable college, and help in choosing a vocation. Pupils whose percentile ratings on academic aptitude and achievement tests are consistently above 50 usually can do successful work in the better colleges, whereas those whose percentile ratings generally fall below the median should be steered away from the more selective colleges or perhaps advised to go directly into an occupation without attempting to enter college.

Ambitious, but dull, pupils are sometimes much upset emotionally if at the end of their secondary school course they are suddenly confronted with the knowledge that they cannot expect to succeed in college or that they must be content with attendance at some minor college rather than apply for admission to an outstanding college which they had hoped to attend. However, if achievement test scores are available for each pupil throughout the secondary school and if these are shown regularly to parents and pupils with an explanation of their meaning, a low ranking pupil will gradually become aware of and come to accept the fact that his abilities are of a different type from those of academically successful students. Thus, on the basis of this impartial evidence, there is an opportunity to make adjustment to a non-academic career by easy stages.

The results of vocational interest tests as well as the scores on academic aptitude and achievement tests are useful in helping pupils to choose a career. The results of such tests should be very carefully interpreted, however, and it should be made clear to the pupil and his parents that these tests do not measure *ability* for different vocations nor show whether or not the individual will be *successful* in a particular vocation.

An eighth function of counselors is to *confer with teachers about individual pupils*. One of the most important aspects of guidance is adjustment, and it is obvious that adjustment between pupils and teachers will be better if each teacher understands the abilities and limitations of the various pupils in his classes. The test scores are valuable both for conferences between counselors and individual teachers, and for staff clinics in which groups of teachers study the problems of different pupils and decide on treatment for their difficulties. One of the essential elements of every testing program is a continuous program of educating teachers in the use of test results. Regardless of how a school's testing program is organized or how many counselors it has, its classroom teachers will do much of the actual guidance work, and the value of tests is almost directly proportional to the interest of the teachers in them and their understanding of the results.

Another function of both counselors and teachers is to *make case studies of certain pupils*. The case study is one of the most useful techniques in a guidance program. Not only is it valuable in personnel work with the pupils but it is an effective way of educating teachers in guidance procedures. The backbone of any case study is evaluation. Tests are needed at the beginning of a study to help determine the nature and degree of the problem which initiated the study, during treatment to measure progress and to redirect training, and at the end to determine the gains made and to indicate what still remains to be done. This function is discussed in detail in Chapter XIV.

A tenth guidance function, particularly in college preparatory schools, is to *aid in decisions concerning when pupils are ready to take end examinations,* such as those of the College Entrance Examination Board. Although the correlation between scores on objective tests and the results of examinations of the type prepared by the College Board is by no means perfect, there is substantial agreement between them. In a study reported by the Educational Records Bureau some years ago, the average correlation between these two types of tests was .67 as compared with a correlation of .63 between school marks and College Board examinations (21). The use of cumulative test records to help decide when students are ready for end examinations is a practical application of tests to guidance and is one that some schools are finding worth while.

The last function of guidance officers which will be mentioned here is to *make reports to colleges and prospective employers*. As already indicated, test results are valuable in reports of both kinds. Test records, together with an appropriate explanation, have been accepted as an integral part of the reports which are sent with the pupil when he is graduated. This is evidenced by the fact that nearly every up-to-date report or transfer form now has space for test results expressed in meaningful, non-technical terms, such as percentiles. It is true that these records are not always understood by the institutions to which they are sent, but it is also true that they are much more generally understood than they were fifteen years ago.

LIMITATIONS TO THE USE OF TESTS IN INSTRUCTIONAL AND GUIDANCE PROGRAMS

Although testing is being used in numerous ways, there are several limitations which restrict the extent and precision of the use of test results. Some tests do not agree very well with the objectives in the organization of modern courses; that is, they do not provide valid measurement of the curriculum with which they are used. No test is perfectly reliable, and there is always a certain amount of sampling error in even the best test administered under ideal conditions. Users of tests sometimes allow themselves to be misled by the labels or names attached to the tests. For example, if one test is called an intelligence test and another is called an achievement test, there is a tendency for users to feel that these tests measure very different things, even when their content is such that there is obviously a great deal of similarity between them. Unless counselors and teachers are aware of these pitfalls, their interpretations of test results are likely to be erroneous.

Probably the most serious limitation to the use of tests in instruction and guidance—and this is particularly true of some of the most promising of the newer tests—is that in many cases no one, not even the test expert, knows just what the relationship of the test data is to future success in various fields. Some of the tests published within the last ten years yield scores, for instance, for such mental traits as verbal, number, space, memory, and reasoning factors. The scores on such tests have a potential value that is very great, but their present usefulness is limited by the fact that we know so little about what the scores mean in terms of the future accomplishment of the individual. The fact that the scores on so many tests cannot be adequately explained in terms of outcomes has caused some persons to become considerably discouraged over the possibility of effective use of tests in guidance. This tendency to be skeptical of the guidance values of some of the newer tests grows out of the knowledge that quantitative test results are really useful for guidance purposes only when they can be expressed in meaningful everyday terms and thus enable one to make a valid qualitative appraisal of the individual and to predict his success in qualitative terms.

How to Improve the Usefulness of Tests

The lack of complete understanding of the scores obtained from tests should not lead to loss of faith in these devices, for at the present stage of measurement work a paucity of consequential data is to be expected. Although some of the objective tests of aptitude and achievement have been in use for about a generation, most of the better tests have been prepared within the last fifteen years and several of the more promising tests have been made available within the last five or six years. Research is the only means by which the prognostic nature of a test can be adequately investigated, but research techniques are often slow and expensive and not enough time has elapsed since the publication of the majority of the good tests for research to discover their relationships to fundamental long-time objectives. It is encouraging to discover that test specialists are showing an increasing awareness of the need for information on the relationship between test data and guidance outcomes and are beginning to take steps to join forces in attacking the problem.

Personnel workers in schools, however, cannot wait until research with tests has supplied answers to many of their questions, for they must meet today the problems of guiding their present students. Nor is it necessary for them to wait, for they can read a great deal of meaning into the scores on the basis of their own experience. For example, the counselors and teachers in a large number of schools have discovered, through their experience with the Cooperative Achievement Tests during the last ten years, critical scores on these tests with respect to success in different colleges. Thus, in a sense, personnel workers faced with the practical job of counseling students from day to day are not infrequently going ahead of the test specialists in discovering the meaning and use of the test results in their own particular situation.

REFERENCES

1. Brueckner, Leo J., and Melby, Ernest O. *Diagnosis and Remedial Teaching.* Boston: Houghton Mifflin Company, 1931. Pp. xviii + 598.
2. Buswell, G. T., and John, Lenore. *Diagnostic Studies in Arithmetic.* Chicago: University of Chicago Press, 1926. Pp. xiv + 212.
3. Foran, Thomas G. *The Psychology and Teaching of Spelling.* Washington, D. C.: Catholic Education Press, 1934. Pp. xi + 234.
4. Gillet, Harry O. "Reading Problems and Guidance in Arithmetic," *Adapting Reading Programs to Wartime Needs,* pp. 206–211. Proceedings of the Confer-

ence on Reading Held at the University of Chicago, Vol. 5. Compiled and edited by William S. Gray. Supplementary Educational Monographs, No. 57. Chicago: Department of Education, University of Chicago, 1943. Pp. viii + 283.

5. Gillingham, Anna, and Stillman, Bessie W. *Remedial Training for Children with Specific Disability in Reading, Spelling, and Penmanship*. New York: Sackett and Wilhelms Lithographing Corp., 1940. Pp. 268.

6. Gray, William H. *Psychology of Elementary School Subjects*. New York: Prentice-Hall, Inc., 1938. Pp. xii + 459.

7. Greene, Edward B. *Measurements of Human Behavior*. New York: The Odyssey Press, 1941. Pp. xxi + 777.

8. Greene, Harry A.; Jorgensen, Albert N.; and Gerberich, J. Raymond. *Measurement and Evaluation in the Elementary School*. New York: Longmans, Green and Co., 1942. Pp. xxiii + 639.

9. Harris, Albert J. *How to Increase Reading Ability: A Guide to Diagnostic and Remedial Methods*. New York: Longmans, Green and Co., 1940. Pp. xx + 404.

10. Hildreth, Gertrude H. *Learning the Three R's*. Minneapolis: Educational Test Bureau, 1936. Pp. x + 824.

11. Hilkert, Robert N. "Parents and Cumulative Records," *Educational Record*, Supplement No. 13 (January 1940), 172–183.

12. Jones, Galen, and Galbraith, Adria. "The Interpretation of Standardized Tests," *School and Society*, LIV (September 20, 1941), 224–227.

13. Lee, J. Murray. *A Guide to Measurement in Secondary Schools*. Chapter VIII, "Use of Tests in Diagnosis and Remedial Instruction," pp. 266–305. New York: D. Appleton-Century Company, 1936. Pp. xv + 514.

14. Lincoln, Edward A., and Workman, Linwood L. *Testing and the Uses of Test Results*. New York: The Macmillan Company, 1935. Pp. xi + 317.

15. McCallister, James Maurice. *Remedial and Corrective Instruction in Reading*. New York: D. Appleton-Century Company, 1936. Pp. xviii + 300.

16. Manuel, Herschel T. *Test Results and Their Uses*. Research Bulletin Number Eight of the Texas Commission on Coordination in Education. Austin, Texas: The Administrative Board of the Texas Commission on Coordination in Education, December 1938. Pp. 39.

17. Mort, Paul R., and Gates, Arthur I. *The Acceptable Uses of Achievement Tests*. New York: Bureau of Publications, Teachers College, Columbia University, 1932. Pp. iv + 85.

18. Paterson, D. G.; Schneidler, G. G.; and Williamson, E. G. *Student Guidance Techniques*. New York: McGraw-Hill Book Co., Inc., 1938. Pp. xviii + 316.

19. Ross, C. C. *Measurement in Today's Schools*. New York: Prentice-Hall, Inc., 1941. Pp. xvii + 597.

20. Strang, Ruth, and Rose, Florence C. *Problems in the Improvement of Reading in High School and College*. Lancaster, Pa.: Science Press Printing Company, 1938 (revised, 1940). Pp. 390.

21. Traxler, Arthur E. "Comparable Tests and School Marks," *1936 Fall Testing*

Program in Independent Schools and Supplementary Studies. Educational Records Bulletin No. 19, pp. 83–109. New York: Educational Records Bureau, January, 1937.

22. Wheat, Harry G. *The Psychology and Teaching of Arithmetic.* Boston: D. C. Heath and Company, 1937. Pp. x + 592.

23. Wood, Eleanor Perry. "Examining the Uses of Examinations," *Harvard Teachers Record,* III (April 1933), 59–66.

24. Woodring, Maxie N., and Flemming, Cecile W. *Directing Study of High School Pupils.* New York: Bureau of Publications, Teachers College, Columbia University, 1935. Pp. vi + 253.

CHAPTER XI

Basic Principles and Main Types of Pupil Personnel Records

Some Basic Principles

THE TERM "PERSONNEL RECORDS," AS USED HERE, INCLUDES ALL THE RECORDS OF THE school that are employed in recording information about individual pupils. It does not include financial and business records, or records and reports that deal with groups rather than with individuals.

According to this definition, certain individual school records, such as the school census and attendance data, which are kept partly for purposes of making group summaries, may logically be regarded as personnel records. Records of this sort, however, will not be included in this discussion. The emphasis will be upon records that are maintained for the purpose of facilitating the guidance of each individual pupil.

We are in a period of transition from haphazard record systems that "just grew" in different schools to systems carefully planned in the light of a study of the conditions and need of each school. A hundred years ago few schools kept any records at all. Largely through the efforts of Horace Mann, the Daily Register was introduced into the schools of Massachusetts in the 1830's and its use gradually spread throughout the country. This one record book, which consists largely of a record of attendance and promotion, continues even to the present day to be practically the sole recording device in many rural schools. As the complexity of urban schools has increased, additional office records and records for transfer of pupil information from department to department, from school to school, and from school system to school system, perforce have been devised. Many of these record forms have grown up without definite plan or coordination and without relationship to records used in other places. So great is the diversity in personnel record systems that the efforts of regional associations and other organizations to bring some order out of the chaos have, in general, met with indifferent success.

Some persons, after examining the poorly planned and unwieldy record systems in vogue in many schools, have been inclined to take a very pessimistic view of the possibility of getting the general rank and file of schools to build efficient and significant personnel records. But anyone who tends to despair over the situation may find considerable solace in a comparison of the present personnel records of any school with the kind that were possible, for instance, two hundred years ago. For example, in his *History of Education,* Cubberley [1] has reported in detail a record that was kept by a Prussian schoolmaster about 1750. This schoolmaster, one Hauberle by name, "with characteristic Teutonic attention to details, has left on record that, in the course of his fifty-one years and seven months as a teacher he had, by a moderate computation, given 911,527 blows with a cane, 124,010 blows with a rod, 20,989 blows and raps with a ruler, 136,715 blows with the hand, 10,235 blows over the mouth, 7,905 boxes on the ear, 1,115,800 raps on the head, and 22,763 *notabenes* with the Bible, Catechism, singing book, and grammar. He had 777 times made boys kneel on peas, 613 times on a triangular piece of wood, had made 3001 wear the jackass, and 1707 hold the rod up, not to mention various more unusual punishments he had contrived on the spur of the occasion. Of the blows with the cane, 800,000 were for Latin words; of the rod 76,000 were for texts from the Bible or verses from the singing book. He also had about 3,000 expressions to scold with, two-thirds of which were native to the German tongue and the remainder his invention."

In contrast to this recital of items which two centuries ago were regarded as important in the guidance of pupils, even the most archaic of personnel records now in use seem fairly valuable. The great need at present is to improve the scope, reliability, and organization of the information collected and recorded about pupils and to train teachers in the intelligent use of this information. The recognition of a number of basic principles should give important impetus to the realization of this goal.

1. *A comprehensive and detailed system of cumulative personnel records is indispensable for the proper functioning of the modern school.* From earliest colonial times down to the beginning of the twentieth century, our schools were mainly rural and village schools. Furthermore, the great majority of the pupils were enrolled in eight-grade elementary schools. This situation had a definite effect on pupil-teacher relationships and on the opportunity for intelligent instruction and guidance, for it was inevitable that the teacher and his pupils should be intimately acquainted. Pupils were often under the same teacher for several years, not merely in one subject, but in all aspects of the life of the

[1] Ellwood P. Cubberley. *The History of Education,* pp. 455–456. Boston: Houghton Mifflin Company, 1920. Pp. xxiv + 849.

school. The contacts of pupils and teacher extended beyond the school, for the teacher knew each pupil in out-of-school relationships. He was in all probability a friend of the pupils' parents. He visited, and sometimes boarded for long periods of time, in each home. The teacher needed no written case history for his pupils. He carried in his mind the history of every one of them. This is not to say that *written* objective records would not have aided the teacher in his work with the pupils. They would have been useful, but they were not indispensable. So he got along either with no permanent records or with the daily register, which was, as already indicated, mainly a record of attendance and promotions.

There were secondary schools consisting first of the Latin grammar schools, later of the academies, and finally of the public high schools, but they were small and tended to be selective. The curricula were limited in scope and the pupils were for the most part those who were getting ready for colleges and professional schools. There was little need, therefore, for either educational or vocational guidance.

With the rapid development of junior and senior high schools during the present century and with the tendency toward departmentalization even in the elementary school, this homely, intimate picture of the school has changed. Departmentalization contributes to the efficiency of instruction even in a small school but as soon as a school has departments, it has teachers seeing only segments of the development of boys and girls. The teacher knows the pupil as a student of English, or a student of mathematics, or as a football player, but he rarely knows the whole individual.

When to this situation there is added another twentieth century influence—namely, the influx of huge numbers of pupils of all economic and ability levels into the schools—there comes into existence a great metropolitan high school, with perhaps two hundred teachers and from five to ten thousand pupils. Each teacher may meet some two hundred pupils in groups of perhaps forty an hour a day for one semester, and then receive an entirely new crowd. The only way of establishing an adequate basis for teacher participation in guidance is to pool the various isolated bits of information that are gleaned by the different persons who have contact with each pupil and to bring them together into one composite picture.

But, one may inquire, when these many items are brought together and put down cumulatively on a record card, does this procedure actually result in a picture of the pupil? When dealing with personality, is not the whole greater than the sum of its parts? The answer is, yes, that is true, but the saving feature of the whole plan is the power of synthesis that is inherent in the human mind. When one takes a long-time cumulative record which has been filled out in detail and studies it with the understanding that comes from experience with such records, one does not get just an impression of a series of details—he has an impression of unity. *One relates a dozen different items and has something new,* an understanding of personality that is not down on the card but is a result of his ability to assimilate a group of facts and to abstract a generalization. Some persons who insist that guidance must be based on an understanding of the whole personality of the individual are critical of the use of tests and cumulative records because they overlook this fundamental point.

2. *The most important purpose of personnel records is to improve the instruction and guidance of each individual pupil.* Personnel records serve various purposes: they contribute to the administration of the school, they form a basis for reports to higher institutions, and they provide data for research. But in setting up a system of personnel records, these purposes are secondary. Each item should be evaluated in the light of its contribution to pupil adjustment and development, and a decision concerning whether or not to include the item in the record should be based first of all on its value to the individual pupil. The items not related to this central purpose that are necessarily added to the personnel-record system should be clearly differentiated from those of major importance, so that they will not be allowed to consume the time and confuse the thinking of persons who are studying the records for the sole purpose of helping the pupil develop normally.

3. *Records are needed that will be continuous over the whole school history from the kindergarten to the junior college, and that will follow the child from school to school.* The bringing together of all available important information about a pupil at any given time and the recording of the facts in one place so that they may be studied is a great help in understanding the child, but the value of the record is increased manyfold if it is cumulative from year to year. It is self-evident that teachers in a higher grade need the benefit of the experience of teachers who have had the pupil in a lower grade. If a complete record of the child's history in a lower school can accompany him when he advances to a higher level, his new school can place him and deal with him to far greater advantage. Status at any given time is important, but for purposes of guiding a pupil, a knowledge of the amount of growth is even more important.

4. *The personnel records for all pupils should be readily accessible to the entire faculty of the school.* The value of personnel records is almost directly proportional to their use by the classroom teacher. They should be open to inspection by the teachers at all times, in fact, if possible, the teachers should be free to go directly to the records without having to utilize the services of a clerk to obtain access to the material. If there are matters of record about certain pupils that are too confidential to be read by everyone, they should be filed in a separate place. *The freedom of use of the main records should not be impaired by the need for recording occasional confidential bits of information.* Needless

to say, the pupils themselves should not have access to each other's record cards but each pupil should have an opportunity to study his own cumulative record in consultation with his faculty adviser.

5. *The records system should be simple enough and well enough organized so that the essential facts about any given pupil will be brought together on one central record card or set of cards in such a way that they may be grasped through a few moments of study by busy teachers and counselors who are not highly trained in interpreting records.* Regardless of the extent and complexity of the procedures used in collecting the original data about each pupil, a plan should be evolved for "boiling down" the essential data and recording it in simple, concise, readable form. The record which the teacher or the counselor uses should be so greatly simplified that the high spots in the whole life of the child can be taken in almost at a glance. Naturally, more extensive and detailed information back of the entries on the cumulative record should be available, but either it should be filed in a different place or it should be arranged in such a manner that it does not interfere with the reading of the main record.

6. *An attempt should be made to keep the records high in reliability and comparability by basing them as far as possible on objective data.* Opinions about pupils are notoriously unreliable and they should have a minor place in the records. Main dependence should be placed on behavior descriptions, physical and mental measurements, and achievement test scores. School marks are useful if their meaning is carefully defined and if the marks are supplemented and interpreted by written comments. Probably the most important single type of data is scores obtained annually or semi-annually on a series of comparable tests.

7. *The records should be uniform in type throughout all the schools of the local system.* Complete uniformity in personnel records may not be either possible or desirable for different schools because of differences in objectives, but the permanent records that are kept in the various schools of one city system should certainly be coordinated. This is particularly important if the elementary school cumulative record goes with the pupil to the junior high school, and the records for both elementary school and junior high school go along with the pupil to the senior high school.

The need for uniformity pertains, of course, to the permanent cumulative record and not necessarily to the "feeders" for the cumulative record, which may conceivably differ from school to school.

8. *The records system should provide for a minimum of repetition of items.* One of the most important reasons why schools hesitate to adopt a really comprehensive and significant system of cumulative records is the amount of clerical work involved in their upkeep. The clerical work can be minimized by planning the system so that needless duplication of items is avoided. A certain

amount of duplication is of course inevitable in large schools, since it is not possible to have a single set of cumulative records placed where they are easily accessible to everyone. Where repetition is necessary, use should be made, wherever possible, of mechanical duplicating devices.

9. *The building of a personnel records system for a given school does not begin with a consideration of the records themselves; it begins with a study of the nature and purposes of the school and of the pupil.* The whole program of the school impinges upon the record system. A good system of records reflects the purposes of the school and what the school is doing. A new records system may perhaps go beyond the immediate program of the school and make provision for the recording of types of information that the school is not at the moment ready to provide, but it should by all means be consistent with the purposes of the school. Therefore, the first step in the revision of personnel records is to obtain a statement of the school's objectives. These objectives should not be vague and ethereal, but should be stated in terms of pupil behavior. They should be stated by each department in the school and they should be specific and detailed rather than general. Once the school has agreed on what it is trying to do, it can proceed to build or to adopt a system of personnel records that will provide for the recording of information about the growth of pupils toward the goals it has set up.

10. *If a school adopts one comprehensive cumulative form as its basic personnel record, it should not only plan this form with meticulous attention to detail, but it should also carefully plan the forms which are to be used in collecting data which will contribute to the main record.* A cumulative record form cannot be regarded as a card for original entry. Obviously, it will seldom, if ever, circulate throughout the faculty so that the various members of the staff may make entries on it. The teachers, counselors, and others will record the information on transient forms of various sorts and they will record it, as a rule, in more detail than it appears on the cumulative record. It is the job of a specially trained staff member to select and summarize the original data and enter it on the permanent card. Obviously, the final entries cannot be more valid, reliable, and meaningful than the original ones. Therefore, the forms for original entry and the directions for filling them out should be set up very carefully.

11. *A detailed manual of directions should accompany the personnel records for the guidance of persons filling out or using the forms.* Some items on the record form, such as the name and address of the pupil, are of course self-explanatory, but others, for example, the personality trait record or the marking system used in the school, require explanation. It is, therefore, desirable to prepare a manual in which the various items will be taken up in order, and directions for recording given and interpretation of the entries explained. An explanation is particularly important if a graphical record of test results is main-

tained, for the meaning of a graph may not be easily apparent to everyone.

12. *There is a natural and logical relationship between the information on reports made to the parents and the information recorded for purposes of permanent record; this relationship should be taken into account in planning both types of forms.* The reports to the parents are less extensive and usually less detailed than the personnel records maintained by the school, and there are, of course, certain kinds of information that the school may not wish to give to the parents. For example, because of the danger of misinterpretation, it is seldom advisable to report I.Q.'s on mental tests to parents. Nevertheless, the reports to the parents and the cumulative records may well have many items in common, and efficiency will be promoted if they are planned in relation to one another.

13. *A system of personnel records must not be static; it must be revised frequently, as a school's theory of education changes.* The reasons why so many schools are now dissatisfied with their records and are trying to do something about them are that during the last few years we have been going through a period of rapid change in educational philosophy and practice and that records systems have been allowed to lag behind other developments. Many schools have, for example, begun to make extensive use of annual programs of comparable tests, but in many cases the cumulative records of the school do not provide adequately for the recording of the test results because they were developed in a period when tests were of minor importance to the school. Similarly, a large number of schools are giving more and more attention to the integration of personality and to social adjustment, but few permanent record systems make extensive provision for records concerning the development of pupils in these respects. A school should reëvaluate its personnel records at frequent intervals, discarding those items which are no longer used and adding others which are needed.

14. *It is imperative that a system of personnel records be associated with a program of teacher education in the use of these records.* The education of the teachers begins with the planning of the records. The building of a new system of personnel records should be an all-faculty job, not alone because of the educational value of the work, but also because no innovations in personnel records can be really successful unless the full sympathy and participation of the teachers is enlisted. Naturally the details of actually drawing up new records will be the work of a selected committee, but the whole faculty should contribute ideas and should help evaluate and revise the new forms before they are put into operation.[2] After the records system is set up, the teachers must be stimulated and encouraged to use the records in connection with their work with their pupils.

[2] For a discussion of procedures followed in one secondary school, see Lester W. Nelson, "Developing a Cumulative Record Card for Local Use," *Guidance in Public Secondary Schools*, pp. 73–78. Educational Records Bulletin No. 28. New York: Educational Records Bureau, October 1939.

One excellent means of promoting the use of records is a series of case studies carried on by the teachers themselves and discussed in a series of carefully planned staff meetings. The nature of a program of this kind will be discussed in some detail in Chapter XIV.

MAIN TYPES OF PERSONNEL RECORD SYSTEMS

The number of different personnel record forms in use in the schools of this country is unknown, but it is unquestionably very large. Surveys of a limited number of schools have identified hundreds of such forms. For example, in a study made some years ago of the office practices of only fifteen secondary schools, Gray[3] discovered 688 different forms which were classified under 177 descriptive titles, only twelve of which were common to all of the fifteen schools. Similarly, Heck[4] found 1515 different items in a study of the record forms of 131 cities in the United States. Only 11.3 per cent of the 1515 items occurred on more than ten forms, and 50.2 per cent of the items occurred only once.

A surprisingly large number of forms is required for the administration of the guidance department of any large city school. Becker,[5] for example, has listed thirty-one forms employed in the Guidance Department of the Samuel Tilden High School, Brooklyn, New York. Similarly, Clark[6] has listed forty-two guidance forms utilized in the Roosevelt High School, Seattle, Washington, although some of the forms have broader uses than for guidance alone.

Nearly all the personnel records used by schools, however, can be classified into a relatively small number of types. We may classify record forms in four different ways—first, according to function; second, according to filing arrangement; third, according to the nature of the centralizing unit; and fourth, according to permanency.

Records Classified According to Function. The grouping of records according to the function they perform is the most familiar way of classifying them. This type of classification for senior high school records has been made effectively by Bristow and Proctor.[7] The groups are as follows: (1) forms dealing with registration and classification of students; (2) attendance records; (3) routine permits and passes; (4) reports to parents; (5) health and physical

---

[3] M. R. Gray. "The Office Practices of High-School Principals." Unpublished Master's Thesis, Department of Education, University of Chicago, 1927, pp. 54–55.

[4] Arch O. Heck. *Administration of Pupil Personnel*, p. 190. New York: Ginn and Company, 1929.

[5] Elsa Becker. *Guidance at Work in a Large City High School.* New York: New York City Board of Education, 1935. Pp. xi + 125.

[6] Frank Jones Clark. *Guidance Working Materials for Junior and Senior High Schools.* Seattle: The Author, Roosevelt High School, 1936.

[7] A. B. Bristow and William M. Proctor. "Senior High School Records and Reports," *Junior-Senior High School Clearing House,* IV (March 1930), pp. 410–432.

training records; (6) special and cumulative record cards; and (7) reports to colleges and standardizing agencies. Among the forms included in the first group are registration cards, pupils' program cards, course-of-study cards, class lists, forms showing distribution of marks, forms for application for change of course, and forms used in granting permit to change course.

In the second group, attendance records, are included the teacher's daily attendance report, the high school admission card, and the attendance investigation card. The third group covers various brief forms for routine passes and permits, such as permit to go to the library, permit to make up lessons missed on account of absence, and card giving permission for early dismissal. The fourth group, reports to parents, includes not only the regular periodic report on work covered, accomplishment, and growth, but also various special reports among which are report regarding absence and tardiness, report regarding deficiency in scholarship, report regarding conduct, and report of suspension.

Health and physical training records, which make up the fifth group, include form for reporting pupils to school physician, form for school nurse to use in reporting health inspection, certificate of disability, record of routine medical examination, and most important of all, the pupil's permanent health record card.

In the sixth class we have what is, without doubt, the most valuable of all the many personnel records that may be maintained by the school, namely, the cumulative record card. This form will be discussed at length and illustrated in the next chapter.

The seventh and last group includes transcript of credits, certificate of recommendation to college, personnel rating blanks, and other forms for reporting to colleges and standardizing agencies. To an increasing degree, cumulative record cards are being used to supplement the usual type of report to colleges. As we will see later, at the present time many influences are working toward a radically different type of report to colleges than has been used in the past.

Personnel records for the elementary school and the junior high school may be classified into the same general categories, with the exception of the final group, but fewer records are ordinarily needed at the elementary school level than at the high school level.

Records Classified According to Filing Arrangement. Another way of looking at records systems is to consider the degree to which they are centralized. At one extreme we may postulate a records system which is completely decentralized—that is, one in which each member of the school staff would keep the records which pertained to his own work and in which no attempt would be made to centralize the information about each child. Obviously, a recording plan of this kind is purely hypothetical, for no present day school could be administered on such a basis. There is a minimum of information about the character of a pupil's work in school which must inevitably be made available in the principal's and the counselor's offices, even though it may in some cases be nothing more than a record of attendance and of marks assigned to the pupils at stated intervals.

The opposite extreme to the recording plan just mentioned would be one in which the teachers and counselors would keep no records at all but would forward all data to the central office to be filed or entered on cumulative records. No school would attempt to apply such a plan, for in practice it would be almost as faulty as a completely decentralized plan.

There is at present a commendable tendency toward greater centralization of personnel records, and some schools have carried this tendency to the point where they attempt to bring together all important information about each pupil on a single cumulative record. It should be clearly understood, however, that back of any really meaningful cumulative record system there is much detailed and non-centralized information in the records of the various individual teachers. It is the possession of these detailed and decentralized records that enables the teachers to prepare valid summary reports for the cumulative records.

Some schools that are convinced of the wisdom of centralized cumulative records do not find it practicable to centralize their records to such a degree that they have only one single cumulative record form. In very large schools, the mere consideration of distance from one part of the plant to the other may make it preferable for certain departments to have their own cumulative records and to report only a very abbreviated summary of their own record to be entered on the cumulative record form in the central office. This is true particularly of health and physical education departments. Consequently, cumulative health records have been developed in a good many schools on a parallel to the more comprehensive cumulative records to be found in the principal's office.

Records Classified According to the Nature of the Centralizing Unit. In general, any one of three plans may be used to bring together and to organize in a central filing system the data about individual pupils. A school may follow the practice of filing loose sheets in cumulative folders, or it may transfer the data annually to a cumulative card or folder, or it may use a combination of the two. Let us see how each one works and consider its advantages and disadvantages.

The cumulative folder should be of the expanding type, sufficiently large to hold an accumulation of several years' data for a given pupil. It may be used for filing teachers' reports about the pupil, a sample of his work, his test papers, anecdotal records, and any other information that will help to give a comprehensive picture of the pupil as a growing individual.

One difficulty in the use of the cumulative folder is that the accumulation of information will probably after a time become unwieldy, so that the very volume of the data, together with the fact that the information is on loose sheets, makes organization difficult. This difficulty may be met to some extent by utilizing a folder that has separate compartments for different kinds of data. Flory and Webb [8] have suggested the use of a cumulative folder with six sub-divisions, as follows: correspondence and reports of conferences, health reports, admission and entrance data, mental records, personality records, and scholastic records. In their article there is no mention of any school system in which a folder of this kind has actually been installed, but the advantages of this type of organization of the data for each individual as contrasted to one large folder in which all the papers for a pupil are filed indiscriminately are obvious.

While a carefully organized folder is no doubt very helpful for a counselor or for anyone who can spend considerable time studying one individual, it is almost impossible for a principal, classroom teacher, or counselor to make a quick appraisal of a pupil through the use of a folder containing many loose papers. It seems desirable, therefore, to have the most significant information recorded on a cumulative record card that can be handled easily and read quickly. Some schools prefer to depend entirely on the cumulative card or set of cards and so do not maintain any cumulative folders at all. This may be a workable plan if the cumulative record card is large and if it is filled out in full, but as Flory and Webb [9] have pointed out, many of the "shorthand" notations on the cumulative record tend to lose much of their meaning for subsequent users of the card when they are completely divorced from the original data from which they were abstracted.

A plan that involves the maintaining of both a system of cumulative record cards and a set of cumulative folders seems to be the ideal arrangement if a school has a sufficient office staff for the handling of such a system. A plan of this kind has three possible variants, which are as follows: (1) the use of the cumulative record as the folder in which the papers containing more detailed information about the pupil are filed; (2) the filing of the cumulative record cards and other information in the same folder; and (3) the maintenance of separate files of folders and record cards. A number of the well-known cumulative record forms can be used in the manner first described, if the school wishes to employ them as file folders as well as record folders. Among these are the cumulative record folder of the American Council on Education, the Behavior Description form of the Progressive Education Association, and the record folder of the Los Angeles City Schools. The main difficulty in the use of

---

[8] Charles D. Flory and James F. Webb. "Cumulative Records for Elementary Schools," *Elementary School Journal*, XXXVIII (December 1937), pp. 278–290.

[9] *Ibid.*

the cumulative card as an individual file folder is that it is not large nor durable enough to hold all the papers, if a serious attempt is made to assemble and retain all the significant information about each pupil. Moreover, the utility of a record card which serves as a file folder will be reduced because the card will tend to become soiled and difficult to read, and if filled with papers, cannot be handled quickly and efficiently, either in entering data or in reading the entries that have already been made.

The idea of providing individual folders for filing cumulative record cards along with other papers seems not to have found its way into practice in many schools, but there is one good illustration of such a plan among the record forms that have been devised in recent years. The Riverside, California, Schools have provided for the filing of an educational record, a social and personal record, and a health record along with special data in an 8½ by 11 inch folder. In an older records plan, the Baltimore Packet Record System, a limited amount of supplementary data could be filed along with the regular cards, if the information was written on 4 by 6 inch cards.

There is a mechanical difficulty in filing cumulative record cards and other papers in the same folder. After a pupil has been in school for several years, his folder will probably become well-filled and rather unwieldy. His cumulative cards cannot easily be consulted without removing the whole folder from the file; yet to take the whole folder out of the file to get one or two items of information about a pupil is time-consuming. Such a plan runs the hazard of discouraging teachers from going to the cumulative records frequently.

Separate files of cumulative record forms and individual folders placed in the same office seem to be the best arrangement. This plan is illustrated by the files of the records office of the University of Chicago Laboratory Schools. Each pupil's cumulative record from the kindergarten through high school is kept on four "master" cards and this cumulative record is paralleled by a large cumulative file folder in which samples of the pupil's work, teachers' reports, correspondence between the school and the parents, and other significant data are filed. A plan of this kind efficiently serves the needs of both the teacher who wishes to obtain a quick general picture of the pupil's work, or to secure without loss of time certain specific items from the cumulative record, and the case worker or counselor who is making a detailed study of the pupil.

Records Classified According to Permanency. Some forms used in guidance departments are designed merely to serve an immediate purpose, such as the summoning of pupils to appear at the counselor's office at a certain time, or interoffice communication about pupils. Although it is true that if these slips are later filed in the counselor's office they will help to round out the picture concerning the pupil, they are less significant and can be eliminated more readily from consideration than certain other forms.

A second, and much more important, class of guidance records includes a variety of forms that are intended to be more or less permanent. Under a system in which a record *folder* is the main vehicle for organizing and preserving in a relatively permanent form the counselor's records about individual pupils, these records will be carefully filed in the folder, will be preserved at least until the pupil is graduated, and will serve as the counselor's principal source of cumulative information about each pupil. If there is a comprehensive system of cumulative record *cards,* on the other hand, many of the data will be transferred to the cumulative cards and the forms for original entry will be much less important as permanent sources of information, although they may well be preserved to supplement the cumulative record cards. Illustrations of the semi-permanent record forms falling into this category are blanks for securing information about students, reports from schools previously attended by the pupil, forms for teacher estimates concerning pupils, forms for pupils' self-estimates, reports on causes of failure, records of interviews, forms for summarizing the results of one testing program, and forms for pupils to use in stating their vocational interests.

A third, and still more important, class of counselor's records consists of forms that are designed to provide a permanent and cumulative picture of pupil development. These cumulative records have so close a relationship to the efficiency of the guidance program that a separate chapter may profitably be devoted to a discussion of them.

CHAPTER XII

Cumulative Records in a Guidance Program

WHAT THE CUMULATIVE RECORD IS

IN CONTRAST TO SOME OF THE TERMS USED TO CHARACTERIZE PUPIL PERSONNEL records, such as school register, report card, transcript of credits, and permanent record card, the term *cumulative record* is a recent addition to educational terminology. Cumulative records are rarely mentioned in the literature prior to 1925, and it is only since 1930 that the term has had common usage. Because of the recent origin of the concept, the term has not become well standardized. From a non-technical standpoint, the words *cumulative record* are properly applied to any record that is formed or becomes larger by successive additions. Thus, all permanent record forms that are designed to cover a period of years, even though they are very sketchy, may be called cumulative records. The term is also used in a restricted sense to designate the newer type of record forms in which emphasis is placed on objective measurements and personality data as contrasted with the older type of permanent record that was confined largely to attendance, school marks, and credits. It is used in a still more restricted sense to apply to the cumulative record forms of the American Council on Education and to adaptations thereof. In the present discussion, the concept *cumulative record* will be used in a rather broad sense and will apply to all records that make provision for the accumulation of significant and comprehensive information about an individual pupil over a period of years, although the illustrations will be drawn mainly from the American Council forms and their adaptations.

VARIATIONS IN RECORD FORMS

Surveys of cumulative record forms, such as those made by Heck (*11*), Troxel and Koos (*36*), and Segel (*26*), show great variation among schools in number and kinds of items included. Differences in local conditions, of course, make a certain amount of diversity in record forms inevitable, but an extremely wide variability in the records of different schools unquestionably creates difficult problems in the exchange of records and in their efficient use by school officers.

Segel classified the items found on the records of 177 school systems into seventeen categories and tabulated the frequency of occurrence of each type of item. The types of items found most frequently were scholarship (marks), school progress, attendance, entrance and withdrawal, home conditions and family history, intelligence test results, social and character ratings, and health. Regardless of the variability in details, it is generally agreed that a good cumulative record should be based as largely as possible on objective data, should be organized into annual divisions, and should present an all-round picture of individual development rather than one narrowly confined to academic achievement.

AMERICAN COUNCIL CUMULATIVE RECORD FORMS

Much of the present interest in the newer and more comprehensive type of cumulative record can be traced to the pioneer work that was done in 1928 by the Committee on Personnel Methods of the American Council on Education, and in particular to the work of Professors Ben D. Wood, of Columbia University, and E. L. Clark, of Northwestern University, in devising the original American Council cumulative record folder. Following the work of that committee, the American Council on Education published four cumulative record forms, including a folder for college students, a folder for secondary school pupils, a card for elementary school pupils, and a card that could be used in either the elementary or the secondary school. Approximately half a million of these record forms were distributed and, in addition, the forms influenced the records of many other organizations and countless local school systems.

In 1940, the Council appointed a committee, with Eugene Randolph Smith as chairman, for the purpose of revising the cumulative record forms to take into account the new trends and progress that had been made in the recording of personnel data by certain other organizations, such as the Progressive Education Association. The Smith committee has prepared revisions which include cumulative record folders for junior and senior high schools, for colleges, for Grades 4, 5, and 6, and for the primary grades. A more detailed explanation of the nature of the cumulative records prepared by the committee will be made later in this chapter.

The Educational Records Bureau Adaptation of the American Council Cumulative Record Form. One of the best-known adaptations of the original American Council form is the Educational Records Bureau cumulative record card for independent schools which was devised in 1933 by Eleanor Perry Wood and Winston B. Stevens. This type of form is illustrated with the records of two pupils in Forms 8A and 8B.

The front of the card, which is made to fit the ordinary letter-size file, is devoted almost entirely to a record of subjects, marks, and credits, and to an extensive test record. The test results are reported in both tabular and graphic form; in fact, one of the distinguishing features of the original American Council form and its adaptations is the gridiron graph in which the results are shown in terms of percentile ratings arranged according to the sigma scale. The back of the card has space for the recording of a variety of less objective data, including information on discipline, home influences and cooperation, mental and emotional factors, physical and athletic development, extracurriculum activities and interests, notable accomplishments and experiences, educational plans, and personality. The whole card is planned for a six-year record, and all the data for any given year are confined to a single column so that the cumulative effect is immediately apparent.

This type of record form is easy to understand and use, except for the fact that the graph of test scores, although the clearest phase of the record to one familiar with graphs of this kind, may seem somewhat puzzling to persons who have had no experience with it. As already indicated, the percentile scale at the left is based on the sigma scale and the distance between successive percentiles is much smaller near the median than at the extremes. The median, or 50th percentile, is marked by the heavy line going horizontally across the graph. The symbols at the top—Jy, Au, S, O, and so forth—stand for the months of the year. As a convenience, the months are grouped according to school years rather than calendar years.

The percentile data that are shown in the table of scores are also entered in the graph. The small dots on the graph show the placement of the various percentiles, the dots being identified by the abbreviated names of the tests printed near them. For example, when the first pupil, David Harris, was in the sixth grade, his Kuhlmann-Anderson mental age, 15–0, corresponded to an independent-school percentile rating of 92 on a test taken in October 1937. The dot has been placed under "O" and opposite the level of 92 in the percentile scale, and has been labeled "K.A.–M.A." to indicate that it stands for the percentile rating on Kuhlmann-Anderson mental age. The percentile shows that the pupil's mental age was up to or above those of 92 per cent of the independent-school seventh-grade pupils who took the Kuhlmann-Anderson test in the fall of 1937.

The percentile points for tests that are in the same subject field from year to year are connected by lines, so that one can readily follow a particular type of aptitude or achievement throughout the whole period covered by the test. For example, one of the lines in the illustration runs from the Metropolitan English percentile in Grade 6 to the Metropolitan English percentile in Grade 7, thence to the English percentile in Grade 8, et cetera. Achievement percentiles are connected by solid lines, academic aptitude percentiles by broken lines, and chronological age percentiles by dotted lines.

The test record of David Harris is an exceptionally favorable one. The graph shows at a glance that all his academic aptitude and achievement scores were well above the independent-school median throughout the six-year history. In fact, except for Latin in Grade 8 and elementary algebra in Grade 9, all his percentiles were above the 84th percentile, or more than one standard deviation above the median for the independent-school population.

The boy's scholastic record is shown near the top of the card. Notwithstanding the limitations in percentage grades unsupported by comments explaining the grades, it is evident that the pupil's school work is in agreement with his very high test record.

The information given on the back of the card, as shown in Form 8B, verifies the impression that Harris is an outstanding boy. Not only is he a good student but he is a leader of his classmates and he is reported to have excellent personal qualities. The boy obviously has the ability and preparation for very successful work in a highly selective college, and one would predict that he will make a fine record in college if he continues to be serious in purpose. It may be observed in passing that a record of this kind furnishes a far better basis for prognosis of college success than is provided by a transcript of credits and an admission form filled out by the school when the pupil is near the end of his secondary school course.

The cumulative record of the second boy, Kenneth E. Johnson, is quite different from the record just examined. Kenneth is slightly, although not significantly, older than the average pupil of the same grade level, and he is in most respects somewhat below average in academic aptitude and achievement as compared with the independent-school group. The majority of the percentile ratings on the achievement tests are below the independent-school median, although few of them are extremely low. There are a few relatively high points, such as physiology-hygiene, in Grade 8, and plane geometry, in Grade 10.

The back of this boy's card shows that he comes from a good home, is in good health, and is inclined to be athletic, that he has had advantages of travel and other experiences, but that he is easygoing, lacks initiative, and has as yet no clearly defined goal. This boy should in all probability be guided away from plans to enter college and an attempt should be made to determine his vocational interests by means of interviews, the Strong Vocational Interest Blank, the Kuder Preference Record, and other procedures.

As a rule, there is considerable correlation in the results of the different tests, so that the points plotted to represent the scores of a pupil tend to fall in the same general area in the graph. Occasionally, however, the graph of percentiles brings out clearly special aptitudes for certain subjects that might otherwise be undiscovered. For example, consider the test record of John R. Belden (Form 8C). This boy's scores on most of the tests taken during a four-year period are in the lower half of the scores of the independent-school group, but his scores on the four science tests—general science, biology, chemistry, and physics—are all in the highest fourth of the independent-school distributions for these subjects. Obviously, as far as knowledge is concerned, the prognosis for this boy's success is much better in science than in the other subjects in which he was tested.

Revision of the American Council Forms. The revised American Council cumulative record folders which have been prepared by the Smith committee are similar to the original ones, in that they retain the organization by years and some of the same categories, but include several important innovations. In general, the revised forms place less emphasis on subjects, credits, and marks, and more emphasis on behavior descriptions and evaluation of personal qualities. They also allow more space for synthesis and interpretation. An illustrative case, entered on the record card for junior and senior high schools, is shown in Form 9.[1]

It will be seen that the card makes provision for a six-year record, which would ordinarily include Grades 7 to 12. There is space near the top of the first page for a summary of the previous school record and for two photographs, the first of which would presumably have been obtained near the time of entrance to the junior high school and the second of which would show the pupil shortly before graduation from high school.

It is intended that the record of academic achievement will consist of much more than grades and credits. Five columns are provided under each year so that each teacher may, if it seems feasible, appraise the pupil with respect to such types of development as work habits, ability to think logically, mastery of technique, oral and written communication, and over-all achievement in the course. If it seems desirable to estimate achievement at the end of each semester, one of these categories can be dispensed with and two of the five columns may be used for appraisal of achievement. The indications of kinds of evaluation are intended as suggestions only and the committee has purposely left the headings to be filled in by the school so that this portion of the card will be quite flexible and can be made to fit into the local situation.

Considerable space in the center of the card is allowed for the record of test

[1] Used with the permission of the American Council on Education.

scores in three areas—academic aptitude, reading, and achievement. Results of other tests, such as personality or interest tests, might also be entered in the space provided for the achievement tests.

Below the test record, space is provided for the interpretation of test results and their relation to academic achievement on a two-year basis. An alternate form of the card is printed in which this space has been given over to a percentile graph for schools which prefer a graphic, as well as a tabular, record of the test results.

Considerable space near the bottom of the front side of the card is allowed for interests and experiences, educational and occupational plans, health and physical characteristics, and discipline. There is also a small segment for an indication of financial aid. Attendance accounts for only a very limited area, since a detailed attendance report is not important for purposes of the cumulative record. The main purpose of noting attendance in a personnel form is to provide a notation of long periods of absence or of frequent tardiness, since these items of information sometimes help in the interpretation of problems of pupil adjustment.

The top portion of the back of the card gives pertinent information concerning home background and family history. Most of the back of the card is taken up with an extensive description of behavior, to which all staff members who are well acquainted with the pupil should contribute. The description of behavior closely parallels the behavior description form developed by one of the Progressive Education Association committees, of which Dr. Smith was chairman. Notes, and post-school and follow-up information complete the card.

The sample record for Raymond Clarence Upton shows how the form may be used to present a comprehensive history of the development of an individual pupil during the junior and senior high school years. This boy entered Grade 7 of the Gillispie Junior High School at the age of eleven years, nine months, after attendance from the kindergarten to the sixth grade at the Packer Elementary School. His work had been average in the elementary school and no special learning difficulties had been noted. He was thought to be in rather poor health. He progressed at a regular rate through the junior and senior high schools, making passing grades in all subjects. During this period, he had three counselors, one throughout the junior high school, another for Grades 10 and 11, and a third for his senior year.

The record of academic achievement in this school system was based on a three-step scale—H for high, U for usual, and L for low. Ratings were assigned in each subject for work habits, ability to think logically, and oral and written communication; achievement marks, in terms of H, U, and L, were assigned at the end of each semester. This boy was rated U in most respects, although he received a number of H's, particularly in mathematics, and several L's, especially in oral and written communication. His ratings for academic achievement tended to be a little better in the senior high school than in the junior high school.

On the whole, the boy had approximately an average test record with rather high percentiles predominating in mathematics. His percentiles in language usage and mechanics of expression were low in the earlier years but they increased somewhat near the end of the high school period.

The boy was small and frail when he entered the junior high school. He was of a nervous temperament and tended to try to compensate for his smallness and weakness in comparison with the other boys by being noisy and by adopting a rather belligerent attitude. His attendance was quite irregular at first because of illness. During the senior high school period, the boy grew rapidly and his health became much improved. These physical factors in turn affected his personality, and he became much more mature, assured, and generally likable.

No clear-cut educational or vocational interests were reported by the boy while he was in junior high school, but during the last two years of senior high school he developed a definite interest in electrical engineering. He had some valuable summer work experiences during the senior high school period.

Raymond's home situation was not favorable. He was one of five children in a family whose economic circumstances were somewhat inferior. His mother and father had been separated shortly before he entered the junior high school, and his father thenceforth saw his family infrequently and took little interest in their support. This situation had a marked effect upon the boy, especially during the first two years of the junior high school.

The description of behavior for this student shows how the judgments of different teachers can be brought together and coordinated to show variations in behavior in different situations during a single school year and to bring out a pattern of development over a period of years. It is interesting to see that in nearly all the categories for which the behavior description form is applicable, this pupil developed from a low or rather mediocre status in Grade 7 to a fairly high position in Grade 12.

It will be observed that in using the description of behavior, it is not necessary for every teacher of the pupil to provide judgments concerning all aspects of his behavior if there are certain categories concerning which an individual teacher may have little or no information. For example, the mathematics teachers and the social studies teachers did not provide descriptions of the behavior of this pupil under the heading of creativeness since the nature of the subjects taught by these teachers was such that they had little opportunity to observe the pupil in situations calling for creativeness.

As one studies a thorough record of this kind, he acquires a feeling of familiarity with the individual's background, aptitudes, achievement, interests, experiences, and personal qualities, even though he may never have seen the pupil or have known anything concerning him previously. When a record of this kind is supplemented by more informal knowledge and information acquired through acquaintance with the student, it becomes an invaluable basis for sound, well-considered, intelligent counseling.

RECORDING TEST SCORES IN TERMS OF A COMMON CRITERION GROUP

For purposes of the cumulative record of test data, some persons prefer a graphic record of test results that is made in terms of *scores* rather than percentiles, so that increments of growth from year to year are more readily apparent. If raw scores are used, it is obviously not advisable to try to graph the results of different tests on the same chart, but if a system of derived scores that take their origin from a common basic group is employed, these scores have elements of comparability that make it feasible to record them on one graph. For example, Flanagan's Scaled Score system devised for the Cooperative Achievement Tests lends itself readily to such a recording plan, and a graphic record form has been set up for these scores. This form may be used also for academic aptitude or intelligence scores if they are first changed to Scaled Scores. The form is printed on one side of an 8½- by 11-inch sheet, and the back of the page contains instructions for using the form. A copy of this record form is shown in Form 10.[2] The Cooperative test scores of Kenneth E. Johnson, which were shown in the table and on the percentile graph in Form 8B, have been entered on this Scaled Score graph.

CUMULATIVE RECORDS EMPLOYED IN DIFFERENT SCHOOL SYSTEMS

A school which is revising its record forms will find it helpful to examine cards which have been published for general distribution, such as those which have just been considered. Some schools may find that records of this kind are so closely adapted to their needs that they can adopt them in their entirety, but no school should decide to take over a ready-made record form without first considering carefully its own objectives and program.

Other schools may find it more desirable to adopt portions of published record forms but to incorporate these portions into a new form of their production. This can be done readily, since the American Council forms and the Educational Records Bureau forms are not copyrighted.

Still other schools may wish to adopt an entirely new approach to their record forms instead of copying parts of any available forms. Even these schools,

[2] Reprinted by permission of the copyright holder, the Cooperative Test Service of the American Council on Education.

however, can obtain valuable ideas concerning arrangement of data on the card from a study of forms that have been prepared either by national organizations, such as the American Council on Education, or by committees in local school systems. In recent years, many schools have printed new record forms that are obviously the results of much thought and work but which are so poorly arranged that much more time is required for a counselor to get the essential information from them than is needed when well-organized forms are used.

It is impossible to present in this book more than a few of the many admirable cumulative records which have been devised by school systems throughout the country. The cumulative records of the following school systems will be shown and briefly discussed: Plainfield, New Jersey, High School; Providence, Rhode Island, public schools; junior and senior high schools of Los Angeles, California; and Minneapolis public schools.

As already indicated, the cumulative record is so extensive and so important that it is necessary for purposes of study to consider it apart from the other records of the school. The consideration of the cumulative record without regard to the other school records, however, may confuse our thinking unless a word of warning is issued. It should be remembered that in the case of every cumulative record, the cumulative form is just one important aspect of a whole complex record system. It does not stand alone but is supported by a whole array of supplementary records.

Plainfield High School—The American Council Cumulative Record Folder in a Visible File. Over a period of years, the Plainfield High School, Plainfield, New Jersey, has developed one of the most advanced guidance programs in the United States.[3] Most of the items on the cumulative record form used at Plainfield are similar to the items on the original American Council cumulative record folder, but the form has been printed on a folder that is adapted to the Remington Rand Kardex visible file. A record which has been filled out is shown in Form 11.[4]

The cumulative record is distorted somewhat in reproduction by the necessity of presenting it in parts which will conform to the size of a book page. To visualize it, the reader should understand that it is so arranged that when it is opened out to its full length all the items are printed on one side of a sheet 11 inches wide and 24½ inches long.

A title insert is used in the visible filing arrangement with each one of the cumulative records. Transparent colored signals placed on the title insert facilitate the rapid and accurate use of the records by administrative officers and teachers.

[3] Galen Jones. "Five Years of Guidance in the Plainfield High School," *Guidance in Public Secondary Schools,* Educational Records Bulletin No. 28, pp. 16–44. New York: Educational Records Bureau, October 1939.

[4] Sample record provided through the courtesy of Miss Adria Galbraith, director of tests and records, Plainfield High School, and used with permission.

A questionnaire which is administered annually to the Plainfield High School pupils in order to gather certain items of information for this cumulative record was presented in Chapter III.

The desirability of having a manual for the cumulative record is emphasized by all specialists in guidance. Most manuals for cumulative records are set up mainly to guide the person making the entries, although they are, of course, helpful to persons studying the records. At Plainfield, a manual for use in recording is not greatly needed since all the work on the records is done under the supervision of one member of the faculty. The school has, however, constructed a brief manual to assist persons who go to the records for information.

Some time ago, a case history similar to the one shown on the illustrative form was discussed in a meeting of the Plainfield High School faculty which was attended by a psychologist from outside the school. Although the amount of information recorded does not seem extensive when one glances at it, the psychologist found that he had been able to glean from the record nearly all the important facts that were brought out in a forty-five minute discussion of the case. This is strong evidence of the efficacy of cumulative records of this type.

Providence Public Schools—American Council Cumulative Record Card, Postindex Adaptation. It is common knowledge that one of the oldest, most firmly established, and most influential guidance programs in the United States has been developed in the Providence public schools, under the direction of Dr. Richard D. Allen, Assistant Superintendent of Schools. Among the many useful forms provided for the guidance program in Providence is an adaptation of the original American Council cumulative record card. The form, as used in Providence, is printed on both sides of an 8- by 9¾-inch sheet, which is then folded into a 5- by 8-inch size (Form 12).[5]

The categories on the Providence form are much like those on the card originally worked out by the American Council on Education with the exception of several minor changes. The record may be used throughout a period of seven years, instead of six. The graphic test record of educational growth is on a rectangular scale, rather than on a sigma scale. The section for personality rating is quite definite and calls for checking appearance and manner, initiative, leadership, emotional control, industry, cooperation, and reliability on a five-point scale. The "date and causes of leaving" have been added to the form, and there is a brief space for a note concerning college record.

Los Angeles Cumulative Record Forms for Elementary School and High School. The Los Angeles cumulative record system consists of two forms, an 8½- by 11-inch card for the elementary school and a cumulative folder for the high school. The high school folder, which is printed on three sides, is reproduced as Form 13.[6]

---

[5] Used with the permission of the Providence Public Schools.
[6] Used with the permission of the Los Angeles City Schools.

In contrast to the traditional emphasis on subjects and marks, it is noteworthy that the front of the cumulative record card for elementary schools contains space for recording data in connection with such headings as health or significant physical traits, mental health or significant mental traits, free time activities or special achievement, parents' plans for pupil, pupil's plan, and interviews, and that the scholastic record is relegated to the back of the card. The scholastic record occupies only a small amount of space, the greater portion of the back of the card being taken up with scholastic capacity and educational achievement test data and trait and attitude ratings.

In the cumulative record for the junior and senior high schools, the top half of the inside portion has to do with the scholastic record and with education achievement test and scholastic capacity test data. In view of the fact that this card is expected to serve six years, it would seem that the space for recording the test data is rather limited.

Several of the divisions that are given on the elementary card also appear on the lower page of the inside section. Thus, data on mental health or significant mental traits should be available in compact form for the entire school period. An important addition is the section for occupational or special interests. The sections in the lower half of the card are somewhat similar to certain parts of the American Council form, although their arrangement is very different.

One of the most interesting parts of the Los Angeles cumulative folder is its back page. This section is an adaptation of the behavior description form which was set up in connection with the Eight-Year Study of the Progressive Education Association. Although the behavior description form is being used extensively and has recently been incorporated into the American Council folder, the Los Angeles school system seems to have been the first school system to take over the form and actually to print it as a part of their own cumulative record system. A similar section appears in a new cumulative record form for use in junior and senior high schools of the United States Indian Service.

Minneapolis Public Schools Cumulative Record Card. The two cumulative record forms of the Minneapolis public schools represent one of the most carefully organized record systems in use in any of the school systems of this country. The cards, which provide for a continuous record from Grade 1 through Grade 12, are reproduced in Forms 14A and 14B.[7]

The front of the first card has spaces for keeping a cumulative record throughout the school history of the pupil with respect to family, health, dental hygiene, and speech and reading disabilities. Data concerning the family record and the health record are to be recorded every two years. The back of the card is for a record of the pupil's history from the kindergarten through the fourth grade. The upper half of the card has spaces for a record of attendance, marks in school

[7] Used with the permission of the Minneapolis Public Schools.

subjects, and scores and percentile ratings on academic aptitude and achievement tests. In the lower part of the card, entries may be made about class behavior, special abilities and interests, personality assets, areas in which the pupil needs help, and procedures which experience with the pupil has shown to be effective in modifying his behavior.

The front of the second card is for a record of the pupil's development from the fifth to the ninth grade, and the back of the card is for his senior high school record. The organization of each side of the second card is similar to that of the back of the first card. Additional spaces are provided on the senior high school form for recording club offices, work outside of school, educational plans, and vocational plans.

One of the most important features of the Minneapolis cumulative record system is an especially well-planned and attractively written manual. The manual, which is printed rather than mimeographed, compares favorably with any other cumulative record manual now available. The directions for filling out the cards are very explicit, but the manual is more than a list of directions. The first section in the manual on "When to Consult the Cumulative Record Card" should be so helpful generally that it is reproduced below.

When to Consult the Cumulative Record Card

The Cumulative Record Card should serve as a means of helping to know pupils as individuals. Although it is not expected that any one teacher will use the card for all these purposes, the following are suggestions regarding how to use it.

Examine the records:

of new pupils to help you get acquainted with them more quickly at the beginning of the term.

of pupils not working up to class level for suggestions as to reason.

of pupils not happy or not well to see if the reasons are apparent and aid can be given.

of pupils of unusual ability to help you in finding extra work for them.

of all pupils in a class before dividing them into small groups for instruction.

of pupils who are absent frequently to find an explanation for their absence.

of pupils who misbehave to discover reason and suggestions as to how to handle them.

of pupils for whom special aid such as lunches, clothing, or scholarship is being considered.

before advising pupils concerning their electives in ninth grade or senior high school.

before advising pupils regarding vocational school courses.

before conferring with parents about their children.

to discover pupils of exceptional talent in such special fields as art, music, athletics, or creative writing.

to determine the capacity of pupils in your group.

to determine the growth made by pupils year by year.

to help you in making out report cards.

The manual also contains a table which shows when and by whom the cards are to be filled out. This is also of enough general value to warrant reprinting.

When and by Whom the Cards Are Filled Out

Section	When	By Whom
Identifying Data (lines 1–3, 12A)	When pupil is enrolled	Clerk in Census Department for kindergarten admits, clerk in school for all other admits
Addresses, Withdrawals, and Readmissions (12A)	When changes occur	Clerk
Family Record (lines 4–11, 12A)	When pupil enrolls or is readmitted (see page 13) and thereafter during fall months of alternate years	Clerk in Census Department for kindergarten admits, clerk in school for all other admits, subsequent entries are made by teachers in elementary schools and home room teachers in junior and senior high schools
Health Record (lines 12–22, 12A)	When medical examination is given (usually every other year)	School nurse
Dental Hygiene Record (lines 23–25, 12A)	Every year during spring months	Dental hygienist
Speech and Reading Disabilities (lines 26–31, 12A)	At end of any period when special help has been given	Speech or reading teacher in Department of Special Education
Identifying Data (line 32, 12B) (line 48, 12C) (line 65, 12D)	When this form is put in use	Clerk
Year and Grade (lines 33, 34, 12B) (lines 49, 50, 12C) (lines 66, 67, 12D)	At time of enrollment and thereafter at end of each semester, for the following semester	Teacher in elementary schools, clerk in junior and senior high schools and vocational schools
Schools (line 35, 12B) (line 51, 12C) (line 68, 12D)	At time of enrollment, at beginning of each semester, and whenever a pupil is transferred	Clerk

Section	When	By Whom
Days Attended, Days Absent, and Teacher or Room (lines 36–38, 12B) (lines 52–54, 12C) (lines 69–71, 12D)	At end of semester and whenever a pupil is withdrawn	Teachers in elementary schools, clerks in junior and senior high schools and vocational schools
Marks in School (section 39, 12B) (section 55, 12C) (section 72, 12D)	At end of each semester	Teacher in elementary schools, clerk in junior and senior high schools and vocational schools
School Ability Tests (line 40, 12B) (line 56, 12C) (line 73, 12D)	Whenever such tests are given	Clerk
Educational Tests (line 41, 12B) (line 57, 12C) (line 74, 12D)	At end of semester	Clerk
Personality Data (line 42–47A, 12B) (line 58–63A, 12C) (line 75–84, 12D)	During second semester of each year, in March or April if possible	Teacher in elementary schools, home room teacher in junior and senior high schools and vocational schools
Counselor's Report (line 64, 12C)	When pupil is in 9A grade	Junior high school counselor
Final Record (Upper right-hand corner of 12D)	When pupil graduates from senior high school	Clerk

Valuable suggestions are given in the manual to aid the teachers in filling out the parts of the card dealing with personality assets and aspects of personality with which the pupil needs help.

The Minneapolis cumulative record cards and manual are the product of the careful work of an able committee. They represent the kind of work that is possible when a school system sets up a thorough and intelligent plan to build its own cumulative record forms to meet local needs.

A Suggested Simplified Cumulative Record

The cumulative record forms that have been discussed in this chapter make provision for a rather extensive recording procedure annually for each pupil.

The very wealth of information provided on such records may cause some schools which have not yet undertaken procedures of this kind to hesitate to adopt them because of the amount of clerical service that seems to be required to keep the records up-to-date. Such schools may wish to begin their cumulative records on a somewhat less ambitious basis. A record form (Form 15) is therefore suggested as an intermediate step between the older type of permanent record form and the modern and extensive cumulative record of the type prepared by the American Council on Education.

This form is similar in many respects to the Educational Records Bureau cumulative record card, but it omits the graph of percentile ratings on the test results and it provides more space for comments and notes. The top portion of the back page is very much like one section of the American Council folder. A section for behavior description is provided, but this is much less extensive than the one on the American Council form.

This form is obviously not original; it consists rather of a rearrangement and "boiling down" of categories which have appeared on other records. Schools are entirely free to make use of any of the ideas presented in the card without obtaining special permission.

BASIC CONCEPTS IN THE CONSTRUCTION OF A CUMULATIVE RECORD SYSTEM

As indicated in the preceding chapter, a committee to devise a cumulative record plan for a school system should begin with a study of the school itself in order to determine what the school is doing and what it hopes to accomplish. The first step is to secure a list of objectives. Once this has been accomplished, the committee will naturally wish to find out what has been done in other places that can be utilized in meeting the recording needs of the local school. An examination of samples of records developed in other school systems will, no doubt, reveal items which are suited to the local situation, but the discovery of these items will not be the major outcome of such a study. The most important result of a study of the more carefully prepared records now available is the development of certain basic concepts which will have a very important influence on the kind of records set up by a school.

Some of the more important concepts which pervade the best cumulative records produced thus far are as follows:

1. *The Concept of the Child as a Developing Organism.* Even the best of records consists of a series of snapshots taken at various points in a child's development. These must be combined in such a way that one studying the records sees not the snapshots but a motion picture—a continuous story of an important segment in the life of an individual.

2. *The Concept of Continuity in Education from the Kindergarten Through*

the Junior College. For administrative purposes we divide the educative process into certain artificial units—elementary school, junior high school, senior high school, junior college, and so forth. Between each two units there is a break calling for adjustments on the part of both pupils and teachers. Continuous records, with provision for passing them freely from one school to another, can do much to improve the articulation between successive units and thus greatly improve both the adjustive and the distributive aspects of guidance.

3. *The Concept of Organization According to Time Sequence.* Some cumulative records present a confused picture; they may contain much useful data, but considerable time and energy must be expended merely in going over the record and in getting the essential facts arranged in relationship one to the other. One of the most helpful contributions to record keeping that has ever been made is the principle of organization according to time sequence. Busy administrators, teachers, and counselors find records in which the data are clearly classified by school years and often by months within each year, a welcome contrast to records that are not arranged chronologically. No school in setting up a new record system can afford to neglect the need for making the cumulative record inherently a growth record.

4. *The Concept of Comparable Measurement.* A cumulative record without measurement is like a picture out of focus—there results a blurred and indistinct impression of the individual, but the whole lacks definiteness and assurance. It may be objected that measurement may very easily give a false impression of definiteness, and that there will be a tendency to read too much into the results. This is probably true if the measurement is made at only one point in the pupil's history and if the interpretation is placed in unskilled hands. But a program of comparable measurements conducted annually by competent persons should result in well-placed confidence, in definite evidence of achievement and growth, tempered by an awareness of the limitations that are involved in all objective data relating to living human beings.

The measurement program should be as broad and as thorough as the resources of the school will permit, for the more inclusive the data, the less the chance of drawing incorrect conclusions. It is desirable for the measurement program to include annual records of anthropometric data, health examinations, academic aptitude tests, achievement tests in all subjects studied by the pupil, and a limited number of personality and interest tests.

5. *The Concept of Graphical Presentation of Numerical Data.* Most persons have rather definite opinions about graphs. Some persons are opposed to them either because they do not understand them or feel that many people cannot make them out; others, among whom are some mathematicians, prefer to deal with numbers rather than graphs, because they know that numbers can be manipulated in ways that graphs cannot. On the other hand, there are those

who want a picture of everything and feel that they can make their interpretations much better if they are able to see data in graph form.

To meet these individual preferences, it is desirable to present data in the cumulative record both numerically and graphically. Aside from personal preference, there is an excellent psychological basis for using graphs to supplement numerical data wherever possible. The principle is really a dual one. In the first place, the mind can apprehend position more quickly than it can apprehend numerical value, and, in the second place, a group of positions can be taken in at a glance, but a group of numbers cannot be digested with one sweep of the eyes. The numbers must be brought into consciousness and interpreted one after another before a generalization can be drawn concerning whether a pupil stands high or low in aptitude, achievement, and so forth. Therefore, in interpreting numbers—for example, test scores or grades—one is forced to go from the particular to the general. In interpreting a graph, however, one may work either way; he may, if he wishes, get his generalization before he particularizes, or even, if he is in a great hurry, generalize without particularizing at all. Thus, one will glance at a series of cumulative records of aptitude and achievement, as entered on the Educational Records Bureau cumulative record card, and say, even while glancing at them, "This boy is high in ability and achievement; this one is low; this one has good ability, but his achievement is not up to capacity"; and so forth.

By no other device could such rapid generalizations be achieved. This point is of great importance and should be carefully considered by every records committee. It is safe to say that the average person—even the average teacher—has to learn to like records, just as he has to learn to like olives. In the beginning, if he is faced with a mass of detail in records, his natural tendency is to avoid them, for they make his head ache and are otherwise distasteful. But if he can go to the record and get a quick picture of the aptitude and achievement of a problem pupil within a few seconds, he will use the records because they save his time and help him in his work. Certainly the use of records should not stop with a general impression concerning only certain aspects of a pupil, but in the beginning the general picture obtained from the graph is the best single point of contact in the popularization of the records within the faculty. Moreover, the general impression given by the graph will continue to be useful even for persons who are very familiar with cumulative records, for each detail is seen in relation to the whole objective record, just as a detail in a picture takes on added meaning when seen against a background.

6. *The Concept of Behavior Description.* One of the outstanding contributions to record keeping has been the observation that if one secures a record of a pupil's behavior, not complicated by the opinion of the person who sets it down, one then has an objective record. The result is not a record that can

readily be treated quantitatively, but nevertheless, in dependability, it compares favorably with a numerical record. Regardless of whether one prefers the anecdotal record plan or the Behavior Description form developed by the Progressive Education Association, or some other plan, provision should certainly be made for the description of behavior in any new cumulative record form that is set up. To neglect this aspect of the record is simply to fail to take into account one of the most fruitful recent trends in the philosophy of education. This is the balance wheel in the records system—or, to change the metaphor, it is the perfect foil for any tendency to overemphasize academic marks and achievement test data.

Finally, there is an emergent concept that will probably affect the recording of the results of measurement in the near future. This concept, which is not yet widely enough recognized to be listed definitely as one that records committees should utilize, is the idea of a common scale for all test data—a scale that is based on a defined group. The best illustration of the application of this concept is in the Scaled Score system used with the Cooperative tests. When school people generally come to realize the advantages of a system of this kind, such a plan may largely replace the recording of test results in terms of raw scores and percentiles.

REFERENCES

1. Allen, Richard D. "Guidance Records in the Secondary Schools," *Junior-Senior High School Clearing House,* IV (March 1930), 432–436.
2. Allen, Wendell C. *Cumulative Pupil Records.* New York: Bureau of Publications, Teachers College, Columbia University, 1943. Pp. vii + 69.
3. Bristow, A. B., and Proctor, W. M. "Senior High School Records and Reports," *Junior-Senior High School Clearing House,* IV (March 1930), 410–432.
4. Davis, Frank G. "Capacity and Achievement," *Bucknell Journal of Education,* XIX (January 1945), 1–13.
5. Embree, R. B. "Cumulative Record System Based on Permanent Standard Scores for Intelligence Quotient and Achievement," *School Review,* XLV (June 1937), 438–446.
6. Fisher, Mildred. "The Cumulative Record as a Factor in Guidance," *Journal of Educational Sociology,* V (February 1932), 344–358.
7. Flory, Charles D. "Cumulative Records for Research Purposes," *Journal of Educational Research,* XXX (November 1936), 157–168.
8. Flory, Charles D., and Webb, James F. "Cumulative Records for Elementary Schools," *Elementary School Journal,* XXXVIII (December 1937), 278–290.
9. Gaw, E. A. "Case-Study Techniques Developed in the Office of a University Dean of Women but Suggestive for Other Personnel Workers," *Journal of Higher Education,* XIV (January 1943), 37–40, 58.
10. Hardy, Ruth G. "Cumulative Records in Citizenship and Personality Development," *National Elementary Principal* (July 1943), 389–395.

11. Heck, Arch O. *Administration of Pupil Personnel*. Boston: Ginn and Company, 1929. Pp. xx + 479.

12. Hilkert, Robert N. "Parents and Cumulative Records," *Educational Record, Supplement No. 13* (January 1940), 172–183.

13. *Individual Inventory in Guidance Programs in Secondary Schools: Study of Present Practices in Selected Schools*. U. S. Office of Education, Vocational Division, Bulletin No. 215; Occupational Information and Guidance Series No. 7. Washington, D. C.: Superintendent of Documents, 1941.

14. Johnson, B. Lamar. "The Permanent Record Form in the Secondary School," *School Review*, XLI (February 1933), 114–122.

15. Jones, Galen, and Galbraith, Adria. "Genesis of a Guidance Program," *School Executive*, LXII (May 1943), 32–34.

16. Learned, William S., and Hawkes, Anna L. Rose. *An Experiment in Responsible Learning*. Bulletin No. 31. New York: Carnegie Foundation for the Advancement of Teaching, 1940. Pp. 61.

17. Learned, William S., and Wood, Ben D. *The Student and His Knowledge*. Bulletin No. 29. New York: Carnegie Foundation for the Advancement of Teaching, 1938. Pp. xx + 406.

18. Leonard, E. A. "Personnel Records in Guidance," *Catholic Education Review*, XXXIX (October 1941), 482–492.

19. Lloyd-Jones, Esther, and Smith, Margaret R. *A Student Personnel Program for Higher Education*. New York: McGraw-Hill Book Company, Inc., 1938. Pp. x + 322.

20. "Personnel Methods," *The Educational Record Supplement*. Washington, D. C.: American Council on Education, 1928.

21. *Pupil Progress Record Forms and Manual*. (Forms for Nursery School Through Sixth Grade.) Margaretta Voorhees, Beaver Country Day School, Chestnut Hill, Massachusetts. 1918 and revisions.

22. Robertson, David A. "The American Council Cumulative Record Forms for Colleges and Secondary Schools," *College Admission and Guidance*, pp. 69–81. Reprinted from *The Educational Record*, American Council on Education, 1932.

23. Rothney, John W. M., and Dearborn, Walter F. *Predicting the Child's Development*. Cambridge, Massachusetts: Sci-Art Publishers, 1941.

24. Ruch, G. M., and Segel, David. *Minimum Essentials of the Individual Inventory in Guidance*. U. S. Office of Education, Vocational Division, Bulletin No. 202; Occupational Information and Guidance Series, No. 2. Washington, D. C.: Government Printing Office, 1938. Pp. 48.

25. Ryan, H. H. "Records and Reports in the Junior High School," *Junior-Senior High School Clearing House*, IV (March 1930), 392–409.

26. Segel, David. *Nature and Use of the Cumulative Record*. U. S. Department of the Interior, Office of Education Bulletin, 1938, No. 3. Washington, D. C.: Government Printing Office, 1938. Pp. 48.

27. Singewald, G. L. "Analysis of Permanent Record Forms Used by Eighty-five Pacific Coast Colleges," *Journal of the American Association of Collegiate Registrars*, XVII (April 1942), 355–356.

28. Smith, Eugene R. "Modernizing Records for Guidance and Transfer," *Educational Record,* Supplement No. 13 (January 1940), 17–33.

29. Smith, Eugene R., Tyler, Ralph W., and the Evaluation Staff. *Appraising and Recording Student Progress.* New York: Harper & Bros., 1942. Pp. xxiii + 550.

30. Strang, Ruth. *Every Teacher's Records.* New York: Bureau of Publications, Teachers College, Columbia University, 1936. Pp. 48.

31. Tansil, Rebecca C. "Development and Appraisal of Cumulative Records at the State Teachers College, Towson, Maryland," *Journal of the American Association of Collegiate Registrars,* XVI (January 1941), 170–186.

32. Thisted, M. N., and Jones, Lonzo. "A Critical Analysis of the Personnel Information Blank in Use in the State University of Iowa," *School and Society,* XXXIII (1931), 540–544.

33. Traxler, Arthur E. "A Cumulative Record Form for the Elementary School," *Elementary School Journal,* XL (September 1939), 45–54.

34. Traxler, Arthur E. (editor). *Guidance in Public Secondary Schools.* New York: Educational Records Bureau, October 1939. Pp. xxv + 329.

35. Traxler, Arthur E. "Cumulative Test Records: Their Nature and Uses," *Educational and Psychological Measurement,* I (October 1941), 323–340.

36. Troxel, Oliver L., and Koos, Leonard V. "An Analysis of High School Record Forms," *Proceedings of the Tenth Annual Meeting of the National Association of Secondary School Principals,* pp. 33–57. Bulletin of the National Association of Secondary School Principals, No. 11. Cicero, Illinois: Department of Secondary School Principals of the National Education Association, 1926.

37. Twente, J. W., and Matter, W. "Study of the Record and Report Forms of Twenty-five Junior High Schools of Kansas," *Kansas University Bulletin of Education,* III (April 1931), 18–19.

38. Williamson, E. G. "Significance for Educational Guidance of Personal Histories," *School Review,* XLIV (January 1936), 41–49.

39. Wood, Ben D. "The Need for Comparable Measurements in Individualized Education," *Educational Record,* Supplement No. 12 (January 1939), 5–12.

40. Wrightstone, J. Wayne. "Cumulative School Record and Pupil Analysis," *Bulletin of the Department of Elementary School Principals,* IX (April 1930), 480–484.

CHAPTER XIII

Reports to the Homes

IT IS NEEDLESS TO EMPHASIZE THE POINT THAT CORDIALITY AND MUTUAL UNDER-standing between the school and the homes of the pupils are important in a guidance program. The relations of the school with the home may take many forms, but the one type of contact that can be counted upon to reach every home served by the school is the periodic report of pupil progress. Reports to the home are therefore a major technique in the functioning of a program of individual guidance.

Report cards are one of the oldest of the forms used by the school, probably antedating all record forms except the school register. The original purpose of report cards was to inform parents how their children were getting along in school, and this has been their main function at all times. The best reporting technique is the one which gives the parent the most complete and reliable information about the school history of his child, within the limits of the time that both teachers and parents can be expected to spend on this matter. The information sent to the home obviously should be based on those kinds of achievement and growth which the school is trying to develop in its students.

Report cards are only one of several devices for informing parents concerning the school achievement and growth of their children. In place of report cards, some schools employ letters written by teachers, letters written by pupils, personal interviews, or visits to the home. Some type of report form, however, continues to have a place in the reporting systems of the great majority of schools.

MARKING SYSTEMS

Although a detailed treatment of the theory and practice of marking falls outside the scope of this book, it is impossible to discuss report cards without giving some attention to it. The traditional plans for grading pupils have been under fire for some years, and the literature relating to marking systems has grown voluminous. The most common marking plans are the percentage system, the symbolic or categorical system, the dichotomous system, and some type of mark, such as the accomplishment quotient, to indicate the relationship of the pupil's achievement to his ability.

The percentage system is the oldest and, in most ways, the least satisfactory plan of marking. Numerous objections against it have been advanced. One of the most important is that its three reference points—0, 100, and the passing mark—are not stable and cannot be rigidly defined. Another valid criticism of this time-honored plan is that it provides for much finer distinctions than human judgment has the capacity to make. Nevertheless, many schools cling fondly to this procedure, even though it is not in harmony with modern techniques of appraisal.

The symbolic or categorical system is one in which letters, such as A, B, C, D, and F, or numbers as I, II, III, IV, and V, are used to characterize the achievement of the pupils. It is usually a five-point system, although sometimes it includes three, seven, or even nine groups. One argument in favor of it when contrasted with the percentage plan is that persons are able to form fairly valid judgments concerning individuals by classifying them into about five groups, whereas an attempt to classify them into 101 groups is futile.

The symbolic system may be clarified and rendered definite by relating it to the normal curve. One common plan for a five-point system is to assign a mark of C to all pupils falling between plus and minus 0.5 sigma; B to those between plus 0.5 sigma and plus 1.5 sigma; D to those between minus 0.5 sigma and minus 1.5 sigma; A to those above plus 1.5 sigma; and F to those below minus 1.5 sigma. In a normal distribution, this results in approximately the following percentages of the different marks: A, 7 per cent; B, 24 per cent; C, 38 per cent; D, 24 per cent; and F, 7 per cent. The marks in this system may be further clarified by paragraph statements supporting them.

The staff members of a considerable number of schools, believing that comparisons among pupils are invidious, have minimized these comparisons as much as possible by adopting a system in which a dichotomy is created. The only grades they assign are *pass* or *fail, satisfactory* or *unsatisfactory, mastery* or *failure to master.* It is stated in favor of this plan that since all pupils who do satisfactory work receive the stamp of official approval, harmful competition is greatly minimized. Nevertheless, it must be admitted that a good many schools that have tried this plan have not found it wholly satisfactory, but have gradually and half unconsciously abandoned it and returned to a symbolic system. The first step away from the dichotomous system is usually the addition of a middle group because of the feeling that *pass* and *fail* does not take care of the situation. A little later, perhaps an honors group is added, and soon the school finds itself using a five-point system, even though its grouping may not be called A, B, C, D, and F. In fact, the attempt to classify the school achievement of all pupils as satisfactory or unsatisfactory is at variance with what we know about the distribution of individuals on any characteristic. They are not readily divided into two clear-cut groups, for they vary all the way from extremely favorable to very unfavorable, and most of them cluster near the average.

Some years ago the accomplishment quotient, or A.Q., popularized by Franzen, had a flurry of popularity which has not entirely disappeared in some places. The A.Q. equals the educational age divided by the mental age, or the E.Q. divided by the I.Q. It is an interesting commentary upon the thinking that is sometimes done about marking that some persons who are vigorously opposed to placing pupils along a scale and comparing them with one another subscribe to the accomplishment quotient, which is simply a ratio between the placement of a pupil on two scales in which he is compared with other pupils. Presumably, the reason that they are willing to accept in one instance what they reject in the other is that they feel that the accomplishment quotient gives every child the same chance to stand high—the dullard as well as the bright pupil. As a matter of fact, it does not. The pupils with high I.Q.'s are placed under a handicap by this plan, so that their accomplishment quotients will probably be lower than those of their less fortunate classmates. One of the bases of this phenomenon is opportunistic. The teachers tend to prod the slow pupils, and to let the bright ones shift for themselves. Consequently, the dullards often do better in comparison with their I.Q. because of more attention, and not from any inward drive. The other basis is statistical. Stated briefly, everyone tends, because of chance errors that are inherent in every measuring instrument, to regress toward the mean of the group on a series of tests. A pupil who makes a very low score on an intelligence test will probably do a little better on subsequent tests of achievement—at least there is a greater chance that he will do better than that he will do worse. Similarly, a pupil whose intelligence score is very high has less chance of making higher average scores on several additional tests than he has of making lower scores.

Moreover, although the accomplishment quotient is a rough measure of working efficiency, it shows nothing about achievement in relation to any defined reference point. At best it may have some limited value when used along with other criteria.

In recent years, some persons have become convinced that all marking systems are inherently bad and have gone on record as being opposed to the assignment of any marks whatsoever to the pupils in their schools. There are three main arguments against the use of marks. The first has its origin in research; the second results from logical inference, supported by experience; and the third arises from mental hygiene.

Beginning with the work of Starch and Elliott about 1912, many studies have been concerned with the reliability of school marks. The evidence of those studies is so well known that it does not need to be presented here. Suffice it to say that Starch and Elliott (*13*), Wood (*16*), Ruch (*12*), and others years ago showed convincingly that the reliability of the ordinary school marks based on the traditional essay-type examinations are too low to satisfy the criteria for individual guidance. Even for examinations three hours in length, the reliability coefficients usually fall within the range .60 to .80. It is true that the reliability of marks can be improved by basing them on the results of objective tests, or by using procedures to objectify the judgments of the instructors, but all too few schools have as yet made a serious attempt to place the grading of their pupils on a more objective basis.

The second objection to marking arises out of the observation that marks are general statements of achievement, whereas specific statements are needed in guidance. It may be stated syllogistically as follows: general statements about pupils are of limited value in a guidance program. Marks are very general summary statements involving a multitude of unanalyzed variables. Therefore, marks have limited guidance value. The validity of the criticism is at once apparent to anyone who conducts a case study of a pupil whose marks are unsatisfactory. One is immediately confronted with the problem of collecting a variety of specific facts about the pupil's achievement which will give the marks meaning, reveal the sources of the difficulty, and provide leads for intelligent remedial treatment.

The third argument against marking is the one most frequently advanced by Progressive schools and is also the one which is most vigorously debated. This objection to marking is that assignment of marks causes pupils to compare themselves with each other, and leads to an unwholesome state of competition in which the less able pupils are predestined to lose and to develop feelings of frustration, inferiority, and inward rebellion. It may be pointed out in reply to this argument that ability to obtain high marks is just one of many ways in which pupils vary and that the elimination of marking will not thereby create a Utopian institution in which all pupils work together on a basis of complete equality. It may also be insisted that children who experience complete frustration because of low marks and who are unable to find a compensatory quality about which to achieve an integration of personality are already mentally and emotionally sick, and are in need of special therapeutic treatment and guidance. Regardless of opinion on this point, the first two arguments against marking are sufficient to give any school pause if it is committed to a practice of indiscriminate marking based on nothing more tangible than teacher opinion and general appraisal on a subjective basis. Marks reach their greatest value when they are supported by objective data and when they provide information con- cering the *specific* strengths and weaknesses of students.

Trends in Forms for Reports to Parents

Several good studies of report forms have been made in recent years. The following outline of the status and trends in reports is based mainly on studies reported by Hill (7), Messenger and Watts (8), Pugsley (10), Hansen (6), Brantley (3), and Metteer (9).

1. *There is growing dissatisfaction with systems of marking that encourage the comparison of pupils with one another.* Nevertheless, this dissatisfaction is probably not yet so widespread as one might think from a survey of articles on the subject. Those who are not satisfied with traditional marking plans seem to be more articulate and more vociferous than those who are. At any rate, studies fail to show that comparative marking has been abandoned in a very large proportion of report cards. In a study of 628 report cards used in the kindergarten and elementary grades of 615 city school systems, for example, Hansen found that 88.89 per cent of all the systems in use were designed to inform parents of the relative standing of the pupil in his class in comparison with other members of the class. Similarly, in 1935, Hill found in a study of 443 report cards distributed from the kindergarten through the high school that all but 8 per cent marked the pupils with either a symbolic scale, a percentage plan, or a combination of the two.

2. *There has been a trend in report cards away from percentage marking toward a scale with fewer points.* This is shown clearly when the findings of Hill (7) in 1935 are compared with those of Chapman and Ashbaugh (4) in 1925. The study by Chapman and Ashbaugh showed that in 1925, 29 per cent of the elementary cards, 23 per cent of the junior high school cards, and 37 per cent of the high school cards used percentages only in marking. In Hill's study, it was found that only 8 per cent of the elementary cards, 12 per cent of the junior high school cards, and 15 per cent of the high school cards employed percentage marking only. Both investigators showed that symbol-per cent scales[1] were utilized in 34 per cent of the cards. Chapman and Ashbaugh re- ported only 31 per cent using symbolic scales in 1925, whereas Hill found 54 per cent using such scales in 1935.

In regard to the nature of the symbolic scales, Messenger and Watts state that a three-point scale is most often recommended in articles on marking and

[1] For example—A, B, C, D, F, defined by percentages, as A = 95–100, and so forth.

reporting. However, Hill (7:119) found that in actual practice, five-point scales were far more common than other types, as shown in Table 5.

TABLE 5. MARKING SYSTEMS EMPLOYED ON 443 REPORT CARDS [2].

Grades	No Marks	Per Cent Only	Symbol—Per Cent Scales			Symbolic Scales		
			Less Than 5 Points	5 Points	More Than 5 Points	Less Than 5 Points	5 Points	More Than 5 Points
	%	%	%	%	%	%	%	%
Kindergarten–primary	29		2	9	2	43	16	
Elementary	3	8	6	24	11	16	34	3
Junior high school		12	5	19	4	6	47	9
High school		15	9	21	11	6	34	5
All	8	9	6	18	7	17	33	4

3. *There is a widespread tendency for report cards to include an evaluation of traits other than subject matter achievement alone.* Most cards now give some space to rating character traits and conduct habits, although in many cards the trait ratings are very general and perhaps not very meaningful. The average number of traits or habits mentioned on the cards studied by Hill were as follows: kindergarten, 8.8; elementary, 5.5; junior high school, 5.1; high school, 4.2; all cards, 5.6.

4. According to Messenger and Watts, *there is a clear tendency to use descriptive rather than quantitative reports.* This tendency may not be wholly commendable. A combination of descriptive and quantitative reporting may be the best plan. Certainly the ultimate purpose of all reporting is complete and accurate description, but quantitative reports may lend greater precision to descriptions, if properly interpreted and used.

5. *In some schools, formal reports are being replaced by notes or letters to parents.* These may be written by the principal, by the teachers, or by the pupils themselves. Many schools follow the practice of supplementing the more formal report of marks with notes and letters. Moreover, according to Hill, four-fifths of the report cards carry some kind of form letter to the parents. Although these messages are sometimes brief and even curt, they usually contain helpful information and suggestions. Hill's list of items discussed in the report letters together with the percentage of cards in which the items appear is as follows (7:118):

[2] Reprinted with Dr. Hill's permission.

Items Discussed in Letter	*Per Cent of 443*
Request for harmony and cooperation	41
Invitation to confer with teachers	35
Invitation to visit the school	32
Request to sign and return the card	31
The importance of regular attendance	20
Explanation of marks	19
Explanation of frequency of issuance	18
The purpose of the report card	14
Meaning of parent's signature—it does not necessarily signify approval	13
Request that parents study card carefully	9
Explanation of absence and tardy excuses	9
Character and citizenship as school aims	8
Importance of home study	5
Purposes and aims of the school	4
Bases of Promotion	4
Explanation of the failing mark	2
Parent-Teacher Association meetings	2
Miscellaneous (20 different items)	14

6. *Noteworthy attempts are made in some of the more recent report cards to analyze and diagnose a pupil's achievements in terms of the objectives of the school.* These attempts, however, are apparently not yet very common. For example, Pugsley found in an analysis of report cards used in certain schools of New York State that reporting was still highly traditional and that main emphasis remained on common knowledge and skills. Of sixty-three report cards examined, only six had some sort of statement of the aims and purposes of education, and in only four was there a clear relationship between the stated aims and the group of items in which accounting was made.

7. Messenger and Watts found that *reports are being sent at less frequent intervals and in some schools only when there is specific occasion for communication with the home.* Hill in his analysis of report cards found that about half of them were sent out six times a year. One-fourth were sent monthly, while 15 per cent were sent only four times a year. An important point in favor of less frequent reports is that the teachers can do a more thorough job of reporting if they are not required to make the reports too frequently.

8. *Attendance continues to be an important item on report cards,* for parents naturally wish to know where their children are and to be assured that they are in school each day that they are sent. Hill found that 96 per cent of the

cards reported on some phase of attendance, the more frequent items being number of times absent and number of times tardy.

9. *Parents are being asked to cooperate in building report cards and also to take part in plans of reciprocal reporting.* In connection with the securing of parental cooperation in building report cards, Ashbaugh (*1*) has suggested items for report cards which were indicated as the choice of parents through questionnaires. These items are as follows: attendance, accomplishment in studies indicated by specific letter grade, class averages as well as individual grades, personal and social traits, and effort.

10. *In some schools, pupils are cooperating in devising report cards and in evaluating their own achievement.* There seems to be a greater tendency to enlist the cooperation of children for informal reporting in the kindergarten and elementary school than in the high school.

In summarizing the findings based on his survey of current practices, Brantley (*3*) said:

The report to parents is in a state of flux in secondary schools today. Some schools still continue to report monthly or quarterly, and include information in regard to scholarship only. An increasing number of schools include a report on conduct as well. In our system, a change is being made whereby a pupil is reported as making satisfactory or unsatisfactory progress in his school subjects and in his personality development. The implication is that the school officials know the capacity, interests, and the ability of the individual so well that they can report on whether or not he is making the most of his opportunities. Such an assumption means that wide use must be made of standard tests, personality ratings, and interest questionnaires. Actually our practice is far removed from our ideal.[3]

CRITERIA FOR REPORT FORMS

In an article on the character of a reporting system, Tibbetts (*14*) has given a good summary of thirteen criteria for report cards. The criteria are as follows:

1. A report which requires a minimum amount of clerical work.
2. A report to which the community is educated.
3. A report which promotes understanding both within the home and the school.
4. A report which will inform parents of progress in all phases, physical and social as well as mental.
5. A report which states in simple terms the philosophy of the school; in other words, the ultimate goals of education.
6. A report which includes adjustment to life as well as to school subjects.
7. A report which sets up a standard of value of work for its own sake rather than for marks or other emoluments.

[3] Quoted with Mr. Brantley's permission.

8. A report which is suitable to the age level for which it is made.
9. A report which is understandable to the child himself.
10. A school record which includes both objective and subjective material.
11. A type of record which in case of transfer, facilitates early and proper adjustment of the child in his new situation.
12. A record and report which shall take into consideration the child as an individual as well as the child as a member of a social group.
13. A type of record and report which will indicate scholastic achievement, individual adjustment, and social growth.

Types of Report Forms with Illustrations

The following illustrative report forms have been selected to represent certain types from a wide variety of forms collected by the Educational Records

Clara Mason No. 5794

PUNISHMENT REPORT
House of Reformation

Date 3/17/41

Reported by F. C. Horner

For Coming to Bldg without Permission

25 lashes
Back 1 grade

W. J. Brown, Supt.
H. of R.

Form 16.

Pupil_____

MEANING OF MARKS E—Excellent .. 90-100 S—Satisfactory 75- 90 P—Poor . . . .65- 75 F—Failure . Below 65	1st Period 4 Weeks	2nd Period 4 Weeks	3rd Period 4 Weeks	4th Period 6 Weeks	Semester
Days Present					
Days Absent					
Times Tardy					
Conduct					
Arithmetic					
Art					
Auditorium					
Civics					
History					
Home Economics or Manual Training					
Language					
Library					
Literature					
Music					
Physical Training					
Physiology-Hygiene					
Science (N.S.& Geog.)					
Reading					
Spelling					
Writing					
Sunday School Credit					

Form 17.

Bureau. So many forms for reports to homes containing helpful suggestions were available, that the problem of selection was a difficult one, and in the case of some of the types represented, the report forms used by several other school systems would have served equally as well as the ones chosen for illustrative purposes.

Old-type Report Card. Before the newer plans for reporting are taken up, it may be well to present one or two illustrations in order to call to mind the

CHARACTER DEVELOPMENT

MEANING OF MARKS: E—Excellent. S—Satisfactory. I—Improving. U—Unsatisfactory.

PERIOD	1st	2nd	3rd	4th	Semester
1. HEALTH Physical appearance and health habits.					
2. SPORTSMANSHIP Attitude of fair play; give and take; loyal cooperation and obedience.					
3. WORK Willingness and diligence in performing tasks; an efficient workman; appreciates dignity of manual labor.					
4. BEAUTY Interest in and love of the beautiful.					
5. THRIFT Care of one's own property, that of the school or others; wise use of time and money; habit of saving; school savings account.					
6. COURTESY Consideration of others; good manners.					
7. NATURE Interest in and love of nature; care of animal and plant life.					
8. LEISURE Worthy use of; worthwhile hobbies and interest; wholesome out-of-school activities.					
9. SERVICE Readiness to assist others; obliging and willing service.					
10. WONDER The imaginative faculty; wholesome curiosity.					
11. COOPERATION Good team worker.					
12. SELF-RELIANCE Independence; self-confidence; accepts responsibility; initiative; doesn't hesitate to try.					

Form 18.

formal type of report that has been used traditionally in our schools. The most reactionary report which came to light in this survey was a brief *punishment report* from a house of reformation. It is reproduced (Form 16) with fictitious names and with the address of the institution deleted.

It is perhaps stretching a point to include this type of report in the present book, for it is highly improbable that even the most unenlightened school would employ such a report at the present time. It is offered as a reminder of a philosophy and practice of dealing with young people that was widely accepted two or three generations ago and that still persists in certain types of institutions. It constitutes an interesting contrast to most of the illustrative report forms which follow.

Form 17 will serve to indicate the main features of the traditional report card that is still used in many schools. It is apparent that this is a monthly report card to inform the parents about the attendance of their child and his achievement in the different school subjects. Achievement is indicated by means of a symbol-per cent scale. The only reference to personality or behavior appearing on the card is the one word "Conduct."

It should be stated that this report form, or even the one shown in Form 16, is not *per se* a bad form if it reflects the educational philosophy of the school in which it is used. Notwithstanding the inadequate and undesirable features of these forms, an attack should not be made upon the cards themselves but rather upon the educational philosophy back of them. The first step in the modernization of report forms is the re-definition of the objectives of the school.

Formal Report Cards Supplemented by Personality Report. Some schools that still retain the formal report card on school achievement have taken a step ahead by supplementing this card with a second report on character or personality. The card shown in Form 18, for example, was devised for optional use as a supplement to the card shown in Form 17.

In this card, twelve character traits have been listed and briefly defined, and provision has been made for marking the pupil as excellent, satisfactory, improving, or unsatisfactory, in each trait. Although certain aspects of this form could be improved, it furnishes some worthwhile information and it helps to keep the attention of the pupils, parents, and teachers from being focused exclusively upon subjects, marks, and credits.

Marks in Each Subject Supported by Comment. In some schools, it is felt that marks are not inherently bad, but that when they stand alone they do not tell enough. Some of these schools have adopted the practice of supporting the mark with a descriptive and interpretative statement written by the teacher. One plan for doing this is to have the mark and supporting comment for each subject written on a separate card. This plan simplifies the administration of the reporting, but it is probably more helpful to the parent in getting a complete picture of the pupil's achievement if all the marks and comments are brought together on a single report form. A simple report form of the latter type used recently in an independent school is reproduced as Form 19.

Since the pages of this report form are 8½ by 11 inches in size, considerable space is allowed for the writing of comments. It will be observed that a three-column arrangement is used, the first for the listing of the subjects, the second for the marks, and the third for the comments. In addition to the usual subjects named, provision is made for reporting on several aspects of English, and on deportment, effort, study habits, and social attitude.

Reports Based on Comments by Teachers. Some schools have gone a step further than the preceding report form in the direction of informality, and have dropped marks from the system, thus making the comments carry the entire burden of informing parents about the achievement and progress of their children. The system of reports used in the Garfield Heights City Schools, Cleveland, Ohio, furnishes one of the best examples of this plan. The three report forms are exhibited as Forms 20–22.[4]

It will be observed that the three major divisions for the comments on the kindergarten pupils are social behavior, self-expression, and health comments. It is interesting to note that in both the kindergarten report and the report form for the elementary division, parents are encouraged to participate in reciprocal reporting through the provision of generous space on the report form for parents' comments.

In the elementary school report, instead of having minute comments on each individual subject, the comments are to be grouped under language—arts, science, and number skills. Both self-expression and social behavior have an important place on the report form. In the helpful manual of instructions which has been made up to accompany the report form, there is a suggested list of desirable social traits to be taken into consideration in connection with the section on social behavior. The list is as follows:

a. Is he industrious?
b. Is he persistent?
c. Is he reasonably accurate?
d. Is he neat?
e. Is he working up to his capacity?
f. Is he developing the ability to concentrate?
g. Is he anxious to improve his work?
h. Is he critical of his own work?
i. Is he open-minded?
j. Does he begin working promptly?
k. Can he work independently?
l. Is he learning to apply newly acquired principles in wider fields?
m. Is he working to achieve a purpose and not just to do something assigned by a teacher?

[4] Used with the permission of the Garfield Heights City Schools.

Mathematics Arithmetic		
Algebra		
English Composition		
Grammar		
Literature		
Speech		
Spelling		
French		
Geography		
History		
Latin		
Science		
Writing		

Form 19.

n. Is he learning to budget his time—a time for work and a time for play?

o. Is he learning to use wisely his leisure time in the classroom?

p. Is he learning how to find things out?

q. Is he learning to organize his materials to make them most useful and effective?

Art		
Crafts		
Music		
Physical Education		
Deportment		
Effort		
Study Habits		
Social Attitudes		

Comments:

Number of school days_____

Absences_____

Latenesses_____

_____
Room Teacher

_____
Director

Form 19 (cont.)

r. Is he learning to speak clearly and effectively?

s. Is he learning to read understandingly and with increasing appreciation?

Suggestions are also made in the manual for recording school activities. This record may frequently take the form of brief anecdotes, like the following:

Garfield Heights City Schools
Kindergarten Division
PUPIL HOME REPORT

_____

(Pupil's Name)

_____   _____

(Teacher's Name)   (Period Ending)

We are submitting the following report concerning the activities of your child in our school. We want this report to serve as a means of helping the school and the home to better understand and guide your child in his school life. The report consists of comments upon the progress of your child, and suggestions regarding the attitudes, habits, and interests which the child is developing during the kindergarten experience.

We want you to feel free to express your reaction to this report in the space provided for this purpose at the close of this letter. All reports must be returned to the teacher for record purposes, except the June report.

Superintendent of Schools

SOCIAL BEHAVIOR:

SELF EXPRESSION: (Rhythms - Art - Music - Dramatization)

Form 20 (front).

HEALTH COMMENTS:

SPECIAL COMMENTS:

PARENT'S COMMENTS

PROMOTION CERTIFICATE: (Parent's Signature

The holder of this report has been assigned

to section _____ for the school year

beginning September, 19_____

_____
(Teacher)

Form 20 (back).

GARFIELD HEIGHTS CITY SCHOOLS

Elementary Schools Division

PUPIL - HOME REPORT

Name _____

Classification _____ Period Ending _____

Teacher _____

Principal _____

Superintendent's Message to Parents

The people of the United States live in a social democracy. If democracy is to best serve the interests of society, citizens generally must be prepared to think and act intelligently. One of the fundamental purposes of public education is to make the American form of government and society a safe adventure. The one best way to do this is for schools to build well-rounded individuals who are developed not only mentally but physically and morally as well.

The City Schools of Garfield Heights are striving toward the attainment of this goal. This informal pupil-home report has been designed to call your attention to the various important phases of your child's development. We suggest that you study it carefully and exchange comments with the teacher of your child. Your cooperation is needed if your child is to profit most from his school experiences.

Herbert G. Menzies

City Superintendent of Schools

The parent plays an important part in the education of the child. We want you to carefully read all the items mentioned on this report. All reports must be returned to the teacher for record purposes, except the June report. A line is provided below for your signature, indicating that you have seen this report. Additional space is provided for any comments you may care to make concerning it. The teacher will appreciate having your reaction.

Parent's Signature _____

Comments:

CERTIFICATE OF ASSIGNMENT:

The holder of this report has been assigned to section _____ for the school year beginning September, 19___

_____ TEACHER.

NOTE:

Form 21 (outside).

Regular attendance is necessary for success in school

Days due this period _____

Days absent this period _____

Teacher comments:

Good health is necessary to good living

	1	2	3	4
Height				
Weight				
Weight Increase				

Health comments

SELF EXPRESSION: (Rhythms-Art-Music-Dramatizations)

SCHOOL ACTIVITIES:

SOCIAL BEHAVIOR:

SCIENCE: (Social - Natural)

NUMBER SKILLS:

LANGUAGE ARTS: (English-Reading-Spelling-Writing)

Form 21 (inside).

Garfield Heights City Schools
Division of Elementary Education

Special Home Report:

Date_____

My dear _____

    We regret to inform you that _____

is doing unsatisfactory work in the following subjects _____

_____

because_____

_____

    If convenient, we should like to schedule a conference with you con-

cerning _____ work on _____

    If this time is not suitable, will you please indicate when you can arrange to call at the school. Please detach the stub below and return it direct to the teacher.

                          Sincerely yours,

                          _____

                                  Principal

_____

Teacher - Room No.

- -

ACKNOWLEDGEMENT

    I have received your report concerning my child's work and will make arrangements to call at the school on

                          _____

                          _____

                        Signature of Parent

Form 22.

John was host for the room one week this period. He was very pleasant at his work. He learned how to greet people and make them welcome. I know he would like to practice being host at home sometime.

John was in the school play. He did his part well. He wasn't always as quiet as he should have been, but I feel sure he intends to improve in this respect.

Spaces are provided in the report for indicating absence, but not tardiness, since it is felt that tardiness is frequently the fault of the parents rather than the child. Cases of excessive tardiness are mentioned in the space for teacher's comments under attendance.

An interesting and valuable feature of the Garfield Heights report form is the report on health, including height, weight, weight increase, and health comments. Helpful suggestions are given in the manual for the comments on health. The health of the pupils is a feature of the report forms to which more schools could well give attention. Hill (7), in his study of "The Report Card in Present Practice," pointed out that such an important educational outcome as health has been neglected in a large proportion of the cards. He stated that over half the cards examined gave no attention to health.

The special report is intended to supplement the regular home report sent at the end of each nine-week period. The teachers are expected to use the special reports in all cases where a student's work is not satisfactory. The special report blank has been constructed in duplicate so that the teacher has a record of all special reports mailed to the home.

If a school decides to change from a system of marking to a system of informal comment, it is faced with the question of whether it should abruptly drop marks throughout the school system or should abandon them gradually. In some situations, gradual abandonment of marks may create less serious problems of adjustment to the new plan for both pupils and parents. In a description of report cards without marks developed in the schools of Laramie, Wyoming, Dawson (5) showed how marks were gradually abandoned there by starting with Grade 1 and extending the new system upward a grade each year.

Letters Substituted for Report Cards. The logical next step in changing from formal to informal reports to parents is to discard all report forms and to send the information by means of letters. Among the schools that have led a movement in this direction is the school system of Newton, Massachusetts (*11*). Since report letters to parents are of course extremely variable, no attempt will be made here to illustrate this type of reporting.

No Stock Form—Mimeographed Forms Made by Each Teacher. Another plan for introducing flexibility into the reporting, which does not involve abandonment of report cards, is to have each teacher construct forms for progress reports for the subjects he teaches in terms of the objectives for that

GRAND JUNCTION PUBLIC SCHOOLS

STUDENT'S OBJECTIVE PROGRESS REPORT

Pupil_____ Year 1937-1938

Subject: ENGLISH, Grade VII

PERIODS

I	2	3	4

1. A check here indicates work is satisfactory in all respects and requires no detailed report.

2. A check here indicates work is *NOT* satisfactory.

KEY:
5—SUPERIOR
4—ABOVE AVERAGE
3—AVERAGE

2—LOWEST ACCEPTABLE WORK
1—FAILURE
Inc.—INCOMPLETE

I. *Scholarship and Class Work.*

Quality of work in English_____

Knowledge of necessary fundamental principles_____

Understanding of new subject matter_____

Neatness and correctness in written work (spelling, punctuation, sentence structure)_____

Clearness in presentation of oral work_____

Notebook work_____

II. *Good Citizenship Traits.*

Study habits_____

Initiative in finding new tasks when those assigned have been finished_____

Carefulness in following directions_____

Behavior and good manners_____

Attendance. Days absent_____

Times tardy_____

Parent's Signature—1st Period   Parent's Signature—2nd Period

Parent's Signature—3rd Period

Teacher

Form 23A.

GRAND JUNCTION PUBLIC SCHOOLS

STUDENT'S OBJECTIVE PROGRESS REPORT

Subject: FRENCH   Pupil_____

     SPANISH   Teacher_____

KEY: (A check mark indicates rank.)

5—SUPERIOR	2—LOWEST ACCEPTABLE WORK
4—GOOD	1—FAILURE
3—FAIR	Inc.—INCOMPLETE

SCHOLARSHIP, KNOWLEDGE AND SKILL

PERIODS

	1	2	3	4

Reading

Applies rules of pronunciation_____

Reads rapidly with expression_____

Translation. (1) Prepared work_____

             (2) Sight work_____

Composition

Oral. Accuracy and fluency_____

Written. Grammatical rules and spelling_____

Important Matters. Positive Response to

Vocabulary building_____

Conjugation of verbs_____

Dictation_____

Memory work_____

Cultural essays about the foreign land_____

GENERAL KNOWLEDGE OF SUBJECT MATTER_____

SCHOOL CITIZENSHIP TRAITS

Daily assignments prepared_____

Uses class time advantageously_____

Makes up work promptly_____

Respects public and private property_____

Attendance. Times tardy_____

             Times absent_____

Parent's Signature—1st Period   Parent's Signature—2nd Period

Parent's Signature—3rd Period

Form 23B.

GRAND JUNCTION PUBLIC SCHOOLS

STUDENT'S OBJECTIVE PROGRESS REPORT

GENERAL SCIENCE

Pupil_____Teacher_____

Division_____Date_____ _____ _____ _____

1st Period   2nd Period   3rd Period   4th Period

KEY: 5—OUTSTANDING ABILITY   2—BELOW AVERAGE

        4—GOOD   1—FAILURE

        3—AVERAGE

PERIODS

	1	2	3	4

Attendance (for home room only).

Days absent_____

Times tardy_____

Times truant_____

General Quality of Work.

Able to apply knowledge to new problems_____

Occupies time to best advantage_____

Good work habits_____

Accurate_____

Attitude.

Shows desire for improvement_____

Attentive_____

Courteous_____

Shows interest_____

Self-reliant_____

Follows directions promptly and cheerfully_____

Tries again and again_____

Dependability.

Punctual in work and appointments_____

Constructive in ideas_____

Dependable without watching_____

*Remarks.*_____

_____

_____

(See other side for further suggestions.)

_____   _____

    Parent's Signature—1st Period   Parent's Signature—2nd Period

_____

    Parent's Signature—3rd Period

Form 23C.

particular subject. There is no stock report form in this system, and the teacher may change his reporting blank as often as the objectives of his courses change. A plan of this kind has been used in the Grand Junction, Colorado, Public Schools. Each teacher made the report blank for his classes, including the objectives that he felt were important and providing spaces for the four marking periods. The pupil was rated on a five-point basis with respect to each objective. The two main divisions were: scholarship of the pupil and good citizenship traits. Three sample forms are shown as Forms 23A–23C.[5]

Two of the strongest features of this plan are its responsiveness to changing objectives and the detailed nature of the information each report gives. The success of this method of reporting depends largely upon the initiative and ability of the teachers in the formulation of the report blanks (*15*).

Growth Report in Terms of Objectives for Each Grade. As already indicated, the report forms that have just been examined illustrate reporting in terms of the objective for each subject as set up by the teacher. Many other schools are now basing their reports on objectives, but in most of these schools, the tendency is to have the objectives formulated by a committee of teachers, and after careful consideration, incorporated into a printed form. Among the report forms that illustrate a rather detailed listing of objectives are those of the Cincinnati Public Schools; the Indianapolis Public Schools; the Long Beach, California, City Schools; the Eaglebrook School, Deerfield, Massachusetts; and the Pasadena, California, City Schools. The growth reports for the Pasadena Elementary Schools will be taken as examples in the present discussion. The report form consists of a four-page folder, 6 by 7 inches in size. There are separate forms for the Kindergarten, Grade 1, Grades 2 and 3, and Grades 4, 5, and 6 combined. Since these are similar in general features, the folder for Grades 4, 5, and 6 only is reproduced here (Form 24).[6]

It will be noted that the report makes provision for an evaluation of the pupil each semester with respect to objectives included under health habits, relationships with others, work habits, and skills and knowledge. A commendable feature of the reporting plan in Pasadena is that it is closely correlated with the cumulative record form used in that school system.

As the name of the form indicates, it is a growth report rather than a report of achievement. Marks are not assigned, but the pupil's development is appraised according to whether or not he is showing satisfactory growth or needs improvement. The specific items in which he has strength or special ability and those in which he needs to improve are designated.

Space is provided on the last page of the folder for both teachers' comments

[5] Used with the permission of the Grand Junction Public Schools.
[6] Used with the permission of the Pasadena City Schools.

GROWTH REPORT

PASADENA CITY SCHOOLS
Pasadena, California

ELEMENTARY SCHOOLS—GRADES 4, 5, 6

Year 194........-194........

Pupil's Name..

School..

Grade................................ Grade................................

To Parent or Guardian:

The teachers in the Pasadena schools strive for the maximum progress of each pupil toward two major goals; the first, that the child shall become a desirable citizen of our democracy; the second, that each child shall meet his or her own reasonable expectations in achievement.

Reports are made to parents in order that home and school may cooperate in realizing these goals. Teachers try to report their estimates of each pupil's progress in understandable terms as a basis for parent, pupil, and teacher planning.

It is hoped that parents will use this report in planning with their children better ways of promoting further progress.

JOHN A SEXSON,
Superintendent of Schools.

Form 24 (outside).

First Semester:

Teacher's Signature..

Placement for next semester—Grade................

Principal's Signature..

Parent's Comments:

Parent's Signature..

Second Semester:

Teacher's Signature..

Placement for next semester—Grade................

Principal's Signature..

Explanation of Symbols:

S Satisfactory Growth for This Pupil
N Needs Improvement
Plus (+) after any sub-head means a strength or special ability
Minus (—) shows wherein the pupil needs to improve
Unmarked items need no special attention at this time

HEALTH AND CITIZENSHIP

	Semester	
	1st	2nd
1 Health Habits (Physical and Mental)		
a. Keeps neat and clean		
b. Is learning self direction		
Behaves well		
Uses energy wisely		
c. Works and plays happily		
2 Relationships With Others		
a. Plays well with others		
b. Is dependable		
c. Is desirably independent		
d. Is courteous		
3 Work Habits		
a. Works well with others		
b. Makes good use of time		
c. Finishes work		
d. Is attentive		
e. Follows directions		
f. Concentrates well		

ATTENDANCE AND PUNCTUALITY

Each absence, however short, may interfere with the pupil's progress.

Days present		
Days absent		
Times tardy		

SKILLS AND KNOWLEDGE

	Semester	
	1st	2nd
1. Oral English		
2. Written English		
3. Handwriting		
4. Spelling		
a. Assigned spelling		
b. Use of spelling in written work		
5. Reading		
a. Reads aloud well		
b. Reads with understanding		
c. Has interest in reading		
d. Reads with good speed		
6. Arithmetic		
a. Uses numbers accurately		
b. Reasons well		
7. Music		
8. Art		
9. Social Studies (History, Geography, Group Living)		
10. Science (Nature Study)		
11. Manual Skills		
12. Physical Education Activities		
a. Skill in games		
b. Sportsmanship		
c. Rhythms		

The foundation of every state is the education of its youth.
—Diogenes.

OMAHA PUBLIC SCHOOLS

PROGRESS
IN
SCHOOL SUBJECTS

Elementary Schools

Report of..

School.................. .... Date.... ......

Grade..... .... { Low
                             { High   ....

Days of School.... .... Days Attended.............

To the Parents:

It is the aim of this report to give a helpful analysis of the child's progress in school. Teachers have noted carefully and specifically the child's own advancement, and have taken into account the fact that normal children differ in the rates at which they learn as well as in their interests which affect learning progress. In this report, therefore, each child is considered as an individual who should be given the opportunities to develop the best in him according to his own personality and individuality.

We hope that you will find this report of interest and value. A conference with the school is welcomed if you feel it would help your child.

Homer W. Anderson,

Superintendent of Schools

The school wishes to cooperate with the home so that boys and girls may be given the best opportunities to grow. It welcomes whatever information the home feels would be helpful to the child.

PARENTS'S COMMENTS

_____

_____

_____

_____

_____

_____

_____

_____

_____
Parent's Signature

Form 25A (outside).

PROGRESS IN SCHOOL

has shown satisfactory growth in _____

_____

_____

_____

_____

_____

Suggestions for improvement _____

_____

_____

_____

_____

_____

PROGRESS IN SCHOOL

Commendations _____

_____

_____

_____

_____

_____

ADDITIONAL COMMENTS

(Suggestion: The child's attitude toward his school, his relation to other children, habits of work, and his acceptance of responsibility may explain his progress in school.)

_____

_____

_____

_____

_____
Teacher

_____
Principal

Form 25A (inside).

The foundation of every state is the education of its youth.
—Diogenes.

OMAHA PUBLIC SCHOOLS

PROGRESS
IN
SCHOOL SUBJECTS

Elementary Schools

Report of _____

School _____ Date _____

Grade _____ { Low _____
High

Days of School _____ Days Attended _____

To the Parents:

It is the aim of this report to give a helpful analysis of the child's progress in school. Teachers have noted carefully and specifically the child's own advancement, and have taken into account the fact that normal children differ in the rates at which they learn as well as in their interests which affect learning progress. In this report, therefore, each child is considered an individual who should be given the opportunities to develop the best that is in him according to his own personality and individuality.

We hope that you will find this report of interest and value. A conference with the school is welcomed if you feel it would help your child.

Homer W. Anderson,
Superintendent of Schools

ADDITIONAL COMMENTS

(Suggestion: The child's attitude toward his school, his relation to other children, his habits of work, and his acceptance of responsibility may explain his progress in school.)

_____

_____

_____
Teacher

_____
Principal

The school wishes to cooperate with the home so that boys and girls may be given the best opportunities to grow. It welcomes whatever information the home feels would be helpful to the child.

PARENT'S COMMENTS

_____

_____

_____

_____
Parent's Signature

Form 25B (outside).

PROGRESS IN SCHOOL

ARITHMETIC—Combinations and tables, problem solving, accuracy

_____

_____

ART—Enjoyment and use of art in school work, appreciation of beautiful things, ability to draw and paint

_____

_____

ENGLISH—Written composition, oral composition, English in conversation, grammar

_____

_____

HEALTH—Cleanliness, posture, interest in play and recreation, sportsmanship

_____

_____

MUSIC—Sings pleasingly, has ability to read music, enjoys singing with group

_____

_____

PROGRESS IN SCHOOL

PENMANSHIP—Writes well, writes with freedom

_____

_____

READING—Understands what he reads, reads well orally, enjoys reading, shows growth in vocabulary

_____

_____

SOCIAL STUDIES (History, Geography, Civics, Elementary Science) Prepares assigned work, gives reports well, takes part in discussions, learns to judge and use information accurately

_____

_____

_____

SPELLING—Learns assigned words, spells well in written work

_____

_____

Form 25B (inside).

The foundation of every state is the education of its youth.
—Diogenes.

OMAHA PUBLIC SCHOOLS

PROGRESS

IN

CITIZENSHIP

Elementary Schools

School _____ Date _____

Report of _____

To the Parents:

School work means training in knowledges and skills. It also means guidance in the development of the child's attitude toward himself, toward other boys and girls, toward the school, and toward society. In general we feel the skills and attitudes through which the child is trained contribute much to character growth and citizenship.

This report gives you the teacher's interpretation of your child's citizenship development as it shows in school. A conference with the school is welcomed if you feel it would help your child.

Homer W. Anderson
Superintendent of Schools

The school wants to cooperate with the home to make it possible for boys and girls to be given the best opportunity to grow.

We welcome whatever information the parents feel would be helpful to the child.

Additional Comments: _____

_____

_____

_____

Teacher _____

Principal _____

Parent's Comments

_____

_____

_____

_____

Parent's Signature _____

Form 25C (outside).

PROGRESS IN CITIZENSHIP

AS AN INDIVIDUAL

1. Work Habits

a. Takes pride in his work _____

b. Is accurate _____

c. Completes his work _____

d. Judges his work thoughtfully _____

e. Is in the right place at the right time, ready for work _____

2. Makes the best of a difficult situation _____

3. Has the desire and willingness to improve himself _____

PROGRESS IN CITIZENSHIP

4. Responds promptly, accurately, and cheerfully to school regulations _____

5. Has grown in self-confidence _____

AS A MEMBER OF A GROUP

1. Is friendly toward other children _____

2. Has ability to work and play harmoniously with the group _____

3. Is willing to share _____

4. Gives courteous attention while others are speaking _____

5. Claims only his share of attention _____

6. Has pride in class accomplishments and school activities _____

Form 25C (inside)

and parents' comments. Thus, reciprocal reporting between the school and the home is encouraged.

Three Report Forms, Two for School Subjects and One for Citizenship. The present section is included here in order to give space to a system of reporting that cannot logically be classified under any of the more general headings. This is the plan used in the Omaha Public Schools, and it is one of the most comprehensive and carefully formulated plans to be found anywhere. There are three main blanks—Forms A and B, which are concerned with progress in the school subjects, and Form C, which deals with progress in citizenship. The teacher is allowed to choose between Forms A and B. The three forms, each of which is set up in a 5½- by 8-inch folder, are presented as Form 25A–25C.[7]

Reports on either Form A or Form B are required twice each semester. Teachers who prefer the personal letter to the report form are expected to use Form A. Although it does not allow them quite the same freedom in expression that a personal letter permits, the nature of the report is much less definitely outlined than would be the case if Form B were used.

A more diagnostic report is provided by Form B, since it has spaces for brief statements in connection with the different school subjects. It is much less formal than the ordinary type of report card.

Form C is to be used at least once each semester in sending to the parents a descriptive report on the child's growth in citizenship. It will be noted that this form provides for a report of his progress as an individual and as a member of a group.

An excellent 21-page manual has been printed for use with the report card. This manual states the purpose and spirit of the report to the parents, and contains a very detailed list of suggestions for the guidance of the teachers in making out the reports of each type. One of the helpful features of the manual is a list of more than 130 comments which the teachers may consult for suggestions in writing their reports. A manual of this kind is, without doubt, an extremely important factor in introducing a new reporting system.

In addition to the forms for making regular reports, there is also a form for special reports on pupils whose progress is not satisfactory.

Dual Systems of Reporting—Rating in Terms of Objectives and Assignment of Marks in the Different Courses. Two of the most important objections to school marks are (1) that they too often represent hasty and unreliable judgments by teachers concerning their pupils, and (2) that usually no one has any very clear idea of what a given mark means. The various items that should be taken into consideration in the assigning of the marks have not been clearly identified and set down so that teachers, pupils, and parents will all know just what the basis of the marks is. If the elements that make up the marks are clearly stated, the

[7] Used with the permission of the Omaha Public Schools.

marks themselves may be useful as summary indices of achievement, and it must be admitted that they are, regardless of their merit, still necessary evils in transcripts sent to many higher institutions. It would probably be desirable for critics of marks to turn their attention not to the marks themselves but to improvement in the methods used by schools in arriving at them and to the need for eliminating the extreme emphasis that is sometimes placed on marks as goals.

If marks are made the lesser phase of a dual system of reporting, their so-called evils will be greatly minimized. The use of a dual reporting plan may be illustrated by reference to a procedure that has been employed in the University of Chicago High School.

The first step in this plan was the formulation of a complete list of objectives for each course through a series of departmental meetings. In addition to the specific objectives for each course, the school as a whole accepted the following objectives for habits of work:

1. Persistence in overcoming difficulties.
2. Tendency to work independently.
3. Promptness in completing work.
4. Application during study.
5. Attention to class activities.
6. Participation in class activities.
7. Effectiveness in following directions.

In the English Department, separate objectives were set up for each course. In each of the other departments, a common list of objectives was accepted for all the courses within the department, although it was recognized that the emphasis on those objectives would vary from one course to another. Report sheets for the different lists of objectives were mimeographed and on each sheet provision was made for rating the pupil on each objective in one of five categories —excellent, good, fair, poor, and very poor.

The plan of making the report was to send a detailed report in terms of the purposes of each course to the parents at the end of each semester. No marks were reported at this time. A week or two after the detailed reports were made, the marks were sent out. The marks were on a five-step scale—A, B, C, D, and F. Since the parents had already had an opportunity to study a detailed analysis of the strengths and weaknesses of the pupil before the marks were received, they were accepted merely as a supplementary and incidental item of information. In fact, it was found that the pupils could usually predict their own marks accurately merely from a study of the analysis of their achievement in terms of the purposes of the course. Three sample report forms developed under this plan are reproduced as Forms 26A to 26C.[8]

[8] Used with the permission of the University of Chicago Laboratory Schools.

THE UNIVERSITY OF CHICAGO

The University High School

SEMESTER REPORT, ENGLISH_____

Student_____Date_____
         Last Name   First Name

NOTE.—This report rates the pupil on his attainment of the purposes of the course and on his habits of work. The ratings are made with reference to standards for the class. Omission of a rating on any item means insufficient evidence.

Purposes	Very Poor	Poor	Fair	Good	Excellent
Language					
1. Adequacy of content in papers and talks					
2. Organization of papers and talks					
3. Paragraph structure					
4. Sentence structure					
5. Vocabulary, diction					
6. Punctuation					
7. Manuscript form and appearance					
8. General accuracy of manuscripts					
9. Spelling					
10. Handwriting					
11. Understanding of grammar					
12. Effectiveness of oral expression					
Reading and Literature					
13. Effectiveness in reading					
14. Range of reading					
15. Acquaintance with literature					
Habits of Work					
16. Persistence in overcoming difficulties					
17. Tendency to work independently					
18. Promptness in completing work					
19. Application during study					
20. Attention to class activities					
21. Participation in class activities					
22. Effectiveness in following directions					

Comments (if any):

Pupil's Grade_____   _____
                                   Instructor

Form 26A.

THE UNIVERSITY OF CHICAGO

The University High School

SEMESTER REPORT, SCIENCE_____

Student_____Date_____

           Last Name   First Name

NOTE.—This report rates the student on his attainment of the purposes of the course and on his habits of work. The ratings are made with reference to standards for the class. Omission of a rating on any item means insufficient evidence.

Purposes	Very Poor	Poor	Fair	Good	Excellent
1. Command of significant information and relationships					
2. Ability to apply principles in new situations					
3. Ability to plan an experiment and to draw conclusions from experiments					
4. Interest in science					
5. Scientific attitude: Openmindedness; habit of not jumping at conclusions; etc.					
6. Effectiveness in logical thinking					
7. Effectiveness in oral expression					
8. Effectiveness in written expression					
Habits of Work					
9. Persistence in overcoming difficulties					
10. Tendency to work independently					
11. Tendency to work effectively with others					
12. Promptness in completing work					
13. Neatness of papers handed in					
14. Application during study					
15. Attention to class activities					
16. Participation in class activities					
17. Effectiveness in following directions					

Comments:

Pupil's Grade_____   ---------------------------

                                       Instructor

Form 26B.

THE UNIVERSITY OF CHICAGO

The University High School

SEMESTER REPORT, SOCIAL STUDIES III------------------

Student------------------------------------Date----------------------

Last Name   First Name

NOTE.—This report rates the pupil on his attainment of the purposes of the course and on his habits of work. The ratings are made with reference to standards for the class. Omission of a rating on any item means insufficient evidence.

Purposes	Very Poor	Poor	Fair	Good	Excellent
1. Acquisition of basic information					
2. Mastery of basic reading skills					
a. ability to recognize main ideas					
b. ability to recognize data pertinent to a given question					
c. understanding of basic social studies concepts					
3. Ability to express ideas orally					
a. presentation					
b. organization					
c. adequacy of content					
4. Ability to express ideas in written form					
a. organization					
b. adequacy of content					
5. Ability to make generalizations and inferences based upon facts					
6. Ability to apply previously acquired information and principles in new situations					
7. Interest in current affairs					
8. Courtesy and cooperation in group situations					
Habits of Work					
9. Persistence in overcoming difficulties					
10. Tendency to work independently					
11. Promptness in completing work					
12. Application during study					
13. Attention to class activities					
14. Participation in class activities					
15. Effectiveness in following directions					

Comments:

Pupil's Grade-----------   ----------------------------------

                                    Instructor

Form 26C.

Detailed reports in terms of the objectives of each course are not only valuable in informing parents about the achievement and progress of their children but they are of great assistance in the individualization of instruction and in guidance, and they have a logical relationship to the cumulative record system of the school. They can be used effectively in individual conferences with both parents and pupils.

The Lincoln School, Teachers College, Columbia University, began a revision of its system of reporting to parents about the same time that the University of Chicago High School began to re-appraise its reporting plan. Working independently, these two experimental schools developed report forms which were remarkably similar in many respects.

JACKSON SECONDARY SCHOOLS		APPRAISAL REPORT				
JACKSON, MISSISSIPPI						
J.P.S. FORM 36		School				
Pupil		Subject				
FACTORS TO BE RATED	VERY HIGH	HIGH	AVERAGE	LOW	VERY LOW
Achievement on tests					
Quality of recitation					
Quality of completed assignments					
Promptness in completing work					
Persistence for mastery					
Self-reliance in work					
Application during study					
Attention to class activities					
Comments (if any) on back of sheet	Date				Instructor	

Form 27.

The Junior High School Goal Book of the Bronxville Public Schools is a still more elaborate system of preparing reports on individual pupils in terms of an extensive and specific list of objectives. Because of its length, no attempt will be

Name of School

Progress Report of _____
Pupil's Name

_____ _____
Grade   Date

This report has been prepared for the purpose of presenting information about the development of the pupil. It is an analysis of strengths and weaknesses made by all the pupil's teachers and is intended to prove helpful for present and future guidance of the pupil concerned. The headings of the columns are abbreviations of the following descriptions of development.

Is Outstanding: The pupil has reached an outstanding stage of development in the characteristic and field indicated: that is, a stage distinctly above that usual for pupils of the same age and similar opportunities.

Is above Usual: The pupil has reached a stage of development somewhat higher than usual, perhaps with promise of eventually reaching a superior level.

Is at Usual Stage: The pupil is at approximately the usual stage of development for age and opportunity.

Is below Usual: The pupil is sufficiently below the usual stage in this field to need particular help from the home and school or greater effort on the part of the pupil.

Is Seriously Below: The pupil is seriously below an acceptable standard in the field indicated.

Advisers and subject teachers are glad to explain or supplement this report by conference with parents. Please arrange appointments by telephone.

Attendance Report through _____

Days Absent _____
Days Tardy _____

RECOMMENDATIONS FOR NEXT YEAR

(Used only on the next to the last report)

At the present stage of the work the pupil seems, in the subjects listed:

Likely to profit by continuance of the subject _____

Able to complete the course but with question of the value of continuing it for another year _____

Likely to be unsuccessful in completing the course _____

(For upper classes only) to show promise for continuing the work successfully at an advanced institution _____

GENERAL COMMENT

This comment is intended to give opportunity for presenting information that will make the picture of the pupil's progress more complete. When there are significant interests, abilities, limitations, or contributions made by the pupils, they will be mentioned.

_____
Adviser's Signature

_____
Parent's Signature if the Report Is Returned

Form 28A (outside).

THE SUBJECT-FIELD OR OTHER RELATIONSHIP OF THE TEACHER AND THE PUPIL IS FOUND UNDER THE DESCRIPTION AND OPPOSITE THE CHARACTERISTIC DESCRIBED.

	Is Outstanding	Is Above Usual	Is at Usual Stage	Is Below Usual	Is Seriously Below
Success in achieving the specific purposes of the course					
Progress in learning how to think					
Effectiveness in communicating ideas — Oral					
Written					
Active concern for the welfare of the group					

General habits of work

Any entry opposite one of the following indicates that the pupil is seriously below an accepted standard in this respect:

Accuracy in following directions	
Efficient use of time and energy	
Neatness and orderliness	
Self-reliance	
Persistence in completing work	
Thoughtful participation in discussion	
Conscientiousness of effort	

REPORTS AND RECORDS COMMITTEE OF THE PROGRESSIVE EDUCATION ASSOCIATION. PRINTED IN U.S.A. R.F.B. 1024

Form 28A (inside).

Name of School -------------------------------

Progress Report of --------------------------------
                     Pupil's Name

------------------------------- -------------------------------
        Grade   Date

This report has been prepared for the purpose of presenting information about the development of the pupil. It is an analysis of strengths and weaknesses made by all the pupil's teachers and is intended to prove helpful for present and future guidance of the pupil concerned. The symbols used are abbreviations of the following descriptions of development.

O. The pupil has reached an outstanding stage of development in the field and characteristic indicated; that is, a stage distinctly above that usual for pupils of the same age and similar opportunities.

H. A stage of development somewhat higher than usual, perhaps with promise of eventually reaching a superior level.

U. Approximately the usual stage of development for age and opportunity.

L. Sufficiently below the usual stage to need particular help from home and school or greater effort on the part of the pupil.

S. The pupil is seriously below an acceptable standard.

Advisers and subject teachers are glad to explain or supplement this report by conference with parents. Please arrange appointments by telephone.

Attendance Report through -------------------------------

            Days Absent -----------

            Days Tardy -----------

RECOMMENDATIONS FOR NEXT YEAR

(Used only on the next to the last report)

At the present stage of the work the pupil seems, in the subjects listed:

Likely to profit by continuance of the subject -----------

Able to complete the course but with question of the value of continuing it for another year -----------

Likely to be unsuccessful in completing the course -----------

(For upper classes only) to show promise for continuing the work successfully at an advanced institution -----------

GENERAL COMMENT

This comment is intended to give opportunity for presenting information that will make the picture of the pupil's progress more complete. When there are significant interests, abilities, limitations, or contributions made by the pupils, they will be mentioned.

Adviser's Signature

Parent's Signature if the Report Is Returned

Form 28B (outside).

EXPLANATIONS OF SYMBOLS: (See complete description on front cover.)

O, is outstanding; H, is above usual; U, is at usual stage; L, is below the usual stage; S, seriously below usual stage.

SPECIFIC WORK HABITS ARE CHECKED ONLY WHEN THEY ARE SERIOUSLY BELOW AN ACCEPTABLE STANDARD.

	English	Social Studies	Mathematics	Science		
Success in achieving the specific purposes of the course						
Progress in learning how to think						
Effectiveness in communicating ideas — Oral						
Effectiveness in communicating ideas — Written						
Active concern for the welfare of the group						
General habits of work						

Any entry opposite one of the following indicates that the pupil is seriously below an accepted standard in this respect:

Accuracy in following directions			
Efficient use of time and energy			
Neatness and orderliness			
Self-reliance			
Persistence in completing work			
Thoughtful participation in discussion			
Conscientiousness of effort			

REPORTS AND RECORDS COMMITTEE OF THE PROGRESSIVE EDUCATION ASSOCIATION. PRINTED IN U.S.A. R.F.B. 1024

Form 28B (inside).

made to reproduce the Bronxville Junior High School Goal Book in this treat-ment of report forms, but it is a plan well worth study by junior high schools that may be revising their own system of reporting to parents.

Schools with large enrollments per teacher may find that detailed reports in terms of the objectives of each course call for more time than teachers can pos-sibly give to this aspect of their work, important though it is. In such schools, simpler forms must of necessity be used. Bolmeier (2), for example, while recognizing the merit of detailed report forms of the type just illustrated, recommended that the average school system provide "a uniform report form which would list the most significant factors of appraisal applicable to most school subjects." He presented an appraisal report used in the Jackson, Mis-sissippi, Secondary Schools, which is reproduced as Form 27.[9]

A Progress Report. Forms prepared by a subcommittee of the Reports and Records Committee of the Progressive Education Association for reporting progress represent an especially modern approach to techniques of reporting to parents. The Progress Report, which is printed in two forms, A and B, is shown reduced in size as Forms 28A and 28B.[10]

The Progress Report makes provision for each teacher to appraise the pupil in five areas: success in achieving the specific purposes of the course, progress in learning to think, effectiveness in communicating ideas, active concern for the welfare of the group, and general habits of work, and allows for indication of serious deficiency in certain special work habits. The principal difference be-tween the two forms is that Form A is arranged with columns for the subject fields and provides for a five-point description under each heading and in re-lation to each area of progress, while Form B has columns for the five descriptive categories and calls for the writing of the names of the subject fields in the proper boxes. Form A is the more conventional, but Form B provides the more graphic picture for the reader and may force more exactness in thinking when the report is made out. Both forms were used experimentally with success by the schools participating in the Eight-Year Study of the Progressive Educa-tion Association.

The Use of Cumulative Records in Reporting. In schools which maintain individual records for their pupils and which are fortunate enough to be able to get the parents to come to the school for individual interviews at regular intervals, it would seem that no report form other than the cumulative record card should be needed. Three essential aspects of an adequate system of re-porting are: ability, present status, and growth. The cumulative record based in part upon objective measurement seems to be more successful in presenting

[9] Used with Dr. Bolmeier's permission.
[10] Used with the permission of Dr. Eugene R. Smith, chairman of the committee.

these three indispensable kinds of information than any other report form that has yet been devised.

The Need for Experimentation with Various Plans of Reporting

Any school which abandons the traditional form of report and begins to search earnestly for better procedures will find itself embarked upon an interesting adventure that calls for a great deal of time and energy on the part of a faculty committee, and that will probably need to be carried on for at least two or three years and perhaps much longer. It is seldom feasible for a school to adopt the report forms devised for some other school system, although valuable ideas can be secured from studying report forms developed in other places, and especially from reviewing the experience of other schools in constructing and using new types of forms.

One of the most striking examples of what may be involved in a search for better reporting techniques is furnished by an experiment described in an article by William L. Wrinkle (*17*), Director of the Secondary School, The Colorado State College of Education. At the time the article was written, the experiment had been going on for six years. The school had tried in succession: (1) detailed reports in terms of objectives; (2) summary statements by the counselors at the close of each quarter in the form of notes and letters written to the parents; (3) scale-type evaluations; (4) conferences with parents; (5) check lists based upon questions that always or nearly always arose in the conferences between parents and teachers; and (6) a simplified evaluation report which would be easily interpreted by the student and his parents and which would focus their attention upon the major objectives of the school. The student evaluation report is shown as Form 29.[11] Since the publication of the article describing the experiment in marking and reporting, the school has continued its exploration of reporting procedures. The most recent evaluation form evolved in the experiment is shown in Form 30.[11]

It is interesting to note that after years of experimentation with a variety of reporting procedures, this school arrived at a relatively simple form for reporting in terms of desired outcomes of the school program. This seems to be in line with the experience of other schools. If any generalization can be made as a result of the survey of report forms presented in this chapter, it is that careful thinking and experimentation on the part of the school faculty seem naturally to lead to reports to parents in terms of the larger general educational objectives, supplemented by the major learning objectives in the various departments of the school.

[11] Used with Dr. Wrinkle's permission.

STUDENT EVALUATION REPORT

The Secondary School of Colorado State College of Education at Greeley

.... 193....

| Student | Curriculum area | Activity | Date |

Fifty desired outcomes of the total school program have been selected for the purpose of evaluation, record and report. The first ten listed below are general outcomes with which all teachers and all areas of the program are concerned. Evaluations of these general outcomes should be indicated by each teacher reporting. From the remaining items each teacher will report on those relating to the area in which he is working.

Five letters are used to indicate evaluations:

H HONORS: He would be noticeably outstanding in a large group of students of similar age and school level.
S SATISFACTORY: He has demonstrated the ability which should be expected of a student of similar age and school level.
N NEEDS TO MAKE IMPROVEMENT: He has not demonstrated the ability which should be expected of a student of his age and school level.
U UNSATISFACTORY: He is very noticeably weak in the demonstration of the ability being evaluated.
O NO EVALUATION: An evaluation cannot be made at this time because (1) the teacher is not sufficiently acquainted with the activities of the student to permit an evaluation, (2) the activity does not permit a demonstration of the ability, or (3) the student has not shown any observed evidence of the ability.

These evaluations are not competitive; they merely indicate how well the student has done certain things which he should do. Specific interpretations of these outcomes are presented in the bulletin "The Interpretation of the Desired Outcomes and Procedures in the Evaluation of the Student."

General Outcomes

—Self-direction
—Social adjustment
—Participation
—Breadth of interests
—Personal attractiveness
—Oral expression
—Written expression
—Basic reading skills
—Location of learning material
—Care of material and equipment

General Arts

—Tool skills and techniques
—Planning, drawing and designing
—Selection of materials
—Application of mathematical skills
—Creative ability

Commercial Education

—Accuracy	Each ability is checked with specific reference to the course in which the student is enrolled—typewriting, shorthand, etc.
—Legibility	
—Neatness	
—Speed	

—Application of mathematical skills
—Ability to apply the skill acquired

Physical Activities

—Health practices
—Coordination and skill in physical activities
—Aggressiveness
—Knowledge of rules and techniques
—Adaptation of techniques

General Language Arts

—Clearness and distinctness of speech
—Poise and self-confidence
—Voice quality
—Choice of reading materials
—Understanding of dramatization
—Understanding of contemporary affairs
—Creative ability

The Foreign Languages

—Comprehension in silent reading
—Rate in silent reading
—Comprehension of the spoken language
—Ability in oral usage
—Interest in language
—Understanding of the contributions of foreign peoples to present civilization

Journalism

—Skills in journalistic writing
—Skills in journalistic reading

Science and Social Studies

—Selection and use of learning techniques and procedures
—Application of the scientific method
—Interpretation and construction of graphic and statistical materials
—Application of mathematical skills
—Understanding of contemporary affairs
—Understanding of related background
—Creative ability

Mathematics

—Accuracy in the use of numbers
—Facility in the use of numbers
—Understanding of mathematical terms and concepts
—Application of the scientific method
—Interpretation and construction of graphic and statistical materials

Music

—Basic skills and understandings
—Interest in development of musical abilities

Additional comments (continue on reverse side)

Teacher..   Supervising Teacher.................. ....

Form 29.

EVALUATION OF STUDENT ACHIEVEMENT AND PROGRESS

COLLEGE HIGH SCHOOL OF COLORADO STATE COLLEGE OF EDUCATION AT GREELEY

------------------------- □ Upper □ Lower Division   Year 1 2 3 4 5 6
      Student

           6   12   36 ( )   2½ 5 10 ( )

-------------------------   ---------------------   -------------------
  Course or Activity   Weeks Enrolled   Periods Each Week

Entered_____Withdrew_____ _____
  (If other than the regular beginning and ending dates)   Date of This Report

All evaluations are in terms of what might be expected normally of students of similar age and school placement. O—Outstanding. S—Satisfactory. N—Needs to make improvement. PN—Has made unusual progress but needs to make further improvement. U—Unsatisfactory. X—Insufficient evidence or does not apply in this course.

_____ 1. *He directs his individual activities effectively*, begins work promptly, makes good use of time, requires minimum of supervision, does more than the minimum, meets responsibilities promptly.

_____ 2. *He intelligently follows plans and directions*, listens to and reads directions carefully, follows and completes plans and directions which have been set up.

_____ 3. *He gets along well with others*, is considerate of rights and wishes of others, is courteous and tolerant, controls his temper, conforms to reasonable social standards.

_____ 4. *He takes an active part in group living*, participates in group planning, volunteers his services, does his share in group activities.

_____ 5. *He speaks correctly and effectively*, speaks clearly, adjusts his voice to the size of the group, has adequate vocabulary to express himself interestingly, speaks with ease and confidence.

_____ 6. *He is careful of his personal appearance*, keeps clean, takes good care of nails, hair and teeth, selects becoming clothes, keeps clothes neat and clean, has good posture, avoids detracting habits.

_____ 7. *He takes good care of personal and school materials and equipment*, shows respect for property, does not waste or damage materials or equipment, returns things when due, reports breakage and loss.

_____ 8. *He observes attendance regulations*, is regular and prompt in attendance, arranges in advance for absence, takes initiative in making up work missed, makes proper use of school health service.

_____ 9. *He reads with ease and understanding*, selects important ideas, understands and evaluates what he reads, reads with reasonable speed.

_____ 10. *He expresses himself correctly and effectively in writing*, expresses ideas clearly, uses correct grammatical forms, punctuates correctly, spells correctly, writes legibly.

Form 30.

----- 11. *He utilizes available sources of learning materials,* selects and uses appropriate sources of information, uses library and library tools effectively, effectively engages in interview and observation.

----- 12. *He uses the problem solving method,* recognizes problems, states problems clearly, collects and records appropriate information, arrives at sound conclusions.

----- 13. *He uses the basic skills in mathematics,* uses accurately the simple fundamental combinations, computes with reasonable speed, uses fractions and per cents correctly, selects correct processes.

14. His achievement of the specific objectives* of this course or activity has been:

☐ Better than ☐ Consistent with ☐ Poorer than what reasonably might have been expected of him.

☐ Such that full credit is not recommended on administrative records.

☐ Such as to justify encouraging enrollment in_____

☐ Such as to justify recommending him for employment as a_____

* The specific objectives of each course and activity have been discussed with the student and used in classroom instruction and evaluation activities. They are available to parents and others who may be interested.

Additional comments citing specific information should be written on the opposite side of this sheet.

Supervising Teacher

Form 30 (cont).

The most encouraging aspect of present day reporting plans is not that perfect report forms have been developed or that the best ways of making reports have been discovered, but that hundreds of schools are experimenting with a variety of new plans and that some of these schools are publishing their experiences so that other schools may benefit by them.

REFERENCES

1. Ashbaugh, E. J. "Parents and Pupils' Report Cards," *Educational Research Bulletin* (April 3, 1929), 143–146.
2. Bolmeier, E. C. "An Analytical Appraisal Report of Pupil Progress," *School Review,* LI (May 1943), 292–299.
3. Brantley, G. D. "An Analysis of Current Practices in the Use of the Report Card," *Bulletin of the National Association of Secondary School Principals,* XXVI, No. 103 (January 1942), 67–76.
4. Chapman, H. B., and Ashbaugh, E. J. "Report Cards in American Cities," *Educational Research Bulletin,* IV (October 7, 1925), 291–293.

5. Dawson, M. A. "Report Card without Marks," *Journal of Education*, CXVIII (December 2, 1935), 532–534.

6. Hansen, Rowena. *Report Cards for Kindergarten and Elementary Grades.* Washington, D. C.: U. S. Office of Education, Leaflet No. 41, 1931.

7. Hill, George E. "The Report Card in Present Practice," *Educational Method*, XV (December 1935), 115–131.

8. Messenger, Helen R., and Watts, Winifred. "Summaries of Selected Articles on Report Cards," *Educational Administration and Supervision*, XXI (October 1935), 539–550.

9. Metteer, W. M. "How California Elementary Schools Report to Parents," *California Journal of Elementary Education*, X (February 1942), 135–151.

10. Pugsley, C. A. "Do Schools Report to Parents in Terms of School Objectives?" *Educational Method*, XV (October 1935), 15–20.

11. "Report Cards Abandoned by Newton Public Schools," *Journal of Education*, CXVI (November 6, 1933), 452.

12. Ruch, G. M. *The Objective or New-Type Examination.* Chapter III: "Objections to the Traditional Examination," pp. 70–111. Chicago: Scott, Foresman and Company, 1929. Pp. x + 478.

13. Starch, Daniel, and Elliott, E. C. "The Reliability of Grading High School Work in English," *School Review*, XX (September 1912), 442–457; "The Reliability of Grading High School Work in History," *School Review*, XXI (December 1913), 676–681; "The Reliability of Grading High School Work in Mathematics," *School Review*, XXI (April 1913), 254–259.

14. Tibbetts, V. H. "Determining the Character of a Record System," *Progressive Education*, XIII (May 1936), 355.

15. Tope, R. E. "Students' Reports," *American School Board Journal*, XC (May 1935), 44.

16. Wood, Ben D. *Measurement in Higher Education.* Yonkers, New York: World Book Company, 1923. Pp. 337.

17. Wrinkle, William L. "Six Years of an Experiment in Marking and Reporting in the Secondary School of the Colorado State College of Education," *Guidance in Public Secondary Schools*, pp. 86–114. Educational Records Bulletin No. 28. New York: Educational Records Bureau, October 1939. Pp. xxv + 329.

CHAPTER XIV

Case-Study Procedures in Guidance

ORIGIN OF CASE STUDIES

THE CASE-STUDY TECHNIQUE, WHICH HAS RECENTLY BEGUN TO ASSUME AN IMPORTANT place in educational procedures, is of ancient origin. It is reported that the oldest known case study is a record of child placement presumably made about 4000 B.C.[1] From that time down to the present, case-study procedures have occasionally been employed, but it was not until the latter part of the nineteenth century that case studies were placed on a well-organized basis in connection with certain professions.

One of the most important developments of the case-study method was in the field of law. Case studies were initiated in the Harvard Law School about 1870 as a device for training students to think about fundamental principles. In the nineteenth century the medical profession began to develop a literature of medicine based on the accurate observation and recording of cases. The case study has now become a fundamental aspect in the training of medical students. Case-study procedures were soon adopted by sociologists because of their obvious value in social investigation. Psychologists were slower to take over the case-study method because, until recently, they have seldom been interested in the whole personality. The case study is now a basic method in both psychology and psychiatry.

Schools did not begin to adopt case-study practices until they had been tried out extensively by several of the other professions. As long as teachers were interested mainly in teaching subject matter to groups of pupils, they had no real need for case studies. The recent tendency, however, to redirect education to take account of individual differences and the emphasis on mental hygiene

---

[1] Ruth Strang. *Counseling Technics in College and Secondary School*, p. 33. New York: Harper & Brothers, 1937.

and guidance have brought into sharp focus the need for understanding each pupil. Consequently, an increasing number of schools are turning to the case-study method as an indispensable aid in making adequate provision for their pupils, particularly for pupils who deviate from the average in any important respect.

What the Case-Study Method Is

The term "case study" has been employed in two types of investigation. A study in which real or assumed situations are presented for discussion as a means of arriving at basic principles in a given field has been called a case study. Law case studies are of this type. A detailed study of an individual, conducted for the purpose of bringing about better adjustment of the person who is the subject of the investigation, is also known as a case study. It is in the latter sense that the term will be employed in this book.

In a case study of this kind, all available data about an individual are surveyed, and the significant items are assembled, organized, and studied in order that the nature and the causes of difficulties may be discovered and that treatment designed to remove the difficulties may be planned and carried out. Thinking will perhaps be clarified if a distinction is made between case studies and case histories. A case history presents the story of an individual in as complete and as objective form as possible. It does not interpret the data and it does not, in itself, bring to a focus the information on the present problems faced by the individual. If the school maintains a complete cumulative-record system, it has a continuous and up-to-date case history for every pupil in the school.

Since the first task in making a case study is to get the facts about the individual, the initial stages of the case study are almost identical with the case history. Thus, if the school has a cumulative-record system, a great part of the arduous work of gathering data for case studies is cared for as a matter of routine. The case study, however, goes far beyond the case history. A case history is largely a clerical task, but keen intelligence and insight are called for in making a case study. The facts available in the case history are marshaled together and interpreted, and a diagnosis is made which will serve as a starting point for treatment.

A question may be raised whether the treatment of the case is a part of or a procedure that follows the case study. The case studies and case-study outlines appearing in recent educational and psychological literature exhibit no uniformity in this respect. Some case studies end with the diagnosis; others report extended treatment and the success that attended the treatment. Notwithstanding the fact that treatment is not included in some case studies, it should be clearly understood that every case study implies treatment; otherwise there would be no point in making the study. After the facts have been analyzed and a tentative diagnosis formulated, treatment should follow and, if possible, should become a part of the case-study record. Whether the treatment is recorded as a part of the case study will depend, to a large extent, on how the case is handled. If the person who initiates the case study also applies the treatment, a record of the treatment will ordinarily be added to the case study. If the case is referred to another person for treatment (for example, if a case of personality adjustment is referred to a psychiatrist), it may not be practicable to report the treatment in the case study. In cases treated by a specialist in psychiatric problems, facts are sometimes discovered which are of such a confidential nature that they should not be set down in writing. In cases of learning difficulty treated in the school, the case study will be much more valuable if it is concluded with a report of the nature of the treatment and of the progress of the pupil during treatment.

Assembling and Organizing Data in a Case Study

In a case study of a pupil, usually the first step is to collect from the school records all important information pertaining to the pupil. The question of whether a given item is important will depend on the nature of the case. If the purpose of the study is to discover the causes of, and to prescribe treatment for, an observed difficulty (for example, inability to deal with situations involving numbers), only those items in the records which may contribute to an understanding of the difficulty are of immediate importance. Even in a specialized case of this kind, however, it is desirable to get a complete picture of the pupil, since a particular difficulty can best be interpreted against the background of his whole personality.

If the study is undertaken, not for the purpose of alleviating special difficulty, but for the purpose of arriving at a thorough understanding of the pupil, so that he may be assisted to better adjustment wherever need may manifest itself, every item of information may be important, and the whole record of the pupil should be carefully scrutinized. In schools maintaining cumulative records, including data on the social history, aptitudes, achievement, and personality, the first step of the investigation will be concerned mainly with the pupil's cumulative-record card.

Although the school records should supply much helpful information, even the best of records will not provide complete data. As a rule, the data are entered at regular intervals and there will usually be a period of several weeks between the time of the last entry on the record and the time of making the case study. The case investigator will, therefore, find it necessary to interview those who have contact with the pupil, including classroom teachers, home-room teacher, physical-education instructor, librarian or study-hall supervisor, adviser, and possibly the parents. Notes should be made after each of these interviews, or better still, each of the teachers and other school officers who are in contact with the pupil should be asked to write out a brief statement concerning the child's attainments, growth, and personality.

A third step is to interview the pupil himself and perhaps to give him additional tests. The school records may sometimes provide all the test data necessary, but, if the case is one of learning difficulty in a certain subject, it is improbable that the survey-test scores in the school records will furnish an adequate basis for diagnosis. For example, if the case is one of reading disability, a diagnostic silent reading test and an oral-reading check test should be employed as a minimum. If the difficulty seems to be in the field of personality, one of the more promising personality inventories, such as the Bernreuter test or the Bell test, may be given, not so much for the purpose of record as for the purpose of securing responses which will form a convenient starting point for interview.

When reasonably complete data about the pupil have been collected, the case should be written up, and a tentative diagnosis and plan of treatment should be formulated. Although a case study could conceivably be conducted without making a written record, the necessity of putting it into writing forces the investigator to clarify his thinking about the individual and provides excellent training in stating, organizing, and interpreting the facts. Even though the plan is to include the progress of treatment as a part of the study, the case should be written up before treatment starts, and, when treatment is applied, this record should be amplified from time to time. When a written record has been made of the case, it will be very helpful to present the case study to the pupil's teachers and to secure their reactions and further suggestions before proceeding with a plan of handling the case.

OUTLINES FOR CASE STUDIES

There is no set way of making a case study. The outlines will vary with the nature of the case and the preferences of the person conducting the study. If the school maintains a cumulative-record system in which comparable data for a pupil are recorded in organized fashion from year to year, it may be desirable to have the outline of the case study up to diagnosis agree with the outline of the cumulative record. Several different outlines have appeared in recent case-study literature, three of which are presented here for illustrative purposes.

Rivlin's Outline for the Case-Study Method [2]

The Complaint
Reason for referring this pupil for special study (Include a detailed account of the incident, if possible, giving the time, place, and circumstances.)
The probable immediate cause of the incident

The approximate length of time during which this type of behavior has been manifested

Any other complaints by the same person or by others

The name and relationship to the child of the person making the complaint (Does this person make complaints about many children?)

The Child

Present status
Age
Sex
Grade—class—teacher's name

Physical appearance
General impression made by the child
Obvious physical or mental limitations
Neatness and condition of clothing
Mannerisms

Personality traits
General emotional tone; for example, cheerful, moody, etc.
Attitude toward his family
Attitude toward his school
Attitude toward his friends
Attitude toward himself, his abilities, and problems
Play life
Hobbies
Educational and vocational ambitions
Marked likes and dislikes
Unusual fears
Any special personal problem?

Educational status
Present school achievements
History of retardation or acceleration
Special deficiencies and proficiencies
Past record in work and conduct

Results of medical examination
Physical defects
Efficiency of sensory organs
General condition of health
Nutritional status
Comparison with normal height and weight
Muscular coordinations
Reduced or exaggerated reflexes
Twitchings, tics, tremors
Peculiarities of gait or speech
Previous health history

The Environment
  The family
    The individuals living at home
    Apparent economic level
    Apparent social status
    Parental methods of discipline
    Parents' emotional disposition
    Attitude toward this child
    Possibilities of securing the home's cooperation
    Record at other social service agencies

  The neighborhood
    Recreational facilities
    Housing and living conditions
    Desirability of his playmates
    Any special obstacle to adjustment

A. J. Jones' Adaptation of Henry C. Morrison's Outline of the Case Method [3]

I. Information
  A. Symptoms
      The first step is always to get at the facts that indicate that the child is a problem case; not his history but the symptoms that have been noted. This involves finding his chronological age, the marks received in various subjects, instances of misconduct, latenesses and absences from school, etc.

      All statements must be actually verified. They must be taken from school records when possible and only first-hand information accepted. The information thus obtained will often be sufficient to show that the case is not a problem one at all. Care should be taken here to exclude all that does not have to deal with present symptoms. History is valuable only as it throws light upon the causes of symptoms, but when gathering data on symptoms, history should be excluded. When the data are all in, they should be written up carefully and summarized.

  B. Examination
      With the symptoms noted, more precise information regarding the case is obtained by various tests and examinations. These are, of course, selected with reference to the needs of the particular case. Some of these are given here:
      1. Psycho-physical
         a. Vision—normal
         b. Hearing—normal

---

[3] Arthur J. Jones. *Principles of Guidance*, pp. 198–204. New York: McGraw-Hill Book Co., Inc., 1934; adapted from: Henry C. Morrison, *The Practice of Teaching in the Secondary School*, pp. 646–666. Chicago: University of Chicago Press, 1931. (Used with permission of the McGraw-Hill Book Co., Inc., and the University of Chicago Press.)

c. Coordination (neuromuscular)—no good tests are available, but careful observation will give helpful data

d. Speech—normal

2. Health
   a. Vital index (height-weight ratio)
   b. Nutrition
   c. Teeth
   d. General physical condition

3. Educational

   Standard tests of various kinds suitable to the grade of the pupil. These are to be used to discover any fundamental weaknesses in his previous training and also to check up on the marks he has received.

4. Mentality

   General intelligence test. It is best to give several types in order to avoid accidental results.

C. Health and Physical History

   Very careful and exact information should be obtained not only of serious illnesses, scarlet fever, measles, etc., but of other illnesses and operations for adenoids, tonsils, and any accidents that may have affected the health or resistance. If possible, a complete record of growth in height and weight and physiological maturity should be obtained and carefully recorded.

D. School History
   1. Promotions
   2. Kind of work done
   3. Changed location—home and school
   4. Quality of schools attended
   5. Relation with individual teachers

E. Family History
   1. Ancestry, parents, brothers and sisters, nationality, mental and criminal history, etc.
   2. Economic status and history
      The previous and present financial and economic situation of the family
   3. Cultural resources of the home
      Education and training of parents; books, music, and cultural atmosphere of the home
   4. Relation with the home—with parents and brothers and sisters
   5. Attitude of parents toward society
   6. Adjustment of parents to American standards
   7. Control exercised by parents of children—kind and amount of control

F. Social History and Contacts
   The pupil's social background outside the school and the home
   1. Church and Sunday school, boy scouts, etc.
   2. Associates

3. Summer camps
4. Gang affiliations
5. Abnormal sex history
6. Court record

II. Diagnosis

This is the working hypothesis of the cause or explanation of the symptoms or the problem and results from a careful analysis of all the data obtained. It is not necessarily delayed until all the evidence is in, for guesses or hypotheses are actually being made and leads followed up at many stages, but the final diagnosis is not actually made until the evidence is in. Possibly, the better statement would be that every guess or lead is followed until the worker is reasonably sure from the evidence that it is correct.

III. Treatment

Out of the diagnosis grows the definite systematic treatment. It often happens that the treatment shows that the diagnosis was not correct. In this case, we must go back for further investigation. In one sense, the treatment may be considered as a step in the verification of the hypothesis; in another, it is itself a guess or an hypothesis set up as a possible remedy that itself needs verification by the final step.

IV. Follow-up

It is very necessary to know the results of the treatment in order to check the accuracy of the diagnosis and to modify, if necessary, the treatment. It also aids in later cases that may be similar in nature.

McCallister's Outline for Case Studies in Remedial Reading [4]

1. Introductory statement—a brief statement which gives the reader the setting of the case
2. Preliminary survey of reading ability
   a. Performance on tests
   b. Reports of instructors concerning schoolwork of pupils
3. Analysis of reading deficiencies
   a. Power of comprehension and interpretation
   b. Rate of reading
   c. Power of perception and recognition
4. Analysis of contributing influences which aid in explaining the origin and cause of deficiencies
   a. Mental ability
   b. Vocabulary
   c. Physical history and health status
   d. School history
   e. Personality traits

[4] James M. McCallister. *Remedial and Corrective Instruction in Reading,* pp. 108–126. New York: D. Appleton-Century Company, Inc., 1936. (Used with permission of the author and the publisher.)

5. Diagnosis of the case—a descriptive statement of deficiencies with explanation of causes
6. Remedial instruction
   a. Plan of instruction
   b. Types of instruction
7. Progress of instruction—an evaluation of the effectiveness of remedial measures
   a. Practice records
   b. Improvement as shown by eye-movement records
   c. Improvement in performance on standardized tests
   d. Reports of instructors concerning school progress
   e. Evaluation of remedial instruction
8. Significant observations—an interpretation of the more significant facts about the case

Strang[5] has classified and discussed the content of case history under the following headings:

> Family history
> Developmental history
> Home and neighborhood environment
> School history
> Vocational and educational plans
> Objective data from tests and observation
> Introspective reports

This outline is simple and clear, and it includes one feature that is omitted from some of the other outlines, namely, "Vocational and educational plans." If this outline were adopted, however, it would probably be advisable to add a section for diagnosis and suggested treatment.

The following outline was set up by a school psychologist as a guide for teacher-advisers in making case summaries, which may be regarded as abbreviated case studies.

> Introductory statement
> Physical condition
> Mental ability
> Achievement in school
> Study habits
> Attitude toward work
> Interests and special abilities
> Personality
> Summary

In connection with the work of a laboratory school, a school psychologist and a psychiatrist cooperated in a series of case studies. The psychologist carried

[5] Ruth Strang, *op. cit.*, pp. 38–40.

on the initial stages of each study and provided a tentative diagnosis. The psychiatrist then took the case over, basing his treatment on a more adequate diagnosis than the psychologist was prepared to make. The outline used by the psychologist in reporting the cases to the psychiatrist could readily be applied to case studies by a classroom teacher. The outline included the following steps:

> Introductory statement—identification, age, school grade, etc.
> Intelligence
> Scores on achievement tests
> School progress
> Summary of teachers' statements
> Learning defects
> Social history
> Health history
> Personality problems
> Observation of pupil
> Summary
> Tentative diagnosis

All the case-study outlines that have been presented in this section have many elements in common. The specific type of outline to be used is not important. Presumably each teacher will wish to formulate his own outline. The main thing is to present the major facts in an orderly fashion and to formulate a plan for using them in understanding and helping the pupil.

THE CASE-STUDY METHOD ILLUSTRATED

Among the books containing valuable case studies of school pupils are those by Reavis, Smithies, Brewer, Sayles, and McCallister.[6] Two significant case studies based on cumulative records were reported by Mrs. Hawkes in Chapter IV of *Guidance in Public Secondary Schools,* published by the Educational Records Bureau. All counselors and teachers planning to make case studies will find it helpful to read Mrs. Hawkes' report. Fifteen case studies written by classroom teachers were included in Chapter XII of the same book.

The following case study was taken from an unpublished report of the writer when he was a psychologist in a laboratory school. The illustration consists of a case study of reading difficulty in which treatment and progress of treatment, as well as the history of the case, are reported. The procedures utilized in the study are not highly technical, and they could readily be employed by either teachers or counselors.

Introductory Statement. Fred entered the sub-freshman class of the high school at the age of 13 years, 1 month. His scores on all reading tests taken at the time of

---

[6] All these books are listed in the references at the end of the chapter.

entrance were rather low and appeared to indicate reading deficiency. He was therefore placed in the corrective reading section of sub-freshman English, in which special attention was given to reading. He did fairly good work in that class and his test scores at the end of the year indicated that he had made considerable progress in reading.

Fred's mother, however, was of the opinion that the boy had gained very little in reading ability during the year. She feared that he was so handicapped in reading that if special steps were not taken he would never be able to do the extensive reading required in the advanced years of high school and in college. The librarian of the high school, likewise, observed evidence of continued retardation in reading. Because of these facts and also because his scores on reading tests were still considerably below the median of his class, special work in reading was undertaken with Fred at the beginning of his freshman year in high school and was continued throughout the year.

General Ability. Fred's scores on intelligence tests during his first year in the high school are shown in Table 6.

TABLE 6.   INTELLIGENCE TEST RESULTS OF A NINTH-GRADE BOY

Test	I.Q.	Norm	Median I.Q. of Class	Quarter Rank in Class [a]
Otis Self-Administering	102	100	107.0	3
Ohio Psychological	105	100	110.4	3
Stanford-Binet Scale	109	100	.....	..

[a] 1 is the highest quarter.

The results of all three tests show that Fred has normal intelligence. His I.Q. was between 100 and 110 on all the tests. On the group tests, he was below the median but above the lowest quartile of his class. On the individual test he showed a mental age of 14 years, 11 months at a chronological age of 13 years, 8 months. The examiner who administered the Binet test to Fred made the following note on his test blank: "Fred is very deliberate in his attack upon problems. He works slowly but is usually correct in his conclusions. His type of response is *reflective.*" There is little doubt that Fred has sufficient mental ability to do acceptable, although probably not outstanding, work in the high school.

Social and School History. Fred is of German stock. His grandparents came to America from Austria and Germany. Three generations on the paternal side have been engaged in the medical profession. Fred has a brother and a sister, both of whom are pupils in the same high school. The economic status of the family is good. A large and comfortable home is maintained and there are two servants. The boy is much interested in a variety of outdoor sports and has playmates his own age.

Fred is large and mature-looking for his age. The school physician examined him and found that his health in general was good. Bitten finger nails were the only evidence of nervousness. The vision in his right eye was found to be quite defective and the physician recommended that he have his eyes retested for glasses. Fred wears glasses now when reading.

If Fred has any serious personality problems, they have not appeared in his work in the high school. He seems to be well adjusted to the social group. Several of his teachers have commented upon his good attitude, his cooperation, and his willingness to profit by criticism.

All of Fred's elementary school training was received outside this school system. His progress through the elementary school was not entirely normal. He repeated one-half year and made up the last half of the sixth grade in the summer. During the first semester that Fred was in the sub-freshman class of the high school he had considerable difficulty with the work. At the end of the first semester he had incomplete work in United States history and art appreciation. His written papers were not good because of weakness in spelling, punctuation, and sentence structure, and he required a considerable amount of reteaching. According to the reports of his teachers, Fred did much better work during the second semester of his sub-freshman year and he has continued to do acceptable work this year. Fred has not had serious difficulty in school except in reading.

Evidences of Reading Deficiency. Scores made by Fred on reading tests since he entered the high school are compared with the test norms and class medians in Table 7.

TABLE 7. SCORES ON STANDARDIZED READING TESTS

Test	When Administered	Score	Grade Norm	Class Median
Monroe Silent Reading				
Rate	Sub-Freshman Year	77	84	109.3
Comprehension	" " "	28	25.4	33.0
Monroe Silent Reading				
Rate	Freshman Year	86	84	.....
Comprehension	" "	30	25.4	.....
Thorndike-McCall	Sub-Freshman Year	47	56.0	61.7
" "	Freshman Year	59	61.5	.....
Inglis Vocabulary	Sub-Freshman Year	38	45.0	47.3
Traxler Silent Reading				
Form 1	Sub-Freshman Year	61	80.0	100.0
Form 3	" " "	71	80.0	.....
Form 4	Freshman Year	81	89.0	.....
Sangren-Woody, Form B	Sub-Freshman Year	61.3	84.0	.....
Form A	" " "	85.4	91.0	.....
Gray Standard Oral Reading	Freshman Year	37.5	48.0	.....

The table shows two general facts concerning the pupil's reading ability. First, Fred was retarded in reading in comparison with the grade norm and the median of his class. Of twelve scores, nine were below standard. In five cases where class medians were available, the pupil's scores were decidedly below the medians.

The second conclusion about Fred's reading skill that can be drawn from the test scores is that there was considerable gain during his sub-freshman year. The gains shown are as follows:

Test	Time Elapsed	Points Gained
Monroe Silent Reading—Rate	12 months	9
" " " —Comprehension	12 "	2
Thorndike-McCall	12 "	12
Traxler Silent Reading	12 "	20
Sangren-Woody	9 "	7

In spite of these gains, however, the fact that Fred was still below the norm on three of the four tests made remedial work during his freshman year advisable.

Fred was observed, while reading, by the librarian and the psychologist early in the present school year and a number of difficulties were noted. These will be brought out in the diagnosis of the case.

Diagnosis of Reading Difficulties. The greatest difficulty revealed in Fred's test scores was a marked slowness in rate of reading. Retardation in rate appeared in every timed reading test administered to him. His rate score on the Monroe Standardized Silent Reading Test in the beginning of his sub-freshman year was 77 as compared with a norm of 84 and a class median of 109.3. His score on this test near the beginning of his freshman year was slightly above the grade norm, but was below the class average. In the Sangren-Woody Reading Test, Fred made rate scores of 16.3 and 16.4 at the beginning and the end of his sub-freshman year. The grade norm is 21. In the various forms of the Traxler Silent Reading Test he read consistently at a rate of about two words a second, whereas the minimum standard for his grade is three words a second. His inferior rate of reading was probably due partly to his slow rate of associating ideas with words. This hypothesis is supported by the fact that the speed with which he did a test of rate of association was considerably lower than the average.

The retardation in rate of reading undoubtedly tended to lower Fred's comprehension scores in some of the tests, particularly the Monroe test. However, his rather low scores on the Thorndike-McCall Reading Scale, which has generous time limits, indicates that he was somewhat retarded in ability to comprehend the meaning of reading material, even when he had plenty of time to ponder over it.

Fred's reading vocabulary was not quite as extensive as that of the median pupil in his class, but it was practically up to the grade norm. In fact, his score on the vocabulary parts of the Sangren-Woody and the Traxler tests equalled or exceeded the norm.

It was discovered early in the individual work with Fred that he manifested a tendency toward that type of reading confusion known as "reversals." That is, he sometimes confused letters which looked alike except that their orientation from left to right was opposite one to the other. This tendency was unquestionably present in the case of *b* and *d*, although it was not noted for any other pairs of letters and was not observed in the case of any pairs of words. The case did not appear to be a very serious one, since no reversals except *b* and *d* were noted.

Fred was not greatly interested in reading when he entered the high school and the training in reading given in the English class during his sub-freshman year did not succeed in building up an interest of this kind. His mother stated at the beginning of the present year that he read very little at home and that she would be glad if he would read just one book and really enjoy it.

Aims of Remedial Work. The purposes of the remedial training in reading given to Fred this year were directly in line with the diagnosis of difficulties. They were as follows:

1. To foster an interest in reading.
2. To build up habits of independent reading.
3. To increase rate of reading as far as native rate of reaction would permit.
4. To develop greater power of understanding reading material.
5. To utilize incidental opportunities to increase the reading vocabulary. Formal training in this respect seemed unnecessary.
6. To overcome the tendency to reverse certain letters.

Treatment of the Case. The remedial treatment of the pupil was planned to achieve the purposes that were outlined. The first and most important needs were to plan a program of reading that would stimulate interest and lead to habits of reading. In this part of the work, the remedial teacher had the full cooperation of the school librarian. At the beginning of the year, the librarian drew up an extensive and varied reading list for Fred and throughout the year she was very helpful in supplying books and making additional suggestions.

The pupil met with the remedial teacher one period each week during the 11:00 o'clock hour. Usually the meeting was held on Wednesday. At this meeting the independent reading of the pupil during the next week was planned. Usually the manner of planning followed was for the remedial teacher to select two or three widely different books from the reading list supplied by the librarian and to have Fred examine them and choose the one that he preferred to read. It was generally planned that the pupil should finish the book and return it at the next meeting on the following week. Sometimes, when the book was exceptionally long or Fred's schedule of regular class work was heavier than usual, more than a week was spent on a book. The pupil reported the amount of independent reading done each week. Usually a few minutes were spent in discussing the content of a book. No attempt was made in connection with this type of reading to check rigidly on Fred's comprehension of the material. It was kept in mind that the purpose was to build up interests in recreative reading and it was felt that the aim would be defeated if the reading was made a task to be done.

As a rule, most of the time in the remedial period was spent on the McCall-Crabbs Test Lessons, Book IV. The plan of using the book was as follows: Five lessons were covered at each meeting. The regular three-minute limit was used for each lesson. After Fred had finished a lesson, he read his answers to the questions to the examiner, marked the ones that were wrong, and translated his raw score into a "G–Score" by means of a table. He then worked out correct answers for the questions he had answered incorrectly, and read aloud and answered the questions that he had failed to cover during the time limit. This oral work at the end of each lesson (except those lessons finished within the time limit) assured the thorough understanding of each lesson. It also gave opportunity for constant check on reversals of *b* and *d,* since the questions were of the four-response type (responses *a, b, c, d*), the pupil indicating his answer by reading the letter preceding the answer he thought was right.

The plan of using lessons that were timed stimulated the pupil to read at his maximum rate. He took much interest in his G–Scores and, with the aid of the teacher, kept a graph of the G–Scores from week to week.

The McCall-Crabbs Test Lessons were sometimes made the basis of informal vocabulary work. The remedial teacher soon found that Fred could nearly always work out the right answer for every question unless the material contained words unfamiliar to him. Occasionally the material was varied by using one of the volumes of *Real Life Stories* instead of the McCall-Crabbs lessons.

After each of the meetings with Fred, the remedial teacher wrote a brief summary of the work carried on during the period. If this entire record were included in the present report it would be needlessly long. The following excerpts illustrate the type of record made:

Friday, October 28. Fred read five of the McCall-Crabbs Test Lessons. Rate slow; comprehension good. (A continuous record of these lessons is kept on another sheet.) He selected and read a story in *Real Life Stories.* His rate was slow —about half a page per minute. He said that the story was interesting. His attitude was excellent.

Wednesday, December 7. Fred returned *The Prince and the Pauper* which he had finished. He had also read 275 pages in *Famous Frontiersmen.* He retained it to finish before next Wednesday. Fred is also going to read short stories for his literature class and will report the titles to me. He read McCall-Crabbs Test Lessons 11 and 12. An improvement in speed was evident. A tendency to confuse *b* and *d,* when these letters stand alone, which had been noted in preceding lessons, was observed again. When it was mentioned to him, he acknowledged the difficulty. I told him not to worry about it and that it would probably disappear with practice in reading. He read aloud the first chapter of Van Loon's *Ancient Man.* He had practically no difficulty with pronunciation and was able to give the thought orally quite well. Fred did the Gates Pronunciation Test without error. I asked him the meaning of several words and found only one that he didn't know. Fred spent the last part of the hour reading ahead in the book, *Famous Frontiersmen.*

Wednesday, April 19. As Fred was absent from school last Wednesday, this was his first meeting with me for two weeks. He returned Hawes' *Mutineer* which he had finished. He said that he found it rather dull at first, but interesting after he got into it. The reading during the period covered McCall-Crabbs Lessons 63–67. The average G–Score was 7.5, the best record he has made thus far. Fred chose the *Story of Ab* to read during the next week.

Progress of Treatment. Fred and the remedial teacher spent a total of thirty class periods (including testing periods) on the work in reading. The pupil was interested in the reading and cooperated with the teacher in every way. Evidence of his interest is found in the amount of independent reading done during the year. The following is a list of books read:

> Britt, *The Boys' Own Book of Frontiersmen*
> DuPuy, *Uncle Sam, Detective*
> Mark Twain, *The Prince and the Pauper*
> Johnston, *Famous Frontiersmen*
> Green, *Roy Andrews, Dragon Hunter*
> Parker, *Book of Electricity*
> Spivak, *Georgia Nigger* (selected independently)
> Gaston, *Modern Lives*
> Driggs, *The Adventures of Arnold Adair, American Ace*
> Garland, *Boy Life on the Prairie*
> Masefield, *Martin Hyde*
> *Hoof and Claw*
> Hawes, *Mutineer*
> Waterloo, *Story of Ab*
> *Lance of Kanana*
> ———— *Electricity for the Farm House*

Fred also read one of Thompson-Seton's books of animal life and several short stories, including some by Poe and one by Conan Doyle.

Near the end of the year the plan of having Fred choose his books from the library rather than from a reading list was adopted. His selections tended to be in the field of science. Although Fred's tastes in fiction are not yet very mature, his interests in non-fiction—especially scientific books—are quite mature. Fred's science teacher reports that he is far ahead of most of his classmates in his understanding of that field.

All ninety-four test lessons contained in the McCall-Crabbs Book IV were read during the year. Occasionally, this work was varied by selections from other material, but Fred showed a preference for reading in the McCall-Crabbs book because he could see his score in reading and could note his progress from week to week.

Results of the Remedial Work. Evidence of Fred's improvement in reading during the remedial period is of four kinds, which are as follows:

1. Gains in G–Score on McCall-Crabbs Test Lessons.
2. Improvement in scores on reading tests.
3. Reports of teachers.
4. Results of observation of the pupil.

McCall-Crabbs G–Score. The authors of the McCall-Crabbs Test Lessons have provided for changing raw scores directly into G–Scores or grade scores. That is, a G–Score of 5.0 on lesson 10 is equal to a G–Score of 5.0 on lesson 15 and every other lesson. Thus, the G–Scores are directly comparable. Some of the lessons do not seem to be very well standardized, but it is probable that if the G–Scores for several lessons are averaged, the errors appearing in standardizing various lessons will tend to cancel each other. At any rate, the scores offer a fairly satisfactory measure of reading ability in terms of grade norms.

Fred's record of G–Scores, with the scores for all the lessons given on any one date averaged, is shown graphically in Figure 4. The pupil's lowest score was 4.3 on October 28, the first time the test lessons were given, and the highest score was 8.0 on May 31, the date on which the test lessons were discontinued. This gain was equivalent to the progress that might normally be expected in 3.7 grades. A part of the improvement was doubtless due to familiarity with the type of lesson used in the McCall-Crabbs books and to better methods of attack on this kind of lesson. These factors do not, however, explain all the improvement. After a number of lessons of this type had been done by the pupil, one can reasonably assume that he had become thoroughly adjusted to the reading situation set up in the lessons and that familiarity with that kind of lesson would thenceforth cause little, if any, gain in score. Nevertheless, he continued to improve to the end of the training period. A genuine gain in reading ability is therefore indicated.

Scores on Reading Tests. Fred's progress in reading ability during the year is indicated by the scores on five reading tests shown in Table 8.

TABLE 8.　IMPROVEMENT IN TEST SCORES DURING REMEDIAL TEACHING

Test	Before Remedial Training	After Remedial Training	Gain in Points	Grade Equiv-alent at End of Period of Teaching
Sangren-Woody Reading	85.4	87.2	1.8	8.3
Thorndike-McCall Reading Scale	59.0	61.0	2.0	8.9
Monroe Silent Reading				
Rate	86.0	89.0	3.0	10.0
Comprehension	30.0	34.0	4.0	12.7
Gray Oral Reading	37.5	46.0	8.5	....
Traxler Silent Reading				
Rate	24.0	24.0	0.0	
Vocabulary	21.0	29.0	8.0	
Comprehension	36.0	42.0	6.0	
Total score	81.0	95.0	14.0	10.0
Average grade equivalent	....	....	....	9.7

Improvement was made on every test. The larger gains were in comprehension, vocabulary, and oral reading. The gain in rate of reading was insignificant according to the results of the Monroe test and the Traxler test. The small gain on the Sangren-Woody test, in which rate of reading is very important, also suggests that Fred did not improve materially in speed of reading. In spite of the fact that the gain in rate was negligible, the remedial training was worthwhile because of the large growth in comprehension.

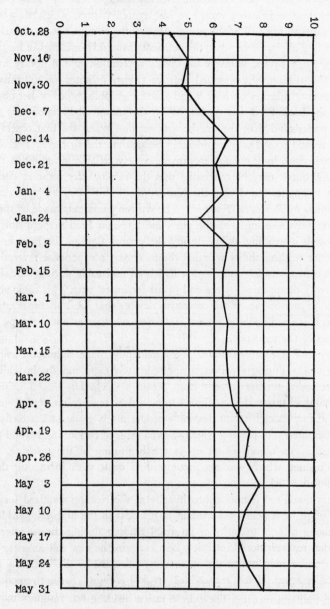

FIGURE 4. G-Scores on McCall-Crabbs Test
Lessons, Book IV.

Reports of Teachers. The comments made by Fred's teachers in the regular reports at the end of the year do not show deficiencies in reading. They indicate that Fred's work was satisfactory except in his written papers, which showed marked deficiencies in spelling and handwriting. Apparently, Fred is not now markedly deficient in reading ability; if he were, the deficiency would be reflected in his class work.

A report made by the librarian on Fred's application in the library may be included in this section. She observed him for twenty minutes on November 22 and again for twenty minutes on May 8 and made a graphic record of her observations. Although the book Fred was reading when the second observation was made was harder to understand than the one he was reading when the first observation was taken, his second record was considerably better than the first one. The observation was not carried on long enough to provide a very reliable sampling of the pupil's study habits, but it may be concluded that the results offer some evidence of improvement in application during the year.

Observations by Remedial Teacher. The written comments made by the remedial teacher after each meeting with the pupil indicate that Fred made a slow, but consistent, growth in reading ability during the period. One of the most encouraging signs of better reading ability was that the tendency to experience reversals—in particular, the confusion of *b* and *d*—that had been noticeable during the fall semester had apparently disappeared by the end of his freshman year. This came about without the use of any of the special corrective devices that are sometimes employed in these cases. It is not known at present, however, whether or not the pupil is permanently cured of the tendency.

Summary and Recommendation. Fred evidently made significant improvement in reading ability during a period of approximately eight months in which he met with the remedial teacher for one class period a week. His largest gains were in power of comprehension. He continued to be a slow reader, but nevertheless he was able to read fast enough to do the work of the ninth grade satisfactorily. He also developed an interest in reading which showed signs of continuing beyond the period of training. Of six objectives set up at the beginning of the teaching, five were reached. The one which was not accomplished dealt with increasing the rate of silent reading.

It appears that Fred is now approximately at the reading standard for the ninth grade, although he is below the median of his class in the high school. He plans to continue doing a large quantity of informal reading during the summer vacation. The remedial teacher should interview him early in the new fall semester in regard to progress and should utilize the opportunity provided by the interview to test his reading ability again. Unless marked loss in skill is found, further remedial instruction will be inadvisable, especially in view of the fact that his written English expression will probably need some special attention. The pupil is mature in his attitude, earnest in purpose, and appears to have reached the point in his development where he can guide himself in his reading.

POINTS TO BE OBSERVED IN MAKING A CASE STUDY

Planning the Case Study. The following points are offered as suggestions for persons who are contemplating the making of a case study for the first time:

1. Select a case in which you are really interested both from the standpoint of the nature of the case and the personality of the individual concerned.

2. If possible, choose a pupil from one of your classes who, you feel, needs attention and help and who will probably cooperate well with you.

3. When considering various pupils, give some thought to the shy, quiet, retiring pupils. Pupils of this type are sometimes more suitable subjects for case study than pupils whose difficulties or behavior cause them to be noticed.

4. Plan only as much as you feel that you can accomplish. If you contemplate a thorough case study, including treatment, it will probably be best to confine your study during the first year to one pupil. If you prefer to make brief case summaries, you can perhaps do several, or even summaries for an entire class if it is small.

Collecting the Data. Some of the main points with respect to collecting the data were set forth earlier in this chapter. An additional point is that in interviewing the pupil and in testing him to get further data about his difficulties, care should be used not to place him on the defensive. He should not be made to feel that he is a culprit or that he is in any way an extreme deviate from his fellow pupils. The meeting ground of the case investigator and the subject should be one of sharing in the solution of the pupil's problems. If the case investigator can enlist the interest of the pupil and can get him to take the initiative from the beginning, the prognosis for the successful solution of the pupil's problems is excellent.

Writing Up the Case. As already indicated, there is no one pattern for writing up the case, but certain general principles should probably be observed.

1. Write objectively, simply, and with directness. Although you should be vitally interested in the case, your report of it should not reflect personal bias. The description of the case should be as objective and the interpretation should be as impersonal as possible. This does not mean that you should avoid interpretation and inference, but it does mean that you should distinguish meticulously between the facts you have discovered and the interpretation or diagnosis based on these facts.

2. In the report of the case, use both general statements and specific illustrations. General statements about intelligence, achievement, and personality are much more convincing if they are supported with some definite data.

3. Eliminate irrelevant items; confine the case report to a few typewritten pages.

Applying and Evaluating Treatment. Persons who are inexperienced in making case studies often find that the study moves along smoothly until they reach the stage of applying treatment, but that this stage presents problems which seem baffling. The observation of a few suggestions may help to clarify these problems.

1. A case investigator should not attempt to apply treatment for difficulties that are entirely outside his experience. If he does make such an attempt, it is probable that he will become involved in an embarrassing situation and that he may do the pupil more harm than good. If the problem is one of learning in his own or a related field, he should be able to handle it. If the problem is one of reading or study difficulty, as many cases are, he should be able to offer the pupil valuable help in reading and studying the content of his own special field and perhaps of other fields. The case investigator can also handle many problems that are volitional, which are caused by lack of interest, or which are of a minor behavior character. If the case involves learning adjustments that are entirely foreign to his experience, or if it includes obscure personality disorders, the investigator should frankly recognize his inability to meet the situation and should conclude his report with a recommendation for referral.

2. During the period of treatment, the case investigator should keep a careful journal record of the progress of treatment. He should not depend upon his memory but should write up each interview with the pupil and each significant observation just as soon as possible. Not all of what is written in the journal will find its way into the case report, but a complete journal record is of inestimable help in making a final report at the end of the period of treatment.

3. If the case is the kind that lends itself to measurement (for example, if it involves achievement in a certain skill or school subject), comparable tests should be administered at the beginning and the end of the treatment. Such tests will take the evaluation of the treatment out of the realm of speculation and will sometimes reveal significant progress under conditions where no conclusions about growth could be made on the basis of observation alone.

4. After a case has been released from treatment, it should be followed up and the individual kept under observation for a few months to make sure that a relapse does not take place. This is especially important in cases involving skills such as reading, spelling, and arithmetic. Some pupils who make marked gains on tests during a period of teaching will tend to return to their old habits later unless they are carefully supervised.

Distribution of Case Studies

If each member of a school faculty should undertake one case study, it may be anticipated that the studies will naturally represent a wide sampling of types of cases. Nevertheless, it will probably be advisable for the faculty to spend some time together in planning the studies to make sure that various kinds are represented. Learning cases in different fields of study will probably account for the largest number of studies. It is to be hoped, however, that some persons will have the temerity to undertake studies of behavior problem cases. Most of the case studies will no doubt be concerned with problem pupils, but a few of them should certainly be directed toward understanding and planning adjustments for very superior pupils. Finally, it will be helpful if some members of the staff will study average pupils in order to investigate the value of case reports for the great middle group in the school population.

VALUE OF CASE STUDIES

Several schools which participated in the Public School Demonstration Project[7] of the Educational Records Bureau experimented extensively with a plan of having case studies carried on and written up by classroom teachers. Their experience indicated that the following values resulted:

1. A considerable number of the pupils in the school who were most seriously in need of careful individual attention and guidance were subjects of detailed study. Not every case study brought about improvement, but it is believed that the net result constituted a real gain.

2. Each case investigator acquired a better understanding of cumulative records and a greater insight into the relationship of these records to the immediate needs of the pupils. It seems probable that the teachers profited as much from the case studies as did the pupils.

3. The case studies formed a basis for group discussions between the different teachers of each pupil. Thus, cooperative work between teachers in different departments, and between teachers and counselors, was fostered.

The preparation of case studies by classroom teachers is relatively a new educational procedure and there is need for further investigation of what can be done in this field. It is highly desirable for schools that are experimenting with case studies to have them presented in written form, for it is through such reports that other schools may be shown how cumulative histories of aptitude, achievement, and personality factors can be made to contribute to the classroom teacher's understanding of individual pupils and to the individualization of instruction. Thus, an accumulation of written case studies may constitute an important contribution to guidance procedures at all levels of the school.

[7] See *Guidance in Public Secondary Schools, Chapter XII.* Educational Records Bulletin No. 28. New York: Educational Records Bureau, 1939.

REFERENCES

Allen, Richard D. *Case Conference Problems in Group Guidance.* New York: Inor Publishing Company, 1936. Pp. x + 152.

Allport, Gordon W. *Personality: A Psychological Interpretation,* "Suggestions for the Preparation of a Case Study," pp. 390–395. New York: Henry Holt and Company, 1937. Pp. xiv + 588.

Babcock, G. M. "Mental Hygiene Approach to Guidance in the Senior High School," *Junior-Senior High School Clearing House,* VI (December 1931), 221–224.

Baker, Harry J., and Traphagen, Virginia. *The Diagnosis and Treatment of Behavior Problem Children.* New York: The Macmillan Company, 1935. Pp. xiv + 393.

Bixler, Roy A. "High School Problem Cases," *Chicago School Journal,* XIII (November 1930), 141–143.

Brewer, John M., and others. *Case Studies in Educational and Vocational Guidance.* Boston: Ginn and Company, 1926.

"Case Studies and Special Curricula Proposed for Secondary Pupils Expecting to Enter College," *Progress Report IV, Study of the Relations of Secondary and Higher Education in Pennsylvania.* Prepared by the Carnegie Foundation for the Advancement of Teaching in cooperation with the Joint Commission of the Association of Pennsylvania College Presidents and the Department of Public Instruction for the Educational Congress, Harrisburg, Pennsylvania, November 4–6, 1931.

Davis, Frank G. *Classroom Teacher's Cumulative Pupil Personnel Record.* Lewisburg, Pennsylvania: Royal Stationery Company, 1944.

Gaw, E. A. "Case Study Techniques Developed in the Office of a University Dean of Women but Suggestive for Other Personnel Workers," *Journal of Higher Education,* XIV (January 1943), 37–40, 58.

Hawkes, Anna Rose. "The Cumulative Record and Its Uses," *Guidance in Public Secondary Schools,* Educational Records Bulletin No. 28, Chapter IV. New York: Educational Records Bureau, 1939.

Hill, Arthur S. "The Use of an Objective Type of Case Study in the Analysis and Prognosis of Pupils' Maladjustment Problems," *Educational Administration and Supervision,* XXI (November 1935), 611–618.

Hirsch, E. C. "Case Method of Dealing with Individual Problems in the Secondary School," *School Review,* XXXVIII (September 1930), 525–531.

Howard, Frank E., and Patry, Frederick L. *Mental Health: Its Principles and Practice,* Chapter XIV, "Methods of Reconstructing Personality and Behavior Problems." New York: Harper & Brothers, 1935. Pp. xvi + 551.

Jones, Arthur J. *Principles of Guidance,* "Case Methods," pp. 198–204. New York: McGraw-Hill Book Co., Inc., 1934. Pp. xvii + 456.

Kuenzel, M. W. "Case-Record System at the Vineland Laboratory," *Training School Bulletin,* XXVIII (May 1931), 41–52.

Ludeman, W. W. "Case Histories for All Pupils," *School and Society,* XLIII (April 11, 1936), 509–510.

McCallister, James M. *Remedial and Corrective Instruction in Reading,* pp. 108-158. New York: D. Appleton-Century Company, Inc., 1936. Pp. xviii + 300.

Mink, Myrtle S., and Adler, Herman M. *Suggested Outline for History Taking in Cases of Behavior Disorders in Children.* 721 S. Wood Street, Chicago: Department of Public Welfare, Series C, No. 9.9. Reprinted from *Welfare Magazine* (March 1926), p. 21.

Morrison, Henry C. *The Practice of Teaching in the Secondary School,* Chapter XXX, "The Problem Pupil—Case Work," pp. 636–666. Chicago: University of Chicago Press, 1931. Pp. x + 688.

Patry, Frederick L. "A Suggested Formulation of Mental Hygiene Case Studies" (in two parts), *Educational Method,* XII (October 1932), 19–25; (November 1932), 89–94.

Reavis, W. C. *Pupil Adjustment in Junior and Senior High Schools.* Boston: D. C. Heath and Company, 1926. Pp. xviii + 348.

Rivlin, Harry N. *Educating for Adjustment,* "The Case-Study Method," pp. 107–114. New York: D. Appleton-Century Company, Inc., 1936. Pp. ix + 419.

Sarbin, Theodore R. "The Case Record in Psychological Counseling," *Journal of Applied Psychology,* XXIV (April 1940), 184–197.

Sayles, Mary B. *Child Guidance Cases.* New York: The Commonwealth Fund, 1932. Pp. xxiii + 584.

Smithies, Elsie M. *Case Studies of Normal Adolescent Girls.* New York: D. Appleton-Century Company, Inc., 1933. Pp. x + 284.

Strang, Ruth. *Counseling Technics in College and Secondary School,* Chapter III, "The Case Study," pp. 32–51. New York: Harper & Brothers, 1937. Pp. x + 159.

Strang, Ruth. *Exploration in Reading Patterns.* Chicago: University of Chicago Press, 1942. Pp. ix + 172.

Strang, Ruth. *The Role of the Teacher in Personnel Work,* Chapter XIV, "The Technic of the Case Study," pp. 289–324. New York: Bureau of Publications, Teachers College, Columbia University, 1935. Pp. xiii + 417.

Symonds, Percival M., and Jackson, Claude E. *Measurement of the Personality Adjustments of High School Pupils,* pp. 76–86; 99–105. New York: Bureau of Publications, Teachers College, Columbia University, 1935. Pp. xi + 110.

Thuemler, Gertrude. "Case Studies," *Indian University, School of Education Bulletin,* VI (March 1930), 53–64.

Traxler, Arthur E. (Editor). *Guidance in Public Secondary Schools.* Educational Records Bulletin No. 28. New York: Educational Records Bureau, 1939. Pp. xxv + 329.

Whitley, R. L. "Case Studies in the Boys' Club Study," *Journal of Educational Sociology,* VI (September 1942), 17–30.

Williamson, E. G. *How to Counsel Students: A Manual of Techniques for Clinical Counselors.* New York: McGraw-Hill Book Co., Inc., 1939. Pp. xx + 562.

Wood, Ben D. "The Major Strategy of Guidance," *The Educational Record,* XV (October 1934), 419–444.

CHAPTER XV

The Role of the Teacher in Guidance

THE RELATIONSHIP OF THE TEACHER TO THE GUIDANCE PROGRAM MAY BE CONSIDERED in two ways. First, there is the obvious connection with guidance which teachers have in school systems where all instructors, or certain selected ones, are designated as guidance officers, each being responsible for a group of perhaps twenty or thirty pupils. Second, there is the connection with guidance which each teacher has in her regular classroom and extracurriculum activities regardless of the system of guidance followed in the school. This chapter will be concerned mainly with the second of these relationships—that which exists in the ordinary daily contacts between teacher and pupils.

It is common knowledge that the average public high school teacher carries a heavy load. He or she must teach from one hundred to two hundred pupils distributed through four, five, or even six classes; participate in the extracurriculum program of the school; prepare lesson plans; read and correct papers; give special help to slow pupils; handle minor behavior problems; make out reports; and often take an important part in the out-of-school life of the community. If participation in a guidance program seems to be just another routine responsibility added to an already heavy load, enthusiasm for the program will naturally be lacking among the teaching staff. A teacher can be expected to contribute wholeheartedly to such a program if the relationship of guidance to the job already being done is clearly understood. It is hoped that the following list of questions and answers will help to clarify this relationship.

I. Is It Desirable to Combine the Functions of Guidance and the Functions of Teaching in the Same Person? Should not Guidance Procedures Be Carried on by Specially Trained Persons?

The answer is that these functions are already combined in the same person. All teachers carry on guidance and will continue inevitably to do so. The question is not whether teachers shall engage in guidance, but whether guidance shall be unplanned and incidental, or planned and purposeful. It is true that the guidance program should be under the direction of one who has specialized in this field and that a staff of specially trained counselors is needed if the program is to reach its greatest effectiveness, but these specialists can succeed only if they have the full and active cooperation of the teachers. In schools that have only one guidance officer, who is frequently on a part-time basis, most of the actual counseling must be done by the teaching staff, because it is physically impossible for one person to keep in close contact with several hundred pupils. Although the principal and the assistant principals often assume much of the work of counseling, it is probable that the most effective guidance can be done when administration and counseling are divorced. The best guidance relationship is obtained when pupil and counselor meet as nearly as possible on an equal footing, with the relationship completely freed of all implications of authority or coercion. Teachers, because of their closer contacts with the pupils, are frequently in a better position to provide the conditions needed for effective counseling than are other members of the staff.

II. If I Try to Do Guidance Work When My Schedule Is Already Full, Will not This Extra Load Reduce My Teaching Efficiency?

It is true that learning to use test results and cumulative records and studying guidance philosophy and the application of guidance techniques does require a considerable amount of a teacher's time at first, and it may call for some reduction in other types of service in the beginning; but in the end it should greatly increase teaching efficiency, for it will lead the teacher to become better acquainted with the abilities and needs of the different pupils and will help the teacher see them as individuals rather than merely as members of a group.

The studying of the philosophy and methodology of guidance is in a sense an extra, although necessary, load for the teacher. The process of guidance, itself, is not, however, an extra load, for it is work that the teacher already engages in and it has for its ultimate goal the same objectives that good teaching has—the maximum adjustment and growth possible for every individual. Under the normal conditions of teaching in a secondary school there can be no sharp dividing line between instruction and guidance. These two processes are inextricably related in every classroom and in every extracurriculum activity in which both pupils and teachers engage.

III. What Can I Do About the Guidance of the Pupils in My Classes, Whom I See in Groups for Forty or Fifty Minutes Each Day, Most of Whom I Did not Even Know by Name Before They Entered the Class, and About Whom I Know Little or Nothing?

This is a live question, presenting a situation which is typical in almost all large public high schools. One might answer the question by asking another—What can you do about *teaching* under such conditions? Even if the teacher were interested only in the formal presentation of subject matter, an adequate job could not be done until he or she had ascertained whether or not the background of the pupils was sufficient to make the class presentations comprehensible. It is obvious that the first thing to be done in meeting the situation for either instructional or guidance purposes is to *study the pupils*. It is here that some of the most important instruments in guidance will be found indispensable. If a comprehensive testing program has been conducted about this time, the results of the test scores will provide information about the present aptitude and achievement of the pupils. If cumulative records have been kept in the school, a variety of information about home background, health, interests, extra-curriculum activities, and growth in achievement, as well as present status of achievement, will be available in compact and readable form. Lacking standardized test scores and cumulative records, the teacher will find the problem of becoming acquainted with the needs of the pupils much more difficult and its solution will depend on the teacher's ingenuity in devising her own methods for getting the necessary information.

Much of the guidance that teachers do is necessarily through group procedures rather than through individual conferences. Alert teachers who have studied their pupils will see opportunities to carry on group guidance in connection with their regular teaching. For example, most pupils need guidance in study habits. The nature of study so varies from subject to subject that probably the most effective guidance in study habits will be carried on in connection with the actual classwork. Time spent on guidance of this type in the classroom is certainly a legitimate function of instruction.

IV. What Can I Do to Help Make the Testing Program of the School Effective?

Teachers can make a very important contribution to the testing program of the school through critically evaluating the achievement tests used in the light of the objectives and content of their courses. Such an evaluation calls for more than general impressions. A detailed checking of each item in the test should be made, with notations indicating whether or not the test question samples something the school is trying to do. Such analyses should be most helpful in interpreting the results of the tests. No test can be expected to fit a particular curriculum exactly, but the correspondence should be fairly close.

The teachers can also aid with the testing program by sending information to the principal, which may be passed along to the publishers, about questions which experience indicates are not valid. The actual experience of teachers in the field with tests is one of the best aids in their revision and improvement.

Still another way in which teachers can assist in securing valid results with tests is to see to it that the new pupils in their classes who have not previously had experience in taking standardized tests are made acquainted with the general nature of objective tests before the tests are administered. A few minutes spent in making an explanation and displaying sample questions to a group of inexperienced pupils may place them in a much better position to show their real ability when the tests are given. Needless to say, the actual forms of the tests which are to be employed in the testing program should not be used for this purpose.

A fourth contribution that the teacher can make to the guidance program is to explain the results to the pupils in either group or individual discussions. It is also legitimate, after the tests have been given, to use some types of scored test papers as teaching devices, but not much time should be spent in this way and care should be used to avoid allowing the tests to determine the content of the courses.

V. What Use Can I Make of Cumulative Records and How Can I Contribute to the Records?

The teacher can use cumulative records in getting the essential facts about the ability and achievement of the class at the beginning of the term and thus within a few days after the course has started (or even before it begins) information will be available that could not be collected in less than several weeks by the usual procedure of gradually becoming acquainted with the pupils through day-to-day contacts. Thus from the beginning the teacher can plan for group activities with some assurance and can also take into account the special needs of individual pupils.

The cumulative records will be a constant source of information for the teacher in connection with individual conferences and special help for the various pupils. Each card should provide an up-to-date case history in summary form. A teacher cannot be expected to carry in mind the essential facts about each pupil, but if the school has a cumulative record system the facts should be looked up when they are needed.

An important part of the cumulative record has to do with social adjustment, personality, mental and emotional factors, activities and interests, accomplishments, experiences, and plans. Tests in these fields are still highly experimental and the main reliance for the filling out of this part of the card must be placed upon observations of persons who have contacts with the pupil. The classroom teachers of each student will have the best opportunity to contribute to this part of the card. Teachers should form the habit of noting down brief anecdotal records about their pupils and of forwarding them to the proper office for entering in condensed form on the pupil's cumulative record. Over a period of years, such uncontrolled observations, collected from a large number of teachers and assembled in the same part of the record card are extremely revealing and provide invaluable data for future guidance.

VI. How Can I Make Maximum Use of Cumulative Test Histories in Diagnosing the Learning Difficulties and Improving the Instruction of My Pupils?

The point which will bear repetition is that the conducting of testing programs and the keeping of cumulative records are only means to an end. These procedures will be valuable in direct proportion to the degree to which the records are used constructively in the improvement of instruction and guidance. After every testing program the scores and percentile ratings of each pupil should be studied in order to find his points of strength and weakness, and in the case of subjects that are continuous over a period of several years, the pupil's growth since the last test was taken should be noted.

One plan for doing this is to have the guidance officer or psychologist make a survey of the test scores of the entire school in order to find the pupils whose growth scores are low and the subjects in which they are deficient, and to refer the cases to the proper teachers for more careful analysis. Pupils who are very slow should be scheduled for special help.

The use of test results in instruction has three distinct aspects, as follows: (1) the improvement of instruction in the regular curriculum of the school; (2) the planning of corrective and remedial work for retarded pupils; and (3) the provision of special programs for superior pupils. In connection with the first aspect, it has been found that a tabulation of the percentage of correct responses made by a class on each item of a standardized test is very useful in helping a teacher see those points that need greater emphasis in instruction. This procedure is to be recommended if it is kept in mind that the purpose is to discover the areas in which groups of children are strong or weak, and then to decide what should be done about the situation. Care should be used to avoid making the specific test items themselves objectives of instruction. Tests are at best samplings of basic skills, information, and understanding, and they should not be permitted to determine the curriculum of the school. The evaluation of responses to particular items and even to whole sections of the test should be in terms of the teacher's objectives for the particular course covered by the test. The fact that the pupils may make low scores on certain parts of the test may not mean that the teacher should give special attention to the matters covered by those parts. It may mean only that the objectives in that particular school are different in some respects from the objectives of the test makers. Nevertheless, the tabulation and study of quantitative data concerning the success of the pupils on the different items in the various tests used is a procedure that some schools are finding very helpful in reappraising and improving their courses. The item-counter unit on the International Test Scoring Machine is a distinct aid to this kind of use of test results, as far as machine-scored tests are concerned.

At the beginning of the year each teacher can profitably spend several hours studying the test histories of the pupils in her class and noting at least the following points: (1) the general level of the academic aptitude and achievement of each pupil in relation to the basic criterion group and to the members of his own class; (2) the achievement of the pupils in the teacher's special field as compared with their achievement in other fields; (3) the achievement of the pupils in the different parts of the test covering the teacher's special field (if this information is available); and (4) the probable readiness of the class as a whole to proceed with the course without the taking of preliminary preparatory steps.

In the planning of remedial and corrective work in connection with a testing program, four steps are ordinarily required of a teacher: (1) a survey of the scores on each test to select the pupils who are low; (2) the diagnosis of the difficulties of the pupil with low scores—a step which may call for the administration of additional diagnostic tests; (3) the planning of corrective teaching either in regular classes or in groups meeting at special times; and (4) the assignment of pupils to these special help groups for the duration of their deficiency. An additional step may also be needed—the provision of individual instruction for pupils who are too handicapped to profit by group instruction, although extensive individual instruction is seldom practicable in a remedial program conducted in public schools, because of the regular teaching load that each instructor carries.

Many studies have been made of diagnostic and remedial work in connection with the basic skills of reading, arithmetic, language usage, spelling, and handwriting, and the more effective methods are fairly well established.[1] In most of the high school subjects, however, the use of test results in analyzing difficulties and in planning special help is still a pioneer field. One of the most significant contributions that could be made by teachers in public schools would be to set up and validate some techniques for doing this type of work.

Much emphasis should be placed on the third aspect of the use of test results—the provision of special programs for superior pupils. Although much theorizing has been done by educators in recent years about the desirability of providing for pupils with exceptional ability, the carrying of these ideas into action has been largely neglected by all except a few schools of the progressive type. Consequently, pupils who according to the results of carefully constructed tests are,

---

[1] For further information on this point see *The Use of Test Results in Diagnosis and Instruction in the Tool Subjects.* Educational Records Bulletin Number 18, revised, pp. 17–35. New York: Educational Records Bureau, 1942.

at high school entrance, above the average for high school graduates in English usage, acquaintance with literature, understanding of the world of science, or other aspects of the work of the secondary school, are usually put through the same routine as their less gifted classmates. If here and there throughout the country, enlightened teachers would, with the consent of their high school principals, courageously break with tradition to the extent of releasing a few of their outstanding pupils from a portion of the regular work of their classes so that they would be free to carry on individual study under guidance, and would keep cumulative records of the progress of these pupils, it is believed that this example would have marked effect in freeing the superior pupils in the schools of the United States from useless and deadening routine.

VII. How Can I Assist in the Adjustment of the Pupils in My Classes to Their In-School and Out-of-School Environment?

This question is directed toward the most vital part of the guidance program. The contributions that a teacher can make to adjustment are innumerable. When it is discovered that a pupil is poorly adjusted, the general rule is to assemble the facts, analyze them, form a tentative hypothesis about the nature of the difficulty, plan treatment, apply it, observe the effect, and revise treatment as needed until the difficulty appears to have been removed. The teacher's most obvious relation to adjustment of pupils is in learning situations. If the pupil's failure is in the teacher's special field, the study of the cumulative record should help the teacher to diagnose the failure, to prescribe and administer treatment, and to effect a cure. If the failure to adjust is due to difficulty with a related field (for example, inability to write up science experiments because of English deficiency) the facts can be marshaled and reported to the proper department. Teachers have long cooperated in adjustment matters of this sort.

Another type of adjustment problem to which teachers can and usually do contribute is the type sometimes known as the "problem of inconvenience." Problems of inconvenience include the minor behavior difficulties that temporarily upset the routine of a classroom. Such problems, being overt in nature, usually do not indicate serious maladjustment on the part of the pupils who cause them, but teachers are ordinarily anxious to help work out adjustments because these matters are so annoying to them. The cumulative record—particularly the less objective part of it—may furnish valuable leads concerning the pupil's behavior and possible ways of modifying it.

All teachers know that there are many matters of personal and social adjustment in which they may aid pupils who seek their advice. Teachers have always helped with this kind of adjustment, but they should remember that in all such cases, they can do a better job if they will utilize the information that can be obtained from complete and carefully kept records.

Much more serious problems of pupil adjustment are liable to be deeply hidden and may escape observation altogether, unless teachers are alert for them. The shy, introverted, imaginative pupil may be more seriously maladjusted than the worst trouble-maker in class. Teachers who have not had courses dealing with psychological and psychiatric problems will be much more competent to assist with the more obscure and difficult problems of adjustment if they will become acquainted with the writings of leaders in these fields, or with recent textbooks and studies dealing with various aspects of child and adolescent psychology. Teachers may thus improve their ability to discover individuals needing guidance in mental hygiene, although they should be careful not to arrive at hasty conclusions about the nature of the difficulties, for psychiatric symptoms usually are not overtly related to their cause but are secondary symptoms developed as a healing process. These symptoms should be recognized and reported but the teacher will seldom, if ever, be prepared to provide adequate interpretation or treatment for them.

Although the adjustive aspects of guidance do have, in some instances, obscure and technical ramifications that call for the assistance of experts, the greater part of the work of guidance is neither mysterious nor highly technical. Good teachers have always been guidance officers, as well as instructors, and they always will be. The philosophy and techniques of a guidance program are for the most part simply a means of helping the school staff do better what it would, by virtue of necessity, attempt to do anyway.

REFERENCES

Bratton, Dorothy. "Classroom Guidance of Pupils Exhibiting Behavior Problems," *Elementary School Journal*, XLV (January 1945), 286–292.

Davis, Frank G. *Classroom Teacher's Cumulative Pupil Personnel Record*. Lewisburg, Pennsylvania: Royal Stationery Company, 1944.

Davis, Frank G., and Raup, Zura. "A Technique for Bringing the Classroom Teacher into the Guidance Picture," *Bucknell Journal of Education*, XVI (November 1941), 9–11, 14–15.

Dunsmoor, Clarence C., and Miller, Leonard M. *Guidance Methods for Teachers in Homeroom, Classroom, Core Program*. Scranton, Pennsylvania: International Textbook Company, 1942. Pp. xvi + 382.

Embree, Royal B., Jr., and Eggersten, Claude. "A Plan for the Induction of Student Teachers into the Training School Guidance Program," *Education*, LX (December 1939), 247–251.

Fahey, George L. "What Every Teacher Can Do for Guidance," *School Review*, L (September 1942), 516–522.

Flory, Charles D.; Allen, Elizabeth; and Simmons, Madeline. "Classroom Teachers Improve the Personality Adjustment of Their Pupils," *Journal of Educational Research*, XXXVIII (September 1944), 1–8.

Hahn, Milton. "The Staff Clinic in the Pupil-Personnel Program," *School Review,* XLVII (January 1939), 32–36.

Herrick, V. E., and Corey, S. M. "Group Counseling with Teachers," *Educational Administration and Supervision,* XXX (September 1944), 321–330.

The Self-Appraisal Program of Guidance in the Junior High Schools of Philadelphia: Handbook for Teachers. Philadelphia: School District of Philadelphia, Board of Public Education, 1944. Pp. 55.

CHAPTER XVI

Follow-up of Students and School Leavers

THERE ARE FOUR DISTINGUISHABLE ASPECTS OF FOLLOW-UP WORK IN GUIDANCE. IN THE first place, there is the incidental follow-up of pupils which counselors and teachers carry on as a part of their normal activities in the school. Counselors frequently follow up interviews with individual pupils to note the effect of advice, or to gather additional information, or to assist the pupil further with his problems of adjustment. Teachers follow up pupils who have had special help with learning problems in order to note progress and forestall recurrence of the difficulties. Individual cumulative record cards are prepared as one phase of the guidance program, and these records may be regarded as a systematic follow-up procedure applied to all pupils—superior, average, and slow. No school could function as a unit without carrying on a considerable number of follow-up activities. Abandonment of these activities would lead to a thoroughly chaotic situation.

A second type of follow-up work is to be found in connection with individual pupils who have served as bases of case studies or who have received intensive remedial help in certain fields. It would be unwise to carry on a detailed case study or to provide remedial teaching for a pupil during a period of a few weeks and then drop the case. Nearly all psychological or psychiatric work in education presupposes that the case of the individual pupil will be followed up over a period of at least a year after the treatment has been discontinued in order to evaluate the results of the work and to note whether further progress is being made, but unfortunately in the busy environment of the school, where dozens of pupils constantly need special attention, this important phase of case-study and remedial work is too often neglected.

A third aspect of follow-up work in guidance is to be found where schools

317

have evolved a systematic procedure for following up pupils from one unit of the school to the next higher one. For instance, a sixth-grade teacher may follow up each of her pupils when they advance to the junior high school, or a junior high school counselor may follow up the pupils in his advisory group throughout the three grades of the senior high school. An illustration of the latter type of provision is furnished by the Providence Public Schools, where the seventh-grade counselors make one-year follow-up studies in cooperation with counselors in Grade 10; eighth-grade counselors carry on two-year follow-up studies in conjunction with the counselors in Grade 11, and counselors at the ninth-grade level conduct three-year follow-up studies jointly with the twelfth-grade counselors. The Providence plan has been explained in detail by Allen (*1*:166–176).

The fourth aspect of follow-up work is the one toward which attention especially needs to be directed, because for the most part guidance programs leave much to be desired as far as this phase of the school program is concerned. This aspect of guidance has to do with the follow-up of graduates and other school leavers. Its importance in the development of a guidance program which actually functions in the lives of the individual young people can hardly be overemphasized. One may well question whether a school has discharged its full guidance responsibility if it gives a pupil careful attention while he is in school, but abruptly terminates its interest in him when he is graduated. Rather, it would seem that the school should help him get adjusted to his post-school environment and that the guidance activities should be "tapered off" gradually.

PURPOSES AND NATURE OF FOLLOW-UP OF SCHOOL LEAVERS

Young people who leave school either by graduation or by dropping out are followed up for one or more of three main purposes. First, there is the natural desire to help the individual with problems of vocational, educational, and social adjustment after he goes from the school and while he is getting himself established elsewhere. As a rule, more attention is given to vocational adjustment than to the other types, although not infrequently adjustment to a vocation depends in part upon the successful resolution of personal factors in the individual's make-up.

A second purpose of follow-up studies is to gather data for use in evaluating the instructional and guidance programs of the local school. This is an extremely important purpose. The chief criterion of the value of a guidance program is its influence on the post-school lives of the individuals who have received the counseling services. The administration of a school can have no clear idea of the worth of its guidance program, or the mistakes that are being made, or the phases which should be stressed more, or those which should be changed, unless data are available concerning outcomes, that is, concerning what is happening to the product of the school.

A third purpose of follow-up studies of school leavers is to gather information of general interest concerning those who have left. Such studies are intended to help all social agencies, including schools, deal with the problems of youth more intelligently. The majority of the comprehensive follow-up studies reported thus far belong in this category. Among these may be mentioned the study conducted by the American Youth Commission in Maryland under the direction of Bell (2); the study by Eckert and Marshall *When Youth Leaves School* (6), carried on as one part of the Regent's Inquiry in New York State; Eurich and Pace's (7) follow-up study of Minnesota graduates; the well-known study of Bell telephone employees made by Bridgman (4); Hale's *From School to College* (9); Thorndike's *Prediction of Vocational Success* (21), and *An Investigation of the Needs of Adults for Further Training* (22) by Trabue and Dvorak.

The great need at present is for the careful planning of continuous follow-up studies to be carried on by local school systems and to serve the first and second purposes mentioned. It is not surprising that during the war period very little in the way of systematic follow-up of school leavers has been done. The war created an abnormal employment situation in which nearly all the boys recently out of school went into one occupation—the armed services of their country—and the entire working population of both sexes was characterized by great mobility, a fact which greatly complicated attempts to follow up individuals. With the gradual transition to peace-time employment conditions, however, follow-up studies are again assuming a potentially important place in all guidance programs.

In follow-up studies of graduates and other school leavers, the following types of information have been found useful in counseling programs:

1. Occupational distribution of school leavers.
2. Occupations in which employment is increasing.
3. Occupations in which employment is decreasing.
4. Time elapsed between school leaving and employment.
5. Success of graduates and non-graduates in employment.
6. Extent to which former students are engaged in the vocations they had in mind in school.
7. Degree to which vocational training pursued in school carries over into life.
8. Influence of such factors as age, sex, intelligence, health, school achievement, home background, and marital status on occupational adjustment.
9. Earnings of school leavers in various occupations.
10. Occupational conditions which have hindered progress.
11. Extent to which graduates are engaged in further study.

12. Success of graduates in higher institutions.
13. Factors that influence the migration of young people.
14. Ways in which students feel that their school training has been most beneficial.
15. Ways in which the school has failed to meet educational or vocational needs.

The two main procedures used in gathering information in follow-up studies are questionnaires and interviews. Both procedures have certain limitations. When questionnaires are used, it is very desirable to obtain a high per cent of replies in order to avoid bias in the data, but unless several successive attempts are made, it is usually found that a considerable proportion of the individuals to whom the questionnaire is sent do not return it. In certain school systems, such as the Providence public schools, which have had much experience with follow-up studies, procedures have been developed for insuring a large proportion of returns.

Interviews are time-consuming and costly and are seldom practicable in the case of individuals who have left the community, but more detailed and perhaps more accurate information can be obtained in this way than by means of questionnaires. In the more recent follow-up plans, there is a tendency to submit a questionnaire to all school leavers and to select from those returning the inquiry forms, a representative sampling to be interviewed.

In both questionnaires and interviews, the replies to questions of opinion about the values of training received in school may, because of what Wrenn (25) has called the "old oaken bucket" reaction, be somewhat too favorable. Everyone tends to remember pleasant and to forget unpleasant experiences. When one has been out of school a few years, his memory of school life tends to be colored by sentiment and he is liable to exaggerate the values derived from the school program. Nevertheless, helpful leads concerning needed improvement in the school are frequently obtained by presenting questions of opinion in the inquiry form.

The treatment of some of the data obtained in follow-up studies is a straightforward clerical job. Data on types of occupation and salaries are of that sort. The analysis of those types of data involving covariance and causal relationship is, however, exceedingly intricate and baffling, and even competent research men sometimes draw questionable conclusions about the relationships of certain factors. It can be shown readily, for example, that number of years of schooling and standing in class are related to vocational success, but one is not justified in inferring a causal relationship without controlling other variables. The correlation may be due to the influence of intelligence upon the factors concerned. This is but one illustration of the need for interpreting the data obtained in follow-up surveys with caution.

THE CONTINUOUS FOLLOW-UP SURVEY

Occasional surveys of school leavers, carried on intermittently, provide a certain amount of useful information for counseling purposes, but they do not satisfactorily meet either the purpose of helping the individual or the purpose of furnishing data on a product of the school. Under the conditions of a haphazard program of this kind, many former students who need help will escape attention, and up-to-date information on the circumstances surrounding school leavers will be lacking.

The ideal follow-up plan is the continuous survey conducted as an integral part of a school's counseling program. Some schools have already inaugurated this type of survey. In the senior high schools of the Providence, Rhode Island, Public Schools, a plan of this kind has been in operation for years. The plan, which has been described in detail by Allen (*1*), involves a follow-up survey of each class, one, three, and five years after the class has been graduated. The class counselor is responsible for making the study, although he may call upon the central office for a certain amount of clerical assistance.

Briefly the mechanics of the plan are as follows: A counselor stays with the same class throughout the three-year senior high school period. In the orientation course at the eleventh- and twelfth-grade levels, he introduces materials to help prepare the class for its own follow-up survey, and he stresses the importance of such surveys to both the individual and the school. The first year after the class is graduated, the counselor drops back to Grade 10 and begins the guidance of another class. At the same time, he makes a one-year follow-up study of his former class. Through the cooperation of class officers, and by means of questionnaires, telephone calls, and interviews, he manages to maintain a proportion of replies that usually reaches 98 to 100 per cent.

The next year the counselor makes no follow-up study, unless he has been responsible for an earlier class, but the following year, when his present counseling group is in Grade 12, he makes a three-year survey of the preceding class. The fourth year, the counselor has a new tenth-grade counseling group and he makes his first follow-up survey of the class just graduated. The next year, the earlier class is ready for its five year follow-up. Henceforth, the counselor has one follow-up study to make each year, but never more than one. Needless to say, the difficulties of securing replies are greater in the three-year and five-year follow-up surveys than they are after an interval of only one year, but even in the five-year follow-up, the counselors customarily manage to get returns from more than 85 per cent of the members of the class.

When all available questionnaires are in, the adviser himself treats them statistically and writes a report of his study, which is then mimeographed in the central office for distribution to all advisers, principals, and staff officers.

Finally, the studies of all advisers of that particular grade are combined to form a composite city-wide study.

A somewhat similar follow-up plan, involving one-, three-, and five-year follow-up studies, was recommended by the Implementation Commission of the National Association of Secondary School Principals as the result of its study of occupational adjustment carried on under the direction of Landy (*10, 11, 12*). The need for follow-up of all school leavers, including drop-outs as well as graduates, was emphasized in that study, which was based upon data obtained from 1,000 school leavers from six representative school systems. The study also pointed to the need for better placement facilities and for post-school counseling service. Only about 5 per cent of the people studied secured their first jobs through the school authorities.

The report on the Occupational Adjustment Study suggested for high schools *A Post-School Occupational Follow-Up and Adjustment Service Plan* involving the following steps:

1. The principal should become aware of the school-leaving intentions of his pupils.

2. At the time of school-leaving, essential factual data should be placed on follow-up cards.

3. A follow-up inventory should be taken at one-, three-, and five-year intervals, by means of a written questionnaire. It is believed that through the use of recommended· procedures, returns can be secured from 90 per cent of the individuals to whom the questionnaire is sent. The returns should be recorded on the original follow-up cards. These cards can readily be sorted for purposes of occupational studies.

4. The school should secure, through the interview technique, additional information which may offer clews concerning the values of given practices, and suggest new ones. The principal should select from the follow-up group a representative sample of individuals to be interviewed. The recommended interview schedule consists of questions, the answers to which, according to experimental evidence, can be secured reliably by means of the interview technique.

5. It is recommended that a selected list of representative employers be compiled and that a suggested employer interview schedule be used with each of these employers.

6. A counseling service for all out-of-school youth should grow out of these interviews. There is a definite need for more adequate counseling of young people who have left school.

A manual was developed which contains specific instructions for using the questionnaire and the interview schedules. Counselors interested in experimenting with procedures for interviewing school leavers and employers can find the suggested interview blanks in the report of the Occupational Adjustment Study (*11*:126–140).

FORMS USED IN FOLLOW-UP SURVEYS

Representative forms which have been used in follow-up studies of high school graduates and other school leavers are shown on pages 324 to 331.[1]

SALIENT CHARACTERISTICS OF A FOLLOW-UP PLAN

The following are among the characteristics of a desirable plan for following up school leavers:

1. It is planned to serve the needs of both the individual and the school.

2. It begins before the students leave school.

3. It is continuous.

4. It includes all school leavers—those dropping out as well as those being graduated.

5. Each class is followed up for at least five years.

6. Procedures are used to insure returns from 80 per cent or more of those to whom the questionnaire is sent.

7. A representative sampling of each group is interviewed in order to obtain more extensive and detailed information than can be included in a questionnaire.

8. Responsibility for making follow-up studies is decentralized so that each class adviser follows up his own classes as they leave school.

9. The adviser's analysis of the data is made available to other school functionaries and is combined with those of other advisers in order to give a complete picture for the school system.

10. Conclusions concerning causal relationships are drawn with caution.

11. The significant items from each individual's return are transferred to his cumulative record card.

12. The follow-up plan is coordinated with a post-school counseling service.

The inauguration of a continuous follow-up service may seem to place a considerable additional burden upon a school staff, but it has been found in practice that a program of this kind is more than worth the additional labor and expense. It helps the school administration, the counselors, the placement office, and the young people who furnish the replies. Perhaps more important than any of these, it benefits the boys and girls still in school, since it helps to bring about needed improvements in the entire school program.

[1] Form 31 used with permission of Providence Public Schools, Providence, Rhode Island; Form 32, by permission of Ralph P. Gallagher, Director of Guidance, Elizabeth Public Schools, Elizabeth, New Jersey.

JUNIOR PLACEMENT SERVICE

PROVIDENCE PUBLIC SCHOOLS

TELEPHONE DEXTER 9400

PLACEMENT OFFICE

Date _____

1. Your name _____

2. Address _____ Telephone _____

3. School or college attended since graduation: Day _____ Evening _____

NAME OF SCHOOL	COURSE	DATE ENTERED	DATE LEFT	REASON FOR LEAVING

4. Working experience since graduation:

FIRM NAME	ADDRESS	DATE ENTERED	DATE LEFT	SALARY	YOUR POSITION

5. Do you like the work you are doing?

    What are its advantages?

    What are its disadvantages?

6. What subjects which you took in school have been most useful to you?

7. Are there any subjects you wish you could have had in high school?

8. Remarks and suggestions:

    All replies will be considered *strictly confidential.* A report will be written for the class as a whole and will not show individual returns.

    If you have suggestions you would like to make to your counselor, please use the reverse side of the questionnaire for a personal note.

Form 31.

Name_____Course_____Year_____

Address_____Phone_____

Married_____Single_____Dependents_____Parents' Name_____

Part A. EMPLOYMENT RECORD.

Job	From	To	Employer	Address	Way Job Was Obtained
1.					
2.					
3.					
4.					
5.					

EMPLOYMENT RECORD (Cont'd).

Job	Name of Person Hiring You	Name of Foreman	Pay Rate	Kind of Work Done	Reasons for Leaving	Employers' Estimates
1.						
2.						
3.						
4.						
5.						

Part B. JOB INFORMATION.

Job	Machines Used, if Any	Tools and Materials Used, if Any	Operations Performed, if Any	Responsibilities, if Any
1.				
2.				
3.				
4.				
5.				

Form 32.

Name_____Course_____Year_____

Part C. EDUCATION BEYOND HIGH SCHOOL

From	To	School	Course	Credit	Remarks

Part D. GRADUATE'S ESTIMATE OF THE VALUE OF SCHOOL TRAINING.
(Rate M, most useful; F, fairly useful; L, least useful.)

Rating	Reasons

____ 1. English_____

____ 2. Mathematics_____

____ 3. Science_____

____ 4. History_____

____ 5. Languages_____

____ 6. Shop work_____

____ 7. Commercial training_____

____ 8. Art_____

____ 9. Music_____

____ 10. Physical education_____

____ 11. Hygiene_____

____ 12. Social activities_____

____ 13. Extracurricular activities_____

____ 14. Other items_____

Subjects that the graduate feels should be taught, with reasons:

_____

_____

_____

_____

Form 32 *(cont.)*

Name_____Course_____Year_____

Part E. PLANS AND ACTIVITIES OF THE GRADUATE.

1. *Graduate's Plans for the Future.*

Occupational	Education or Re-training	Other Plans, if Any

2. *Leisure Time Activities of the Graduate.*

Hobbies	Athletics	Musical	Club	Other

3. *Significant Achievements of the Graduate.*

Occupational	Civic or Political	Social

4. *Ways in Which the School Can Help the Graduate Now.*

Form 32 (cont.)

Name_____Course_____Year_____

Part F.   OBSERVATIONS OF THE INTERVIEWER.

1. *Home Conditions of the Graduate.*

_____
_____
_____
_____
_____

2. *Physical Condition of the Graduate.*

_____
_____
_____

3. *Mental Outlook of the Graduate.*

_____
_____
_____

4. *Interviewer's General Impressions of the Graduate.*

_____
_____
_____
_____
_____
_____
_____

Graduate Interviewed by_____Date_____194__

Form 32 (cont.)

Year
in
college

{ Freshman ------

Sophomore------

Junior   ------

Senior   ------ }

Name---

College or university--

Are any of your present courses selected with a vocation in mind?-----------

If so, what vocation?--

When did you decide on this vocation?--------------------------------------

Did you select any of your high-school courses with this vocation in mind?------

----

Was your high-school preparation adequate for the work that you are now

taking?------If not, how was it weak? (Be specific.)-----------------------

----

Do you find it necessary to work harder in college than you worked in high school?

------Comment:--

Have you received any honors or awards in college?------If so, what were they?

Have you taken part in any extra-curriculum activities?------If so, what ones?

(Include athletics.)--

Have you held office in any organization?------If so, what?------------------

----

In the light of your present experience, could you have planned your work in

the University High School so that it would have been more profitable to you?----

In what way?--

Form 33.

		Year in college	Freshman ------
			Sophomore ------
			Junior ------
			Senior ------

Name_____

College or university_____

Is the school year divided into semesters or quarters?_____

		Courses	Hours	Marks	Grade points
S e m e s t e r	First	------------------------------	------	------	------
		------------------------------	------	------	------
		------------------------------	------	------	------
		------------------------------	------	------	------
		------------------------------	------	------	------
		------------------------------	------	------	------
o r	Second	------------------------------	------	------	------
		------------------------------	------	------	------
Q u a r t e r		------------------------------	------	------	------
		------------------------------	------	------	------
		------------------------------	------	------	------
	Third	------------------------------	------	------	------
		------------------------------	------	------	------
		------------------------------	------	------	------

Total grade points_____Grade points possible_____

Rank in class: Percentile_____If not available, in what quarter of the class does this student rank? Upper_____Upper middle_____

Lower middle_____Lower_____

Has the student received any honors during the present year?_____

If so, what?_____

_____

Have you any evidence concerning citizenship of the student?_____

If so, check one of the following: Low_____Average_____High_____

Comment:_____

_____

Form 34.

REFERENCES

1. Allen, Richard D. *Organization and Supervision of Guidance in Public Education,* pp. 166–176, 297–308, 331–369. New York: Inor Publishing Company, 1937. Pp. xxii + 420.

2. Bell, Howard M. *Youth Tell Their Story.* Washington, D. C.: American Council on Education, 1938. Pp. 274.

3. Booker, Ivan A. "From High School Senior to College Freshman," *Secondary Education,* VII (April 1938), 52–55.

4. Bridgman, Donald S. "Success in College and Business," *Personnel Journal,* IX (June 1930), 1–19.

5. Cramer, Buell B. "Following-up High School Graduates," *Occupations,* XVIII (December 1939), 182–187.

6. Eckert, Ruth E., and Marshall, Thomas O. *When Youth Leave School.* New York: McGraw-Hill Book Co., Inc., 1938. Pp. 360.

7. Eurich, Alvin C., and Pace, C. R. *A Follow-up Study of Minnesota Graduates from 1928 to 1936.* Minneapolis, Minnesota: University of Minnesota Committee on Educational Research, 1938. Pp. 41.

8. *Follow-up of Secondary School Graduates.* Leads to Better Secondary Schools in Michigan, No. 1. Lansing, Michigan: Michigan Study of the Secondary School Curriculum, State Board of Education, 1943. Pp. 70.

9. Hale, Lincoln B. *From School to College.* Yale Studies in Religious Education, XI. New Haven, Connecticut: Yale University Press, 1939. Pp. xxiv + 446.

10. Landy, Edward. "Principals Offered Follow-up Program," *Occupations,* XIX (January 1941), 266–272.

11. Landy, Edward, and others. *Occupational Adjustment and the School.* Bulletin No. 93. Washington, D. C.: National Association of Secondary School Principals, 1940. Pp. 160.

12. Landy, Edward; Beery, John R.; Hayes, Byron C.; and Long, C. Darl. *The Occupational Follow-up and Adjustment Service Plan.* New York: The Occupational Adjustment Study of the National Association of Secondary School Principals, 1940. Pp. 96.

13. Long, C. Darl. *School-leaving Youth and Employment.* Teachers College Contributions to Education, No. 845. New York: Bureau of Publications, Teachers College, Columbia University, 1941. Pp. viii + 84.

14. Odom, Charles L. "Closing the Gap between School and College," *Occupations* XX (December 1941), 194–197.

15. Pace, C. Robert. *They Went to College.* Minneapolis, Minnesota: University of Minnesota Press, 1941. Pp. xiv + 148.

16. Proctor, W. M. "Intelligence and Length of Schooling in Relation to Occupational Level," *School and Society,* XLII (December 1935), 783–786.

17. *Report of Problems and Progress.* General College, University of Minnesota. Minneapolis, Minnesota: Folwell Hall Bookstore, 1939. Pp. 258.

18. Smith, Hugh A. "College Records and Success in Life," *Education*, XLVII (May 1927), 513–529.

19. Southwick, Arthur F. "Survey of Wooster Graduates," *Occupations*, XVIII (January 1940), 266–274.

20. Strang, Ruth. "Recent Issues in Student Personnel Work," *Personnel Journal*, XIII (August 1934), 101–107.

21. Thorndike, E. L., and others. *Prediction of Vocational Success*. Institute of Educational Research, Teachers College, Columbia University. New York: The Commonwealth Fund, 1934. Pp. xxiv + 284.

22. Trabue, M. R., and Dvorak, B. J. "A Study of the Needs of Adults for Further Training," *Bulletins of the Employment Stabilization Research Institute*, Vol. III, No. 3. Minneapolis, Minnesota: University of Minnesota Press, 1934.

23. Viteles, M. S. "Validating the Clinical Method in Vocational Selection," *Psychological Clinic*, XVIII (May–June 1929), 69–77.

24. Williamson, E. G., and Darley, J. G. *Student Personnel Work*, Chapter IX. New York: McGraw-Hill Book Co., Inc., 1937. Pp. xxiv + 313.

25. Wrenn, Gilbert C. "A Critique of Methods Used in Follow-up Studies of Students," *Harvard Educational Review*, X (May 1940), 357–363.

26. Zeran, F. R. "Significance of Follow-up Activities in Guidance Service," *Education in a Nation at War*, pp. 293–296. Schoolmen's Week Proceedings. University of Pennsylvania Bulletin, Vol. XLII, No. 36. Philadelphia: University of Pennsylvania, June 26, 1942.

CHAPTER XVII

Guidance in the Adjustment of Individuals

A GUIDANCE PROGRAM OBVIOUSLY CONSISTS OF MORE THAN THE TECHNIQUES DISCUSSED in this book. Familiarity with and skill in using these techniques should greatly increase a counselor's effectiveness, but it should be clear to everyone that the techniques are tools or means to an end, and that intelligence, understanding, sympathy, and insight are required of a counselor in the application of these techniques to the guidance of individual boys and girls.

The science of guidance is applied by counselors and teachers who are not highly trained in psychology more readily to the *distributive* phases of guidance than to the adjustive aspects. One who is well informed concerning the educational and vocational opportunities for young people and who has command of the procedures for obtaining broad and accurate information about individuals can guide students toward the most appropriate kinds of educational and occupational choices with confidence and with a large measure of success. This aspect of guidance, of course, contributes to the adjustment of the individual, but these adjustive functions are indirect and may not be fully realized by either counselor or student.

Even though many persons participating in a school guidance program have had little professional training for counseling, they can be very helpful to individual pupils in connection with the *overt, immediate problems of adjustment*. The more common general areas into which these problems fall are pupil-teacher relationships, relationships with other pupils, relationships between pupils and parents, study difficulties, and minor behavior difficulties. This type of problem is usually specific, and ordinarily it is either recognized by pupil and counselor from the outset or it emerges and is identified in the course of one or two interviews. Not infrequently, this type of problem can be solved quickly through the planning of a definite and immediate course of action.

More important adjustment problems are deep seated, are woven into the fabric of the individual's personality, are not overtly related to symptoms, and are to be resolved largely through growth and development over a considerable period of time. It is in this area that the average counselor is most likely to fall down on the job because of lack of knowledge and skill in psychotherapy. There is danger that he will either completely overlook the maladjustment and do nothing about it or will misinterpret the difficulty and try to apply treatment directly to the symptoms. Even when he correctly diagnoses the difficulty, he may get into deep water if he tries to prescribe and direct a program of treatment himself.

There is no easy solution for the lack of preparation of a large proportion of school guidance functionaries to handle difficult and obscure cases of maladjustment. But consideration of certain fundamentals may sharpen the awareness of counselors to these problems and help them avoid some of the pitfalls.

What Is Adjustment?

Occasionally in the use of the term adjustment we imply that the most desirable state of adjustment is one in which the individual is perfectly happy and satisfied with all aspects of his life, and one in which he has reached the level in all his contacts with his environment that he would be glad to see persist through his life. Seldom, if ever, is this kind of adjustment achieved by an individual in all his relationships, and it would not be a desirable kind of adjustment even if it were realized. Complete adjustment in all aspects of life would lead to extreme mental and physical stagnation. Much of the motive power of living would be lost.

A certain degree of lack of adjustment is wholesome and stimulating. Man's realization that he has not reached the adjustment level he desires is one of the great driving forces both for individuals and for social groups. Much of the work of the world is done by those who are somewhat unadjusted but who are striving for better adjustment. In fact, some of the most outstanding contributions to our civilization, particularly in the fields of literature and music, have been made by men who were decidedly neurotic. This is not to imply that the eradication of maladjustment and the bringing about of better adjustment all along the line is not desirable, but it is well to keep in mind the fact that adjustment is always relative and that occasional evidence of maladjustment is usual and does not set one off from the normal group.

In the last analysis, the best integrated and adjusted individuals seem to be those who have established some reasonable goals in line with their interests and abilities and who have settled down to work toward those goals seriously and steadily but without unusual tension. It is highly desirable for advisers to keep in mind the *integrative and adjustive nature of purposeful behavior* in connection with the therapeutic aspects of their counseling work.

THE DANGER OF LABELS

In every area in which thinking is done, vocabulary is, of course, extremely important, not only as a vehicle of thinking but as a guide to and a determiner of thinking. The truth of this observation is especially apparent when the personality adjustment of an individual is being considered. To the lay mind, the word *psychoneurotic* has a connotation that is especially damning to the individual concerned; yet it is a generic term which covers everything from mild neuroses to personality aberrations that call for institutional treatment. In reality it has little meaning until the nature of the difficulty is defined.

An illustration of the need for especial care in the application of technical terms to individuals is found in the cases of some of the returning veterans. The Armed Forces have designated a considerable number of men as unfit for military service because of psychoneuroses. Where a given individual is concerned, this may be significant with respect to his ability to adjust to civilian life, or it may have little or no significance. There is a positive correlation between external conditions—between physical, mental, and emotional pressure—and neurotic tendency. Many individuals who cannot withstand, over a long period, rigorous and exacting conditions such as those found in military life get along very well in a civilian environment. It is probably no exaggeration to state flatly that every individual without exception may become neurotic if he is placed in an environment which subjects him to continuous emotional tension or to a continuous series of problems which he cannot solve.

It is of the utmost importance for counselors to keep in mind one basic tenet of modern psychology. This tenet is that individuals can never be clearly separated into the normal and the abnormal or into the emotionally adjusted and the neurotic, but rather that *abnormal psychological phenomena are either exaggerations or disguised developments of normal psychological phenomena.* Counselors who keep this important principle constantly in mind will be in much less danger of allowing the jingle fallacy resulting from names and labels to obscure their thinking concerning individual cases.

MECHANISMS OF ESCAPE FROM REALITY

Major problems which seem insoluble to the individual concerned are the chief source of emotional disorders. The characteristic abnormal reaction to a baffling problem is some type of retreat from reality. Avoidance of reality may be attempted in many ways. Some of the milder forms of escape are *rationaliza-*

tion, or the advancement of plausible but incorrect reasons to justify a course of action or explain a failure; *phantasy,* or daydreaming in which one achieves imaginary fame or success, performs wonderful feats, or renders outstanding service; and *projection,* or attempts to divert attention from one's own problems by dwelling on those of others. These means of avoiding the facing of problems are undesirable, but they are very common among normal individuals. Their mechanism is not highly complex, and school counselors should be able to recognize them and to help individuals who are being advised understand how they function and how they can be overcome.

A more serious mode of escape from difficult problems or unwelcome situations is the development of temporary *mental or physical ills or incapacities* which force the individual out of the activities he wishes to avoid. For example, a boy who fears he will fail a difficult examination may develop an upset stomach on the morning of the examination day and have to spend the day in bed; or an extremely timid girl who is frightened at the thought of having to make a talk in her English class may come down with a nervous headache. These mechanisms of escape may take place not merely once but each time a difficult situation is encountered. Occasionally they represent deliberate malingering, in which case they are more reprehensible but not so serious psychologically. Not infrequently, however, the individual is made actually sick by the difficulty he faces. He is not pretending illness, and he is probably not even aware of the relationship between his indisposition and his desire to escape an intolerable situation.

Hysterical-like symptoms such as those just described are liable to be baffling, but they are not insoluble in a counseling situation in which the counselor is able to enlist the active cooperation of the individual in analyzing his symptoms and going to the root of the trouble. In rare instances, however, the mechanism of hysteria may be completely beyond the counselor's experience and beyond any contribution he can make to a treatment of the case, except to report what he observes.

The outward manifestation of hysteria in the technical sense is a disease symptom. The number of diseases that may be simulated by a hysterical person is almost infinite. An inquiry into the mechanism of hysteria would call for an extensive study of the theories of various psychologists, including especially Janet (9) and Freud (2). The explanation advanced by Freud is interwoven with his concept of sex as the great motivating force in human life. Regardless of what theory is accepted, the modern treatment of hysteria calls for analysis by an expert in psychology or psychiatry and a program of re-education.

It is not probable that school counselors will encounter cases of major hysteria, for the withdrawal reactions of children and adolescents in school are rarely so extreme. An awareness of the symptoms of marked maladjustment may help counselors occasionally, however, to recognize incipient abnormal tendencies and to take steps to bring these cases to the attention of specialists in the early stages when adjustment can readily be brought about.

One of the primary functions of counselors is to help young people learn to meet problems frankly and courageously, and to accept frustration philosophically. All persons have limitations; no one can excel in everything. Failure can be reduced by setting goals that are within the capacity of the individual, but even under the best planning possible, every individual will have his failures and everyone will meet some problems—vocational, social, or personal—which are clearly insoluble as far as he is concerned. When one of these immovable barriers is encountered, an individual may either persistently refuse to accept the reality of the situation until he experiences a disintegration of personality or he may find compensatory activities and other outlets around which he can achieve such an integration of personality that he may emerge from the experience stronger than before. Everyone will agree that the counselor has extremely important work to perform in this connection, but no one has ever been able to give him a blue print of how to proceed, although it may be helpful to list the steps in a usual counseling situation where the primary purpose is therapeutic.

STEPS IN COUNSELING FOR ADJUSTMENT

The traditional concept of counseling is the giving of advice. According to this concept, a student goes to his counselor with a problem, or the counselor calls him in, and then the counselor talks the situation over with the student and out of his broader knowledge and more mature experience offers suggestions for the student to consider and presumably to act upon. This will no doubt always be an important phase of counseling, for in the experience of every student there may arise emergencies of urgent and immediate import concerning which the advice of an experienced and understanding friend is greatly needed. The need for early resolution of the difficulty may outweigh the desire to make the counseling relationship a growth experience for the individual.

These instances, however, are exceptional. In the more common counseling situation, the modern emphasis is upon the sharing of experiences and not upon the counselor's accepting responsibility for the solving of problems. The more skillful counselor who is seeking to help the student to better adjustment is likely to let the individual do the larger share of the talking while, by means of timely questions, he shrewdly and subtly directs the line of thinking until, in the end, the student himself will seem to have thought the problem through and to have decided upon a course of action almost independently. It is here that counseling loses much of its scientific character and takes on the guise of a highly sensitive art.

This approach to counseling not only is likely to be more successful in the immediate situation, but it has for its more remote objective the development in the individual of a confident, independent, and thoughtful attitude that will lead him to make a determined effort to solve his own problems whenever they arise.

The following list indicates the steps that may take place during successful counseling for adjustment:[1]

1. The student asks his counselor for help and states the situation as he sees it.
2. The counselor and student discuss the situation until the problem is clearly defined.
3. The counselor leads the student to talk about the problem at length. In the beginning, the individual's statements about the problem will in all probability be negative. That is, he will talk about how difficult the problem is or how unendurable the situation, and how thoroughly disgusted he is with the whole business.
4. Instead of criticizing this attitude, the counselor accepts it as normal and logical. He does not show approval, but he avoids creating antagonism by trying to force a different attitude at this point.
5. After the individual has "talked himself out," the counselor, by means of appropriate suggestions, leads him to begin consideration of the positive side of the situation.
6. The counselor accepts the positive suggestions of the individual calmly and thoughtfully, and voices approval when the individual seems to be on the right track.
7. As the subject talks on the positive side, he begins to develop insight and to formulate a plan of action.
8. The counselor allows the individual to do most of the planning, but keeping in mind the accumulated information he has about this student, he tries to steer him into a course of action consistent with his abilities and with the problem at hand.
9. The individual puts his plan into action, thereby acquiring further understanding of the problem.
10. He develops an integrated and successful program of action, loses his need for the counselor, and terminates the guidance relationship as far as it applies to this problem.

This outline of the development of a counseling situation is, of course, very general, and in actual practice certain steps frequently will be merged and will not occur in exactly this sequence. The important point is for the adviser to see that the subject takes positive and appropriate action which is self-initiated and

[1] For a more detailed outline and discussion, see Carl R. Rogers, *Counseling and Psychotherapy.* Boston: Houghton Mifflin Company, 1942. Pp. xiv + 450.

is therefore likely to persist and to contribute to the personal growth of the individual.

CHARACTERISTICS AND PROFESSIONAL TRAINING DESIRABLE FOR COUNSELORS

The techniques discussed in the other chapters of this book will, when used intelligently, provide much of the data for a dependable guidance program. Familiarity with these procedures will help the work of every counselor, but the point which will bear repetition is that close attention to them does not alone constitute guidance. It is through the intelligence, understanding, skill, and personality of the counselor himself that life is given to these techniques. The personal qualities of a school's counselors are among the most important determiners of the excellence of its guidance program. Probably not more than one-fourth of the teachers in a school have the qualities required for superior work in the guidance of young people. The characteristics needed for successful counseling of individuals include:

1. An intelligent view of the philosophy of individual guidance and the relation of guidance to a broad educational program.
2. A genuine interest in and liking for people.
3. Ability and willingness to know and understand individuals before attempting to guide them.
4. A sincere and business-like attitude, tempered by a sense of humor.
5. An easy and cordial manner in meeting and talking with people.
6. Ability to approach the main problem in a discussion without abruptness but without vacillation.
7. Ability to control the interview and still take a self-effacing position.
8. Skill in asking the right questions at the right time and in keeping silent at the right places during an interview.
9. Awareness of one's own strengths and limitations as a counselor, combined with a willingness to undertake what one is competent to do, and to admit inability to provide treatment for certain individuals.
10. Sufficient knowledge of various theories of personality to understand what different kinds of overt behavior may mean in terms of maladjustment.

With regard to the last category, many counselors—perhaps the majority— have not specialized in psychology. Much of their training in psychology must be acquired through in-service reading and experience. Their reading is certain to bring them into contact with various theories concerning the organization of personality, including those of Jung, Kretschmer, Adler, and Freud. Jung has stressed introversion-extroversion; Kretschmer, constitutional types; Adler, compensation and struggle for power; Freud, sex, broadly defined, and psychoanalysis. Freud's theories are likely to be both highly intriguing and very confusing for one not professionally trained in psychiatry. The usual first reaction is to reject and even to ridicule Freud's whole point of view, for his analysis of maladjustment in terms of repressed sex impulses—in particular, his emphasis upon infantile sex drives—seems at first thought to be farfetched and even bizarre. Without question, there has been a great deal of misinterpretation and exploitation of Freud's theories by incompetent charlatans, and there has been, and still is, much popular misinformation about his contribution to psychology.

Nevertheless, Freudian psychology is so closely interwoven with modern psychiatry that guidance people in schools cannot choose to ignore Freud if they expect to enlist the cooperation of experts in the handling of difficult and obscure cases. The principal contributions to and applications of Freudian psychology have in recent years passed from Germany to America. A competent and especially thorough and critical appraisal of Freud's work from the American point of view is to be found in the writings of Karen Horney (8).

Those who are specialists in psychology are likely to have their moments of doubt as they contemplate the guidance scene in the United States and observe thousands of classroom teachers, whose training has been in English or mathematics or social studies, performing guidance functions and making certain tentative explorations and probings into the personality of the pupils they counsel. They are inclined to wonder sometimes, even though they do not voice their fears, whether more harm than good may not come from such an arrangement. The whole thesis of this book, however, is that counselors who are not psychologists are entirely capable of performing the *distributive functions* of guidance and many of the *less involved adjustive functions,* provided they will get acquainted with and use the techniques for knowing individuals. Every guidance program should be so organized that the services of one or more specialists in mental therapy are available for the handling of the more involved cases. Counselors can contribute to the treatment of these cases by observing pupils accurately and with some understanding of the problems involved, and by reporting their observations to these specialists. They can increase their effectiveness in this regard by means of carefully selected professional reading and through summer-session and extension courses in mental hygiene.

REFERENCES

1. Barker, Lewellys F. *Psychotherapy.* New York: D. Appleton-Century Company, Inc., 1940. Pp. x + 218.
2. Beeley, Arthur L. "Freud and Psychoanalysis," *Social Service Review,* V (March 1931), 10–27.
3. Brown, J. F., and Menninger, Karl A. *The Psychodynamics of Abnormal Behavior.* New York: McGraw-Hill Book Company, Inc., 1940. Pp. xvi + 484.

4. Buswell, G. T. "Experimentation and Personality Development," *Elementary School Journal*, XLIII (March 1943), 393–397.

5. Fenton, Norman. *Mental Hygiene in School Practice*. Stanford University, California: Stanford University Press, 1943. Pp. xvi + 456.

6. Frank, Lawrence K. "Projective Methods for the Study of Personality," *Journal of Psychology*, VIII (1939), 389–413.

7. Geisel, John B. *Personal Problems and Morale*. Boston: Houghton Mifflin Company, 1943. Pp. vii + 435.

8. Horney, Karen. *New Ways in Psychoanalysis*. New York: W. W. Norton and Company, Inc., 1939. Pp. 313.

9. Janet, Pierre. *Major Symptoms of Hysteria*. New York: The Macmillan Company, 1929. Pp. x + 345.

10. Kanner, Leo. *Child Psychiatry*. Springfield, Illinois: Charles C. Thomas, 1942. Pp. xviii + 528.

11. McKinney, Fred. *Psychology of Personal Adjustment: Students' Introduction to Mental Hygiene*. New York: J. Wiley and Sons, Inc., 1941. Pp. xi + 636.

12. Maslow, A. H., and Mittelmann, Bela. *Principles of Abnormal Psychology*. New York: Harper & Brothers, 1941. Pp. x + 638.

13. May, Rollo. *The Art of Counseling: How to Gain and Give Mental Health*. Nashville, Tennessee: Cokesbury Press, 1939. Pp. 247.

14. Mikesall, William Henry. *Mental Hygiene*. New York: Prentice-Hall, Inc., 1939. Pp. xvi + 456.

15. Murray, Henry A., and the workers at the Harvard Psychological Clinic. *Explorations in Personality*. New York: Oxford University Press, 1938. Pp. xiv + 761.

16. Rogers, Carl R. *Counseling and Psychotherapy*. Boston: Houghton Mifflin Company, 1942. Pp. xiv + 450.

17. Sherman, Mandel. *Mental Conflicts and Personality*. New York: Longmans, Green and Co., 1938. Pp. viii + 319.

18. Sherman, Mandel. *Basic Problems of Behavior*. New York: Longmans, Green and Co., 1941. Pp. viii + 440.

19. Spencer, Douglas. *Fulcra of Conflict*. Yonkers, New York: World Book Company, 1938. Pp. xii + 306.

20. Strecker, Edward A. *Fundamentals of Psychiatry*. Philadelphia: J. B. Lippincott Company, 1942. Pp. xvii + 201.

CHAPTER XVIII

Reading Resources for Counselors

CONTRIBUTIONS TO PERSONNEL WORK IN THE SCHOOLS ARE TO BE FOUND IN AN extensive body of literature. No counselor can be expected to be acquainted with all the books, monographs, and studies that are related to personnel work, but he will be aided materially in meeting the great variety of day to day problems of advising pupils if there is available in the professional library of the school a selected list of reading resources to which he can turn when he does not know the answer to a particular problem. This chapter represents an attempt to provide such a list.

CHILD PSYCHOLOGY AND MENTAL HYGIENE

It is highly desirable for the counselor to have some training in psychology, since he is engaged in a type of work for which a knowledge of psychology is very important. Regardless of his professional background in this field, the availability of some of the better reference books in child and adolescent psychology will assist his work, and the counselor's library should contain such books. The handbook on child psychology edited by Murchison (*129*) is one of the most complete reference works in this field up to 1933. Among the more recent textbooks on child psychology are those by Pressey and Robinson (*136*), Morgan (*128*), Jersild (*96*), and Skinner and Harriman (*157*). The first part of the book by Pressey and Robinson deals with development through the first twenty years, and the second part discusses the guidance and fostering of learning. Morgan's book, which is in its third edition, provides a general treatment of the subject written in somewhat more popular style. Among the topics covered in Jersild's book are the development of language, emotions, the development of social behavior and learning, the growth of understanding, the measurement and prediction of individual differences in mental ability, personality and character, and some aspects of applied child psychology. The book edited by Skinner and Harriman represents a collaboration of several psychologists. It presents the problems of child psychology and describes the methods employed in the scientific study of children. Luella Cole's revised book (*35*) contains one of the most recent and thorough treatments of the psychology of adolescence.

Books that are somewhat more specialized than the general text in child psychology and that deal in considerable detail with basic aspects of personality are also useful in the counselor's library. One of the most thorough and scholarly books of this kind is Allport's authoritative presentation *Personality: A Psychological Interpretation* (*3*). Part IV on the "Analysis of Personality" and Part V on "Understanding Personality" should be of special interest to counselors.

The counselor should be acquainted with the relation of mental hygiene to personal guidance, and although he will find this approach discussed in some of the general references on child psychology, several books dealing with mental hygiene can profitably be included in this library. One of the best-known books of this kind is Sherman's *Mental Hygiene and Education* (*155*). This book is planned to aid teachers and counselors in understanding the emotional and personality problems of their pupils and in instituting treatment. It also describes problems that teachers and counselors should not treat but should refer to a psychiatrist. Another useful book on the subject is Howard and Patry's *Mental Health* (*91*). Some of the topics in this book include the detecting and preventing of unwholesome mental patterns, the creating of healthy minds, the mental hygiene of family relationships, the mental hygiene of childhood and youth, methods of reconstructing personality and behavior problems, and sex as related to mental hygiene. Symonds' book *Mental Hygiene of the School Child* (*176*) is a non-technical treatment of mental hygiene that should be helpful to counselors. Among the more recent worth-while books on this subject are Cutts and Moseley's *Practical School Discipline and Mental Hygiene* (*43*), Crow and Crow's *Mental Hygiene in School and Home Life for Teachers, Supervisors, and Parents* (*40*), Fenton's *Mental Hygiene in School Practice* (*61*), Klein's *Mental Hygiene* (*104*), and Tiegs and Katz's *Mental Hygiene in Education* (*181*).

Closely related to books on mental hygiene are references on behavior problems and maladjustments, such as Louttit's *Clinical Psychology* (*120*) and Morgan's *The Psychology of the Unadjusted School Child* (*127*). The latter is a non-technical book intended to help teachers and counselors guide children into habits of mental health and to change habits likely to have deleterious effects from the standpoint of mental hygiene. *Counseling and Psychotherapy* by Rogers (*143*) is a stimulating book on the therapeutic aspects of counseling. It contains much interesting illustrative material taken directly from recordings of counseling interviews.

Those who wish to make a still deeper exploration into abnormal psychology as a basis for understanding normal individuals who need guidance in adjustment could profitably read *The Psychodynamics of Abnormal Behavior* by Brown (*22*).

EDUCATIONAL GUIDANCE, COUNSELING, AND PERSONNEL WORK

There are now many books that deal specifically with guidance, counseling, and personnel work at all levels of the school. Among the books which have been available for some years, one useful in becoming orientated to high school guidance is Koos and Kefauver's *Guidance in Secondary Schools* (*106*).

One of the most comprehensive general treatments of guidance is found in Part I of the Thirty-Seventh Yearbook of the National Society for the Study of Education entitled *Guidance in Educational Institutions* (*75*). This report was prepared by the National Society's Committee on Guidance. Among the topics that should assist the counselor in understanding pupils are: appraisal of student characteristics and needs, appraisal of certain aspects of study achievement, counseling with students, and guidance in personality development.

Strang has published two books designed to help college and secondary school counselors to understand and guide their students. The larger of these, *Behavior and Background of Students in College and Secondary School* (*167*), summarizes results of investigations relating to adolescent problems, physical characteristics, intelligence, achievement, personality, attitudes, interests, social and economic background, and expenditures of time and money. It provides a background of understanding that will aid in the use of the other book, which is a small volume entitled *Counseling Technics in College and Secondary School* (*168*), and is concerned with the discussion of technics of work with individuals. These two books used together should improve the counselor's procedures of bringing together the information about each student and should help him to understand the significance of the facts he has collected. More recently Strang has published *Pupil Personnel and Guidance* (*169*) in order to focus the attention of administrators and teachers on child development instead of subject matter. The book is suitable for use by counselors at all levels of the school. In cooperation with Hatcher, Strang has provided help for rural-school counselors in a new book, *Child Development and Guidance in Rural Schools* (*170*).

Two books concerned mainly with counseling problems at the college level are *Student Personnel Work—An Outline of Clinical Procedures* (*189*) by Williamson and Darley and *A Student Personnel Program for Higher Education* (*118*) by Lloyd-Jones and Smith. The former book is an exposition of the possibilities of developing and utilizing the scientific techniques in the educational and vocational guidance of the individual. The latter book is an up-to-date and comprehensive statement of the whole guidance program in colleges. It contains a good chapter on student records.

An unusually objective approach to personnel work is found in Williamson's *How to Counsel Students* (*188*). Clinical procedures are emphasized in this book which is based on personnel work in colleges, but which has many implications for the guidance and counseling of secondary school pupils. A more elementary book prepared especially for secondary school personnel workers is Williamson and Hahn's *Introduction to High School Counseling* (*190*).

Other recent books on high school guidance are *Guidance in the Secondary School* by Hamrin and Erickson (*79*), *Personnel Work in High School* by Germane and Germane (*69*), and *Testing and Counseling in the High-School Guidance Program* by Darley (*46*). All three books are suitable for use either as texts in courses on guidance in departments of education, or as references for counselors and teachers in service.

Guidance and Personnel Services in Education by Anna Y. Reed (*141*) contains an especially broad and thorough discussion of the guidance field. This new book, which is based on a long period of practical experience, covers guidance and personnel services prior to 1916, information on educational and occupational opportunities and community resources, information about the individual, methods of utilizing informational data, organization and administration, and a final division, retrospect and prospect.

The *Inor Group Guidance Series* by Richard D. Allen and others (*1*) provides one of the most comprehensive treatments of guidance in the secondary school that is to be found anywhere. This series of four volumes makes available for counselors a very extensive list of practical suggestions dealing with a variety of guidance problems. The first two volumes are on group guidance, but they have many implications for understanding the individual. The third volume, entitled *Self-Measurement Projects in Group Guidance,* should be very useful in helping the counselor understand individual pupils and in making it possible for pupils better to understand themselves. The fourth volume on *Organization and Supervision of Guidance in Public Education* is of especial interest to administrators and guidance directors.

A *Group Guidance Series* under the authorship of Bennett and Hand (*13*), like the *Inor Group Guidance Series,* contains one volume that is planned to help the student in self-analysis. This volume, entitled *Design for Personality,* is an attempt to assist the student to evaluate himself as objectively as possible. It introduces the pupil to sound techniques of evaluation, including measurement.

Some counselors prefer to make use of a very definite and detailed outline for diagnosing pupils. Baker and Traphagen have provided such an outline in their book *The Diagnosis and Treatment of Behavior Problem Children* (*6*). This book presents and explains the Detroit Scale for the diagnosis of behavior problems, discusses in detail the significance of each of the sixty-six items included, and illustrates its application by reporting several case studies.

Teachers, of course, have an important place in guidance programs. Some schools use their classroom teachers as guidance officers, but whether or not the teachers are expected to work in this capacity, they inevitably take on, at times, some of the functions of counselors. Among the many books that are valuable for teacher counselors is a counseling manual by Elliott and Elliott entitled *Solving Personal Problems* (57). This book discusses the kind of personal counseling which should be the responsibility of teachers and parents. It should be of particular interest to persons not highly trained in techniques of counseling. A book by Cox and Duff is concerned with the teacher's place in guidance. This book, *Guidance by the Classroom Teacher* (39), is planned to assist teachers in re-orientating themselves and their work to the hypothesis that education is essentially guidance by the classroom teacher. It discusses a variety of practical problems that teachers must meet if they assume the role of guidance officers. Strang has also made a valuable contribution to this area in her book, *The Role of the Teacher in Personnel Work* (166), and Dunsmoor and Miller have recently published a helpful book entitled *Guidance Methods for Teachers in Homeroom, Classroom, and Core Program* (54).

VOCATIONAL GUIDANCE

Although educational and vocational guidance cannot be clearly differentiated, certain books are so closely related to the vocational guidance aspect of personnel work that special attention should be drawn to them. Among these are Culbert and Smith's *Counseling Young Workers* (41), Forrester's *Methods of Vocational Guidance* (63), Gardiner's *How You Can Get a Job* (68), Hoppock's *Job Satisfaction* (89), Keller and Viteles' *Vocational Guidance Throughout the World* (100), Kitson's *How to Find the Right Vocation* (103) and *I Find My Vocation* (102), Lane's *Vocations in Industry* (110), Lincoln's *Teaching about Vocational Life* (117), Myers' *Principles and Techniques of Vocational Guidance* (131), Rosengarten's *Choosing Your Life Work* (144), *Occupational Counseling Techniques* by Stead, Shartle, and others (163), and Williamson's *Students and Occupations* (187). Four comparatively recent books in this field are *Principles of Employment Psychology* by Burtt (25), *Prognosis, Guidance, and Placement in Business Education* by Dame, Brinkman, and Weaver (44), *The Dynamics of Vocational Adjustment* by Super (175), and *Vocational Guidance for Girls and Women* by Zapoleon and Moore (200). In his book, *History of Vocational Guidance,* Brewer (21) has traced the development of vocational guidance from the time of Frank Parsons to the present.

A very helpful continuous service with respect to vocational opportunities, trends, and guidance is provided in Science Research Associates publications (151). This organization issues a variety of publications which are finding their way into thousands of junior and senior high schools in the United States. The Institute for Research (*28*) also publishes an extensive series of monographs covering more than a hundred different occupations. The *Occupational Index, Inc.* (*134*) publishes abstracts dealing likewise with a variety of occupations. These pamphlets indicate the nature of the occupation, the abilities and training required, earnings, trends in employment, and advantages and disadvantages of the occupation.

Studies Related to Guidance

Counselors cannot be expected to keep up with all the hundreds of studies that have some bearing on the understanding and guidance of the individual child, but they should be familiar with the more significant investigations. Studies of conditions, particularly the economic conditions faced by American youth, have an especially close relationship to guidance. An extremely important series of studies has been issued since 1935 by the American Youth Commission of the American Council on Education. At least five of the books reporting these studies should be in the library of every counselor. The first of these, *How Fare American Youth?* (*138*), prepared by Rainey and others, presents a basic analysis and a statement of various problems of youth. The second, *Youth Tell Their Story,* by Howard M. Bell (*10*), is an unusually comprehensive and significant study of the life and work of young people. Another book prepared by Bell in this series, *Matching Youth and Jobs* (*11*), is a practical statement of the functioning of occupational adjustment programs and is based on careful research in representative areas. A fourth book prepared under the auspices of the Commission discusses public youth work programs, including the Civilian Conservation Corps, the Work Projects Administration, and the National Youth Administration. This book, *Youth Work Programs,* by Lorwin (*119*), also considers the implications of national defense plans in connection with work programs. The general report of the American Youth Commission, *Youth and the Future* (*198*), summarizes the recommendations of the Commission and presents a philosophy of youth guidance and a plan for the future training of youth, the significance of which can scarcely be overestimated. This book, which was published in January 1942, takes into account the influence of our entry into the war on the occupational adjustment of youth in the immediate future, and also tries to predict long-time trends and to suggest needed steps to meet the problems which will arise in the postwar period. A study guide entitled *Looking Ahead with Youth* was prepared by Chambers for use with the general report.

Certain chapters in *High School and Life* (*162*), a study carried on under the direction of Spaulding in connection with the Regents' Inquiry into the

Character and Cost of Public Education in the State of New York, present a challenging picture of the status and needs of vocational guidance in secondary schools.

One of the weaknesses in many guidance programs is the lack of an adequate plan for following up pupils after they leave school. Most counselors recognize this weakness and desire suggestions for correcting it. A noteworthy follow-up study carried on by Landy and others (*108, 109*) under the auspices of the National Association of Secondary School Principals, was described briefly in Chapter XVI. An attempt was made in the study to discover the means by which a secondary school can get valid information about the degree of occupational adjustment of pupils who leave the school and clues concerning desirable changes in the guidance and educational programs of secondary schools.

Studies of child behavior also contain important suggestions for counselors. The most extensive series of studies of this kind that has yet been published was issued by the Character Education Inquiry several years ago. This series includes three books: *Studies in Deceit* by Hartshorne and May (*82*); *Studies in Service and Self-Control* by Hartshorne, May, and Maller (*83*); and *Studies in the Organization of Character* by Hartshorne, May, and Shuttleworth (*84*). The studies were based on carefully planned and frequently ingenious measurement and the results were presented and interpreted thoroughly. Another widely read study of behavior is Wickman's *Children's Behavior and Teachers' Attitudes,* an extensive study of the behavior of school children and of teachers' attitudes toward behavior problems. Suggested procedures for re-education in attitudes are included in this book and the study is summarized in a briefer book entitled *Teachers and Behavior Problems* (*186*).

In recent years there has been much discussion among psychologists and statisticians concerning the number and nature of the factors that make up mental ability. Although few counselors, unless they have had considerable training in mathematics, can be expected to understand the details of the technical discussions concerning the components of mental ability, the conclusions of the studies in this field, if they are to be of any practical value, must eventually be utilized in guidance. The most thorough study leading toward an actual measurement of a variety of mental factors is included in Thurstone's monograph *Primary Mental Abilities* (*180*). Studies of this kind should have a place in the libraries of all counselors who are contemplating the experimental use of such tests as the Chicago Tests of Primary Mental Abilities.

Longitudinal or follow-up studies of the development of pupils are of special interest to counselors who are trying to gain an understanding of the individual child. In this connection, three investigations that come to mind at once are Freeman and Flory's study of the mental and physical growth of the University of Chicago Laboratory School children (*65*), the Harvard Growth Study conducted by Dearborn and Rothney (*49*), and the study of the relations of secondary and higher education in Pennsylvania carried on under the auspices of the Carnegie Foundation for the Advancement of Teaching and reported in *The Student and His Knowledge* by Learned and Wood (*113*). This study of the results of high school and college examinations administered in 1928, 1930, and 1932 should be read by every counselor.

Interests and Their Measurement

The field of interests is one of the broad categories that counselors must explore before they are fully equipped to understand the individual child. Probably the most thorough summary of studies of interests up to a few years ago is Fryer's *The Measurement of Interests* (*66*). Strong has carried on the most sustained study of interests that are related to vocational choice. His findings are reported in his books *Change of Interests with Age* (*171*) and *Vocational Interests of Men and Women* (*172*). The latter book should be in the possession of everyone who administers and attempts to interpret the Strong Vocational Interest Blank. A somewhat different approach to the measurement of interests has been described by Kuder in an article entitled "The Stability of Preference Items" (*107*), which should be read by persons who undertake to use and interpret his *Preference Record*.

Testing in a Guidance Program

In order to study the individual child adequately, the counselor must of course be familiar with the meaning, interpretation, and uses of test results. Many books on testing are available and the counselor should certainly have one or more of these at hand. For all-round usefulness in a counseling program, one of the most valuable books on testing is *The Construction and Use of Achievement Examinations* by Hawkes, Lindquist and Mann (*85*). This manual, which pertains particularly to the secondary school, was prepared with the collaboration of experts in the theory and practice of achievement testing. An exceptionally practical book having to do with the uses of tests in a guidance program is *Student Guidance Techniques* by Paterson, Schneidler, and Williamson (*135*) which includes a presentation of diagnostic techniques based on objective records. It contains also a selected list of tests with extensive information about each one. Many of the achievement tests listed are those published by the Cooperative Test Service. Guidance officers using the Cooperative tests should have at hand Flanagan's bulletin on their system of *Scaled Scores* (*62*).

Among the newer textbooks on testing, *Educational Measurement and*

Evaluation by Remmers and Gage (*142*) is especially helpful because of its broad, thorough, and explicit treatment of the problems and procedures of evaluation. The practical approach and simple, clear treatment of Ross' *Measurement in Today's Schools* (*145*) should commend this book also to counselors who are trying to become orientated to the whole field of measurement. The books by Greene, Jorgensen, and Gerberich (*72, 73*) on measurement and evaluation in the elementary and secondary schools are also helpful.

Bingham's *Aptitudes and Aptitude Testing* (*16*) is one of the best reference works on aptitude measurement. It contains a thoughtful presentation of the theory of aptitude and a comprehensive survey of the various types of aptitude tests. Viteles' *Industrial Psychology* (*184*) is a valuable source of information on aptitude measurement in connection with industry.

Counselors who have the problem of selecting tests for various purposes should have access to Buros' Mental Measurements Yearbooks (*23, 24*). These yearbooks not only provide an extensive and detailed listing of the newer tests but also contain hundreds of reviews written by measurement specialists. Although some of the reviews are subjective and reflect the personal bias of the writers, the reviews as a whole provide the best appraisal of objective tests available anywhere.

CASE STUDIES

Books dealing wholly or in part with case studies are very valuable references in connection with any guidance program. Among the books of this type are Reavis' *Pupil Adjustment in Junior and Senior High Schools* (*139*), Smithies' *Case Studies of Normal Adolescent Girls* (*161*), Sayles' *Child Guidance Cases* (*150*), and McCallister's *Remedial and Corrective Instruction in Reading* (*121*). Reavis presents the case study techniques used some years ago in the University of Chicago High School. Smithies' book is a reference volume for guidance workers and teachers who are dealing with high school girls. It contains a chapter on the technique of case-study work and eleven case studies. Sayles' book contains detailed reports on eight case studies, each of which consists of two parts—initial study and treatment. The case studies reported are much more extensive than most counselors can undertake, but some of the same techniques can be applied to less extensive studies. One part of McCallister's book gives an outline for case studies of retarded readers and three illustrative studies.

Some years ago Brewer published a book entitled *Case Studies in Educational and Vocational Guidance* (*18*) which is suitable for use in an educational and discussion program concerning the case study. It presents 138 cases classified under such headings as Attitude toward School Work, Problems of a Personal or Social Nature, and Problems in Readjustment and Promotion. In each instance, the nature of the case is stated and questions relative to its solution are formulated. The Educational Records Bureau's report of the Public School Demonstration Project, *Guidance in Public Secondary Schools* (*182*), contains a chapter in which fifteen case studies prepared by classroom teachers are presented.

CUMULATIVE RECORDS

Because of the increasing emphasis on cumulative records in guidance programs, reports dealing with the nature and use of cumulative records are of unusual interest to personnel workers. As stated in Chapter XIV, a very illuminating article on the value of cumulative records in case studies is "The Cumulative Record and Its Uses," by Anna L. Rose Hawkes which was published in *Guidance in Public Secondary Schools* (*182*), and which shows by means of two careful and very detailed case studies some of the ways in which cumulative records can be used in a guidance program in the secondary school. Several cumulative records are presented and explained by Learned and Hawkes in *An Experiment in Responsible Learning* (*112*), which is one of the series of publications growing out of the Study of the Relations of Secondary and Higher Education in Pennsylvania.

A comprehensive survey of the cumulative record in schools throughout the country is given in Segel's *Nature and Use of the Cumulative Record* (*152*). *Minimum Essentials of the Individual Inventory in Guidance* by Ruch and Segel (*146*) also has important implications for the kinds of information that should go into cumulative records. A doctor's dissertation, *Cumulative Pupil Records* by Wendell C. Allen (*2*), is also a helpful contribution.

VISUAL AIDS TO GUIDANCE

Since projectors for 16 mm. sound film are now standard equipment in many colleges and secondary schools, instructors of guidance courses, guidance directors, and persons in charge of guidance workshops should be alert to opportunities to use guidance films in promoting understanding of pupil behavior, problems encountered by young people, and procedures of organizing and administering guidance. Films such as *Choosing Your Vocation* (*201*), *Guidance in Public Schools* (*202*), and *Guidance Problem for School and Home* (*203*) can be used to advantage in educating counselors and teachers in guidance procedures. Titles of other films which might be useful in a school's guidance program can be checked in the Educational Film Catalog, published monthly during the college year by the H. W. Wilson Company, 950 University Avenue, New York City. It would be desirable for guidance specialists to give increased attention to the preparation of this type of special aids for a training program in guidance techniques.

BIBLIOGRAPHIES

In order to keep posted on the ever-growing literature on guidance and personnel work, counselors should have access to some of the more important bibliographies in this field. Two mimeographed bibliographies have been published by the National Association of Deans of Women under the title *Guide to Guidance* (78). A list of "Selected References on Guidance" prepared by Hutson (92) appears annually in the September number of the *School Review*. Every three years the American Educational Research Association devotes one of its numbers of the *Review of Educational Research* to a summary of research and an extensive bibliography in the field of pupil personnel, guidance, and counseling. For those who wish to be brought up-to-date at more frequent intervals concerning the literature dealing with the aspects of personnel work having to do with vocational counseling, Science Research Associates issues each month a *Vocational Guide* (151), which contains a selection and classification of current vocational literature. Similarly, the *Occupational Index, Inc.* (134), issued four times a year, lists new pamphlets, books, and articles on occupations, with each reference carefully annotated and thoroughly indexed.

A SELECTED LIBRARY FOR COUNSELORS

1. * Allen, Richard D., and others. *Inor Group Guidance Series.* New York: Inor Publishing Company, Inc., 1933 and 1934. Volume I, *Common Problems in Group Guidance;* pp. xx + 186; $1.95. Volume II, *Case Conference Problems in Group Guidance;* pp. x + 152; $1.55. Volume III, *Self-Measurement Projects in Group Guidance;* pp. xviii + 274; $2.25. Volume IV, *Organization and Supervision of Guidance in Public Education;* pp. xxii + 420; $3.65.

2. Allen, Wendell C. *Cumulative Pupil Records.* New York: Bureau of Publications, Teachers College, Columbia University, 1943. Pp. vii + 69. $1.85.

3. Allport, Gordon W. *Personality: A Psychological Interpretation.* New York: Henry Holt and Company, 1937. Pp. xiv + 588. $3.00.

4. Appel, Kenneth E., and Strecker, Edward. *Practical Examination of Personality and Behavior Disorders.* Adults and Children. New York: The Macmillan Company, 1936. Pp. xiv + 219. $2.25.

5. Arlitt, Ada Hart. *The Adolescent.* New York: McGraw-Hill Book Company, Inc., 1938. Pp. ix + 242. $2.00.

6. Baker, Harry J., and Traphagen, Virginia. *The Diagnosis and Treatment of Behavior Problem Children.* New York: The Macmillan Company, 1935. Pp. xiv + 393. $3.00.

Starred references are especially recommended.

7. Barker, Roger G.; Kounin, Jacob S.; and Wright, Herbert F. *Child Behavior and Development*. New York: McGraw-Hill Book Company, Inc., 1943. Pp. viii + 652. $4.00.

8. Bear, Robert M. *The Social Functions of Education*. New York: The Macmillan Company, 1937. Pp. xiii + 434. $2.25.

9. Becker, Elsa G. *Guidance at Work in a Large City High School*. New York: New York City Board of Education, 1935. Pp. xi + 125.

10. Bell, Howard M. *Youth Tell Their Story*. Washington, D. C.: American Council on Education, 1938. Pp. 273. Paper, $1.50; cloth, $2.00.

11. Bell, Howard M. *Matching Youth and Jobs*. Washington, D. C.: American Council on Education, 1940. Pp. xiii + 277. $2.00.

12. Bender, Eric. *Way of Life Series*. New York: Row, Peterson and Company, 1941–42. Thirty-five books in series. $0.96 each; $0.58 for five or more.

13. * Bennett, Margaret E., and Hand, Harold C. *Group Guidance Series*. New York: McGraw-Hill Book Company, Inc., 1938. Volume I, *School and Life;* pp. xiii + 185; $1.24. Volume II, *Design for Personality;* pp. xiii + 222; $1.36. Volume III, *Beyond High School;* pp. xv + 227; $1.36. Teacher's Manual, *Group Guidance in High School;* pp. iv + 111; $1.00.

14. Bentley, John E. *Problem Children*. New York: W. W. Norton and Company, 1936. Pp. xxiii + 437. $2.75.

15. Bergstresser, John L. "Counseling and the Changing Secondary School Curriculum," *The Bulletin of the National Association of Secondary School Principals of the National Education Association,* XXIV (May 1940), 1–112.

16. * Bingham, Walter Van Dyke. *Aptitudes and Aptitude Testing*. New York: Harper & Brothers, 1937. Pp. x + 390. $3.00.

17. Bingham, Walter Van Dyke, and Moore, Bruce V. *How to Interview*. New York: Harper & Brothers, 1934 (revised edition). Pp. 308. $3.00.

18. Brewer, John M. *Case Studies in Educational and Vocational Guidance*. Boston: Ginn and Company, 1926. Pp. xxiv + 243. $2.00.

19. Brewer, John M. *Education as Guidance*. New York: The Macmillan Company, 1932. Pp. x + 668. $3.00.

20. Brewer, John M., and Landy, Edward. *Occupations Today*. Boston: Ginn and Company, 1943. Pp. vi + 376. $1.64.

21. * Brewer, John M., and others. *History of Vocational Guidance*. New York: Harper & Brothers, 1942. Pp. viii + 344. $3.00.

22. * Brown, J. F. *The Psychodynamics of Abnormal Behavior*. New York: McGraw-Hill Book Company, Inc., 1940. Pp. xvi + 484. $3.50.

23. * Buros, Oscar K. *The Nineteen Thirty-Eight Mental Measurements Yearbook*. New Brunswick, New Jersey: Rutgers University Press, 1938. Pp. xiv + 415. $3.00.

24. * Buros, Oscar K. *The Nineteen Forty Mental Measurements Yearbook*. Highland Park, New Jersey: The Mental Measurements Yearbook, 1941. Pp. xxiii + 674. $6.00.

25. Burtt, Harold Ernest. *Principles of Employment Psychology*. New York: Harper & Brothers, 1942 (revised). Pp. xii + 568. $4.00.

26. Caliver, Ambrose. *Vocational Education and Guidance of Negroes.* United States Office of Education Bulletin No. 38, 1937. Pp. x + 138. (Out of Print.)

27. Cardall, Alfred J. *A Wartime Guidance Program for Your School.* Guidance Plans and Methods, No. 12. Chicago: Science Research Associates, 1943. Pp. 104. $1.00.

28. * *Careers: Research Monographs.* Institute for Research, 537 South Dearborn Street, Chicago, Illinois. $0.75.

29. Chambers, M. M. *Youth Serving Organizations: National Nongovernmental Organizations.* Washington, D. C.: American Council on Education, 1941. Pp. 237. $2.50.

30. Chapman, Paul W. *Guidance Programs for Rural High Schools.* Washington, D. C.: United States Office of Education, 1940. Pp. 58.

31. Chave, E. J. *Personality Development in Children.* Chicago: University of Chicago Press, 1937. Pp. xiii + 354. $2.50.

32. *Child Development and the Curriculum.* Thirty-Eighth Yearbook of the National Society for the Study of Education, Part I. Bloomington, Illinois: Public School Publishing Company, 1939. Pp. x + 441. Cloth, $3.25; paper, $2.50.

33. Clark, Florence E. *The Printing Trades and Their Workers.* Scranton, Pennsylvania: International Textbook Company. Pp. 132. $2.00.

34. Clark, Harold F., with the assistance of Mervyn Crobaugh, Wilbur I. Gooch, Byrne J. Horton, and Rosemary Norris Kutak. *Life Earnings in Selected Occupations in the United States.* New York: Harper & Brothers, 1937. Pp. xx + 408. $5.00.

35. * Cole, Luella. *Psychology of Adolescence.* New York: Farrar & Rinehart, Inc., 1942 (revised). Pp. xviii + 660. $3.25.

36. * Cooperative Test Service. *The Cooperative Achievement Tests: A Handbook Describing Their Purpose, Content, and Interpretation.* New York: Cooperative Test Service, 1936. Pp. 39. $0.25.

37. Cooperative Test Service. *A Booklet of Norms.* New York: Cooperative Test Service, 1938. Pp. 85. $0.25.

38. Cooperative Test Service. *Cooperative Achievement Tests.* New York: Cooperative Test Service, 1945. Pp. 76. Gratis.

39. Cox, Philip W. L., and Duff, John C. *Guidance by the Classroom Teacher.* New York: Prentice-Hall, Inc., 1938. Pp. xxv + 535. $3.00.

40. Crow, Lester D., and Crow, Alice. *Mental Hygiene in School and Home Life for Teachers, Supervisors, and Parents.* New York: McGraw-Hill Book Company, Inc., 1942. Pp. xii + 474. $3.00.

41. Culbert, Jane F., and Smith, Helen R. *Counseling Young Workers.* New York: Vocational Service for Juniors (95 Madison Avenue), 1939. Pp. xii + 212. $1.75.

42. Cunliffe, Rex B.; Field, George; Herbert, Edward; O'Brien, James J.; and Stiglitz, Hanna. *Guidance Practices in New Jersey.* Rutgers University

Studies in Education, No. 15.   New Brunswick, New Jersey: School of Education, Rutgers University, 1942.   Pp. xviii + 148.

43.   Cutts, Norma, and Moseley, Nicholas. *Practical School Discipline and Mental Hygiene*. Boston: Houghton Mifflin Company, 1941. Pp. x + 324. $1.90.

44.   Dame, J. Frank; Brinkman, Albert R.; and Weaver, Wilbur E. *Prognosis, Guidance, and Placement in Business Education*. Cincinnati: South-Western Publishing Company, 1944. Pp. vi + 216. $2.00.

45.   Darley, John G. *Clinical Aspects and Interpretation of the Strong Vocational Interest Blank*. New York: Psychological Corporation, 1941. Pp. 72. $1.00.

46. * Darley, John G. *Testing and Counseling in the High-School Guidance Program*. Chicago: Science Research Associates, 1943. Pp. 222. $2.60.

47.   Davidson, Percy Erwin, and Anderson, H. Dewey. *Occupational Mobility in an American Community*. Stanford University, California: Stanford University Press, 1937. Pp. vii + 203. $3.25.

48. * Davis, Frank G., and Davis, B. Carnall. *Guidance for Youth*. Boston: Ginn and Company, 1937. Pp. xii + 387. $1.56.

49.   Dearborn, W. F., and Rothney, J. W. M. *Predicting the Child's Development*. Cambridge, Mass.: Sci-Art Publishers, 1941. Pp. 360. $4.50.

50.   Dearborn, W. F.; Rothney, J. W. M.; and Shuttleworth, F. K. *Data on the Growth of Public School Children*. Monographs of the Society for Research in Child Development, Vol. 3, No. 1. Washington, D. C.: National Research Council, 1938. Pp. 136. (Out of Print.)

51.   DeSchweinitz, Dorothea. *Occupations in Retail Stores*. Scranton, Pennsylvania: International Textbook Company. Pp. 411. $2.75.

52.   Detjen, Mary E. (Ford), and Detjen, Erwin W. *Home Room Guidance Programs for the Junior High School Years*. Boston: Houghton Mifflin Company, 1940. Pp. 509. $2.00.

53. * *Dictionary of Occupational Titles*. Part I, *Definitions of Titles,* June, 1939; pp. xxxii + 1287; $2.00. Part II, *Titles and Codes,* June, 1939; pp. xxvi + 330; $1.00. Part III, *Conversion Tables,* June, 1939; pp. ii + 259; $1.00 (out of print). Part IV, *Entry-Occupational Classification,* 1941; pp. 108. U. S. Employment Service, U. S. Department of Labor. Also *Occupational Titles Supplement,* Edition II, July, 1943. Pp. viii + 525. $0.60. Division of Occupational Analysis and Manning Tables, Bureau of Manpower Utilization, War Manpower Commission. Washington, D. C.: Government Printing Office. (For sale by the Superintendent of Documents.)

54. * Dunsmoor, Clarence C., and Miller, Leonard M. *Guidance Methods for Teachers in Homeroom, Classroom, and Core Program*. Scranton, Pennsylvania: International Textbook Company, 1942. Pp. xvi + 382. $2.50.

55.   Eckert, Ruth E., and Marshall, Thomas O. *When Youth Leave School*. The Regents' Inquiry into the Character and Cost of Public Education in the State of New York. New York: McGraw-Hill Book Company, Inc., 1938. Pp. xviii + 360. $3.00.

56.   Edwards, Alba M. *A Socio-Economic Grouping of the Gainful Workers of*

the United States. Washington, D. C.: Government Printing Office, 1938. Pp. vi + 264.

57. Elliott, Harrison S., and Elliott, Grace L. *Solving Personal Problems.* New York: Henry Holt and Company, 1936. Pp. viii + 322. $2.00.

58. Endicott, Frank S. *One Hundred Guidance Lessons.* Scranton, Pennsylvania: International Textbook Company, 1937. Pp. xi + 236. $1.34.

59. Fenton, Norman. *The Counselor's Approach to the Home.* School Case Work Manuals, No. 1. Stanford University, California: Stanford University Press, 1943. Pp. 32. $0.50.

60. Fenton, Norman. *The Counselor's Interview with the Student.* School Case Work Manuals, No. 2. Stanford University, California: Stanford University Press, 1943. Pp. 36. $0.50.

61. * Fenton, Norman. *Mental Hygiene in School Practice.* Stanford University, California: Stanford University Press, 1943. Pp. xvi + 455. $4.00.

62. * Flanagan, John C. *Scaled Scores.* New York: Cooperative Test Service, 1939. Pp. v + 41. $0.25.

63. Forrester, Gertrude. *Methods of Vocational Guidance—with Specific Helps for the Teacher of Business Subjects.* Boston: D. C. Heath and Company, 1944. Pp. xx + 460. $3.00.

64. * Freeman, Frank N. *Mental Tests.* Boston: Houghton Mifflin Company, 1939 (revised). Pp. x + 460. $2.75.

65. Freeman, Frank N., and Flory, Charles D. *Growth in Intellectual Ability as Measured by Repeated Tests.* Monograph of the Society for Research in Child Development, Vol. II, No. 2. Washington, D. C.: National Research Council, 1937. Pp. xii + 116. $1.00.

66. Fryer, Douglas. *The Measurement of Interests.* New York: Henry Holt and Company, 1931. $3.60.

67. Gallagher, Ralph P. *Guidance Service Standards for Secondary Schools.* Trenton, New Jersey: New Jersey Secondary School Teachers Association, 1937. Pp. 50. $0.25. (Requests for copies should be sent to the treasurer of the Association, Lester D. Beers, Plainfield High School, Plainfield, New Jersey.)

68. Gardiner, Glenn L. *How You Can Get a Job.* New York: Harper & Brothers, 1934 and 1938. Pp. ix + 226. $1.50.

69. * Germane, Charles E., and Germane, Edith G. *Personnel Work in High School.* New York: Silver Burdett Company, 1941. Pp. xv + 599. $4.00.

70. Gesell, Arnold, and Thompson, Helen. *The Psychology of Early Growth.* New York: The Macmillan Company, 1938. Pp. 290. $5.00.

71. Greene, Edward B. *Measurements of Human Behavior.* New York: The Odyssey Press, 1941. Pp. xxi + 777. $3.75.

72. * Greene, Harry A.; Jorgensen, Albert N.; and Gerberich, J. Raymond. *Measurement and Evaluation in the Elementary School.* New York: Longmans, Green and Company, 1942. Pp. xxiii + 639. $3.75.

73. Greene, Harry A.; Jorgensen, Albert N.; and Gerberich, J. Raymond. *Meas-*

urement and Evaluation in the Secondary School. New York: Longmans, Green and Company, 1943. Pp. xxvi + 670. $3.75.

74. Greenleaf, Walter J., and Brewster, Royce E. *Public High Schools Having Counselors and Guidance Officers.* Washington, D. C.: United States Office of Education, Misc. 2267, 1939. Pp. 40.

75. *Guidance in Educational Institutions.* Thirty-Seventh Yearbook of the National Society for the Study of Education, Part I. Bloomington, Illinois: Public School Publishing Company, 1938. Pp. viii + 314. Cloth, $2.50; paper, $1.75.

76. "Guidance in Public Schools," *Teachers College Record,* XL (October 1938), 1–79.

77. *Guidance Manual for the High-School Victory Corps.* Washington, D. C.: U. S. Office of Education, Victory Corps Series, Pamphlet No. 4, 1943. Pp. vi + 38. $0.20.

78. *Guide to Guidance.* Volume I: An Annotated Bibliography of 1938 Publications of Interest to Deans, Counselors, and Advisers (Compiled by Margaret Carrigan); Volume II: An Annotated Bibliography of 1939 Publications of Interest to Deans, Counselors, and Advisers (Compiled by Elizabeth Broad). Washington, D. C.: National Association of Deans of Women of the National Education Association. $0.50 each.

79. * Hamrin, Shirley A., and Erickson, Clifford E. *Guidance in the Secondary School.* New York: D. Appleton-Century Company, 1939. Pp. xii + 466. $3.00.

80. Hamrin, Shirley A., and others. *Guidance Practices in Public High Schools.* Bloomington, Illinois: McKnight & McKnight, 1940. Pp. 68. $0.50.

81. Hand, Harold C. *Campus Activities.* New York: McGraw-Hill Book Company, Inc., 1938. Pp. xvi + 357. $3.00.

82. Hartshorne, Hugh, and May, Mark A. Volume I, *Studies in Deceit.* New York: The Macmillan Company, 1928. Pp. xxi + 306. $4.50.

83. Hartshorne, Hugh; May, Mark A.; and Maller, Julius B. Volume II, *Studies in Service and Self-Control.* New York: The Macmillan Company, 1929. Pp. xxiii + 559. $2.75.

84. Hartshorne, Hugh; May, Mark A.; and Shuttleworth, F. K. Volume III, *Studies in the Organization of Character.* New York: The Macmillan Company, 1930. Pp. xxv + 503. $2.75.

85. * Hawkes, Herbert E.; Lindquist, E. F.; and Mann, C. R. *The Construction and Use of Achievement Examinations.* Boston: Houghton Mifflin Company, 1936. Pp. vii + 497. $2.50.

86. Hawkins, Layton S., and others. *Occupational Information and Guidance.* Washington, D. C.: U. S. Office of Education, 1939. Pp. 181.

87. Heck, Arch O. *The Education of Exceptional Children.* New York: McGraw-Hill Book Company, Inc., 1940. Pp. xviii + 536. $3.75.

88. Hilkert, Robert N. "Parents and Cumulative Records," *Educational Record,* XXI (Supplement No. 13, January 1940), 172–183.

89. *Hoppock, Robert. *Job Satisfaction.* New York: Harper & Brothers, 1935. Pp. xxi + 303. $3.50.

90. Hoppock, Robert, and Shaffer, Robert H. "Job Satisfaction: Researches and Opinions of 1940–1941," *Occupations,* XXI (February 1943), 457–463.

91. *Howard, Frank E., and Patry, Frederick L. *Mental Health.* New York: Harper & Brothers, 1935. Pp. xvi + 551. $3.50.

92. *Hutson, Percival W. "Selected References on Guidance," *School Review,* XLI (September 1933), 539–546; XLII (September 1934), 540–546; XLIII (September 1935), 540–546; XLIV (September 1936), 539–546; XLV (September 1937), 540–546; XLVI (September 1938), 539–546; XLVII (September 1939), 540–546; XLVIII (September 1940), 540–546; XLIX (September 1941), 541–547; L (September 1942), 529–535; LI (September 1943), 428–433; LII (September 1944), 431–436.

93. Hutson, Percival W., and Webster, Arthur D. "An Experiment in the Educational and Vocational Guidance of Tenth-Grade Pupils," *Educational and Psychological Measurement,* III (Spring, 1943), 3–21.

94. International Business Machines Corporation, Test Scoring Machine Department. *Methods of Adapting Tests for Machine Scoring: International Test Scoring Machine.* New York: International Business Machines Corporation, 1938. Pp. 24. Gratis.

95. Jager, Harry A. "Guidance for Essential Occupations and the Armed Forces," *Bulletin of the National Association of Secondary School Principals,* XXVII (April 1943), 51–56.

96. *Jersild, Arthur T. *Child Psychology.* New York: Prentice-Hall, Inc., 1940 (revised and enlarged). Pp. xiv + 592. $3.00.

97. *Jones, Arthur J. *Principles of Guidance.* New York: McGraw-Hill Book Company, Inc., 1934 (second edition). Pp. xxviii + 456. $3.00.

98. Jones, Galen, and Galbraith, Adria. "The Interpretation of Standardized Tests," *School and Society,* LIV (September 20, 1941), 224–227.

99. Kefauver, Grayson N., and Hand, Harold C. *Appraising Guidance in Secondary Schools.* New York: The Macmillan Company, 1941. Pp. xiv + 260. $3.50.

100. Keller, Franklin J., and Viteles, Morris S. *Vocational Guidance Throughout the World.* New York: W. W. Norton, 1937. Pp. xiii + 575. $3.25.

101. Kelley, Truman L., and Krey, A. C. *Tests and Measurements in the Social Sciences.* New York: Charles Scribner's Sons, 1934. Pp. xiv + 635. $3.00.

102. Kitson, Harry Dexter. *I Find My Vocation.* New York: McGraw-Hill Book Company, Inc., 1937 (revised edition). Pp. xvi + 227. $1.40.

103. *Kitson, Harry Dexter. *How to Find the Right Vocation.* New York: Harper & Brothers, 1938 (revised edition). Pp. xii + 215. $2.50.

104. Klein, David B. *Mental Hygiene.* New York: Henry Holt and Company, 1944. Pp. xii + 498. $2.80.

105. Koos, Leonard V. "Some Essentials in Student Personnel Work," *Junior College Journal,* X (May 1940), 602–609.

106. * Koos, Leonard V., and Kefauver, Grayson N. *Guidance in Secondary Schools.* New York: The Macmillan Company, 1932. Pp. xii + 640. $2.75.

107. Kuder, G. F. "The Stability of Preference Items," *Journal of Social Psychology,* X (February 1939), 4-50.

108. Landy, Edward, with the collaboration of Beery, John R.; Hayes, Byron C.; and Long, C. Darl. *Occupational Adjustment and the School.* Bulletin of the National Association of Secondary School Principals, Volume 24, No. 93. Washington, D. C.: National Association of Secondary School Principals, 1940. Pp. 160.

109. * Landy, Edward; Beery, John R.; Hayes, Byron C.; and Long, C. Darl. *The Occupational Follow-up and Adjustment Service Plan.* New York: The Occupational Adjustment Study of the National Association of Secondary School Principals, 1940. Pp. 96.

110. Lane, May Rogers. *Vocations in Industry.* Scranton, Pennsylvania: International Textbook Company. Volume I, *Agriculture, Forestry and Animal Husbandry;* pp. 155; $1.50. Volume II, *Mining and Mineral Industries;* pp. 204; $2.00. Volume III, *Manufacturing and Mechanical Industries;* pp. 467; $3.50.

111. Lane, May Rogers. *Manual to Accompany Vocations in Industry.* Scranton, Pennsylvania: International Textbook Company. Pp. 111. $2.00.

112. Learned, William S., and Hawkes, Anna L. Rose. *An Experiment in Responsible Learning.* Bulletin Number 31. New York: Carnegie Foundation for the Advancement of Teaching, 1940. Pp. 61. Gratis.

113. * Learned, William S., and Wood, Ben D. *The Student and His Knowledge.* Bulletin No. 29. New York: Carnegie Foundation for the Advancement of Teaching, 1938. Pp. xx + 406. Gratis.

114. Lee, J. Murray. *Guide to Measurement in Secondary Schools.* New York: D. Appleton-Century Company, 1936. Pp. xii + 514. $2.75.

115. * Lefever, D. Welty; Turrell, Archie M.; and Weitzel, Harry I. *Principles and Techniques of Guidance.* New York: Ronald Press Company, 1941. Pp. xviii + 522. $3.00.

116. Lincoln, Edward A., and Workman, Linwood L. *Testing and the Use of Test Results.* New York: The Macmillan Company, 1935. Pp. xi + 317. $2.25.

117. Lincoln, Mildred E. *Teaching about Vocational Life.* Scranton, Pennsylvania: International Textbook Company. Pp. 630. $3.50.

118. * Lloyd-Jones, Esther McD., and Smith, Margaret Ruth. *A Student Personnel Program for Higher Education.* New York: McGraw-Hill Book Company, Inc., 1938. Pp. x + 322. $2.75.

119. * Lorwin, Lewis L. *Youth Work Programs.* Washington, D. C.: American Council on Education, 1941. Pp. xi + 195. $1.75.

120. Louttit, Chauncey M. *Clinical Psychology:* A Handbook of Children's Behavior Problems. New York: Harper & Brothers, 1936. Pp. xx + 695 $3.50.

121. McCallister, James M. *Remedial and Corrective Instruction in Reading.* New York: D. Appleton-Century Company, 1936. Pp. xviii + 300. $2.00.

122. McClintock, James A. *Personnel Procedures in the Secondary School.* New York: The Psychological Corporation, 1940. Pp. xv + 183. $2.00.

123. McConn, Max. "Educational Guidance Is Now Possible," *Educational Record,* XIV (October 1933), 475–499.

124. McKinney, Fred. *Psychology of Personal Adjustment.* New York: John Wiley and Sons, 1941. Pp. xii + 636. $3.50.

125. McKown, Harry C. *Home Room Guidance.* New York: McGraw-Hill Book Company, Inc., 1934. Pp. xxii + 447. $3.00.

126. Moore, Bruce V., and Hartmann, George W. *Readings in Industrial Psychology.* New York: D. Appleton-Century Company, 1931. Pp. 560. $5.00.

127. Morgan, John J. B. *The Psychology of the Unadjusted School Child.* New York: The Macmillan Company, 1936 (revised). Pp. viii + 340. $2.25.

128. * Morgan, John J. B. *Child Psychology* (third edition). New York: Farrar & Rinehart, Inc., 1942. Pp. xii + 588. $3.00.

129. Murchison, Carl (editor). *Handbook of Child Psychology* (second edition, revised). Worcester, Mass.: Clark University Press, 1933. Pp. 956. (Out of Print.)

130. Murray, Sister M. Teresa Gertrude. *Vocational Guidance in Catholic Secondary Schools.* New York: Teachers College, Columbia University, Contributions to Education, No. 754, 1938. Pp. 163. $1.60.

131. Myers, George E. *Principles and Techniques of Vocational Guidance.* New York: McGraw-Hill Book Company, Inc., 1941. Pp. xii + 377. $3.00.

132. Myers, George E.; Little, Gladys M.; and Robinson, Sarah A. *Planning Your Future* (second edition). New York: McGraw-Hill Book Company, Inc., 1934. Pp. xiv + 419. $1.50.

133. New Jersey State Teachers' Association. *A Discussion Outline in Guidance.* W. C. Compher, Association Treasurer, New Brunswick Senior High School, New Brunswick, New Jersey. Pp. 40.

134. * *Occupational Index, Inc.* New York University, Washington Square, New York 3, N. Y. $5.00 a year.

135. * Paterson, D. G.; Schneidler, G. G.; and Williamson, E. G. *Student Guidance Techniques.* New York: McGraw-Hill Book Company, Inc., 1938. Pp. xviii + 316. $3.00.

136. * Pressey, Sidney L., and Robinson, Francis P. *Psychology and the New Education.* New York: Harper & Brothers, 1933 (revised, 1944). Pp. xxv + 654. $3.00.

137. "Pupil Personnel, Guidance, and Counseling," *Review of Educational Research.* Volume III, Number 3 (June 1933); Volume VI, Number 2 (April 1936); Volume IX, Number 2 (April 1939); Volume XII, No. 1 (February 1942).

138. Rainey, Homer P., and others. *How Fare American Youth?* New York: D. Appleton-Century Company, 1937. Pp. ix + 186. $1.50.

139. Reavis, William C. *Pupil Adjustment in Junior and Senior High Schools.* Boston: D. C. Heath and Company, 1926. Pp. xviii + 348. $2.00. (Out of print.)

140. Reavis, William C. *Programs of Guidance.* National Survey of Secondary Education Monograph No. 14. U. S. Office of Education Bulletin No. 17, 1932. Pp. vi + 144.

141. * Reed, Anna Y. *Guidance and Personnel Services in Education.* Ithaca, New York: Cornell University Press, 1944. Pp. xi + 496. $4.75.

142. * Remmers, H. H., and Gage, N. L. *Educational Measurement and Evaluation.* New York: Harper & Brothers, 1943. Pp. x + 580. $3.25.

143. * Rogers, Carl R. *Counseling and Psychotherapy.* Boston: Houghton Mifflin Company, 1942. Pp. xiv + 450. $3.60.

144. Rosengarten, William. *Choosing Your Life Work.* New York: McGraw-Hill Book Company, Inc., 1936 (revised edition). Pp. xxiii + 353. $2.50.

145. * Ross, C. C. *Measurement in Today's Schools.* New York: Prentice-Hall, Inc., 1941. Pp. xviii + 597. $3.25.

146. * Ruch, Giles M., and Segel, David. *Minimum Essentials of the Individual Inventory in Guidance.* U. S. Office of Education, Vocational Division Bulletin No. 202, Occupational Information and Guidance Series No. 2, 1940. Pp. vi + 84. $0.15.

147. Russell, John Dale. *Student Personnel Services in Colleges and Universities.* Proceedings of the Institute for Administrative Officers of Higher Institutions, 1940. Chicago: University of Chicago Press, 1941. Pp. 300. (Out of print.)

148. Ryan, W. Carson. *Mental Health through Education.* New York: The Commonwealth Fund, 1938. Pp. 328. $1.50.

149. Ryans, David G. *The First Step in Guidance: Self-Appraisal.* New York: Cooperative Test Service, American Council on Education, 1941. Pp. 35. $0.10.

150. Sayles, Mary B. *Child Guidance Cases.* New York: The Commonwealth Fund, 1932. Pp. xxiii + 584. $2.50.

151. * Science Research Associates publications: *Vocational Trends,* a monthly magazine of occupational facts and forecasts ($2.50 a year); *Vocational Guide,* a monthly selection and classification of current vocational literature ($4.00 a year); *Occupational Monographs,* a study issued every month outlining basic trends and characteristics in an industry, trade, or profession ($5.00 a year); *Reprint and Abstract Service,* a reproduction each month of inaccessible or costly vocational materials ($2.50 a year); *Research Department,* research facilities for handling special problems, questions, and requests. Science Research Associates, 228 South Wabash Avenue, Chicago 4, Illinois.

152. * Segel, David. *Nature and Use of the Cumulative Record.* United States Department of the Interior, Office of Education Bulletin No. 3. Washington, D. C.: Government Printing Office, 1938. Pp. 48. Gratis.

153. Segel, David, and Proffitt, Maris M. *Pupil Personnel Services as a Function of State Departments of Education.* Studies of State Departments of Educa-

tion, Monograph No. 5.   U. S. Office of Education, Bulletin No. 6, 1940.   Pp. vi + 84. $0.15.

154.   Shaffer, Laurance F.   *The Psychology of Adjustment*.   Boston: Houghton Mifflin Company, 1936.   Pp. xix + 600. $3.50.

155.   * Sherman, Mandel.   *Mental Hygiene and Education*.   New York: Longmans, Green and Company, 1934.   Pp. xi + 295. $2.25.

156.   Shoobs, Nabum E., and Goldberg, George.   *Corrective Treatment for Unadjusted Children*.   (*Principles and Practice* by Shoobs, *Manual* by Goldberg).   New York: Harper & Brothers, 1942.   Pp. viii + 240. $3.00.

157.   * Skinner, Charles E., and Harriman, Philip L. (editors).   *Child Psychology and Modern Education*.   New York: The Macmillan Company, 1941.   Pp. xii + 522. $3.00.

158.   Smith, Charles M., and Roos, Mary M.   *A Guide to Guidance*.   New York: Prentice-Hall, Inc., 1941.   Pp. xvi + 440. $3.00.

159.   * Smith, Eugene R. (Chairman).   *Fourth Report of the Committee on School and College Relations*.   New York: Educational Records Bureau, 1943.   Pp. 55. $0.25.

160.   * Smith, Eugene R., and Tyler, Ralph W.   *Appraising and Recording Student Progress*.   Adventure in American Education, Volume III.   New York: Harper & Brothers, 1942.   Pp. xxiii + 550. $3.00.

161.   Smithies, Elsie M.   *Case Studies of Normal Adolescent Girls*.   New York: D. Appleton-Century Company, 1933.   Pp. x + 284. $2.00.

162.   Spaulding, Francis T.   *High School and Life*.   The Regents' Inquiry into the Character and Cost of Public Education in the State of New York.   New York: McGraw-Hill Book Company, Inc., 1938.   Pp. xviii + 378. $3.00.

163.   Stead, William H.; Shartle, Carroll L.; and others.   *Occupational Counseling Techniques*.   Published by the Technical Board of the Occupational Research Program.   New York: American Book Company, 1940.   Pp. x + 274. $2.75.

164.   * Stoddard, George D.   *The Meaning of Intelligence*.   New York: The Macmillan Company, 1943.   Pp. ix + 504. $4.00.

165.   Stoddard, George D., and Wellman, Beth L.   *Child Psychology*.   New York: The Macmillan Company, 1934.   Pp. xii + 419. $2.75.

166.   Strang, Ruth.   *The Role of the Teacher in Personnel Work*.   New York: Teachers College, Columbia University, 1935.   Pp. xvi + 332.   (Out of print.)

167.   * Strang, Ruth.   *Behavior and Background of Students in College and Secondary School*.   New York: Harper & Brothers, 1937.   Pp. xiv + 515. $4.00.

168.   * Strang, Ruth.   *Counseling Technics in College and Secondary School*.   New York: Harper & Brothers, 1937.   Pp. x + 159. $2.00.

169.   * Strang, Ruth.   *Pupil Personnel and Guidance*.   New York: The Macmillan Company, 1940.   Pp. xiv + 356. $2.00.

170.   Strang, Ruth, and Hatcher, Latham.   *Child Development and Guidance in Rural Schools*.   New York: Harper & Brothers, 1943.   Pp. xvi + 218. $2.50.

171.   Strong, Edward K., Jr.   *Change of Interests with Age*.   Stanford University, California: Stanford University Press, 1931.   Pp. xix + 235. $4.00.

172. * Strong, Edward K., Jr. *Vocational Interests of Men and Women.* Stanford University, California: Stanford University Press, 1943. Pp. xxix + 746. $6.50.

173. Studebaker, John W. "Vocational Guidance in Wartime," *Occupations,* XX (April 1942), 482–492.

174. Sturtevant, Sarah M.; Strang, Ruth; and McKim, Margaret. *Trends in Student Personnel Work.* Teachers College Contributions to Education, No. 787. New York: Teachers College, Columbia University, 1940. Pp. 110. $1.85.

175. Super, Donald E. *The Dynamics of Vocational Adjustment.* New York: Harper & Brothers, 1942. Pp. xiv + 286. $3.00.

176. * Symonds, Percival M. *Mental Hygiene of the School Child.* New York: The Macmillan Company, 1934. Pp. xi + 321. $1.75.

177. Teeter, Verl A. *Occupational Life.* A Work Guide for Students. New York: McGraw-Hill Book Company, Inc., 1937. Pp. vi + 137. $0.60.

178. * Terman, Lewis M., and Merrill, Maud A. *Measuring Intelligence.* Boston: Houghton Mifflin Company, 1936. Pp. x + 319. $2.60.

179. Thorndike, E. L. *Human Nature and the Social Order.* New York: The Macmillan Company, 1940. Pp. xx + 1020. $6.00.

180. Thurstone, L. L. *Primary Mental Abilities.* Psychometric Society, Psychometric Monographs No. 1. Chicago: University of Chicago Press, 1938. Pp. ix + 121. $2.00.

181. * Tiegs, Ernest W., and Katz, Barney. *Mental Hygiene in Education.* New York: Ronald Press Company, 1941. Pp. xiv + 418. $2.75.

182. Traxler, Arthur E. (editor). *Guidance in Public Secondary Schools.* A Report of the Public School Demonstration Project in Educational Guidance. Educational Records Bulletin No. 28. New York: Educational Records Bureau, 1939. Pp. xxvi + 330. Paper, $2.00; cloth, $2.50.

183. Uhl, Willis L., and Powers, Francis F. *Personal and Social Adjustment.* New York: The Macmillan Company, 1938. Pp. xi + 475. $1.40.

184. Viteles, Morris S. *Industrial Psychology.* New York: W. W. Norton and Company, 1932. $6.50.

185. Wallin, J. E. Wallace. *Personality Maladjustments and Mental Hygiene.* New York: McGraw-Hill Book Company, Inc., 1935. Pp. xii + 511. $3.00.

186. Wickman, E. K. *Teachers and Behavior Problems.* New York: The Commonwealth Fund. Pp. 40. $0.25.

187. Williamson, E. G. *Students and Occupations.* New York: Henry Holt and Company, 1937. Pp. xxiv + 438. $2.50.

188. * Williamson, E. G. *How to Counsel Students.* New York: McGraw-Hill Book Company, Inc., 1939. Pp. xx + 562. $3.75.

189. * Williamson, E. G., and Darley, J. G. *Student Personnel Work—An Outline of Clinical Procedures.* New York: McGraw-Hill Book Company, Inc., 1937. Pp. xxiv + 314. $3.00.

190. * Williamson, E. G., and Hahn, M. E. *Introduction to High School Counseling.* New York: McGraw-Hill Book Company, Inc., 1940. Pp. x + 314. $3.00.

191. Winn, Ralph B. (editor). *Enyclopedia of Child Guidance.* New York: Philosophical Library, Inc., 1943. Pp. xvi + 456. $7.50.

192. Wood, Ben D. "Criteria of Individualized Education," *Occupations,* XIV (May 1936), 781–786.

193. * Wood, Ben D. "The Need for Comparable Measurements in Individualizing Education," *Educational Record,* Supplement No. 12, XX (January 1939), 14–31.

194. Wood, Eleanor Perry. *Achievement Testing in Public and Independent Secondary Schools.* Educational Records Bulletin No. 11. New York: Educational Records Bureau, 1933. Pp. 70. $1.50.

195. Woodhouse, Chase Going. *Business Opportunities for the Home Economist.* New York: McGraw-Hill Book Company, Inc., 1938. Pp. xii + 262. $2.50.

196. Wrenn, C. Gilbert, and Bell, Reginald. *Student Personnel Problems.* New York: Farrar & Rinehart, Inc., 1942. Pp. xiv + 236. $2.00.

197. Yale, John R. *Occupational Filing Plan: How to Build an Occupational Information Library.* Guidebook. Seventy-five file folders; fifteen out cards. Chicago: Science Research Associates, 1944. Pp. 120. $6.00.

198. * *Youth and the Future.* The General Report of the American Youth Commission (Owen D. Young, Chairman; Floyd W. Reeves, Director). Washington, D. C.: American Council on Education, 1942. Pp. xix + 296. $2.50.

199. *Youth Education Today.* Sixteenth Yearbook of the American Association of School Administrators of the National Education Association. Washington, D. C.: National Education Association, 1938. Pp. 510. $2.00.

200. Zapoleon, Marguerite W., and Moore, Louise. *Vocational Guidance for Girls and Women.* U. S. Office of Education, Vocational Division Bulletin No. 214, Occupational Information and Guidance Series, No. 6, 1941. Pp. vi + 162.

GUIDANCE FILMS

201. *Choosing Your Vocation,* by Harry D. Kitson. 10 minutes. Sound. Chicago: Encyclopaedia Britannica Films, Inc., 1931.

202. *Guidance in Public Schools,* by Richard D. Allen. 20 minutes. Sound. Chicago: Encyclopaedia Britannica Films, Inc., 1931.

203. *Guidance Problem for School and Home.* 18 minutes. Sound. New York: Bureau of Publications, Teachers College, Columbia University, 1935.

APPENDIX

Guidance and Placement of Persons Whose Education Has Been Interrupted[1]

ALTHOUGH AN EDUCATIONAL GUIDANCE PROGRAM IS NORMALLY CONCERNED MAINLY with pupils in school and individuals who have recently been graduated from or have dropped out of school, another group especially needs the advice of counselors in schools and colleges. This group consists of more mature individuals whose education has been interrupted and who desire counsel concerning further educational opportunities, and advice about the desirability of returning to school as contrasted with immediate entry upon a new vocation, and concerning related problems. In normal times a comparatively small number of such individuals is likely to seek the advice of school counselors each year.

The transition from war conditions to a peace-time economy and social structure, which is now under way and which will probably continue for several years, has changed this formerly small and numerically unimportant group to one of staggering proportions and critical importance. It challenges guidance resources as never before. The national government has clearly recognized the need for counseling and has made provision for the establishment of counseling services, particularly in connection with the Veterans Administration, but this is a situation which calls for the mobilization of the total counseling resources of the nation. The full cooperation of counselors in schools and colleges is needed. The guidance personnel in education may be counted upon to undertake this responsibility with unusual zeal, for the relationship of sound advice to the immediate adjustment problems of young men and women who have so recently made great sacrifices for the common good is apparent to all.

[1] Under present conditions it is virtually impossible to provide an up-to-date treatment of this important topic in a book. Plans for the education of veterans and others whose schooling was interrupted by the war are going ahead so rapidly that some of the statements in this chapter may be obsolete before the book is printed, or soon thereafter. It was therefore decided to publish this chapter, which was written in November 1944, as an appendix so that it could be more easily revised to take into account new developments.

The young people whose education was interrupted by the war fall into two general classes—war veterans and employees in war industries. The first group is the larger and is the one toward which most of the guidance efforts are properly being directed. The individuals in this group have matured rapidly under the stress of war. Their outlook upon their environment is, in many respects, more adult than that of young people of comparable age in civilian life. A large proportion of them have had their knowledge of the world greatly extended by a long period of service in different parts of the earth. Many have acquired intricate technical skills while in the Armed Forces. The majority are anxious to get established vocationally, and, if they resume their education for a time, they will want courses which will contribute to their vocational adjustment. All these young people face problems of re-adjustment to civilian life and to the environment of their family and friends. Some are physically handicapped and some have acquired neuroses during the strain of military life, but these form but a small per cent of the total number.

The second group, war-industry employees, contains a large proportion of young women. The group has had experiences during the war which are, on the whole, probably less maturing than those of the men and women in the Armed Forces. Their experiences have been less varied in matters broadly educational. Some of them are exceptionally highly trained in technical skills. They have become accustomed to living on a comparatively high economic level and, in many instances, their re-adjustment to a lower postwar wage scale will not be made easily. Because of the marked cutbacks in war industries attendant upon the end of the war in Europe, many of these young people who left school to take jobs are considering the possibility of resuming their education. The counseling problem here is not so acute as it is in the case of the war veterans but it is one that deserves a place in guidance programs.

There seems to be complete unanimity of opinion that an intelligent, practical, well-informed counseling program of national proportions is essential throughout the long period of transition from war to peace. Never before have the guidance people of the country had such an opportunity to utilize their training. Never before have they been put to such a test. They must use every precaution to see that the advice they give to each individual who comes to their attention is as nearly right as is humanly possible. The young men and women whom they counsel are at a point where they must make critical decisions that will frequently have life-time import. There can be very little margin for error.

What procedures can a counselor follow to prepare himself to participate in this important guidance program? One step is to get acquainted with the provisions which the National and State governments have made for the education of war veterans. The Federal provisions for the education of veterans are set forth in Chapter IV of Public Law 346, popularly known as the "G.I. Bill."

The complete text of the law should be read for details, but the general provisions applicable to education may be summarized briefly as follows: Any man or woman is eligible who was discharged or released under conditions other than dishonorable, who has served ninety days or more in active military or naval service since September 16, 1940, exclusive of time spent in the service academies or special college training programs of the Army or Navy, whose education was interfered with by entrance into the Service, or who desires a re-training or refresher course. That education was interfered with is presumed for all veterans who were not over twenty-five when they entered the Armed Services.

A person who is eligible under the law may take a refresher or retraining course limited to one year or its equivalent in part-time study; or one year of education or training which, upon satisfactory completion, may be extended to equal the veteran's length of service beyond ninety days but not to exceed a total of four years. Time spent in special service courses is subtracted from the total.

The government pays the institution providing the training for the veteran its usual tuition fee, and includes also laboratory, library, health, infirmary, books, supplies, and other necessary expenses, not to exceed five hundred dollars for the ordinary school year. Veterans without dependents are allowed financial aid of fifty dollars a month while in school, and those with dependents, seventy-five dollars a month. The subsistence allowance includes one month's leave with pay for each calendar year. There is an implication, but not a requirement, in this provision that a veteran will follow an accelerated program with eleven months of education during the year.

There is also opportunity for a program of part-time work and part-time education with lesser tuition fees and subsistence allowance to be determined by the Administrator of Veterans' Affairs.

A veteran who wishes to take advantage of the provisions of the law must initiate his course not later than two years after either the date of his discharge or the termination of the war, whichever is the later, and must complete the course within seven years of the end of the war. He may study at any institution included in lists to be prepared by the appropriate state agencies or approved by the Administrator of Veterans' Affairs, provided the institution will accept him.

The law is being administered by the Veterans Administration through its fifty-two regional offices. Wherever possible, existing educational resources are to be utilized. The law states that "The term 'educational or training institutions' shall include all public or private elementary, secondary, and other schools furnishing education for adults, business schools and colleges, scientific and technical institutions, colleges, vocational schools, junior colleges, teachers colleges, normal schools, professional schools, universities, and other educational institutions, and shall also include business or other establishments providing apprentice or other training on the job . . ." The law does not permit federal supervision or control of existing educational institutions except that which has been already provided for under previous laws.

Public Law No. 16 requires that the Veterans Administration give training to disabled veterans which will prepare them for employment and obtain positions for them. As a result of Public Law No. 16 and Public Law No. 346, the Veterans Administration is contracting with colleges and universities to handle a part of the counseling load. A minimum unit for any contract is one counselor, one psychometrist, and one clerk. Into the same office the Veterans Administration places a vocational appraiser (counselor) and a trained officer. It is believed that such a unit should be able to handle approximately seventy-five veterans a month.

There are fifty-four Veterans Administration offices in the United States with rating boards which establish the rights of the veteran under these two laws. An advisement unit is then notified that the veteran has applied and what his rating is. The advisement unit then gets in touch with the veteran for counseling. If he has rights under Public Law No. 16, the Government supplies traveling expenses to the nearest advisement unit. The advisement unit maintains living quarters for the veteran while he is going through the counseling process.

The Veterans Administration has set up procedures, forms, and a manual which must be followed in the advisement unit. Any rehabilitation plan under Public Law No. 16 must be approved by the vocational appraiser and put into effect by the training officer who will finally place the veteran.

It is apparent that almost all the younger returning service men and women who are honorably discharged will have an opportunity for at least a year of further education at government expense and some of these young men and young women may be sent to school for a much longer period. Will this fact cause the educational facilities of the country to be overwhelmed? This seems unlikely if careful planning is done ahead of time, even though the over-all enrolment in higher institutions will go up sharply. Surveys indicate that between half a million and a million Service men and women plan to take advantage of the provisions of the law, exclusive of those wishing shorter refresher courses to prepare them for immediate employment. It is estimated that in the average community of a million people, a maximum of about five thousand returning veterans will desire education in any one year. In the average community of thirty thousand, perhaps one hundred thirty-five men and women who have been in the Service may ask for further education at government expense in one year. This would not seem to be an especially difficult burden, but the guidance of these young people into the right kind of education will call for careful consideration of all the factors involved. Certain communities will have more Service people wanting additional education than other communities of similar size. Moreover, provisions for education of veterans, adopted by legislatures in different states, may affect the situation from one state to another.

This brings us to a second type of preparation that may be made by a counselor, or perhaps more appropriately by the guidance functionaries of an entire school system. This is to try to estimate the probable annual demand for further schooling in the local community on the part of those whose education has been interrupted. In large cities and in communities that have a large mobile population of war workers, such estimates are likely to be considerably erroneous, but in smaller communities which have a stable population information may be obtained concerning the plans of nearly every individual in this group and the prediction of educational demands may be highly accurate.

A third step is to survey the facilities for the further education of individuals whose education has been interrupted. One should look first into the educational opportunities in the local community. The types of courses offered by local colleges and special provisions in the way of accelerated courses and vocational training for veterans and other mature students should be noted. The local public school system should be encouraged to make special provision at the high school level for further education of returning veterans who will not be content to go back to the regular high school environment with boys and girls much younger in years and experience than themselves. Some city school systems—for example, the Pittsburgh, Pennsylvania, Public Schools—are setting up special high schools for this older group.

Counselors should also become acquainted with educational provisions for returning veterans and others in nearby centers, as well as with the leading institutions for various types of professional and vocational education throughout the nation. It should be kept in mind that veterans do not have to attend school or college in their local community but may have their training financed at government expense in any educational institution to which they apply and are admitted, regardless of location in the United States.

A fourth step is to survey the employment opportunities in the local community and to try to predict those which will probably be available two or three years after the war ends. Probable country-wide trends in work opportunities in different vocations should also be studied thoroughly. The group whose education has been interrupted will make greater demands upon counselors for vocational advice than for any other type of counseling, and the value of the advice given will depend largely upon the accuracy and recency of the information available to counselors.

A fifth step that the counselor can take is to become acquainted with the requirements of different occupations and with the composition of "job families." The counselor may already have accumulated much information of this kind in connection with his usual guidance activities but it is improbable that the requirements of occupational counseling of high school youths will have called for as broad or as thorough a knowledge of a vocational field as will be needed in the guidance of this more mature group. In this connection, everyone who participates in this type of counseling should have access to the Dictionary of Occupational Titles (7).

The Dictionary was described briefly in Chapter II. The definitions found in Part I for thousands of different jobs are of great value, for these definitions are stated definitely and specifically in terms of the detailed work performed on the job. Thus, a counselor is provided with a basis for deciding whether or not a job is in line with the aptitudes and interests of the persons being advised even though the counselor may have had no first-hand experience with the job in question. Moreover, through the use of Volume II on Titles and Codes, which classifies jobs into groups or families, a counselor can see the relationship of the previous work experience of the individual to a variety of jobs. The potential usefulness of Part IV of the Dictionary in counseling the younger veterans should not be neglected. This part makes possible the classification and placement of men who have had little or no work experience.

A sixth, and very important, step in the preparation of one who expects to counsel those whose education has been interrupted is to become thoroughly acquainted with all sources of information concerning the abilities and achievements of an individual and with techniques for obtaining further information. For purposes of summarizing information relative to the background of returning veterans and appraising the vocational significance of their technical training in the Armed Forces, the Army has developed Army Separation Qualification Record, WD AGO Form 100, and Counselor's Interview Memorandum, WD AGO Form 100–1. The Navy has prepared somewhat similar forms. Form No. 100 provides for a record of civilian education, Service education, civilian occupation, and military specialties. It is planned that by means of the standard code system employed in the Dictionary of Occupational Titles, the form will indicate the relationship of the technical work experience of the individual to different job families.

The upper half of the Counselor's Interview Memorandum will contain the individual's Army test scores. Spaces are provided in the lower half of the sheet for the judgments of the counselor with respect to additional school or training and suggested field of work.

Some war veterans will have taken the United States Armed Forces Institute Tests (26) while in the Service and their scores, translated into terms of national norms, may be used in counseling. Those individuals who have not taken these tests and who contemplate further education should have the appropriate ones, or other suitable tests, administered to them.

The Armed Forces Institute Tests are published on two levels, high school and college. Each level consists of two series, tests of general educational development and tests of achievement in different subjects. There are two forms of each test, a form specially reserved for administration by the Armed Forces and a form which may be obtained by professional personnel in colleges and secondary schools.

At each level, the tests of general educational development consist of Test 1: Correctness and Effectiveness of Expression; Test 2: Interpretation of Reading Materials in the Social Studies; Test 3: Interpretation of Reading Materials in the Natural Sciences; and Test 4: Interpretation of Literary Materials. At the high school level, there is also Test 5: General Mathematical Ability.

The available subject tests prepared by the Armed Forces Institute cover English, college level; commercial correspondence, college level; engineering drawing, college level; English literature and composition, high school level; business English; French, lower level; first-year algebra, high school level; advanced algebra, high school level; plane geometry, high school level; physics, high school level; chemistry, high school level; American history, high school level; first-year bookkeeping and accounting, high school level; first-year typewriting, high school level; and first-year Gregg shorthand, high school level.

Although the Armed Forces Institute Tests should do much to help educational institutions to meet the problems of guidance and placement of men whose education has been interrupted, some colleges are preparing their own batteries of tests for use with this group and other entering students. For example, in the summer of 1944, the University of Chicago inaugurated a system of educational achievement tests, instead of high school credits, as a basis of placing students in the College. Not only will individuals who can pass the tests be admitted to the College, regardless of whether or not they have the customary number and kinds of high school credits but, also, those whose test results indicate intellectual equipment in some particular field better than their credit records show will be placed higher in the college program. Thus, war veterans entering or returning to college will receive full recognition for skills and knowledge achieved during war service.

For individuals who do not plan to continue their formal education and whose main need is vocational guidance, the problem of selection of suitable and useful tests is more difficult than it is in the case of those who are continuing school. Most persons who desire advice concerning vocational choice want to be helped first of all to discover what their own aptitudes and abilities are. A certain amount of information on this question can be obtained from the record of work experience of individuals who have held jobs, but among the war veterans are many boys who went directly from high school into the Armed Forces and who have had little or no work experience. Frequently, these young men will ask for a test to show their vocational aptitudes. Such requests point directly to the need of a vocational aptitude test consisting of a single booklet having multiple-scoring features, which will provide an indication of aptitudes for a wide sampling of occupations. No such test is at present in general use, although a Counseling Battery, consisting of those individual tests which have the greatest commonality among numerous specific batteries, has been developed by the Division of Occupational Analysis and Manning Tables, Bureau of Manpower Utilization, War Manpower Commission. This single battery can be administered to an individual and can be scored for a large number of occupations.

The Counseling Battery and similar tests yet to be devised may ultimately come into general use, but at present the measurement of vocational aptitude is carried on almost entirely through the giving of a variety of tests covering verbal aptitude, numerical aptitude, scientific aptitude, mechanical aptitude, clerical aptitude, and aptitudes for other special fields. Such a series of tests requires much time for administration, scoring, and interpretation. Aptitude tests of these types were described in Chapter IV.

Among the most useful tests in a program of guidance for war veterans and others who may turn to educational counselors for advice are tests of interests, such as the Strong Vocational Interest Blank for Men and the Kuder Preference Record. These two tests were listed and discussed in Chapter VI. Both tests yield results which may be expressed on individual graphic record sheets in the form of a profile. Illustrative records are shown in Figures 5, 6, and 7.

Figures 5 and 6 show the scores of two young men on the Strong Vocational Interest Blank. The tests were scored with twenty-seven of the available thirty-four occupational scales. The names of the occupations are given in the column near the left-hand margin of the sheet. There is a column in which the standard scores may be shown numerically, adjacent to the occupations. The standard score scale is also printed across the top of the sheet, and letter ratings (A, B+, B, B—, C+, and C) are applied to different standard score levels. The standard scores of each man are shown by the crosses opposite the various occupations and below the appropriate numbers printed at the top of the sheet.

The shaded area for each occupation indicates a range within which scores are not very dependable. Crosses falling to the right or left of the shaded areas are likely to be more nearly indicative of the true interests of the individual than crosses within this range.

In general, ratings of *A* indicate close agreement between the interests of the individual taking the test and those of men successfully engaged in the occu-

Name _DAVIS, JOHN R._

Group	Occupation	Standard Score	C					C+	
			16	18	20	22	24	26	28
I	Artist	9							
	Psychologist	9							
	Architect	13							
	Physician	12							
	Dentist	13							
II	Mathematician	10							
	Engineer	32							
	Chemist	32							
III	Production Mgr.	50							
IV	Aviator								
	Farmer								
	Carpenter								
	Printer								
	Math.-Sci. Teacher	38							
	Policeman								
	Forest Service								
V	Y. Physical Dir.								
	Personnel Mgr.	48							
	Y.M.C.A. Secy.	30							
	Social Sci. Teacher	34							
	City School Supt.	15	X						
	Minister	15	X						
VI	Musician	21			X				
VII	C. P. A.	51							
VIII	Accountant	59							
	Office Worker								
	Purchasing Agent	45							
	Banker	31							
IX	Sales Manager	49							
	Real Estate Slsmn.	38							
	Life Insur. Slsmn.	37							
X	Advertising Man	27						X	
	Lawyer	22				X			
	Author-Journalist	17		X					
XI	President	42							
I	Group I								
II	Group II								
V	Group V								
VIII	Group VIII								
IX	Group IX								
X	Group X								
	Occupational Level								
	Masculinity-Femininity								
	Interest Maturity								

FIGURE 5.

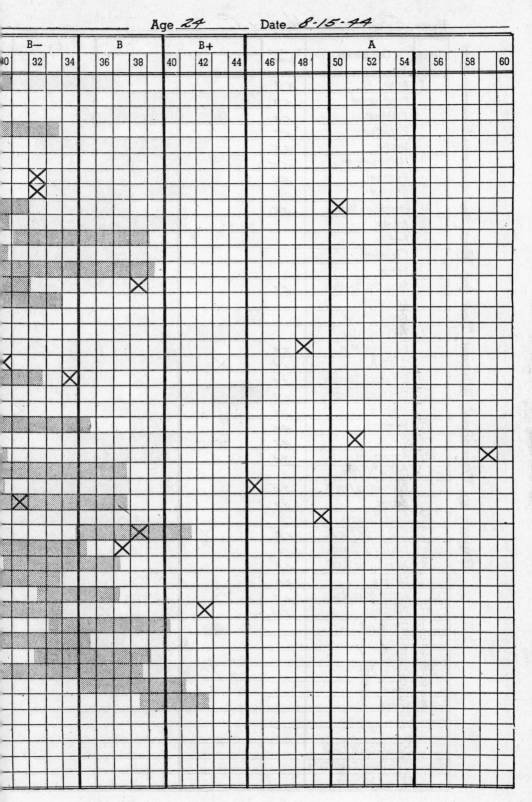

FIGURE 5 (cont.).

Report on Vocational Interest Test for Men (See other side for explanation)

Name EDWARDS, HENRY C.

Group	Occupation	Standard Score	C						C+	
			16	18	20	22	24	26	28	
I	Artist	39								
	Psychologist	57								
	Architect	53								
	Physician	51								
	Dentist	45								
II	Mathematician	45								
	Engineer	54								
	Chemist	60								
III	Production Mgr.	38								
IV	Aviator									
	Farmer									
	Carpenter									
	Printer									
	Math.-Sci. Teacher	51								
	Policeman									
	Forest Service									
V	Y. Physical Dir.									
	Personnel Mgr.	33								
	Y.M.C.A. Secy.	17	✗							
	Social Sci. Teacher	22				✗				
	City School Supt.	19		✗						
	Minister	29							✗	
VI	Musician	46								
VII	C. P. A.	32								
VIII	Accountant	30								
	Office Worker									
	Purchasing Agent	20			✗					
	Banker	12								
IX	Sales Manager	8								
	Real Estate Slsmn.	18		✗						
	Life Insur. Slsmn.	9								
X	Advertising Man	28							✗	
	Lawyer	30								
	Author-Journalist	37								
XI	President	24					✗			
I	Group I									
II	Group II									
V	Group V									
VIII	Group VIII									
IX	Group IX									
X	Group X									
	Occupational Level									
	Masculinity-Femininity									
	Interest Maturity									

FIGURE 6.

Age _28_ Date_ 9.12.44

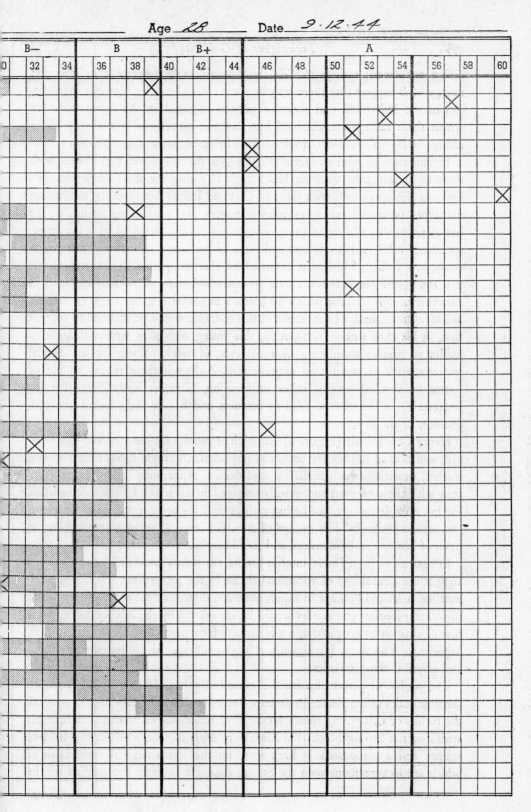

FIGURE 6 (cont.).

pation concerned; ratings of $B+$ show considerable agreement in interests; ratings of B suggest that there may be some correspondence between the inter-ests of the individual and those of persons engaged in the occupations for which these ratings are obtained but that the agreement is not very close; ratings of $B-$, $C+$, and C indicate little or no agreement in interests.

The interests of John R. Davis (Figure 5) apparently agree very closely with those of accountants, since he has a high A rating for this occupation. His interests also agree well with those of Certified Public Accountants, production managers, personnel managers, sales managers, and purchasing agents, for he has A ratings in all five of these occupations. There seems to be some corre-spondence between his interests and those of presidents of manufacturing con-cerns, as a rating of $B+$ was obtained for this occupation. It seems probable that the agreement between Davis' interests and those of persons engaged in the other occupations for which his blank was scored is either slight or entirely lacking. On the basis of the results of this test, one would be inclined to suggest that, in his choice of an occupation, this young man give serious thought to public or private accounting or some type of work calling for managerial interests, such as production management. Although these results should of course be checked against other information, it seems fairly clear that his interests lie in the general field of business and not in the sciences, the pro-fessions, or the arts.

Henry C. Edwards (Figure 6) has high A ratings for chemist and psycholo-gist, and also A ratings for architect, physician, engineer, mathematics-science teacher, musician, mathematician, and dentist. Apparently his interests agree well with those of men successfully engaged in all nine of these occupations. He has no $B+$ ratings, but he has ratings of B for artist, production manager, and author-journalist. His ratings of $B-$, $C+$, and C are concentrated in the fields of business, salesmanship, and social service.

In contrast to John Davis' interest profile, the scores made by Henry Edwards suggest the desirability of vocational choice in the professions, science, or engi-neering. It should be kept in mind, however, that in actual counseling practice the Strong interest test results would be considered by the adviser as only one part of a much larger picture, made up of information concerning background, experience, education, intelligence, achievement, special aptitudes, and health and physical characteristics.

The profile of percentiles for the same individual, Henry C. Edwards, on the nine scales of the Kuder Preference Record is shown in Figure 7. In general, the results of this young man's Kuder Preference Record tend to confirm his scores on the Strong blank. He has a very high interest score in the field of science and a comparatively high score on the computational scale, both of which are in agreement with the Strong data. He is above the median on the musical scale, a finding which one would expect on the basis of the Strong profile. He is also slightly above the median in mechanical interests. His scores fall below the median in the persuasive, artistic, social service, and clerical scales, which results tend, on the whole, to conform to the Strong results. The only point where there is a clear-cut difference is a percentile slightly above 90 on the literary scale on the Kuder Preference Record as compared with a rating of *B* on the author-journalist scale of the Strong blank.

Throughout the work of educational counselors with returning service men, there should be very close cooperation with the Advisement Unit of the Veterans Administration and the counseling program of the United States Employment Service. The first Advisement Unit established under the program of the Veterans Administration was opened at the College of the City of New York in June, 1944. It is planned that each community will have an Advisement Unit, for while the problem is a national one, the veterans' postwar adjustment must be met and solved in the local community. The adjustment of the veteran to peace-time conditions necessarily depends upon the utilization of local institutions and agencies, administered by those who knew him as a civilian and who are trained and prepared to understand his problems and needs.

The problems of counseling those who have seen extensive military service abroad are social and psychological quite as much as they are vocational. Unusual tact, understanding, and foresight are needed in the counseling of disabled veterans. In general, these men should, as far as possible, be advised against following a natural desire to go into employment while the present labor shortage makes it possible for them to get jobs, but be guided instead into a program of education which will make it possible for them to take permanent positions later and to maintain themselves vocationally after a return to peace-time employment conditions. From the therapeutic, as well as the vocational standpoint, it is imperative that extreme care be used to see that these men undertake educational programs that are within their capacity and through which they can develop self-confidence and normal readjustment to civilian living.

The vast program of counseling persons whose education has been interrupted is so important, both to the individual man or woman who needs advice and to our national welfare, that it is desirable for counselors who expect to participate in this program to spend time in obtaining special training in short courses now being offered by certain colleges in cooperation with the Veterans Administration.

REFERENCES

1. Baer, Max F. "When the Boys Come Marching Home," *Occupations*, XXII (October 1943), 10–16.

2. Bingham, Walter V. "Personnel Classification Testing in the Army," *Science,* C (September 29, 1944), 276–280.

3. Brown, Francis J. "Postwar Education for Ex-service Personnel," *Adult Education Journal,* II (October 1943), 178–182.

4. Cartwright, Morse A. *Marching Home: Educational and Social Adjustment after the War.* Published for the Institute of Adult Education. New York: Bureau of Publications, Teachers College, Columbia University, 1944. Pp. iv + 44.

5. Davenel, George F. "Aid for Post-War Employment," *Personnel Journal,* XXIII (October 1944), 122–129.

6. David, Paul T. *Postwar Youth Employment.* Prepared for the American Youth Commission. Washington, D. C.: American Council on Education, 1943. Pp. x + 172.

7. *Dictionary of Occupational Titles,* Parts I, II, and IV, and Supplement, Edition II. Division of Occupational Analysis and Manning Tables, Bureau of Manpower Utilization, War Manpower Commission. Washington, D. C.: Government Printing Office, 1939–1943.

8. Educational Policies Commission (Alexander J. Stoddard, Chairman). *A Program of Education for Returning Veterans.* Washington, D. C.: National Education Association, 1944. Pp. 40.

9. Evans, George R. "The Army Separation Classification and Vocational Counseling Program," *Occupations,* XXIII (November 1944), 69–74.

10. Gray, Carl. "The Gray Plan for Post-War Reemployment," *Occupations,* XXII (October 1943), 3–9.

11. Jager, Harry A., and Zeran, Franklin R. "Community Adult Counseling Centers," *Occupations,* XXIII (February 1945), 263–308.

12. Keesling, C. M. "Education for Our Returning Veterans," *Journal of the National Education Association,* XXXIII (October 1944), 166.

13. Kitson, Harry D. "Vocational Guidance for the War-Dislocated," *Teachers College Record,* XLV (May 1944), 526–531.

14. Layton, Warren K. "Counseling the Returning Veteran," *School and Society,* LX (September 30, 1944), 209–211.

15. Lindgren, H. C. "The Navy Counsels the War-Disabled," *Occupations,* XXIII (December 1944), 133–135.

16. McGrath, E. J. "Navy Off-Duty Education and Postwar Educational Readjustment," *Harvard Educational Review,* XIV (March 1944), 91–104.

17. Manuel, Herschel T. *Measurement and Guidance in Time of War.* Research Bulletin Number Fifteen of the Texas Commission on Coordination in Education. Austin, Texas: The Administrative Board of the Texas Commission on Coordination in Education, April 1942. Pp. 23.

18. "Pursuit of Learning Broadcasts: Education for Veterans," *Education for Victory,* III, No. 7 (October 3, 1944), 21–25.

19. Ryan, T. A., and Johnson, Beatrice R. "Interest Scores in the Selection of Sales-

men and Servicemen: Occupational vs. Ability-Group Scoring Keys," *Journal of Applied Psychology,* XXVI (August 1942), 543–562.

20. Sackett, Everett B.   "Fitting the Veteran to the Academic Mold," *Occupations,* XXII (May 1944), 471–474.

21. "School Plan for Adjustment of Veterans and War Workers" (A Symposium by Bess D. Ellis, R. M. Handville, R. D. Fleming, A. J. Cloud, C. T. Silva, and Harry E. Nelson), *Occupations,* XXIII (October 1944), 5–13.

22. Shartle, Carroll L.; Dvorak, Beatrice J.; Heinz, Carl A.; Osborn, Martha L.; Keller, Kathleen; Giese, Willis E.; Pimm, Walter B.; Nichols, William O.; Lewis, Leon; and others.   "Ten Years of Occupational Research," *Occupations,* XXII (April 1944), 387–446.

23. *Special Aids for Placing Military Personnel in Civilian Jobs.* Washington, D. C.: Government Printing Office, February 1944.

24. *Special Aids for Placing Navy Personnel in Civilian Jobs.* Washington, D. C.: Government Printing Office, May 1943.

25. Strong, Edward K., Jr. *Vocational Interests of Men and Women.* Stanford University, California: Stanford University Press, 1943.   Pp. xxix + 746.

26. *United States Armed Forces Institute Tests.* New York: Cooperative Test Service of the American Council on Education, 1944.

27. Ward, Raymond S.   "How to Use Part IV of the 'Dictionary,'" *Occupations,* XXII (October 1943), 39–41.

28. Weintraub, Ruth G., and Tough, Rosalind.   "The Post-War Soldier Retrains," *Harvard Educational Review,* XIV (May 1944), 202–209.

Accomplishment quotient, 237

Achievement tests, *see* Tests, achievement

Adjustment, danger of labels in, 336; nature of, 335–336; steps in counseling for, 338–340; teacher's role in, 314–315

Adjustment Inventory, 103, 110–111

Administration of tests, 158–159

Administrative uses of tests, 185–187

American Council Civics and Government Test, 93

American Council on Education cumulative record forms, 216, 219–222

American Council on Education French Reading Test, 81

American Council on Education German Reading Test, 82–83

American Council on Education Personality Rating Scale, 148

American Council on Education Psychological Examination, 48, 52–53

Anecdotal records, *see* Records, anecdotal

Aptitude, and intelligence, 45–46; assumptions concerning, 43–45; definition of, 42–43

Aptitude tests, *see* Tests, aptitude

Aspects of personality, 104, 116

A-S Reaction Study, 103, 109

Attitude, definition of, 105; tests and scales for measurements of, 105, 117, 120

Attitude Scales, 105, 117

Barrett-Ryan-Schrammel English Test, 78

BEC Personality Rating Schedule, 131, 151

Behavior Description, 151

Behavior Description Plan of Eight-Year Study of Progressive Education Association, 147

Bennett Mechanical Comprehension Test, 50, 60

Bronxville Public Schools Junior High School Goal Book, 273

California Test Bureau, adaptation of tests to scoring machine, 167

California Test of Mental Maturity, 47–48, 53–54

California Test of Personality, 104, 119–120

Cardall-Gilbert Test of Clerical Competence, 51, 62

Carnegie Units limitations of, 21

Case studies in guidance, 284–307; applying and evaluating treatment, 304; assembling and organizing data in, 286–287; collecting data for, 303; distribution among types of cases, 304–305; explanation of case-study method, 285–286; history of, 284–285; illustrated, 293–302; outlines for, 287–293; planning, 303; points to be observed in making, 303–304; reading references on, 351–352; value of, 305; writing up the case, 303

Character Education Inquiry, 99

Chicago Reading Tests, 70–71

Chicago Tests of Primary Mental Abilities, 48–49, 50, 54

Child psychology and mental hygiene, references on, 343–345

Clerical aptitude, tests of, 50–51, 62

Colgate Personal Inventory Rating Scales, 103

College Entrance Examination Board Scholastic Aptitude Test, 48

Colorado State College of Education secondary school experiment with report forms, 279–282

Committee on School and College Relations, Fourth Report, 17

Community opportunities for youth, 15

Cooperative American History Test, 90–91

Cooperative Ancient History Test, 91

Cooperative Biology Test, 88

Cooperative Biology Test, Educational Records Bureau Edition, 88–89

Cooperative Chemistry Test, 89

Cooperative Chemistry Test, Educational Records Bureau Edition, 89

Cooperative Economics Test, 93

Cooperative Elementary Algebra Test, 84–85

Cooperative English History Test, 91–92

Cooperative English Tests, 78–79

Cooperative French Tests, 81–82

Cooperative General Achievement Tests, 93–94

Cooperative General Culture Test, 94

Cooperative General Mathematics Test for High School Classes, 87

Cooperative General Science Test, 88

Cooperative German Tests, 83

Cooperative Intermediate Algebra Test, 85

Cooperative Latin Tests, 83–84

Cooperative Literary Acquaintance Test, 80

Cooperative Literary Comprehension and Appreciation Test, 80

Cooperative Literary Comprehension Test, 80

Cooperative Mathematics Test for Grades 7, 8, and 9, 86

Cooperative Mediaeval History Test, 92

Cooperative Modern European History Test, 92

Cooperative Physics Test, 89–90

Cooperative Physics Test, Educational Records Bureau Edition, 90

Cooperative Plane Geometry Test, 85

Cooperative Reading Comprehension Test, 71

Cooperative Science Test for Grades 7, 8, and 9, 90

Cooperative Solid Geometry Test, 85–86

Cooperative Spanish Tests, 84

Cooperative Test in Secondary School Mathematics, 87

Cooperative Test of Social Studies Abilities, 92–93

Cooperative Test Service, 69, 167, 222

Cooperative Trigonometry Test, 86

Counseling, for adjustment, 334–342; use of results of tests in, 194–198

Counseling veterans, preparation for, 367–380

Counselors, characteristics and professional training needed by, 340–341; selected library for, 353–365; types of reading references for, 343–353

Cowan Adolescent Personality Schedule, 112–113

Cumulative records, *see* Records, cumulative

Detroit Mechanical Aptitudes Examinations, 50, 60–61

Detroit Scale for the Diagnosis of Behavior Problems, 148

Diagnosis, general procedures in use of tests in, 189–194; principles governing use of objective tests in, 187–189

Dictionary of Occupational Titles, 17, 356, 371

Distributions of test scores illustrated, 175, 176, 178, 179

Downey Will-Temperament Test, 102

Dunlap Academic Preference Blank, 107, 113

Durrell-Sullivan Reading Capacity and Achievement Tests, 71

Educational Records Bureau, xiii; cumulative record form, 216–219; description of program, 171–172; scoring procedures used by, 172–174

Eight-Year Study of the Progressive Education Association, 24, 70

Elizabeth, New Jersey, public schools follow-up schedule for graduates, 326–329

Elwell-Fowlkes Bookkeeping Test, 94

Escape mechanisms, 336–338

Extracurriculum opportunities for youth, 15

Follow-up program, 317–333; aspects of, 317–318; continuous features of, 321–323; forms used in, 323, 324–331; main characteristics of, 323; purposes and nature of, 318–320; types of information obtained by, 319–320

Foreign Language Prognosis Test, 51, 63

Free association method of personality testing, 101

Garfield Heights city schools report forms, 247, 250–255

Gates Basic Reading Tests, 71–72

"G.I. Bill," educational provisions of, 368–369

Grand Junction, Colorado, public schools report forms, 256–259

Guidance, bibliographies on, 353; case-study procedures in, 284–307; cooperation in, 12; costs of, 9–11; in adjustment, 334–342; influences that have created programs of, 4–6; kinds of information needed in, 20–25; main divisions of, 3; meaning of, 2–4; of persons whose education has been interrupted, 366–381; reading references on, 345–347; records and reports in, 202–283; relation to education in a democracy, 13; relation to teaching, 7–9; role of teacher in, 308–316; staff organization for, 6–9; studies related to, 348–350; use of test results in, 194–199; visual aids to, 352, 365; vocational, *see* Vocational guidance

Guidance movement, background of, 1–6

Haggerty-Olson-Wickman Behavior Rating Schedules, 130, 131, 150

Henmon-Nelson Tests of Mental Ability, 47, 54–55

Hill School, The, fall testing program, 159–161

Individual students, information needed about, 20–25; procedures for collecting information, 25–41

Inglis Tests of English Vocabulary, 80–81

Instructional uses of tests, 187–194

Intelligence, definitions of, 45; relation to aptitude, 45

Intelligence quotient, constancy of, 45–46; limitations to use with adolescents and adults, 46

Interest measurement, inventories for, 106–107, 112, 113, 114, 115, 118, 119, 373–379; reading references on, 350

Interest Questionnaire for High School Students, 107, 113

International Business Machines Corporation, 11, 166

International Test Scoring Machine, 11–12, 165–170

Interview as means of collecting information, 25–28

Introversion-Extroversion in Young Children, 130–131, 150

Inventory of Activities and Interests, 104, 115

Iowa Algebra Aptitude Test, 51, 62

Iowa Every-Pupil Tests of Basic Skills, 75–76

Iowa Plane Geometry Prognosis Test, 51, 63

Iowa Silent Reading Tests, New Edition (Revised), Advanced Test, 72

Iowa Silent Reading Tests, New Edition (Revised), Elementary Test, 72

Iowa state testing program, 12

I.Q., see Intelligence quotient

Jackson, Mississippi, public schools appraisal report, 273

Junior Scholastic Aptitude Test, 48, 55

Kent-Rosanoff Association Tests, 101, 114

Knauber Art Ability Test, 49, 58

Kuhlmann-Anderson Intelligence Tests, 47, 55

Kwalwasser Test of Musical Information and Appreciation, 50, 59

Kwalwasser-Ruch Test of Musical Accomplishment, 50, 59–60

Law Aptitude Examination, 51

Lee Test of Algebra Ability, 51, 62

Lee Test of Geometric Aptitude, 51, 63

Lincoln Diagnostic Spelling Test, 81

Lists of test scores illustrated, 175

Los Angeles city schools cumulative record forms, 224–225

Luria-Orleans Modern Language Prognosis Test, 51, 64

McAdory Art Test, 49–50, 58

McCall-Crabbs Test Lessons, 299–301

MacQuarrie Test of Mechanical Ability, 50, 61

Manual and mechanical aptitude, tests of, 50, 60–61

Marking systems, 235–239, 240

Mean, how to find, 182

Median, definition of, 180; how to find, 180–181

Meier-Seashore Art Judgment Test, 49–50, 58–59

Mental hygiene, influence upon guidance movement, 4–5

Metropolitan Achievement Tests, 76–77

Michigan Vocabulary Profile Test, 81

Minneapolis public schools cumulative record cards, 225–228

Minnesota Manual Dexterity Test, 50

Minnesota Personality Scale, 113

Minnesota Vocational Test for Clerical Workers, 50–51, 62

Mode, how to find, 182

Modern School Achievement Tests, 77

Moss Scholastic Test for Medical Students, 51

Music aptitude, tests of, 50 59–60

National Clerical Ability Tests, 94

National Teacher Examinations, 51

Nebraska Personality Inventory, 104, 114

Nelson-Denny Reading Test, 72–73

Normal curve, 43–45

Occupational Adjustment Study of National Association of Secondary School Principals, 322–323

Occupational Index, Inc., 348, 353, 361

Ohio State University Psychological Test, 47, 55–56

Omaha public schools report forms, 262–268

Opportunities for youth, nature of, 14–16; sources of information about, 16–19

Orleans Algebra Prognosis Test, 51, 62–63

Orleans Geometry Prognosis Test, 51, 63

Otis Quick-Scoring Mental Ability Tests, 47, 56

Otis Self-Administering Tests of Mental Ability, 47, 56

Pasadena city schools report forms, 259–261

Percentiles, explained, 182; how to find, 182–184

Personal Audit, 104, 108–109

Personal Data Sheet, 102, 121

Personal Index, 115–116

Personality, attempts to measure, 99; defined, 99–100; procedures for appraising, 100–107

Personality Inventory, 103, 111–112

Personality Inventory for Children, 104, 112

Personality Rating, 131, 150–151

Personality Schedule, 103, 120

Personality tests, see Tests, personality

Personnel records, see Records, pupil personnel

Philanthropy, influence upon guidance movement, 4

Pintner General Ability Tests: Verbal Series, 47, 56–57

Plainfield, New Jersey, high school, 223–224; costs of cumulative records in, 11–12; cumulative record folder, 223–224; questionnaire for students, 32–41; testing program, 170–171

Pre-Engineering Inventory, 51

Preference Record, 107, 114–115, 373, 378–379

Pressey Reading Tests, 73

Pressey X-O Tests, 102, 116–117

Professions, tests of aptitudes for, 51

Progressive Achievement Tests, 77

Progressive Education Association, progress reports, 274–277, 278

Progressive Reading Tests, 73

Providence public schools, costs of guidance in, 10; cumulative record card, 224; follow-up program, 318, 321–322, 324–325

Psychoneurosis, 336

Public Law No. 16, educational provisions of, 369

Public Law No. 346, educational provisions of, 368–369

Public School Demonstration Project, 352
Pupil report forms, *see* Reports to parents

Quartile, how to find, 181
Questionnaire, as means of collecting information, 28–41; for high school pupils, 29–31

Rating scales, advantages and limitations of, 130–131; annotated list of, 148–152
Reading resources for counselors, 343–365
Reavis-Breslich Diagnostic Tests in the Fundamental Operations of Arithmetic and in Problem Solving, 87
Records, anecdotal, 131–146; characteristics of, 132–133; definition of, 132; filing, 139–140; forms for, 135–139; illustrations of, 144–146; limitations and cautions in preparation of, 140–142; relation to personality ratings and behavior descriptions, 147–148; steps in setting up plan for, 134–140; summarization of, 140; values and uses of, 142–144
Records, cumulative, 215–234; American Council forms revised, 219–222; American Council on Education form, 216; basic concepts in construction of, 229–232; Cooperative Test Service form, 222; costs of, 10–11; definition of, 215; Educational Records Bureau form, 216–219; forms used in various school systems, 222–229; graphic presentation of data, advantages of, 230–231; reading references on, 352; suggested simplified form, 228–229; teacher use of, 311–314; use in reports to parents, 278–279; variations in, 215–216
Records, pupil personnel, 202–214; basic principles, 202–209; classified according to filing arrangement, 210–211; according to function, 209–210; according to nature of centralizing unit, 211–213; according to permanency, 213–214; main types of, 209–214
Religion, influence upon guidance movement, 4
Remedial and corrective instruction based on diagnosis of test results, 192–194, 313
Reporting procedures for tests, 174–184
Reports and Records Committee of the Progressive Education Association, 24, 147, 151
Reports to parents, 235–283; criteria for, 242; dual systems of, 268–273; forms based on comments by teachers, 247–255; forms based on marks supported by comments, 245–247; growth reports in term of objectives, 259–261; letters to parents substituted for, 255; mimeographed forms prepared by different teachers, 255–259; need for experimentation with, 279–282; old-type forms, 243–246; progress reports in eight-year study, 274–277, 278; separate forms for progress in school and progress in citizenship, 262–268; trends in, 239–242; types of, with illustrations, 243–278; uniform report on main objectives, 273, 278; use of cumulative records in, 278–279

Results of tests, *see* Tests, use of results of
Revised Minnesota Paper Form Board Test, 50, 61
Revised Stanford-Binet Scale, 46–47, 57
Riverside, California, city schools cumulative record, 213
Rochester Athenaeum and Mechanics Institute, anecdotal records in, 132, 140
Rorschach Psychodiagnostik, 101, 117–118

Sangren-Woody Reading Test, 73
Scale for Evaluation of School Behavior of Children Ten to Fifteen, 130, 150
Scaled Scores, 70
Scales for the Measurement of Social Attitudes, 105, 120
School Inventory, 103–104, 111
School orientation books, 18
School subjects, tests of aptitudes for, 51–52, 62–64
Science Research Associates, 17–18, 347–348, 353, 362
Scientific aptitude, tests of, 50, 60
Scoring procedures for tests, by service agency, 171–174; hand, local, 164–165; machine, local, 165–171
Seashore Measures of Musical Talent, Revised Edition, 50, 59
Self-marking Test, 116
Shank Tests of Reading Comprehension, 73–74
Sigma scale, relation to normal distribution, 44
Social change, influence upon guidance movement, 5
Specific Interest Inventory, 106, 118
Stanford Achievement Tests, 77–78
Stanford Scientific Aptitude Test, 50, 60
Statistical procedures in school testing program, 179–184
Stenquist Mechanical Aptitude Tests, 50, 61
Study of Values, 106, 109–110
Supervisory uses of tests, 185–187

Teacher, contribution to pupil adjustment, 314–315; contribution to testing program, 310–311; role in guidance, 308–316
Teacher's Rating Scale for Pupil Adjustment, 131, 149
Terman-McNemar Test of Mental Ability, 47, 57
Test of Personality Adjustment, 117
Testing program, costs of, 11, 167, 170; general directions to pupils concerning, 159–161; planning and conducting, 157–159; reading references on, 350–351; state-wide, 12
Tests, achievement, annotated list of, 70–95; business subjects, 94–95; Cooperative, 69–70, 71, 78, 79, 80, 81, 82, 83–87, 88–93, 94; elementary school, 68–69, 75–78; English, 78–81; foreign languages, 81–84; general, 93–94; general culture, 94; mathematics, 84–87; reading, 70–75; science, 88–90; secondary school

and junior college, 69–70, 71, 72, 73, 74, 75, 78–95; social studies, 90–93

Tests, administrative uses of, 185–187; how to administer, 158–159; how to select, 155–156; information for students about, 161–162; instructional uses of, 187–194; reporting procedures for, 174–184; scoring, *see* Scoring procedures for tests; supervisory uses of, 185–187

Tests, aptitude, annotated list of, 52–64; art, 49–50, 58–59; clerical, 50–51, 62; foreign language, 63–64; general academic, 46–48, 52–58; general academic two-axis, 47–48; general academic yielding one mental age and I.Q., 46–47; general academic yielding several diagnostic scores, 48; kinds of, 45; manual and mechanical, 50, 60–61; mathematics, 62–63; music, 50, 59–60; professions, 51; school subjects, 51–52; scientific, 50, 60; special fields, 48–52, 58–64

Tests, personality, adjustment questionnaires, 102–104; annotated list of, 108–121; attitude tests and scales, 105; disguised and partially disguised, 101–102; free association, 101; interest inventories, 106–107; reliability of, 107; uses of, 107–108; validity of, 107

Tests, use of results of, 185–201; administrative and supervisory, 185–187; by teacher, 187–189; diagnostic, 189–192; general procedures in, 189–194; improvement of, 199; in counseling, 194–198; in providing for pupils of high ability, 194; instructional, 187–194; limitations to, 198–199; need for plan of, 163; principles basic to, 187–189

Tests in Fundamental Abilities of Visual Arts, 59
Tests of Honesty, 112
Thompson Business Practice Test, 95
Traxler Reading Tests, 74
Turse-Durost Shorthand Achievement Test, 95
Tweezer Dexterity Test, 50

United States Armed Forces Institute Tests, 70, 371–372
United States Indian Service cumulative record card, 225
University of Chicago High School report forms, 269–273
University of Chicago Laboratory Schools records office, 213

Van Wagenen Reading Scales, 74
Van Wagenen-Dvorak Diagnostic Examination of Silent Reading Abilities, 74–75
Veterans' Administration, 368–369, 379
Vineland Social Maturity Scale, 148, 149
Visual aides to guidance, 352, 365
Vocational guidance, need for long-time planning, 16; reading references on, 347–348; relation of follow-up studies to, 318–319; for individuals not planning to continue their formal education, 372–379
Vocational Interest Blanks, 106, 118–119, 373–378
Vocational Interest Inventory, 106, 112
Vocational Inventory, 106, 114
Vocational orientation and exploratory courses, 18–19

Washburne Social Adjustment Inventory, 104, 121
Wiggly Block Test, 50
Winnetka Scale for Rating School Behavior and Attitudes, 130, 151–152
World Book Company, adaptation of tests to machine scoring, 167

Yale Educational Aptitude Tests, 48, 49, 50, 57–58
Yale Legal Aptitude Test, 51

INDEX OF NAMES

Aamodt, Geneva P., 62, 66

Achilles, Paul S., 28

Adams, Clifford R., 108, 109, 121

Adkins, Dorothy C., 121

Adler, A., 340

Adler, Herman M., 307

Allen, Elizabeth, 315

Allen, Richard D., 10, 76, 95, 224, 232, 306, 318, 321, 332, 346, 353, 365

Allen, Wendell C., 232, 352, 353

Allport, Floyd H., 103, 109

Allport, Gordon W., 103, 109, 110, 121, 126, 306, 344, 353

Alster, Benjamin, 104, 116

Anderson, H. Dewey, 356

Anderson, Hedwin C., 119, 127

Anderson, H. R., 90, 91, 92, 93

Anderson, Rose G., 55, 65

Anderson, Roy N., 64

Andrew, Dorothy M., 62, 64

Appel, Kenneth E., 353

Appelt, E. P., 82

Arlitt, Ada Hart, 353

Ashbaugh, E. J., 239, 242, 282

Babcock, G. M., 306

Babcock, Virginia, 88

Baer, Max F., 379

Baker, Harry J., 60, 61, 64, 148, 149, 152, 306, 346, 353

Ball, Rachel S., 151, 153

Barker, Lewellys F., 341

Barker, Roger G., 354

Barr, A. S., 152

Barrett, E. R., 78

Bartlett, Russell S., 90

Baxter, Edna Dorothy, 122

Bear, Robert M., 354

Beck, Samuel J., 101, 118, 122, 123

Becker, Elsa, 209, 354

Beckman, R. O., 109, 122

Beeley, Arthur L., 341

Beers, F. S., 79

Beers, Lester D., 90

Beery, John R., 332, 360

Bell, Howard M., 319, 332, 348, 354

Bell, Hugh M., 103, 110, 111, 122

Bell, Reginald, 365

Bender, Eric, 354

Bender, I. E., 122

Benjamin, John O., 118, 122

Bennett, Elizabeth, 114, 125

Bennett, George K., 60, 64, 115, 123

Bennett, Margaret E., 346, 354

Bentley, John E., 354

Benton, Arthur L., 60, 64

Berg, Harry, 90

Bergstresser, John L., 354

Bernreuter, Robert G., 103, 111, 112, 122

Bickel, Charles L., 89

Bingham, Walter V., 18, 25, 42, 64, 351, 354, 380

Bixler, Harold H., 76

Bixler, Roy A., 306

Blatz, William E., 152

Bliss, Walton B., 18

Blose, Carl, 94

Bolmeier, E. C., 278, 282

Booker, Ivan A., 332

Bott, E. A., 152

Bowes, Fern H., 152

Bradshaw, Francis F., 148, 152

Brainard, Paul P., 106, 118

Brandenberg, G. C., 117, 126

Brantley, C. D., 239, 242, 282

Bratton, Dorothy, 315

Breslich, E. R., 87

Brewer, John M., 19, 293, 306, 347, 351, 354

Brewster, Royce E., 358

Bridgman, Donald S., 319, 332

Brigden, R. L., 113, 122

Brinkman, Albert R., 347, 356

Brintle, S. L., 119, 127

Bristol, Radcliffe W., 87

Bristow, A. B., 209, 232

Britton, Ralph D., 161

Broad, Elizabeth, 358

Brown, Francis J., 380

Brown, Fred, 112, 122

Brown, J. F., 341, 345, 354

Brown, Marion, 132, 142, 152

Brown, W. Gordon, 89

Bruce, Harold W., 63

Brueckner, Leo J., 199

Buros, Oscar K., 49, 53, 54, 57, 64, 99, 122, 351, 354

Burtt, Harold E., 347, 354
Buswell, G. T., 199, 342

Calandra, Alexander, 93
Caliver, Ambrose, 355
Cardall, Alfred J., 355
Carpenter, M. F., 79, 80
Carrigan, Margaret, 358
Carter, Harold D., 122
Cartwright, Morse A., 380
Chambers, M. M., 348, 355
Chapman, H. B., 239, 282
Chapman, Paul W., 355
Charters, W. W., 142, 143, 152
Chave, E. J., 105, 120, 122, 128, 355
Cheshire, Leon E., 84, 85
Cheydleur, F. D., 81
Clark, E. L., 216
Clark, Florence E., 355
Clark, Frank J., 209
Clark, Harold F., 355
Clark, Willis W., 53, 73, 77, 104, 119, 120, 128
Cleary, Elizabeth J., 19
Cleeton, Glen U., 106, 112, 122
Cloud, A. J., 381
Cole, Luella, 344, 355
Congdon, Nora A., 112, 123
Connor, William L., 76
Cook, W. W., 78, 79
Corey, Stephen M., 123, 316
Corre, Mary P., 32
Cowan, E. A., 112
Cox, Philip L. L., 347, 355
Craig, Gerald S., 77
Cramer, Buell B., 332
Crawford, A. B., 48, 51, 57, 64
Crissy, William J. E., 64
Crobaugh, Mervyn, 355
Crockett, Alex C., 60
Croon, Charlotte W., 90, 91, 92, 93
Crow, Alice, 344, 355
Crow, Lester D., 344, 355
Cruikshank, Ruth M., 60, 64
Cubberley, Ellwood P., 203
Culbert, Jane F., 347, 355
Cunliffe, Rex B., 355
Cunningham, Bess V., 56
Cureton, Edward E., 80
Cutts, Norma, 344, 356

Dame, J. Frank, 347, 356
Darley, John G., 113, 123, 333, 345, 346, 356, 364
Darnell, Alice H., 86
Davenel, George F., 380
David, Paul, 380
Davidson, H. H., 118, 124
Davidson, Percy E., 356
Davis, B. Carnell, 356

Davis, Frank G., 232, 306, 315, 356
Davis, Frederick B., 71, 78, 80, 95
Dawson, M. A., 283
Dearborn, Walter F., 233, 350, 356
Denny, E. C., 72
DeSchweinitz, Dorothea, 356
Detjen, Erwin W., 356
Detjen, Mary E. (Ford), 356
Doll, Edgar A., 148, 149, 152
Downey, June E., 102, 123
Downing, Chester M., 81
Drake, Margaret J., 115, 123
Droba, D. D., 123
Duff, John C., 347, 355
Dunlap, Jack W., 113, 119, 123, 126
Dunsmoor, Clarence C., 19, 315, 347, 356
Durost, Walter N., 56, 95
Durrell, Donald D., 71
Dvorak, August, 74
Dvorak, Beatrice J., 319, 333, 381
Dwyer, Paul S., 119, 123

Ebaugh, Franklin, 118, 122
Eckert, Ruth E., 95, 319, 332, 356
Edwards, Alba M., 356
Eggersten, Claude, 315
Eigerman, Hyman, 80
Ellingson, Mark, 152
Elliott, E. C., 238, 283
Elliott, Grace L., 347, 357
Elliott, Harrison S., 347, 357
Ellis, Bess D., 381
Elwell, Fayette H., 94
Embree, Royal B., Jr., 232, 315
Endicott, Frank S., 357
Engelhart, Max D., 70, 71, 96
Erickson, Clifford S., 19, 346, 358
Estabrooks, G. H., 106, 119, 129
Eurich, Alvin C., 319, 332
Evans, George R., 380

Fahey, George L., 315
Farwell, H. W., 89
Feder, Daniel D., 129
Fee, Mary, 128
Fenton, Norman, 342, 344, 357
Ferguson, Leonard W., 123
Ferguson, M. L., 64
Field, George, 355
Fisher, Mildred, 232
Fisher, Vivian E., 123, 128
Fitzpatrick, F. L., 88
Flanagan, John C., 70, 86, 96, 103, 111, 123, 222, 357
Fleming, R. D., 381
Flemming, Cecile W., 123, 201
Flemming, E. G., 123
Fletcher, Stevenson W., 86
Flory, Charles D., 212, 232, 315, 349
Foran, Thomas G., 199

Forlano, George, 104, 116, 126
Forrester, Gertrude, 347, 357
Fowlkes, John Guy, 94
Frank, Lawrence K., 123, 342
Franzen, Raymond, 237
Freeman, Frank N., 131, 149, 349, 357
Freud, Sigmund, 337, 340, 341
Froelich, Clifford, 114, 123
Fryer, Douglas, 123, 350, 357

Gage, N. L., 17, 42, 65, 97, 351, 362
Galbraith, Adria, 32, 153, 200, 223, 233, 359
Gallagher, Ralph P., 32, 323, 357
Gardiner, Glenn L., 347, 357
Garretson, Oliver K., 113, 123
Gates, Arthur I., 71, 77, 200
Gaw, E. A., 232, 306
Gehlmann, Frederick, 119, 124
Geisel, John B., 342
Gentry, Curtis G., 106, 114
Gerberich, J. Raymond, 200, 351, 357
Germane, Charles E., 19, 346, 357
Germane, Edith G., 19, 346, 357
Gesell, Arnold, 357
Ghiselli, Edwin E., 64
Gibbons, Charles C., 115, 123
Giese, Willis E., 381
Giffen, Lowell L., 124
Gilbert, Jane, 62
Gillespie, F. H., 117, 126
Gillet, Harry O., 199
Gillingham, Anna, 200
Goldberg, George, 363
Gooch, Wilbur I., 355
Gorham, T. J., 51, 64
Gottschalk, Winston M., 90
Graham, Frederick B., 76
Gray, Carl, 380
Gray, M. R., 209
Gray, William H., 200
Gray, William S., 200
Greenberg, Jacob, 81, 84
Greene, Edward B., 81, 96, 200, 357
Greene, Harry A., 62, 63, 72, 75, 200, 351, 357
Greenleaf, Walter J., 17, 358
Guilford, J. P., 104, 114, 124
Guilford, Ruth B., 104, 114, 124

Haggerty, M. E., 150
Hahn, M. E., 19, 316, 346, 364
Hale, Lincoln B., 319, 332
Hamalainen, Arthur E., 152
Hamrin, Shirley A., 19, 346, 358
Hand, Harold C., 346, 354, 358, 359
Handville, R. M., 381
Hansen, Rowena, 239, 283
Hardy, Ruth G., 232
Harriman, Philip L., 343, 363
Harris, Albert J., 200
Harrower-Erickson, M. R., 123

Hartmann, George W., 361
Hartshorne, Hugh, 112, 124, 349, 358
Hatch, Roy, 77
Hatcher, Latham, 345, 363
Hathaway, Starke R., 124
Hattwick, L. W., 154
Hawkes, Anna L. Rose, 233, 293, 306, 352, 360
Hawkes, Herbert E., 96, 350, 358
Hawkins, Layton S., 358
Hayes, Byron C., 332, 360
Hayes, Margaret, 130, 150, 152
Heck, Arch O., 209, 215, 233, 358
Heinz, Carl, 381
Henmon, V. A. C., 54, 55, 65, 79, 81, 82
Herbert, Edward, 355
Herrick, V. E., 316
Herring, John P., 125
Hertz, Marguerite R., 101, 117, 118, 123, 124
Hespelt, E. Herman, 83, 84
Hespelt, Miriam V., 83
Hildreth, Gertrude, 76, 99, 124, 200
Hilkert, Robert N., 89, 196, 200, 233, 358
Hill, Arthur S., 306
Hill, Clyde M., 18
Hill, George E., 239, 240, 241, 255, 283
Hirsch, E. C., 306
Hitchcock, C. S., 89
Hoppock, Robert, 347, 359
Horn, Ernest, 75
Horney, Karen, 341, 342
Horton, Byrne J., 355
Howard, Frank E., 306, 344, 359
Hull, Clark L., 65
Humm, Doncaster G., 124
Hunsicker, A. L., 124
Hutson, Percival W., 353, 359

Inglis, Alexander, 80, 81, 96
Iorns, Martin E., 124

Jackson, Claude E., 307
Jager, Harry A., 359, 380
Janet, Pierre, 337, 342
Jarvie, L. L., 152
Jersild, Arthur T., 343, 359
John, Lenore, 199
Johnson, B. Lamar, 233
Johnson, Beatrice R., 380
Johnson, O. E., 152
Johnson, Ralph C., 159
Johnson, Reynold B., 166
Jones, Arthur J., 289, 306, 359
Jones, Galen, 32, 153, 200, 223, 233, 359
Jones, Lonzo, 234
Jones, Mary Cover, 122
Jorgensen, Albert N., 72, 200, 351, 357
Joyal, A. E., 126
Judd, Charles H., 19
Jung, C. G., 340

Kanner, Leo, 342
Katz, Barney, 344, 364
Kaulfers, Walter V., 65
Kawin, Ethel, 131, 149
Keesling, C. M., 380
Kefauver, Grayson N., 3, 19, 345, 359, 360
Keller, Franklin J., 347, 359
Keller, Kathleen, 381
Kelley, Truman L., 77, 359
Kelley, V. H., 72
Kent, Grace H., 101, 114, 124
Keys, Noel, 96, 115, 116, 125
King, Harold V., 78, 84
Kitson, Harry D., 347, 359, 365, 380
Klein, David B., 344, 359
Klopfer, Bruno, 101, 118, 123, 124
Knauber, Alma J., 58, 65
Kogan, Leonard O., 119, 124
Kohlstedt, K. D., 126
Koos, Leonard V., 3, 19, 215, 234, 345, 359, 360
Kounin, Jacob S., 354
Kretschmer, E., 340
Krey, A. C., 359
Krieger, Laura B., 77
Kroll, Abraham, 123
Krugman, Morris, 123
Kuder, G. Frederic, 107, 114, 115, 124, 350, 360
Kuenzel, M. W., 306
Kuhlmann, F., 55, 65
Kutak, Rosemary, 355
Kwalwasser, Jacob, 59, 60, 65

Laird, D. A., 103, 125
Lake, Jeannette S., 19
Land, George A., 83
Landy, Edward, 322, 332, 349, 360
Lane, Mary Rogers, 347, 360
Laslett, H. R., 114, 125
Layton, Warren K., 380
Learned, William S., 96, 233, 350, 352, 360
Lee, Doris M., 63, 65
Lee, J. Murray, 62, 63, 65, 200, 360
Lefever, D. Welty, 360
Leigh, Robert D., 93
Leonard, E. A., 233
Leonard, Sterling A., 79
Lepley, William M., 108
Lester, Helene, 119, 125
Lewerenz, Alfred S., 59, 65
Lewis, Don, 59, 66
Lewis, Leon, 381
Likert, Rensis, 61, 65
Lincoln, A. L., 55, 81
Lincoln, Edward A., 200, 360
Lincoln, Mildred E., 347, 360
Lindgren, H. C., 380
Lindquist, E. F., 75, 79, 80, 90, 91, 92, 96, 350, 358

Link, H. C., 115, 125
Litterick, William S., 87
Little, Gladys, 361
Lloyd-Jones, Esther McD., 153, 233, 345, 360
Loftus, John J., 104, 116
Long, C. Darl, 332, 360
Long, John A., 84, 85, 86
Longstaff, Howard P., 62
Loofbourow, Graham C., 115, 116, 125
Loomis, H. H., 89
Lorge, Irving, 111, 120, 125
Lorge, Sarah Wolfson, 82
Lorwin, Lewis L., 348, 360
Louttit, Chauncey M., 344, 360
Ludeman, W. W., 306
Lundholm, H. T., 85, 87
Luria, Max A., 64
Lurie, W. A., 125
Lutz, Rose E., 86

McAdory, Margaret, 58, 65
McAndrew, William, 18
McBroom, Maude, 75
McCall, William A., 125
McCall, William C., xiv, 115, 128
McCallister, James M., 200, 291, 293, 307, 351, 361
McClintock, James A., 361
McConn, C. Max, 97, 361
McCormick, C. F., 153
McGeoch, J. A., 116, 125
McGoldrick, Joseph D., 93
McGrath, E. J., 380
McKim, Margaret, 364
McKinley, John C., 124
McKinney, Fred, 342, 361
McKown, Harry C., 361
McNamara, Walter J., 113, 123
McNemar, Quinn, 57, 65
MacQuarrie, T. W., 61
Maller, Julius B., 99, 116, 124, 125, 349, 358
Manger, C. W., 109, 125
Mann, C. R., 96, 350, 358
Mann, Horace, 202
Manuel, Herschel T., 200, 380
Marshall, Mortimer V., 65
Marshall, Thomas O., 319, 332, 356
Marston, L. R., 150, 153
Martin, Margaret P., 85, 87, 93, 94
Martin, Vibella, 132, 142, 152
Maslow, A. H., 342
Mathews, E., 121
Matter, W., 234
May, Mark A., 112, 124, 349, 358
May, Miriam, 78
May, Rollo, 342
Meier, Norman C., 58, 59, 65
Melby, Ernest O., 199
Menninger, Karl A., 341
Merrill, Maud A., 57, 66, 364

Messenger, Helen R., 239, 240, 241, 283
Metteer, W. M., 239, 283
Mikesall, William H., 342
Miller, Alice, 83
Miller, Donald H., 88
Miller, Lawrence W., 120, 125
Miller, Leonard M., 315, 347, 356
Mink, Myrtle S., 307
Mittelmann, Bela, 342
Mollenkopf, William, 87, 94
Moore, Bruce V., 25, 354, 361
Moore, Louise, 347, 365
Morgan, John J. B., 343, 344, 361
Morrison, Henry C., 289, 307
Morrison, Thomas F., 88
Mort, Paul R., 77, 200
Moseley, Nicholas, 344, 356
Mosher, Raymond D., 18
Moss, F. A., 65
Munroe, Ruth, 123
Murchison, Carl, 343, 361
Murray, Henry A., 125, 342
Murray, Sister M. Teresa Gertrude, 361
Myers, George E., 347, 361

Nash, Elizabeth A., 151
Nelson, Harry E., 381
Nelson, Lester W., 208
Nelson, M. J., 54, 55, 65, 72
Neprash, J. A., 120, 126
Neymann, C. A., 126
Nichols, Calvin J., 19
Nichols, William O., 381
Noll, Victor H., 89

O'Brien, James J., 355
O'Connor, Johnson, 50
Odegard, Peter H., 93
Odom, Charles L., 332
Ojemann, R. H., 120, 126
Olson, Willard C., 150, 153
Orleans, Jacob S., 62, 63, 64
Orleans, Joseph B., 62, 63, 65
Osborn, Martha L., 381
Otis, Arthur S., 56

Pace, C. Robert, 319, 332
Parsons, Frank, 347
Partington, J. E., 93
Paterson, Donald G., 62, 79, 200, 350, 361
Patry, Frederick L., 306, 307, 344, 359
Pearson, Carl A., 90, 93, 94
Pedersen, Ruth A., 110, 126
Perry, James D., 60, 64
Petersen, Ann Nappi, xiv
Peterson, Bertha M., 126
Pimm, Walter B., 381
Pintner, Rudolph, 56, 104, 116, 126
Piotrowski, Z. A., 118, 123, 126
Piper, Alva H., 62
Poland, Roberta C., 90

Popper, Emma, 83
Powers, Francis F., 364
Powers, N. E., 153
Powers, S. R., 88, 89
Pressey, L. C., 116
Pressey, S. L., 73, 116, 126, 343, 361
Proctor, W. M., 209, 232, 332
Proffitt, Maris M., 362
Pugsley, C. A., 239, 241, 283

Quasha, William, 61, 65

Rainey, Homer P., 348, 361
Randall, J. A., 132, 142, 153
Raths, Lois, 132, 142, 153
Raup, Zura, 315
Reavis, William C., 87, 293, 307, 351, 362
Reed, Anna Y., 19, 346, 362
Reeves, Floyd W., 365
Remmers, H. H., xi, xiii, 17, 42, 65, 97, 105,
    117, 126, 351, 362
Richardson, H. D., 65
Riggs, Winifred C., 126
Rivlin, Harry N., 287, 307
Roberts, Katherine E., 151, 153
Robertson, David A., 153, 233
Robinson, Francis P., 343, 361
Robinson, Sarah A., 361
Rogers, Carl R., 104, 117, 126, 339, 342, 344,
    362
Roos, Mary M., 363
Rorschach, Herman, 117, 118, 126
Rosanoff, A. J., 101, 114, 124
Rose, Florence C., 200
Rosengarten, William, 347, 362
Roslow, Sidney, 109, 115, 123, 127
Ross, C. C., 200, 351, 362
Ross, Carroll G., 87
Rothney, J. W. M., 126, 233, 350, 356
Rubenstein, Boris B., 118, 124
Ruch, Giles M., 59, 77, 233, 238, 283, 352, 362
Rugg, Harold O., 153
Ruggles, Richard, 109, 126
Rulon, P. J., 131, 151, 153
Russell, John Dale, 19, 362
Ryan, H. H., 233
Ryan, T. A., 380
Ryan, Teresa M., 78
Ryan, W. Carson, 362
Ryans, David G., 66, 126, 362

Sackett, Everett B., 381
Saetveit, Joseph G., 59, 66
Saint Clair, Walter F., 127
Sangren, Paul V., 73, 97
Sarbin, Theodore R., 119, 127, 307
Sayles, Mary B., 293, 307, 351, 362
Schneidler, Gwendolyn G., 200, 350, 361
Schrammel, H. E., 78
Schultz, Richard S., 109, 127

Seashore, C. E., 58, 59, 66
Seder, Margaret, 53, 66, 86, 97, 119, 127
Seegers, J. Conrad, 127
Segel, David, 119, 127, 215, 216, 233, 351, 362
Selover, Margaret S., 93, 97
Semenoff, Boris, 59, 66
Shaffer, Laurance F., 363
Shaffer, Robert H., 359
Shank, Spencer, 73
Sharkey, Vincent J., 113, 127
Shartle, Carroll L., 347, 363, 381
Shaw, Amy I., 77
Sherman, Mandel, 127, 342, 344, 363
Shoobs, Nabum E., 363
Shuttleworth, F. K., 124, 349, 356, 358
Siceloff, L. P., 84, 85, 86, 87
Siceloff, Margaret McAdory, 58, 66
Silance, E. B., 117, 126
Silva, C. T., 381
Simley, Irvin T., 18
Simmons, Madeline, 315
Sims, Verner M., 127
Singewald, G. L., 233
Skinner, Charles E., 343, 363
Smith, Carroll M., 19
Smith, Charles M., 363
Smith, Eugene R., 17, 24, 151, 153, 216, 220, 234, 278, 363
Smith, Helen Parker, 19
Smith, Helen R., 347, 355
Smith, Hugh A., 333
Smith, Margaret R., 153, 233, 345, 360
Smithies, Elsie M., 293, 307, 351, 363
Southwick, Arthur F., 333
Spaney, Emma, 85, 93
Spaulding, Francis T., 363
Spaulding, Geraldine, 78, 79, 81, 82, 83, 84
Spence, Ralph B., 77
Spencer, Douglas, 127, 342
Spitzer, H. F., 75
Spranger, Eduard, 106
Stagner, Ross, 127
Stalnaker, John M., 70, 97
Starch, Daniel, 238, 283
Stead, William H., 347, 363
Stein, M. L., 61, 66
Stenquist, J. L., 61, 66
Stevens, Winston B., 217
Stewart, Francis J., 106, 118
Stiglitz, Hanna, 355
Stillman, Bessie W., 200
Stoddard, George D., 64, 66, 363
Storment, Robert C., 124
Strang, Ruth, xiii, 19, 132, 153, 200, 234, 284, 292, 307, 333, 345, 347, 363, 364
Strecker, Edward A., 342, 353
Strong, Edward K., Jr., 118, 119, 127, 350, 363, 364, 381
Studebaker, John W., 364
Stull, DeForest, 77

Sturtevant, Sarah M., 364
Sullivan, Elizabeth T., 53
Sullivan, Helen Blair, 71
Super, Donald E., 127, 347, 364
Sweet, Lennig, 127
Swineford, Frances, 127
Symonds, Percival M., 63, 66, 77, 113, 127, 307, 344, 364

Tansil, Rebecca C., 234
Taylor, Wallace, 91, 92
Teeter, Verl A., 364
Terman, Lewis M., 57, 66, 77, 364
Terry, Paul W., 19
Thisted, M. N., 234
Thompson, Helen, 357
Thompson, James M., 95
Thompson, William A., 115, 127
Thorndike, E. L., 319, 333, 364
Thorpe, L. P., 104, 119, 120, 128
Thuemler, Gertrude, 307
Thurstone, L. L., 46, 52, 54, 66, 103, 105, 120, 128, 349, 364
Thurstone, Thelma Gwinn, 46, 52, 54, 66, 70, 71, 96, 120, 128
Tibbetts, V. H., 242, 283
Tiegs, Ernest W., 53, 54, 66, 73, 77, 104, 119, 120, 128, 344, 364
Toops, Herbert A., 55, 56, 66
Tope, R. E., 283
Torgerson, T. L., 62, 66
Totten, Helen, 154
Tough, Rosalind, 381
Towne, Laura, 82
Townsend, Agatha, 55, 66, 81, 94, 97
Trabue, M. R., 319, 333
Traphagen, Virginia, 148, 149, 152, 306, 346, 353
Traxler, Arthur E., 54, 55, 66, 67, 74, 97, 110, 111, 115, 119, 120, 125, 128, 164, 200, 234, 307, 364
Triggs, Frances O., 115, 128, 129
Troxel, Oliver L., 215, 234
Tubbs, William R., 128
Turell, Archie M., 360
Turney, Austin H., 110, 128
Turse, Paul L., 95
Tuttle, Harold S., 120, 128
Twente, J. W., 234
Tyler, H. T., 128
Tyler, Ralph W., 97, 132, 153, 363

Uhl, Willis L., 364
Underhill, O. E., 88

Vaillant, Paule, 81
Van Alstyne, Dorothy, 151, 152, 153, 154
Van Wagenen, M. J., 74
Vaughn, Kenneth W., 51, 67

Vernon, Philip E., 109, 110, 117, 121, 128
Viteles, Morris S., 333, 347, 351, 359, 364
Voorhees, Margaretta, 233

Walker, M. J., 81
Wallin, J. E. Wallace, 364
Walston, Rosa Lee, 80
Wang, C. K. A., 109, 128
Wantman, M. L., 64
Ward, Raymond S., 381
Washburne, J. N., 121, 128
Waterman, Alan T., 90
Watson, Richard E., 90, 93
Watson, Robert J., 123, 128
Watson, Thomas J., 166
Watts, Winifred, 239, 240, 241, 283
Weaver, Wilbur E., 347, 356
Webb, James F., 212, 232
Webster, Arthur D., 359
Weedon, Vivian F., 106, 128
Weintraub, Ruth G., 381
Weitzel, Harry I., 360
Wellman, Beth L., 363
Wheat, Harry G., 201
Whitely, Paul L., 110, 117, 125, 128, 129
Whitley, R. L., 307
Wickman, E. K., 150, 349, 364
Will, Lucy M., 83
Williams, Robert H., 84
Williamson, E. G., 19, 119, 129, 200, 234, 307, 333, 345, 346, 347, 350, 361, 364
Willing, M. H., 79

Willis, Mary, 80, 90, 92, 93, 94
Willoughby, Raymond R., 120, 129
Winn, Ralph B., 365
Wittenborn, J. R., 129
Wolfle, Dael, 129
Wood, Ben D., xiii, 69, 93, 96, 97, 132, 142, 146, 154, 166, 216, 233, 234, 238, 283, 307, 350, 360, 365
Wood, Eleanor Perry, xiii, 201, 217, 365
Woodhouse, Chase G., 365
Woodring, Maxie N., 201
Woodward, Grace L., 151
Woodworth, Robert H., 88
Woodworth, R. S., 102, 120
Woody, Clifford, 73
Woodyard, Ella, 58, 66
Workman, Linwood L., 200, 360
Wrenn, C. Gilbert, 320, 333, 365
Wright, Herbert F., 354
Wrightstone, J. Wayne, 92, 97, 121, 129, **234**
Wrinkle, William L., 279, 283

Yale, John R., 365
Young, C. W., 106, 119, 129
Young, Owen D., 365

Zahn, D. Willard, 132, 142, 154
Zapoleon, Marguerite W., 347, 365
Zeran, F. R., 333, 380
Zimmerman, John G., 90, 93, 94
Zubin, Joseph, 129
Zyve, D. L., 50, 60, 67

J